Wissenschaftliche Untersuchungen
zum Neuen Testament · 2. Reihe

Herausgeber / Editor
Jörg Frey (Zürich)

Mitherausgeber / Associate Editors
Friedrich Avemarie (Marburg)
Markus Bockmuehl (Oxford)
James A. Kelhoffer (Uppsala)
Hans-Josef Klauck (Chicago, IL)

317

Jonathan D. Worthington

Creation in Paul and Philo

The Beginning and Before

Mohr Siebeck

JONATHAN D. WORTHINGTON, born 1978; 2005 Master of Divinity; 2006 Master of Theology at Reformed Theological Seminary (Jackson, Mississippi, USA); 2010 PhD in New Testament Studies at Durham University (Durham, England); Director of University and Youth Ministries in Bon Accord Free Church of Scotland in Aberdeen, Scotland.

ISBN 978-3-16-150839-4
ISSN 0340-9570 (Wissenschaftliche Untersuchungen zum Neuen Testament, 2. Reihe)

Die Deutsche Nationalbibliothek lists this publication in the Deutsche Nationalbibliographie; detailed bibliographic data are available on the Internet at *http://dnb.d-nb.de*.

© 2011 by Mohr Siebeck, Tübingen, Germany.

This book may not be reproduced, in whole or in part, in any form (beyond that permitted by copyright law) without the publisher's written permission. This applies particularly to reproductions, translations, microfilms and storage and processing in electronic systems.

The book was printed by Laupp & Göbel in Nehren on non-aging paper and bound by Buchbinderei Nädele in Nehren.

Printed in Germany.

This work is dedicated to
Lynsey,
my most treasured of God's creations.
Hebrews 6:10

Preface

Is there a relationship between protology (one's interpretation of creation) and what can be called "pre-protology," i.e., one's interpretation of God's pre-creational purposes? This question, which lies at the heart of this book, was sparked in a café in 2007 in Aberdeen, Scotland. Having already done some research into creation ("from nothing") in early Judaism and Christianity, I was aware of the tendency of Philo of Alexandria to interpret Genesis 1–2 in connection with God's "pre-existent" thoughts, a doctrine partially culled from Plato's *Timaeus*, but partially (and importantly) from Genesis 1–2 itself. While then reading Ephesians 1 over a cup of coffee, a curious flicker ignited: Would the understanding of God's "predestining" activity discussed in this passage – in which God "chose us in Christ *before* the foundations of the world," i.e., before Genesis 1 – have been related to a Pauline interpretation of Genesis 1 itself. Though tantalizing, such a query seemed to fall outwith my project. I placed the small curiosity under the mental bushel nebulously labeled "for a future project."

As I sipped my coffee, I had no idea that throughout the next few years of research Paul's use of the wording and motifs of Genesis 1–2 and 5 in 1–2 Corinthians and Romans (not Ephesians 1), as well as Philo's in *De opificio mundi*, would render it impossible to keep that curiosity from shining out. For example, Paul uses the "image"-motif from Gen. 5:3 in Rom. 8:29, but there he is not explaining what God had done in creation (as in 1 Cor. 15:48a and 49a), nor even what God does in the new creation (as in 1 Cor. 15:48b and 49b), but specifically what God had "*pre*-marked out" ("pre-destined") before the original creation. Was it from the text of Genesis itself that Paul gleaned testimony not only to the Beginning but also to the Before, perhaps in a manner not wholly dissimilar to Philo? What was going on hermeneutically as well as theologically? Is it significant that in 1 Corinthians, in which Paul uses Genesis 1, 2, and 5 at many significant points, he employs the central theme and wording of that great creation passage – or, rather, that great "before creation" passage – in Proverbs 8 to express that God's wisdom was "pre-marked out" ("pre-destined") before the ages for our glory (1 Cor. 2:7)? At more points than those just mentioned my attempts to wrestle with Paul's perception of God's *creational* activity were repeatedly interupted by his communication of God's *pre-*

creational intentions. As I focused on *how* Paul culled his protology from that sacred text that he shared with Philo – i.e., the beginning of Genesis – that flicker from the Aberdonian café had to be placed on a stand; indeed, it became the very flame that burns at the heart of this book. (A close contingent of this heart is the nexus between eschatology – the End – and protology.) This book explores the Beginning and Before, and a bit Beyond.

Many people have my gratitude regarding the present study. Any flaws remain mine alone, and what value and propriety this book does contain would not be the same without Professor Dr. Francis Watson's care for it in its form as a PhD dissertation at Durham University, England. His sharp insights, gentle prods, and humble challenges were always of timely help. Also, Professor Dr. Jörg Frey and Dr. Henning Ziebritzki, along with the editorial staff of Mohr Siebeck, deserve my thanks for seeing something of worth in this work and for investing in it by making it part of *WUNT* II series. Professor Dr. John Barclay and Dr. Jutta Leonhardt-Balzer deserve my thanks for their helpful suggestions concerning this and further connected research. A particular and warm gratitude extends to two scholars, Dr. Jason Maston and Dr. Brian Mattson, whose friendship and theological erudition greatly improved both my thesis and person, and whose families have been a true family to mine.

A deep and abiding gratefulness is indebted to my parents, Everett and Kirby Worthington, who for many years have been committed to my further education and who have practiced that commitment in no insignificant way! Also to Lynsey's parents, Vince and Jill Franz, my appreciation goes for constantly opening their hearts and home to us. Our life in Aberdeen, Scotland would also not be as rich and full as it has been without the faithful and exceedingly hospitable community of Bon Accord Free Church of Scotland, who have put up with me for 5 years as their Director of University and Youth Ministries. Singling out Donald and Anne Smith simultaneously recognizes their particular care for us while it does not deny the love of all others for whom we are so greatly appreciative. It is humbling to consider those literally around the world who have prayed for us and for my work these years.

Anya, my daughter born during an early stage of this study, should be thanked as one of my greatest sources of delight during the stresses and intensity of this research. And now Lydia, born during the final stage of this book's completion, reminds me of the powerful yet delicate creativity of our God. It is with all of my heart that my deepest and most profound thanks and love within the whole realm of creation extends to my wise wife, Lynsey. Though *soli Deo gloria* through Jesus Christ, my Lord!

Aberdeen, April 2011   Jonathan D. Worthington

Table of Contents

Preface VII

Introduction 1
Beginnings 1
Recent Treatments of Paul's View of Creation 3
Paul as a Reader of Genesis in Comparison with Philo 13
Paul's and Philo's Three-Strand Hermeneutic of Creation 17

Chapter 1: Before the Beginning? 21

1.1 Proverbs 8:22–31 and Before Genesis 1 23
1.2 Philo's "Before":
    God's Pre-Creational Deliberation for Goodness' Sake 27
    1.2.1 The Presence in Philo of a Pre-Creational Plan
          and the *Timaeus* of Plato (*Op.* 16, 26–28) 29
        (a) Philo's Timing of "In the Beginning":
            Before the Beginning (*Op.* 26–28) 31
        (b) The Purpose of God's Pre-Creational Intentions:
            For Goodness' Sake (*Op.* 16) 34
    1.2.2 Philo's Content of God's Pre-Creational Plan:
          The Invisible, Beautiful Paradigm (*Op.* 29 and 129–30) 38
        (a) Philo's First Reading of the Before:
            An Invisible Earth and Gen. 1:1–5 (*Op.* 29) 38
        (b) Philo's Second Reading of the Before:
            Invisible Green in Gen. 2:4–5 (*Op.* 129–30) 41
1.3 Paul's Before:
    God's Pre-Creational Deliberation for our Glory 45
    1.3.1 The Presence in Paul of a Pre-Creational Plan
          and the Text of Proverbs 8 (1 Cor. 2:7) 51

		(a)	The Presence of God's Pre-Set Intentions (1 Cor. 1:18–2:5, 2:7)..53

           (a) The Presence of God's Pre-Set Intentions
               (1 Cor. 1:18–2:5, 2:7) 53
           (b) The Timing and Text(s) of "Before the Ages":
               Prov. 8:23, Genesis 1, and Before (1 Cor. 2:7) 57
      1.3.2 Paul's Content of God's Pre-Creational Wisdom:
           Christ, His Cross, and a Plurality of Preparations
           (1 Cor. 1–2, 15, and Rom. 8:29–30) 64
           (a) Paul's First Presentation of the Before:
               Mediator, Means, and Goal of Glory
               (1 Cor. 1:24, 30, and 2:7, 9) 65
           (b) Paul's Second Presentation of the Before:
               Method and Members from Image to Glory
               (1 Cor. 15:49 and Rom. 8:29–30) 69

1.4 Comparisons and Conclusions:
     Philo and Paul on Before the Beginning... 75

Chapter 2: The Beginning of the World 78

2.1 Genesis 1, God's Desire, the World's Goodness 79

2.2 Philo and Paul on Genesis 1:2–5:
     The God Who Spoke Light 81

      2.2.1 Philo's Reading of Genesis 1:2–5:
           A Special Light and its Bodily Dimming (*Op*. 30–35) 83
      2.2.2 Paul's Reading of Genesis 1:2–5:
           A Special Light and its Facial Glory (2 Cor. 4:6) 89

2.3 Philo and Paul on Genesis 1:6–31:
     Six Days of Ontic Order and Divine Design 98

      2.3.1 Philo's Reading of Genesis 1:6–31 (*Op*. 36–68) 98
           (a) The Second Day:
               Philo on Genesis 1:6–8 (*Op*. 36–37) 99
           (b) The Third Day:
               Philo on Genesis 1:9–13 (*Op*. 38–44) 100
               (i) On vv. 9–10:
                   Primordial Ooze, Good Land (*Op*. 38–39) 100
               (ii) On vv. 11–13:
                   Illustration of the Seed (*Op*. 40–44) 105
           (c) The Fourth Day:
               Philo on Genesis 1:14–19 (*Op*. 45–61) 107

		(i)	The Theological Delay of the Luminaries (*Op*.45–46) 108

                    (i)   The Theological Delay
                          of the Luminaries (*Op*.45–46) 108
                    (ii) The Teleological Ends
                          of the Luminaries (*Op.* 53–61) 110
            (d)   The Fifth Day:
                  Philo on Genesis 1:20–23 (*Op.* 62–63) 112
            (e)   The Sixth Day:
                  Philo on Genesis 1:24–26 (*Op.* 64–68) 113
            (f)   Summary: Philo's Beginning of the World 115
      2.3.2 Paul's Reading of Genesis 1:6–31 (1 Cor. 15:35–41) 115
            (a)   "Sowing the Seed" of God's Creative Power
                  (1 Cor. 15:36–38a) 118
            (b)   Days 2–6: Paul's Cosmology
                  and Genesis 1 (1 Cor. 15:38b–41) 121
                    (i)   The Third Day (Gen. 1:11–13):
                          Two Themes of Genesis 1 (v. 38bc) 121
                    (ii) The Other Days:
                          the Language of Genesis 1 (vv. 39–41) 124
                          1. The Fifth and Sixth Days: Paul's Zoology
                             and Gen. 1:20–27 (v. 39) 127
                          2. The Second Day: Paul's Cosmology
                             and Gen. 1:6–8, 9–10 (v. 40) 128
                          3. The Fourth Day: Paul's Astronomy
                             and Gen. 1:14–19 (v. 41) 131
            (c)   Summary: Paul's Beginning of the World 134

2.4   Comparisons and Conclusions:
      Philo and Paul on the Beginning of the World 135

Chapter 3: The Beginning of Humanity 138

3.1   The Image of God: Genesis 1:27 139

      3.1.1 Philo's Reading of Genesis 1:27 141
            (a)   Philo's First Reading of Genesis 1:27
                  (*Op.* 69–88) 142
                    (i)   Gen. 1:27ab: "Imaging" and "Resembling"
                          God (*Op.* 69–71) 143
                    (ii) God's Foresight in Humanity's Tardiness
                          (*Op.* 77–78 and 82) 145
            (b)   Philo's Second Reading of Genesis 1:27
                  (*Op.* 134–35) 147

			(i)	Philo's Re-Reading of the Beginning of the World (*Op.* 131–33) 148
			(ii)	Philo's Re-Reading of the Beginning of Humanity (*Op.* 134) 149
		(c)	Summary: Philo's Reading of Genesis 1:27 151	
	3.1.2	Paul's Reading of Genesis 1:27 151		
		(a)	Paul's First Application of Genesis 1:27: Man, the Image and Glory of God (1 Cor. 11:7–12) ... 152	
			(i)	Paul's Application of the Beginning of Humanity (1 Cor. 11:7–12b) 152
			(ii)	Paul's Cosmogonic Perspective (1 Cor. 11:12c) 156
		(b)	Paul's Second Application of Genesis 1:27: Christ, the Image of God (2 Cor. 4:4–6) 157	
			(i)	Paul's Re-Application of the Beginning of Humanity (2 Cor. 4:4) 158
			(ii)	Paul's Cosmogonic Perspectives (2 Cor. 4:6) 161
		(c)	Summary: Paul's Reading of Genesis 1:27, in Comparison with Philo's Readings 162	
3.2	The Man of Dust: Genesis 2:7 164			
	3.2.1	Philo's Reading of Genesis 2:7 166		
		(a)	Philo's Negative Reading: "Earthly" Man in Comparison (*Op.* 134–35) 166	
		(b)	Philo's Positive Reading: "First Man" *per se* (*Op.* 136–50) 170	
		(c)	Summary: Philo's Reading of Genesis 2:7 172	
	3.2.2	Paul's Reading of Genesis 2:7 172		
		(a)	Paul's Positive Reading: A Glorious Adam *per se* (1 Cor. 11:7–9, 12:12–30, 15:39–40) 173	
			(i)	Adam as God's Original "Image and Glory" (1 Cor. 11:7–9) 173
			(ii)	Adam's "Flesh" and Earthly "Body" as having "Glory" (1 Cor. 15:39–40) 175
			(iii)	God's "Desired" Construction of the Original Human Body and the World: Comparing 1 Cor. 11:7–12 and 15:37–42 with 12:12–30 176
		(b)	Paul's Negative Reading: The Inglorious Adam in Comparison (1 Cor. 15:44b-47) 180	

		(c)	Summary: Paul's Reading of Genesis 2:7, in Comparison with Philo's Reading 184

3.3 The Image of Adam: Genesis 5:3 185
    3.3.1 Philo's Reading of Genesis 5:3 188
        (a) Ontological Adam-like Nobility (*Op.* 145) 188
        (b) Ethical Adam-like Nobility (*QG* 1.81) 190
        (c) Summary: Philo's Reading of Genesis 5:3 191
    3.3.2 Paul's Reading of Genesis 5:3 191
        (a) The "Image" of Adamic Ontology
            (1 Cor. 15:48–49) 192
        (b) The Glory of the New Adamic "Image"
            (2 Cor. 3:18) 195
        (c) The New Adamic "Image," the Cosmos,
            and the Before (Rom. 8:29) 198
        (d) Summary: Paul's Reading of Genesis 5:3,
            in Comparison with Philo's Readings 202

3.4 Comparisons and Conclusions
    Philo and Paul on the Beginning of Humanity 203

Conclusion 205

Bibliography 211

Index of Ancient Sources 233
Index of Modern Authors 250
Index of Subjects 254

Introduction

Beginnings

Beginnings are important to the apostle Paul. His own beginning in the knowledge of the resurrected Christ gave to him a sense of humility and divinely purposed vigor in life and mission (1 Cor. 15:8–10). The beginning of the Galatians' faith and life in the Spirit set the standard, Paul urges them, according to which their lives should follow (Gal. 3:2–3). The beginning of the Mosaic Law in relation to the beginning of the Abrahamic promise – the Law beginning four centuries after the promise – shaped Paul's understanding of their whole relationship (Gal. 3:17–19). The beginning of sin and death through Adam's disobedience in Genesis 3 is clearly important for Paul's construal of the common human plight "in Adam" and of the gracious salvation "in Christ" (1 Cor. 15:21–22; Rom. 5:12–21). But what about *before* that fatal beginning of sin in the world, that world from which its inhabitants were supposed to perceive the eternal power and divine nature of their Creator, and worship him (Rom. 1:20)? Was the ultimate Beginning of all things – creation itself – at all important in Paul's thinking and letter-writing?

This book focuses on Paul's letters to the Corinthian and Roman Christians. Within those few correspondences alone, Paul quotes, alludes to, and builds upon the beginning of Genesis on numerous occasions. In order to humble the Corinthians, Paul turned their attention to God as creative Cause (1 Cor. 11:12c; cf. 2 Cor. 5:18a) and to the Father's causation of creation through Christ (1 Cor. 8:6). Also for the Romans, though in their case with the intention of deepening their understanding of guilt and praise, Paul introduced the general notion that God created all things (Rom. 1:20 and 11:36, respectively).[1] Yet Paul also brought to his readers' attention God's more specific creations: of light (2 Cor. 4:6), of seeds and plants (1 Cor. 15:37–38), and of bodies throughout heaven and earth (1 Cor. 15:40) including sun, moon, and stars (1 Cor. 15:41), and fish, birds, and beasts (1 Cor. 15:39). Paul used the language and motifs of the Begin-

---

[1] A much more inclusive presentation of the "creation motifs" in Romans 1–8 can be found in Adams, 2000, 153–55; cf. *idem,* 2002, 19–43.

ning to explain God's creation of humans as God's image (1 Cor. 11:7b; cf. 2 Cor. 4:4), God's fashioning of Adam from the dust (1 Cor. 15:44–47), and God's assembling of the human (i.e., Adamic) body (1 Cor. 12:12–26) with its own peculiar flesh (1 Cor. 15:39) and even glory (1 Cor. 15:40b; cf. 11:7–9). It was from the texts of the Beginning that Paul drew the gender-dynamics of difference and interdependence (1 Cor. 11:7–12) as well as the ontic nature of sexual union (1 Cor. 6:16). He even presented to both the Corinthians and Romans God's built-in anthropological principle by which all further humans were propagated according to Adam's image (1 Cor. 15:48–49; cf. 2 Cor. 3:18; Rom. 8:29).[2] All of these references to various aspects of the ultimate Beginning are *in addition* to Paul's more pronounced and well-known treatment of Adam's sin and its consequences according to Genesis 3.

What themes are connected to these texts of creation? Paul's uses of the Beginning (before sin) mentioned above touch on such important, interconnected subjects as Christology, anthropology (including bodily ontology, gender relations, and sexual ethics), ecclesiology, and eschatology. By this fact alone it seems that a systemic treatment of Paul's understanding of creation could have wide ramifications. A more modest observation is that if all of these statements are indeed based on Genesis – and I shall argue throughout the study this very point concerning a selection from these texts – then Paul provides comments not only on Genesis 1–2 as a whole and in general, but also on the particular texts of Gen. 1:2–3, 11–12, 14–19, 20–21, 24–25, 26–28, 2:7, 18, 21–23, 24, and 5:3 – and that is only within his Corinthian and Roman correspondences! It is tempting to immediately compile all of his treatments of these texts into a sort of Pauline commentary on creation. This book takes a step prior to such an endeavor.

This is not an exhaustive study of Paul's theology of creation. Rather, through select passages from those mentioned above I will tease out some of Paul's underlying interpretive tendencies when he employs terms and motifs from his scriptural texts of creation. Paul has more to say about creation than is often thought, though the depth and complexity of his protology is easily missed because of the brief and scattered nature of his references and allusions. However, by placing Paul's references to creation next to the formal and developed commentary on Genesis 1–2 written by one of his contemporaries, Philo of Alexandria (c. 20 BCE–50 CE), more about Paul's own reading of creation can be discerned and legitimately compared with Genesis' creation texts than may be possible by only study-

---

[2] Though this principle was first enacted in Gen. 5:3, and thus in one sense has a *post-sin* origin, Paul initially treats it as a simple matter of human ontology (1 Cor. 15:48a, 49a; see chapter 3 below). Since it was built by God within the fabric of Adam's and Eve's frames *before* sin, it can legitimately be treated as a pre-sin creation text.

ing Paul. Though there are important differences between Philo's and Paul's treatments of creation, and these will be explored at the end of each major section below, a broad hermeneutical similarity can be discerned between these two interpreters, as can a similar treatment of particular texts.

The proposal is this: *Paul's interpretation of creation, like Philo's in his commentary, contains three interwoven aspects: the beginning of the world, the beginning of humanity, and God's intentions before the beginning.* Note what the thesis is and is not. The central proposition is not that Paul's interpretation of creation is like Philo's. They display too many significant differences to make such a simplistic claim. The observation is that Paul's interpretation of creation has three interwoven aspects: two of the Beginning (of the world and of humanity) as well as the Before. A subordinate (but important) observation is that this general hermeneutic of creation is also found in Philo's commentary on Genesis 1–2.

Three basic questions are raised by the assertions above, and they each must be answered before we begin to analyze the three strands of Paul's and Philo's interpretations of creation in the chapters that follow. Firstly, how is this study related to other attempts to comprehend Paul's view of creation? Secondly, why approach this fuller treatment of Paul's understanding of creation by comparing his and Philo's readings? And finally, how will this study of Paul's and Philo's three-strand hermeneutic of creation unfold?

Recent Treatments of Paul's View of Creation

Scholars who have commented on Paul's view of creation in general and/or Paul's view of Adam in particular have often misconstrued his outlook due to underdeveloped engagement with each of the ways he interprets the protological texts and concepts. The majority of applicable details from these presentations of Paul's view of creation and of Adam are more effectively engaged throughout this book itself since they typically arise concerning particular texts of Paul (e.g., 1 Cor. 15:45; 2 Cor. 4:4, 6; Rom. 8:29) rather than as systematic treatments of his exegesis of the early texts in Genesis. A few general examples will suffice in order to demonstrate from different angles that a deeper and broader engagement with Paul's handling of the creational texts themselves will fill in an existing gap in scholarly discussion.

Though virtually everyone would agree that Paul believed that in fact God did create the world, there has been little attention paid to Paul's understanding of creation before Genesis 3. As we will see, some say (somewhat casually) that Paul really did not think much about creation and existence prior to sin. Not fitting into that perspective, Herman Ridderbos considered creation "fundamental" to Paul's thinking about sin and the gospel "even though little separate attention is paid" to the original creation in his letters.[3] In light of the "little separate attention" that Paul supposedly grants to creation, Ben Witherington is not surprised that "commentators have often noted how very little Paul has to say about creation or creatures prior to the Fall."[4] Ridderbos' modifier "separate" has been dropped, and now it appears that Paul did not say much of anything about creation, whether in connection with other doctrines or not. Apparently in agreement with the commentators, Witherington explains:[5]

When Paul talks about creation, he is speaking of creation as it now exists, groaning under the burden of futility to which the Fall subjected it. When Paul reflects on the world, he is almost always reflecting on a world gone wrong or a world the form of which is passing away (1 Cor. 7:31).

Due to Paul's emphasis on the power and pervasiveness of sin, on Adam as sinner, and on "this present age" as evil and passing away, it is indeed tempting to convert the (alleged) notion that Paul *says* very little about creation prior to the Fall into the notion that, as Witherington favorably records of the plurality of commentators, Paul "*has very little to say* about creation." Twenty years prior to Witherington, J. Reumann had suggested "that Paul's expectation of an imminent end scarcely made creation a matter of importance to him."[6] If so, then indeed Paul would likely have very little to say about anything prior to the fundamental event of the universe: Adam's disobedience.

These few examples represent little more than passing comments on Paul's view of creation. When there has been a greater effort to say more about how Paul construes the creation of the world, attention has typically focused upon two statements in Paul's undisputed letters: Rom. 4:17c and 1 Cor. 8:6. From 1 Cor. 8:6 it is argued that Paul believed "all things" were created "through Christ" (cf. Col. 1:15–16).[7] From Rom. 4:17c it is argued that he believed God "called non-being into being" – i.e., some sort of

---

[3] Ridderbos, 1975, 105. The term "separate" is unfortunate, for it implies that any attention to creation that is related to another topic is somehow less meaningful. It may tend toward an unwarranted restriction of the Pauline evidence.

[4] Witherington, 1994, 9.

[5] Witherington, 1994, 9.

[6] Reumann, 1973, 90. Cf. the favorable appraisal of Reumann's sentiments in Aymer, 1985, 82.

[7] E.g., Cox, 2007, 141–61 (on 1 Cor. 8:6), 161–92 (on Col. 1:15–20); Gibbs, 1971, 59–73 (on 1 Cor. 8:6), 94–114 (on Col. 1:15–20).

creatio ex nihilo by divine *fiat*.[8] In the study below I will not discuss either of these texts.

Although 1 Cor. 8:6 is most likely a reference to creation (as well as to redemption)[9] – to its (their) source, goal, and mediation – I have not selected it for his study because it does not betray a treatment of specific texts within the beginning of Genesis. Likewise in relation to Rom. 4:17c, even if this is a reference to creation (see below) it is similarly too broadly construed to be of relevance for this particular study of Paul's interpretive moves regarding the text. In my opinion, rather than referring to creation Paul's statement in Rom. 4:17c – "the God who called non-existing things as existing things" (καλοῦντος τὰ μὴ ὄντα ὡς ὄντα) – is most adequately explained as a gloss of Gen. 17:5, which Paul just quoted in v. 17a, and particularly as a gloss of God's use of the perfect tense within that quote. That is, God claimed "I *have* established [τέθεικα] you father of many nations," though he had not yet actualized even one child, let alone "many nations." But Abraham believed in this God who "called the non-existent things [*sc.* no-children and no-nations] *as* [ὡς] the existent things [*sc.* the already established 'many nations']." This construal makes the best sense out of both Paul's language and context. Yet even though Rom. 4:17c is not a reference directly to God's act of creation, God's assumed enactment of this "call" can certainly be *compared* to a creative act. Indeed, in his letter to the Corinthians Paul himself unites childbirth (to which he is referring in Rom. 4:17c) to the creation account of Genesis 1–2, putting both under the same rubric of the all-powerful causation of the Creator: "all things are from God" (1 Cor. 11:12; cf. vv. 7–12).[10]

---

[8] Many derive creation from Rom. 4:17c: e.g., Becker, 2007, 165, 167, 168; Wright, 2002, 498; Adams, 2002, 35; Schwarz, 2002, 168; Byrne, 1996, 159–60; Haffner, 1995, 47; Stuhlmacher, 1994, 74; Witherington, 1994, 233; Ziesler, 1989, 132; Dunn, 1988, 236–37; Käsemann, 1980, 122–23; Cranfield, 1975, 244–45. This is critiqued by, e.g., Schreiner, 1998, 237; Moo, 1996, 282; Morris, 1985, 209; Murray, 1959, 146–47; Sanday and Headlam, 1896, 107.

[9] Contra Murphy-O'Connor, 1978A, 253–67, who argues against a creational understanding of 1 Cor. 8:6 (cf. Kuschel, 1992, esp. 285–91). His treatment has not been well received by many: cf., e.g., Thiselton, 2000, 635–38; Fee, 2007, 90 n. 15; Cox, 2005, 172; Dunn, 1998B, 267.

[10] Ironically, it is only when one understands Rom. 4:17c as a gloss of Abraham's situation to which God spoke that a greater ultimacy of "nothingness" (and consequently of God's affect on it) may be derived from Paul's use of it here than otherwise could be derived if this were a direct reference to creation itself. In the ancient world, creation of "non-being into being" typically did not assume an ultimate or absolute "nothing" (*nihil*): see 2 Mac. 7:28a (cf. v. 28b and v. 23 with v. 28a); Plato, *Soph.* 265c; Philo: *Spec.* 4.187; *Migr.* 183; *Mos.* 2.100 (though these references in Philo should be compared with his use of an ultimate "nothing" in *Plant.* 7; *Somn.* 1.63–64; *Mos.* 2.267). So e.g., May, 1994 (on Philo specifically see pp. 9–21); cf. Radice, 2009, 144–45; Schwarz, 2002, 173; Runia,

Neither 1 Cor. 8:6 nor Rom. 4:17c betrays a treatment of a specific text of Genesis. Therefore, although general ideas about Paul's view of creation can be either exegeted or derived from these confessions, Paul's specific *reading* of the creation text cannot be discerned from either. Yet these two have been the most common texts of discussion when contemplating Paul's view of creation.

Recently, P. Bouteneff set himself to analyze "how Paul might have understood creation and how that understanding may be derived from aspects of the Hexaemeron [i.e., 'six day,' Genesis 1] account."[11] Though he feels unable to attribute to Paul "a fully formed 'theology of creation'," Bouteneff does see certain aspects of Paul's reading of Genesis as highly significant, "groundbreaking," "seminal."[12] But on actual analysis of Paul's understanding of Genesis 1 itself, he too only mentions Rom. 4:17c and 1 Cor. 8:6.[13] In fact, the main significance Bouteneff presents in Paul's interpretation of creation actually does not have to do with the creation of the world, but with the fallen person of Adam.[14]

Because of the enormous scope of Bouteneff's task, he cannot be faulted with treating only a few carefully selected passages in Paul.[15] (Faults within his conclusions based upon his few texts, however, can be found – see below.) I single out Bouteneff because his claims of what is

---

2001, 152–53 (cf. *idem,* 1986, 289); Fergusson, 1998, 12; Clifford and Collins, 1992, 13 (cf. Clifford, 1994, 141); Sacks, 1990, 4; Goldstein, 1983, 307; Winston, 1979, 38–40; Wolfson, 1947, 1.300–10.

The result of this general setting of the use of "nothing" in Paul's day is that if Rom. 4:17c actually were a direct reference to creation itself, we would not know whether "non-being" was ultimate or not, and the thought context of Paul's broader time-period would tempt us toward a non-ultimate "nothing." But since "non-being things" (an interesting plural) refers to the non-existence of children – which is absolute – had by Abraham and Sarah, God's relationship to *that* "non-being" should be seen as more ultimate than his relationship to the "nothing" or "non-being" of other explicitly creational contexts. Granted, Paul's reference is still not to the actual divine *activity* of bringing nations into being, but rather to his claim in Gen. 17:5. But Paul surely believes that what gives God's "call" power is the fact that God then *caused* what he claimed. Thus Paul's understanding of *God's causation*, a causation which in this context brings an *absolute* "non-being" into "being" exactly as he claims – an understanding that can be *derived* from Rom. 4:17c – is ironically closer to a robust view of *creatio ex nihilo* than would be discernible if Paul were explicitly speaking in Rom. 4:17c of God's activity in Genesis 1–2.

[11] Bouteneff, 2008, 36.
[12] Bouteneff, 2008, 33.
[13] Bouteneff, 2008, 37–38.
[14] Bouteneff, 2008, 33, 38–43.
[15] Bouteneff analyzes the "ancient Christian readings of the biblical creation narratives" from the creation texts themselves, through their use in OT, early Jewish, and NT writings, through Tertullian, Origen, and the Cappadocian fathers, finally ending with Gregory of Nyssa in the 390s CE.

desired do demonstrate what has been lacking, even though this deficit continues in his own work. He wanted to demonstrate "how Paul might have understood creation" (which, like others, he did only through 1 Cor. 8:6 and Rom. 4:17c) and "how that may be derived from aspects of the Hexaemeron account." I agree that the latter is particularly desirable, but even Bouteneff's treatment leaves a wide door of opportunity into which this present study will enter in detail. A full-length discussion of Paul's interpretation of the creation of the world will simultaneously challenge the broad generalizations regarding Paul's lack of regard for the original creation and add understanding where it has merely been lacking. In chapter 2, "The Beginning of the World," I seek to provide just such a fuller analysis of Paul's reading of God's creation of the cosmos according to Genesis 1. This will also have the benefit of providing Paul's own broader hermeneutical framework for his understanding of God's more particular creation of Adam and humanity.

Some treatments of Paul's more specific view of Adam (rather than of creation as a whole) sound a similar tone to Reumann's and Witherington's mentioned above. While it is true that Robin Scroggs (among many others) has offered the brief idea, deduced from Rom. 3:23, that like many of his contemporaries Paul acknowledges a "glory once enjoyed by Adam,"[16] even this verdict is tempered by this perspective:[17]

Taken with the events of Christ and the church, Paul is directly concerned with the new creation which God is bringing to man and the cosmos. He is only secondarily interested in the old creation which is passing away.

What this subordination of interest – "secondarily interested" – means for Scroggs comes out in his subsequent practical approach and then in his confession. In practice, when Scroggs expounds the "old creation" he only discusses the post-sin creation, thereby not showing much of an interest himself in Paul's view of Adam (or creation) before sin.

This approach to Paul's view of Adam is reminiscent of C.K. Barrett's practice only a few years prior. Barrett thought it important "to ask what Saul the Jew will have made of the figure of Adam," but he then began his own search with Paul's understanding of "the myth of Eden" regarding the "Fall" rather than of the prior creation of Adam. Even though Barrett considered his research to have "traced [Paul's] story from its beginning,"[18] Paul's "beginning" was "when Man upset the balance of God's creation" and how "creation is *now* perverted and subjected to vanity; the reign of

---

[16] Scroggs, 1966, 73 (cf. 73 n. 42). Cf. Dunn, 1980: "By virtue of his creation in the image of God [Adam] was given a share in the glory of God, the visible splendor of God's power as Creator" (102).

[17] Scroggs, 1966, 72 (on the new creation see pp. 61–72). Cf. Whiteley, 1964, 17.

[18] Barrett, 1962, 92.

evil beings."[19] But what about *before* Adam's disobedience and his introduction of cosmic disaster? Is Paul interested? Though Scroggs is surely right that "the context of Paul's whole theology indicates that the Apostle wrestles mightily with Gen. 1–3,"[20] in practice he, like Barrett, only really looks at Paul's view of the Adam of Genesis 3 in any depth.

Barrett himself had presented not many more than two general comments concerning Paul's view of pre-sin Adam: "Adam was created by God for life,"[21] and Adam had "minor sovereignty" (i.e., over animals).[22] Barrett's confession was clear, however, about what Paul did *not* claim about the pre-sin Adam: "the first man, Adam, is *never* said by Paul to bear the image of God."[23] (It should be noted that this claim was more easily asserted since Barrett judged that 1 Cor. 11:7 was simply "not relevant" to his study of what Paul "will have made of the figure of Adam,"[24] even though that passage is built on the assumption that the man of Genesis 2 – i.e., Adam – *was* precisely "God's image and glory"; see chapter 3 below).

In a similar manner to Barrett, even though Scroggs mentions in passing the glory which Adam must have enjoyed prior to his sin, in confession he is confident of Paul's attitude toward the pre-sinful Adam:[25]

> The Apostle is consistently *silent* about Adam's status prior to his sin. The reason for this must be... that Paul knows *only* Christ as the exhibition of God's intent for man and thus has *nothing* to say about what Adam was before the fall or might have been had he not sinned.

Again Scroggs confesses: "*Nowhere* in [Paul's] Epistles is Adam the perfect man before his sin. Paul knows *only* the Adam of sin and death."[26] Paul "knows *only*" the sinful Adam and "knows *only*" Christ as "the exhibition of God's intent." One may wonder if Paul's ignorance of the pre-sin (i.e., the created) Adam is due to a lack of contemplating Genesis 1–2 – despite Scroggs' earlier (unsubstantiated) claim that he can discern in Paul's letters a "mighty wrestling" with Genesis 1–3 – or is due to Paul seeing God's creation of Adam in Genesis 1–2 as sinful and not exhibiting "God's intent." The former is more likely the case for Scroggs, though he does not draw out the implications of these bold claims.

A similar analysis of Paul's view of Adam can be found in S. Kim. Parallel to Barrett and Scroggs, Kim also points to a primary negativity to-

---

[19] Barrett, 1962, 13.
[20] Scroggs, 1966, 97–98.
[21] Barrett, 1962, 19.
[22] Barrett, 1962, 88.
[23] Barrett, 1962, 88 (emphasis added).
[24] Barrett, 1962, 97.
[25] Scroggs, 1966, 91 (emphasis added); cf. p. 59.
[26] Scroggs, 1966, 100 (emphasis added). Cf. Dunn, 1973, 136 (and 136 n. 28).

ward Adam in Paul's writings, but he actually does tie this attitude more closely to Paul's reading of a pre-sin text. Kim writes:[27]

> For Paul Adam is *always* a sinner. For him Adam means simply the fallen first man. He knows no glorious Adam before his fall as some Rabbis fantastically depicted. What Adam was before his fall *does not interest him*. In contrast to Christ in whom Paul saw the image and glory of God and the eternal life restored, Adam is from the beginning the fallen *Stammvater* [i.e., progenitor] of fallen humanity. That is why even in Gen 2.7 Paul can see only the ignoble, weak and mortal Adam.

Does this mean that Paul saw Gen. 2:7 as God's creation of a "fallen first man," a "sinner"? In harmony with Barrett's and Scroggs' presentation of Paul's view of the creation of Adam and with Reumann's and Witherington's presentation of Paul's view of the creation of the world, Kim does not think that Paul "knows" or is "interested in" the pre-sin creation. Not only does Paul say nothing but he even "knows" nothing about Adam as a good created human.

James Dunn argues that "Adam plays a larger role in Paul's theology than is usually realized.... Adam is a key figure in Paul's attempt to express his understanding both of Christ and of man."[28] Adam-Christology is "one of the principal load-bearing beams in the superstructure of Pauline Christology."[29] Paul's pervasive "in Christ" language is even essentially connected to his Adam-Christology.[30] Dunn writes, "Adam christology can thus be seen to form an extensive feature in Paul's theology. More importantly, it provides an integrating framework both for Paul's christology and for his entire gospel."[31] In light of this (extreme) importance attributed to Paul's use of Adam for his theology, it certainly would seem "necessary," as Dunn argues, "to trace *the extent of the Adam motif* in Paul if we are to appreciate the force of his Adam christology."[32]

Before one gets too excited about the prospect of someone actually tracing "the extent of the Adam motif" in Paul, however, G. Fee counters that "neither the nature nor the extent of so-called Adam Christology is a matter on which all are agreed."[33] While critical of a "maximalist" recognition

---

[27] Kim, 1980, 264 n. 1 (emphasis added).
[28] Dunn, 1980, 101; affirmed by van Kooten, 2008, 70.
[29] Dunn, 1998A, 231.
[30] Dunn, 1998A, 233; cf. Ridderbos, 1975, 60–61.
[31] Dunn, 1998A, 233. Cf. Black, 1954: "The Second Adam doctrine provided St Paul with the scaffolding, if not the basic structure, for his redemption and resurrection christology" (173; also quoted with favour by Dunn, 1980, 308 n. 39).
[32] Dunn, 1980, 101 (emphasis added).
[33] Fee, 2007, 513. Even more critically, Fee writes of the "overblown emphasis on a so-called Adam Christology" which "goes considerably beyond the biblical account itself and thus takes Paul's Christology where Paul himself does not go" (272).

of "Adam Christology" represented by Dunn (as well as by N.T. Wright),[34] but also of a "minimalist" approach that only sees Adam in Paul's three explicit uses of his name (1 Cor. 15:21–22, 45–47, and Rom. 5:12–21), Fee dubs his approach "middling" and includes Paul's references to "image" in 1 Cor. 15:49, 2 Cor. 3:18, 4:4–6, and Rom. 8:29. Fee adds that Paul's notions of "new creation," "image of God," and "second Adam" are "so important" as an aspect of "Pauline soteriology."[35]

Yet even Dunn's "maximalist" and Fee's "middling" approaches to Paul's concept of Adam leave a lot to be desired for a treatment of Paul's understanding of the original creation of humanity. It is not surprising that Fee does not deal with 1 Cor. 11:7–12 at all, for while it is protological (and pre-sin) it is not Christological, and his task is specifically Christological. Fee does briefly mention a general loss or "distortion" of the divine image by Adam.[36] But the only other hint which Fee gives toward Paul's understanding of the original Adam or creation regard his brief statements about 1 Cor. 15:49: "the goal of the first creation will be finally realized in the second"[37] and the "ultimate goal of salvation" is "re-creation into the divine image."[38] While this may be true, because this "Adamic" aspect of Fee's study does not engage much with Paul's view of the *first* Adam it presents a wide berth for a study that does.

In Dunn's tracing of "the extent of the Adam motif" in Paul, he argues that "Paul's understanding of man as he now is is heavily influenced by the narratives about Adam in Gen. 1–3."[39] This is reminiscent of Scroggs' assertion (see above). Although Dunn had previously and self-consciously followed Scroggs in claiming that "it is the risen Jesus who is the image of God, *not* any *Urmensch*, let alone the first Adam"[40] and that "Adam in Paul is *always* fallen man,"[41] his subsequent work seems to take more account of what Paul actually writes (or at least implies) about the pre-sin Adam. Adam is one of Paul's metaphors for "man's salvation,"[42] and that salvation, as Dunn summarizes it, is "the fashioning or reshaping of the believer

---

[34] Fee, 2007, 513–14. See Dunn, 1980, 98–128; *idem*, 1998B, 199–204; Wright, 1992, 18–40, 57–62, 90–97. Fee's comments here are also approved and somewhat employed by van Kooten, 2008, 70–71.

[35] Fee, 2007, 486.

[36] Fee, 2007, 114–19 (on "Jesus as Second Adam" in 1 Corinthians), 486.

[37] Fee, 2007, 119. On 2 Cor. 3:18, 4:4, 6 see pp. 180–85, and on "Jesus as Second Adam" in Romans see pp. 271–72.

[38] Fee, 2007, 484–88.

[39] Dunn, 1980, 101.

[40] Dunn, 1973, 136 (quoting Scroggs, 1966, 91, at 136 n. 28).

[41] Dunn, 1973, 136 n. 28.

[42] See Dunn, 1980, 101–13.

into the image of God."[43] For Paul's pre-sin Adam Dunn deduces harmony with and knowledge of God (Rom. 1:18–25),[44] glory (Rom. 3:23),[45] and image-bearing (1 Cor. 15:49; 2 Cor. 3:18; Col. 3:10; Eph. 4:24).[46] Dunn even almost takes into consideration 1 Cor. 11:7 in relation to this last observation, but he then relegates it to an "untypical" thought of Paul.[47] (Dealing with 1 Cor. 11:7 in more detail, as we will in chapter 3, actually would have helped Dunn in this particular task of analyzing "the extent of the Adam motif in Paul").

Dunn thus draws out of various Pauline phrases more implications for Paul's view of the pre-sin Adam than many others had done. Yet Dunn's claim to have "examined the influence *of the creation* and fall narratives on Paul's understanding of man"[48] still leaves significant room for an even fuller treatment of what Paul thinks about God's creation of Adam. Dunn's portrayal of Paul's view of pre-sin Adam certainly allows for deeper exploration of how this aspect of the Beginning relates to Paul's broader reading of God's creation of the entire world according to Genesis 1.

Bouteneff treats Paul's understanding of Adam as well. As we saw above, Bouteneff's treatment of Paul's reading of the Hexaemeron account as a whole turned out to be more limited than even he had expressly desired.[49] With Paul's understanding of Adam too, Bouteneff only briefly explores Paul's more particular interpretation of Adam *as created*, dealing only with Paul's use of Gen. 2:7c in 1 Cor. 15:45. There Bouteneff shows how Paul contrasts the man made from dust with Christ, and he concludes (helpfully) that "our resurrection in immortality is neither bodiless nor ours by right or by nature but is entirely ['in Christ']."[50] After this one statement, however, and in line with the emphasis in Barrett, Scroggs, Kim, Dunn, and Fee, Bouteneff mainly treats Paul's use of Adam as a sinner. Such an *emphasis* in each interpreter is legitimate enough, for the majority (i.e., two out of three) of Paul's explicit uses of "Adam" by name (1 Cor. 15:21–22 and Rom. 5:12–21) do treat him as the bringer of the sinful sting of death. But the claims that are then made concerning Paul's view of Adam, claims that are based on incomplete treatments of what Paul writes, tend to outrun the noted evidence and run in the wrong direction in relation to the wider evidence.

---

[43] Dunn, 1980, 105. Cf. Fee's "ultimate goal of salvation" as "re-creation into the divine image" (2007, 484–88).
[44] Dunn, 1980, 101.
[45] Dunn, 1980, 102–03, 106 (cf. *idem*, 1988, 1.178–79; *idem*, 1998A, 231–32).
[46] Dunn, 1980, 105.
[47] Dunn, 1980, 105, 308 n. 31.
[48] Dunn, 1980, 105.
[49] Bouteneff, 2008, 36.
[50] Bouteneff, 2008, 44; see 43–44.

To give another example of this last criticism, Bouteneff draws a conclusion that harmonizes with the chorus above (i.e., with Barrett, Scroggs, early Dunn, and Kim) concerning Paul's understanding of the pre-sin beginning in Adam:[51]

> [R]*ather than* Adam being a model or image for humanity or even the first real human being, it is Christ who is both. Christ is the first true human being, and *Christ is the image of God and the model for Adam*. Indeed, there is *no* mention of the person of Adam as created in God's image. Genesis 1:26 and 2:7 are distinct for him: Paul's Adam is *not* so much the first human being as he is the first human to sin.

Bouteneff appears to qualify this last statement. He admits that Paul "sees that the human person is in God's image (1 Cor. 11:7)." But he immediately counters that even so "Paul does not write of Adam as glorious or image-bearing but, *rather*, as the 'man of dust' (1 Cor. 15:47)."[52] Bouteneff adds another falsely dichotomized alternative (used by Barrett, Scroggs, Dunn, and Kim; see above): *rather* than Adam being "glorious or image-bearing," for Paul "it is *Christ* who is the image of God (Col. 1:15; Heb. 1:3) and to whose image humanity must conform (Rom. 8:29)."[53]

It is true that the goal and hope of a Christian is to be conformed to Christ's "image" and not to that of the first Adam (1 Cor. 15:49, see chapter 3). But does Paul's labeling of Christ's status as "image of God" or of Adam's status as "man of dust" really imply that Adam, in his creation, was thereby for Paul *not* "glorious or image-bearing"? This question (among others) is best answered by a more robust engagement with Paul's material than has heretofore been presented, an engagement that takes into consideration Paul's complex and diversely-related comments as well as the sacred source upon which he bases them.

How is this study related to other attempts to understand Paul's view of creation? As seen above, some scholars hail the fruitfulness of exploring Paul's view of the creation of Adam and of the world while others imply that such a pursuit would be futile. The lack of detail in any of these scholars mentioned above regarding Paul's full treatment of either the beginning of humanity or of the beginning of the world opens the way for the usefulness of the present study. Paul's language of creation in his letters to the Corinthian and Roman Christians suggests more than has been previously offered, and it corrects or qualifies what many have proposed. Yet it is not only the case that a fuller engagement with Paul's own language of creation will be of such benefit. As I will now argue, it is also the case that a comparison between Paul's somewhat scattered treatments of scriptural texts of creation and the contemporary but more formal and systematic

---

[51] Bouteneff, 2008, 45 (emphasis added).
[52] Bouteneff, 2008, 45 (emphasis added).
[53] Bouteneff, 2008, 45 (emphasis original).

treatments of the same creational texts by Philo of Alexandria can help us recognize, highlight, and analyze important and intertwined complexities in Paul's perspectives on creation.

Paul as a Reader of Scripture in Comparison with Philo

The mention of a comparison between Paul's and Philo's readings of creation raises our second question: why are we approaching this fuller treatment of Paul's understanding of creation in such a manner? In general, studying Paul's interpretation of scripture is helpful for interpreting his thought. He often refers to scripture as proof of a point and he often shapes a particular statement on a (or some) text(s). So, for example, regarding the relationship between Paul's scripture interpretation and his Christology, Francis Watson rightly explains: "In Paul, scripture is not overwhelmed by the light of an autonomous Christ-event needing no scriptural mediation. It is scripture that shapes the contours of the Christ-event."[54] In this regard, and with a particular eye toward our specific purpose, even though Christ is much more important to Paul than is Adam, nevertheless Paul can explain *Christ* as "the last *Adam*" (1 Cor. 15:45). This is a textual claim as well as a Christological one; it is virtually meaningless without the knowledge of what, for example, "Adam" means for Paul.

Paul and Philo share a common footing when standing up to announce their perspectives to their own readers. Concerning both men, the Jewish scripture "condition[s] [their] perception of the world"[55] and is "the 'determinate subtext that plays a constitutive role' in shaping [their] literary production" as well.[56] In light of this, a deep engagement with their readings is necessary for discerning their views of reality.[57]

Though it is generally agreed that Philo is important to an understanding of NT interpretation, the exact relationship between Philo, Paul, their writings, and some sort of shared background is still debated.[58] Some have

---

[54] Watson, 2004, 17.

[55] Hays, 1989, 16 (also quoted favorably in Watson, 2004, 17–18).

[56] Hays, 1989, 18.

[57] Watson (2004) rightly observes that Paul's interpretation is a two-way street, "an interaction rather than a unilinear movement" (5), that "the Christ who sheds light on scripture is also and above all the Christ on whom scripture simultaneously sheds its own light" (17; see 14–17). Throughout this study I will demonstrate this sort of reciprocal hermeneutic; my present emphasis on the direction from scripture to Christ and reality does not undercut the importance of the return direction.

[58] Since a fuller bibliography and engagement with various studies will be found throughout our study, a mere sample of recent applicable scholarship will be listed here. For Philo as generally important for NT and Pauline studies cf. Hurtado, 2004, 73–92 (on

been criticized for reading Philo (and other ancient Jewish writers) in light of Pauline categories.[59] Others can be faulted with reading Paul in light of Philonic categories that are foreign to Paul.[60] One thing that Philo and Paul both clearly demonstrate through their writings, however, is a deep engagement with the same scriptural texts. John Barclay writes,[61]

> The Jewish philosopher Philo and the Jewish apostle Paul were contemporaries whose paths never crossed and whose minds moved within startlingly different frameworks. Both, however, were profoundly engaged in the interpretation of the Jewish Scriptures... [and a] comparison which gives attention to the differences as well as the similarities between these two figures seems well justified.

This common ground of scripture engagement will be our focus for comparison.

For both Paul and Philo, God created the world and humanity. It was the same text of Genesis which they both read as saying so and how. Philo's commentary on Genesis 1–3, *De Opificio Mundi* ("*Op.*"), has a definite emphasis on creation in 1:1–2:7.[62] His comments on the text therein are not

---

Paul see 75–77); Sterling, 2004, 21–52 (on Paul see 41–43); Nickelsburg, 2004, 53–72 (on NT see 69–70). See also Runia, 1993, 63–86 (on Paul see 66–74).

[59] Levison (1988) argues that "'motifs' of an 'Adam speculation' or 'Adam myth' ...discerned in Early Judaism" (e.g., by Davies [pp. 14–15], Jervell [pp. 15–16], Barrett [p. 16], Brandenburger [pp. 17–18], Scroggs [pp. 18–20], Dunn [pp. 20–21], Wright [pp. 21–23]) "do not exist" (13), and the erroneous perpetuation of this myth is fuelled by previous scholars having typically interpreted the Jewish authors through the lenses of Pauline categories (14–23). In Levison's estimation, this practice has skewed an understanding of Philo's concept of Adam, as well as the Adam-theologies of Ben Sira, *Jubilees*, Josephus, *4 Ezra*, etc. This was also the basic criticism which J. Neusner (1978), amid a mostly positive review, levelled against Sanders' *Paul and Palestinian Judaism* (177–91). Cf. the critique of Sanders in Watson, 2004, 6–13. Watson argues that "if there are ambiguities and tensions in the scriptural texts, one would expect a degree of interpretative diversity rather than an almost universal conformity to a single 'pattern'" (13).

[60] For the judgment that it was *not* Philo or Philonic ideas behind the Paul-Corinthian debate and that such construals misunderstand Paul (and perhaps also Philo) see Schaller, 2004, 42–51 and Hultgren, 2003, 343–57. For some who are thereby criticized for seeing Philonic (or Philonic-type) and/or Platonizing interpretations of reality and Gen. 2:7 (and 1:27) as behind the issue in 1 Cor. 15:45–49 see Pearson, 1973 (esp. 11–12, 17–21); *idem*, 1983, 73–89; Horsley, 1976, 269–88; *idem*, 1977, 224–39; *idem*, 1978, 203–231 (esp. 206–07); Davis, 1984 (esp. 49–62); Sellin, 1986, 156–89; Theissen, 1987, 353–67; Sterling, 1995, 355–84; *idem*, 2004, 41–43. See chapter 3 for more particular critiques of some of these construals of the issue, and particularly regarding van Kooten's recent (2008) presentation of Paul's treatment of Gen. 1:27 and 2:7 in a Philonic manner.

[61] Barclay, 2006, 140. On the fundamental importance of the scriptures to ancient Jewish people generally see Barclay, 1996A, 424–26.

[62] The beginning of *Op.* introduces creation rather than sin (§§1–12), and the conclusion summarizes five theological-creational doctrines and no hamartological ones (§§170–72). Philo's commentary on 1:1–2:7 then occurs in §§13–147, obviously the ma-

allegorical (thereby making them easier to compare with Paul's comments), are from a very similar time period to Paul's, and are especially discernible as they take the form of an explicit and formal commentary. A deliberate and contemporary commentary on God's creation according to Genesis provides a very helpful foil against which we may compare Paul's occasional (but not few) comments on the same sacred texts.

There seems to be a general growth in recognition that treating Paul and Philo as readers of shared scripture is a fruitful way to discuss their thoughts, both alone and in comparison.[63] F. Watson has recently encouraged and demonstrated the benefits of a "three-way conversation" between Paul, non-Christian Jewish writers (including Philo), and the shared scriptural texts to which each turns in order to understand and explain their world.[64] Richard Hays has called for greater attention to "Pauline hermeneutical strategies" and has argued for the "study of Paul's exegesis of scripture" as a healthy way forward in Pauline discussion.[65] David Runia has written that "there is a growing consensus among Philonic scholars that Philo saw himself first and foremost as an exegete of Mosaic scripture, and that a sound way to start understanding him is to begin at the level of his exegetical expositions."[66] This claim regarding Philo has been criticized for neglecting the importance of Philo's philosophical understanding,[67] though it need not be understood in such a manner. Comparing any two exegetes on a particular passage, e.g., George van Kooten and Gordon Fee on 1 Cor. 15:45, will simultaneously link the two different thinkers as fellow readers of the same text, will show certain commonalities between them, and yet will also bring to light some of the philosophical and theological differences which both interpreters bring to the "conversation." Toward a similar complex of ends, this study places Philo and Paul in "conversation" over (and with) their shared scripture.

---

jority of the commentary, while the remainder of the commentary (§§151–69) encompasses the naming in 2:19 (§§148–50), the woman in 2:21–23 (§§151–52), and the garden, temptation, and sin in 2:8–9, 3:1–24 (§§153–69). Thus, though *Op.* is technically a commentary on Genesis 1–3, it is not inappropriate to summarize it as a commentary on Genesis 1–2:7.

[63] See the helpful approach by Loader, 2004, regarding the issue of sexuality and gender in Philo's and Paul's (and the NT's) reading of the LXX (and especially of Genesis 2).

[64] See Watson, 2004, and his method on pp. 1–6.

[65] Hays, 1995, 85–86.

[66] Runia, 1990, XI.72.

[67] See e.g., Berchman, 2000, 49–70.

With regard to this particular issue of "using" Philo's perspective as a comparison piece with NT, and especially with Pauline texts, Berndt Schaller argues:[68]

> If such efforts are to contribute something real to the case, then this requires an approach wherein the textual evidence and its factual peculiarities on both sides are accurately recorded, reflecting existing overlaps and disparities in detail and not hastily constructing relationships of a religion-historical and tradition-historical nature.

Schaller is clear that he is not condemning history-of-religion and tradition-historical approaches to Paul and Philo *per se*, but his call for certain care in accurately reflecting both Philo and Paul with their own peculiarities is important. Watson similarly argues that exegesis of selected non-Pauline Jewish texts "must be carried out with no less care and attention to detail than one devotes to Paul's own texts," for they each "fully repay a 'close reading,' and each has a theological and hermeneutical interest of its own which must be brought to the fore if comparison with the Pauline readings is to be fruitful."[69]

In light of the very real dangers of illegitimately pressing either Philo or Paul into the other's categories, and since the focus below is on Philo and Paul as interpreters of the same sacred text of the Beginning, it is therefore appropriate that their shared scripture is what sets the structure of comparison. Thus, after drawing to the surface some potential points of interpretation raised by each text itself, I will then present Philo's exegesis and then Paul's on that particular creation text. This procedure is clearly attractive regarding Philo's interpretation of creation, for, since we will almost exclusively look at Philo's commentary on Genesis 1–2, to follow his text's order is to follow his own order. This will help guard against an "artificial category" being imposed on Philo's exegesis.

One might question the validity of this approach for Pauline interpretation. Although such an organization may have the appeal of producing an orderly view of Paul's reading of particular biblical creation texts, unlike Philo Paul is not writing a systematic commentary. His comments occur in different contexts and in a different order from the text of Genesis. His use of the creation of light from Gen. 1:2–3 comes two verses *after* his use of the anthropological title from Gen. 1:27, "image of God." As both of these are in 2 Corinthians (4:4, 6), they both come *after* Paul's reading of Gen.

---

[68] Schaller, 2004, 151 (translation mine): "Aber wenn solche Bemühungen wirklich in der Sache etwas einbringen sollen, dann verlangt dies ein Vorgehen, das die textlichen Befunde und ihre sachlichen Eigentümlichkeiten auf beiden Seiten genau registriert, vorhandene Überschneidungen wie bestehende Unterschiede eingehend reflektiert und nicht vorschnell Zusammenhänge religionsgeschichtlicher und traditionsgeschichtlicher Art konstruiert."

[69] Watson, 2004, 3.

2:7 in 1 Cor. 15:44–47 and Gen. 5:3 in 1 Cor. 15:48–49. Thus, while keeping Philo's voice liberated enough to converse with the texts in the order that he presents them, are we merely binding Paul to an inappropriate and artificial exploration of his "reading" of creation?

No. The text of Genesis sets its "anthropogony" in the larger context and movement of its "cosmogony"; i.e., the more specific texts about the "birth" or creation of the human (Gen. 1:26–28, 2:7, 5:1–3) only come after and in the context of the broader text concerning the "birth" or creation of the cosmos (Gen. 1:1–25; 2:4–6). The general connection in Philo's and Paul's day between the broader world and the particular human within it has been highlighted by scholars from many perspectives: e.g., Graeco-Roman philosophical, Jewish apocalyptic, sociological.[70] Paul and Philo both demonstrate through their exegesis of Genesis' creation-texts that there is not merely a conceptual connection between *cosmos* and *anthropos*; there is a hermeneutical connection as well. That is, the creation of the more particular humanity takes place in concert with the creation of the broader world. Paul demonstrates this in an especially clear way in 1 Cor. 15:35–49 (though it can also be seen in a slightly different form in 1 Cor. 11:7–12, 2 Cor. 4:4–6, or even Romans 8 – see below). There Paul presents God's creation of heaven and earth and all that is in them (vv. 37–41), within which "humans" are but one of the many (vv. 39–40), as conceptual prolegomena to his more specific treatment of the creation of Adam (vv. 45–47) and the propagation of subsequent humans in Adam's image (vv. 48–49). Paul's argument and use of the texts from the beginning of Genesis follow the same basic order and logic of the biblical narrative as well as of Philo.

Both readers can set the prior and broader work of God in the beginning of the world as the context for their construal of the beginning of humanity. It is also the case that Paul, like Philo and their scripture before them, uses similar language to describe the creation of the world and the creation of humanity. Hence introducing a structure of comparison based on Genesis itself, a structure which then introduces Philo's and Paul's exegeses of the applicable scriptural text of the Beginning – both of the world (chapter 2 below) and of humanity (chapter 3 below) – will help preserve the integ-

---

[70] There was a general Graeco-Roman trend in connecting cosmos and anthropos: so Martin, 1992, 3–15, 17; cf. Runia, 2001, 227, 254 (cf. *idem*, 1986, 555); van den Hoek, 2000, 65, 67, 67 n. 12; Steenburg, 1990, 102, 104; Sandmel, 1983, 24; Tobin, 1983, 45, 45 n. 19, 49, 125; Kim, 1980, 191. (On this in Philo see Radice, 2009, 134; *idem*, 1989, 122.) Beker (1980) and Barrett (1962) trace out some connections between the human and the world in terms of apocalyptic thought. Adams, 2000, 3–7 summarizes a number of sociological approaches to NT writings which see a close connection between the world and the human.

rity of each interpreter's own treatment of the sacred Word to which they both submit.

Paul's and Philo's Three-Strand Hermeneutic of Creation

As mentioned in the beginning, this thesis is that Paul's interpretation of creation contains three interwoven aspects: the beginning of the world, the beginning of humanity, and God's intentions before the beginning. In this broad respect Paul's hermeneutic of creation is similar to Philo's manner of interpreting the same texts of creation within his formal commentary. Now that answers have been provided for how this study relates to other attempts at understanding Paul's view of the creation of the world and the creation of Adam, as well as for why it is helpful to approach this fuller treatment of Paul's understanding of creation via a comparison between his and Philo's readings, I will briefly conclude this introduction with an answer to the third question: How exactly will this study of Paul's and Philo's three-strand interpretation of creation unfold?

As we have seen, many portrayals of Paul's view (or non-view) of Adam as a *created* being, and especially of the world as a created thing, are underdeveloped and/or developed in the wrong direction. In chapter 3, "The Beginning of Humanity," I will offer a detailed study of how Paul actually interprets the beginning of humanity according to Genesis in comparison with how Philo does likewise. The focus will be on Philo's and then Paul's uses of "the image of God" from Gen. 1:27 (for Philo in *Op.* 69–88 and 134; for Paul in 1 Cor. 11:7 and 2 Cor. 4:4), of the creation of the human person particularly as it relates to Gen. 2:7 (for Philo in *Op.* 134–50; for Paul in 1 Cor. 11:7–9, 12:12–30, 15:39–40, and 15:44–47), and of the creative principle of the propagation of humanity according to the "image" of Adam from Gen. 5:3 (for Philo in *Op.* 145 and *QG.* 1.81; for Paul in 1 Cor. 15:48–49, 2 Cor. 3:18, and Rom. 8:29).

Above I spent more time developing the usefulness of the present study with regard to Paul's more specific view of the creation of Adam than to Paul's more general view of the creation of the world. This is partly because more scholars have set themselves to the former task than to the latter. Another reason for this emphasis on humanity rather than the world is because both Philo and Paul treat the creation of humanity in more detail than they do the creation of the world. This may simply be because they are both humans and are both writing to humans. But their anthropological emphases are probably also due to their shared scripture. It crowns humanity with a peculiar glory and honor that other creatures were not granted. Both Philo and Paul recognize this quality of the Beginning. But an engagement with Paul's and Philo's readings of the beginning of humanity is only the final third of this study. Chapters 1 and 2 offer a necessary correction to the majority's tendency to focus *only* on the beginning of humanity. But to get to this human beginning – whether in Genesis itself, or in Philo's construal, or in Paul's – one should travel through their understandings of the beginning of the world itself.

Thus Chapter 2, "The Beginning of the World," will seek to fill-in the definite gap in Pauline discussion by setting aside Paul's general acknowledgment of Christ's mediation of creation (1 Cor. 8:6) as well as the general statement of God's relationship to "non-existent things" (Rom. 4:17c) and by focusing on Paul's treatment of specific texts within Genesis 1. In comparison with Philo's more elaborate treatment of the beginning of light on day one (*Op.* 30–35 on Gen. 1:1–5) and the beginning of the rest of the visible cosmos on the second through sixth days (*Op.* 36–68 on Gen. 1:6–25), we will focus on Paul's treatment of the creation of light (Gen. 1:2–3) in 2 Cor. 4:6 and of the remainder of God's creation of heaven and earth (Gen. 1:1–27) in 1 Cor. 15:35–41. Remaining focused on Paul's and Philo's readings of the text of Genesis 1 will add significant hermeneutical and theological context to our subsequent consideration in chapter 3 of Paul's and Philo's more particular readings of God's creation of Adam as or according to "God's image," as the man "of dust," and as the progenitor of humanity in "his image."

Thus far I have only mentioned two of Paul's and Philo's interlocking strands that they recognize when interpreting the Beginning: the world and humanity. Like Philo, Paul has a third aspect of his interpretation of creation. It is this third aspect which is something of the tie that binds the other two into one united treatment of creation. As I will demonstrate throughout all three chapters, both Paul and Philo consider what was determined in God's mind *before* he created this empirical world to be an important aspect of the Beginning of the world and humanity. In chapters 2 and 3, I will draw attention to how both interpreters see behind God's creative activity a certain "desire" and "purpose" according to which the creation of the world and humanity then began. These are Paul's and Philo's *implicit* testimonies to the Before, i.e., to God's pre-creative reasoning and intention. Although not explicitly labeled as taking place "before" creation, for Paul as for Philo it is in both the beginning of the world (chapter 2) and the beginning of humanity (chapter 3) that God's desire and purpose nevertheless function as that which propels and shapes God's creative activity.

Both Paul and Philo also have certain *explicit* and definable ideas about what took place in the Creator's mind before he created the visible world according to the beginning of Genesis. Both interpreters unambiguously label these divine plans and determinations as "before" creation. Such overt notions of "the Before" will occupy us in chapter 1, "Before the Beginning?" I will analyze Philo's explicit Before in *Op.* 16, 26–29, and 129–30 and then Paul's explicit Before in 1 Cor. 2:7–9 and Rom. 8:29–30. Although it may be tempting to see these Befores in Philo and Paul as merely external impositions onto Genesis of previously formed theories – Philo's shaped by Plato's *Timaeus*, Paul's shaped by Prov. 8:22–31 and the Christ-event – there is a peculiar exegetical fact in both interpreters that restrains us from such a conclusion. Both Philo and Paul actually use the language and categories from *Genesis* to communicate the content of the Before. This fact necessitates a detailed examination of how their theories of *before* creation really are intimately bound to their readings of Genesis' texts of the *beginning* of creation.

Far from having little to say about the pre-sin Beginning, Paul's interpretation of creation proves to be far more important to him as he explains God's reality than is often realized. We will now see this by demonstrating that Paul's interpretation of creation, like Philo's in his commentary, contains the three tightly interwoven strands of the beginning of the world, the beginning of humanity, and both the implicit and explicit intentions of the Creator before the beginning. And a cord of three strands should not be quickly broken.

Chapter 1

Before the Beginning?

In the beginning God existed before he created the world. Was he doing or thinking anything before he began to create? Did he deliberate over just how fast light should travel? Did he have any desires or plans for how human history should develop or end? If "time" began with the creation of space, then is it even philosophically legitimate to consider "before" creation? Do such questions even have a place in a study of how two ancient interpreters read and applied the beginning of a book that says, "In the beginning God made...," with no mention of his previous purpose? Or does Genesis testify in some way to God's pre-creational designs?

Many people find it natural to ask about the Before when contemplating the Beginning, even those who are not basing their knowledge on Genesis 1. Steven Hawking, the notable modern physicist, asks in the beginning of *A Brief History of Time*, "What do we know about the universe, and how do we know it? Where did the universe come from, and where is it going? Did the universe have a beginning, and if so, what happened *before* then?"[1] Concerning Genesis 1, Francis Watson voices what many biblical scholars assume, suggesting that "[i]f God's action is comprehensible to the extent that this narrative presupposes, then it should provide indications of [God's] purpose for the reader to develop."[2] These are not only modern queries and suggestions, however, regarding existence and the Beginning.

Writing nearly two-thousand years before Hawking and Watson, both Paul of Tarsus and Philo of Alexandria considered it important that God's acts are preceded by his thoughts. This general conviction included God's "thoughts" existing *before* his "acts" of creation. This feature of Paul's and Philo's thinking – i.e., that God deliberated before he created – is particularly noteworthy for an investigation of their interpretations of Genesis' creation account, for it is precisely in the language and motifs of Genesis that Philo and Paul each convey God's ultimate *pre*-deliberations. This suggests that their understandings of God's *pre*-creational thoughts were, in some way, connected to their interpretation of his *creative* activity as described by Genesis.

---

[1] Hawking, 1988, 1.
[2] Watson, 1994, 145.

This chapter contends that Paul's concept of God's intentions *before* creation, like Philo's, is an important aspect of his interpretation of the beginning of both the world at large and humanity in particular. The question posed in the chapter's title – "Before the Beginning?" – is thus not merely valid when analyzing Paul's and Philo's interpretations of creation; it is vital. Both interpreters give evidence that Genesis' Beginning casts their minds to the Before.

The words "In the beginning God..." could themselves easily prompt questions about the Before. The God who acts within the statement has the privilege of being in the Before.[3] So Ps. 89:2 (LXX) says, "*Before* [πρό] the mountains were brought about and the earth and the inhabited-world were formed, from the age until the age *you exist*." In Gen. 1:1 the God who was already there began to act. Since before an action there is often an intention, a deliberation, perhaps even a plan,[4] it is easy to query whether the pre-existent God had a plan before he created heaven and earth.

Around Philo's and Paul's day, many writers mused about this very question of the Before.[5] Much in the ancient Jewish discussion was prompted by the text that can be considered the scriptural "mother" of pre-protological contemplation: Prov. 8:22–31.[6] Proverbs 8 has a number of

---

[3] Wenham, 1987, 12.

[4] So Scroggs, 1966, 4. F. Watson (1994) writes, "[I]n reading any account of a series of actions carried out by an agent, it is natural and legitimate for the question *why?* to arise in the reader's mind, whether or not the narrative acknowledges the question by providing an explicit answer to it" (145). For a discussion of God's act of creation in Genesis 1 as rooted in intentionality see Jenson, 1999, 7. Jenson discusses this interpretation of creation by Basil the Great (*Homilies on the Hexaemeron* ii.7) and Thomas Aquinas (*Summa Theologiae* i.34.1). As Jenson himself observes, however, in Genesis 1 it is not God's thought *per se* that creates but God's spoken word. Cf. Martin Luther, *Lecture on Genesis* (WA 42), 13:13. Following Luther's criticism of Aquinas, Jenson writes that "God's act to create is certainly an act of intellect and will, as the majority tradition has said," but "it is the kind of such act that is not enclosed within the subject but takes place as communication" (7). God's communicative act of creation is similutaneously not reduced to but yet connected with intention.

[5] For the Before in Qumran see Schnabel (1985) on 1QS 3.15–18, where creation accords with God's "glorious design" which he "established *before* they existed," and on 1QH³ 1[9].7ff, where "*before* creating" everything God's knowledge and wisdom were planning (200; see 200 n. 209 for more texts). Cf. Endo, 2002, 115 for more examples from Qumran. Endo also lists for the Before elsewhere in ancient Judaism: *1 En.* 9:11; *2 En.* 25:3; 33:3; 4 Ezra 6:1–6; 7:70; 8:52; *2 Bar.* 14:17; 54:1; *T. Mos* 1:12–13, etc. (115). One may add *1 En.* 39:11 ("even before the world was created, [God] knew what is forever and what will be from generation to generation"); 46:1–2; 47:3; and 48:3–7 (esp. vv. 6–7 which use words such as "hidden," "before creation," and "wisdom"; cf. 1 Cor. 2:6–9 below).

[6] See Hengel, 1974, 1.153–75. Endo (2002) says that in the contexts of the passages listed in my previous note (n. 5), "Prov 8:22–31 is more or less mentioned" (115).

lexical and conceptual overlaps with Genesis 1 itself. This is particularly relevant for us for at least three reasons. One, Proverbs 8 has been influential in guiding a number of ancient thinkers (e.g., Sirach, Wisdom of Solomon, Philo) into thoughts about before the beginning.[7] Two, these contemplations of pre-existence are almost always done in correlation with the use of phrases and themes from Genesis 1–2.[8] And three, like the text of Genesis itself, the text of Prov. 8:22–31 (and v. 23 in particular) is common ground for Philo and Paul. For example, Philo quotes Prov. 8:23 in *Ebr.* 30–31 and Paul alludes to it in 1 Cor. 2:7. (See below for substantiation.) Prov. 8:23 plays a formative role in both Philo's and Paul's understanding of what took place *before* the beginning, and both interpreters also use Genesis' own language and motifs to further explain this Before and its effects.

Philo and Paul each testify, both explicitly and implicitly, to an understanding of pre-creation. Both readers incorporate into their explanation of God's creative activity a testimony to a certain governing intentionality – a "purpose," a "desire" – that is not explicitly labelled as "before" but is nonetheless *implicitly* regarded as prior to a specific creation. These statements will be explored below in chapters 2 and 3 since they are thoroughly interwoven into Paul's and Philo's comments that are more directly on God's acts of creating the world and humanity. In this first chapter, however, I will demonstrate the presence and content of an *explicit* Before – i.e., what they label "before" – in Philo's commentary on Genesis 1 and in Paul's letters to the Corinthians and Romans. Both readers present a definite and definable divine plan, whether, simplistically put, for structural enactment (so Philo) or historical enactment (so Paul).

To now gain our bearing on Philo's and Paul's treatment of Genesis' Beginning and Before, I will make a few observations on Prov. 8:22–31 itself and on its connection to Genesis 1.

1.1 Proverbs 8:22–31 and Before Genesis 1

According to Paul and Philo, Genesis (written by Moses) would have been recorded before Proverbs (written by Solomon).[9] Though numerous scholars today do not follow this notion of authorship, it carries a hermeneutical significance that one must consider when analyzing Philo and Paul. For interpreters like these two, any scriptural testimonies to creation that come

---

[7] Hengel, 1974, 1.99 n. 300, 1.162–63; Steenburg, 1990, 101–02; Harrington, 1996.

[8] See the discussion in Kugel, 1998, 44–47.

[9] Aristobulus mentions Solomon's authorship of Proverbs, particularly of Prov. 8:22–23, preserved in Eusebius' *Pr. Ev.* 13.12.9–11. Cf. Hengel, 1974, 1.166; Kugel, 1998, 44.

after Moses' time (e.g., Psalms 24 and 104), and thus Proverbs 8, would most likely be read as referring to the event as it was primarily and initially described in Genesis 1–2. This would be further confirmed if there was shared language. Gen. 1:1–2 LXX says,

In the beginning [ἐν ἀρχῇ] God made [ἐποίησεν] the heaven and the earth [τὸν οὐρανὸν καὶ τὴν γῆν]. And the earth [ἡ γῆ] was invisible and un-constructed [ἀόρατος καὶ ἀκατασκεύαστος], and darkness was upon the abyss [τῆς ἀβύσσου], and the Spirit of God was bringing itself upon the water [τοῦ ὕδατος].

In Prov. 3:18–20 we read (with lexical similarities to Genesis 1–2 italicized) that "wisdom" is

...a *tree of life* [ξύλον ζωῆς] to all who hold fast to it, and for those who stay themselves on it, as upon the Lord, [wisdom is] secure. God in wisdom [τῇ σοφίᾳ] founded *the earth* [ἐθεμελίωσεν τὴν γῆν], and he prepared *the heavens* [ἡτοίμασεν δὲ οὐρανούς] in understanding [ἐν φρονήσει]; in discernment [ἐν αἰσθήσει] he burst the *abyss*es [ἄβυσσοι], and clouds let flow dew.

Like 3:18–20, Prov. 8:22–31 draws the reader back into the realm of creation in an attempt to show the surpassing greatness (and thus the desirability) of this particular wisdom.[10] In Prov. 8:22–25 LXX below (with italics for lexical similarities to Genesis 1 and "before" [πρό]) "wisdom" says,

The Lord created [ἔκτισεν] me, *the beginning* [ἀρχήν] of his ways for his works. *Before* the age [πρὸ τοῦ αἰῶνος] you founded me [ἐθεμελίωσέν με], *in the beginning* [ἐν ἀρχῇ]. *Before* the *making* of *the earth* [πρὸ τοῦ τὴν γῆν ποιῆσαι], and *before* the making of the *abyss*es [πρὸ τοῦ τὰς ἀβύσσους ποιῆσαι], before the coming forth of the springs of *the waters* [πρό...τῶν ὑδάτων], before [πρό] the mountains were placed, and before [πρό] all the hills, you bore me.

Prov. 8:22–25 evokes Gen. 1:1–2. Not only do they share the general theme of creation, but they correspond at a number of lexical points: "beginning," "in the beginning," "make," "the earth," "abyss," "water." The simple fact that the Lord "created" wisdom to be "the beginning" of his works (v. 22) would probably recall Genesis 1, even though ἔκτισεν and ἀρχήν refer to wisdom rather than to "the heavens and the earth." But what follows in vv. 23–25 even more firmly roots its readers back in the text of Genesis 1, "in the beginning."

God's establishment of wisdom is simultaneously "in the beginning" (ἐν ἀρχῇ, v. 23b; Gen. 1:1a) and also "before the age" (πρὸ τοῦ αἰῶνος, v. 23a). Though this appears contradictory at first – was wisdom founded *before* or *in* the beginning? – the text then explains. Although wisdom existed "in the beginning" (v. 23b), it was actually there "*before* the making of the earth" (v. 24a). When Gen. 1:1 records "In the beginning," but just

---

[10] For the link between Prov. 3:19 and 8:22–31 cf. Scott, 1965, 70–71; Fee, 2007, 611 n. 42.

before it reports that "God made...the earth," *that* is the moment when wisdom was present and set in place. This "time" was also *before* "the making of the abysses" (v. 24b) and *before* "the waters" (v. 24c), both of which were already present by Gen. 1:2. When contemplating "the beginning," Prov. 8:23–24 posits that it was only after God's wisdom was firmly set that his creative acts then transpired as Genesis 1 relays them.

The six references to "before" (πρό) in Prov. 8:23–25 are enmeshed in the language of the beginning of Genesis 1. In Prov. 8:26–31 the word "before" ceases to be used, but the theme persists. Wisdom continues her autobiography in relation to creation, and the references remain in the language of Genesis 1 (italicized below):

The Lord *made* [ἐποίησεν] countries and uninhabited places and outermost dwellings of what is under *heaven*. When he was preparing *the heaven* [ἡτοίμαζεν τὸν οὐράνον] I was together with him, and also when he was separating his throne upon the winds. When he was *making* [ἐποίει] strong the clouds above, and was fixing the fountains of what is under *heaven* as certain, and was *making* [ἐποίει] strong the foundations of *the earth* [τὰ θεμέλια τῆς γῆς], I was joined beside him. I myself was the one in whom he delighted each *day* [καθ' ἡμέραν]. And I rejoiced in his presence all the time when he rejoiced in the inhabited world after *complet*ing [συντελέσας] it; and he rejoiced in the sons of men.

Wisdom overtly claims to have προ-existed creation (vv. 22–25), and she continues to press upon the reader her contemporary presence already at those very creative moments that were recorded, originally, in Genesis 1.

Wisdom was related to God in his creative work, and it was wisdom in whom God delighted. God's "daily" delight – perhaps on each of the six "days" – could easily recall God's blessing (Gen. 1:22, 28–30) and appraisal (1:31) of his whole inhabited creation after he "completed" it (συντελέω, 2:1–3). That is, on each day God saw "goodness," even "beauty" (καλός), in his newly forming world, and after humans began to inhabit it God celebrated all things together as "exceedingly beautiful" (Gen. 1:31).[11] Wisdom recalls that after "completing" (συντελέσας) the inhabited world God "rejoiced" in both it and humanity. Proverbs 8 recalls Genesis 1, being inextricably bound up in its language and themes.[12]

Unlike a number of psalms which merely relay the protology of Genesis 1 in other words,[13] and unlike Genesis 1 itself which merely prompts an implicit question of the Before, Proverbs 8 explicitly mentions something about *pre*-protology. Although Proverbs 8 falls short of providing either an actual pre-creational structural plan or program of action, it has given an unambiguous textual foothold to scripture-interpreters who think it impor-

---

[11] Hengel (1974) sees Proverbs 8, and especially wisdom as God's "companion" (ἁρμόζουσα, 8:30) as communicating purposeful creational "beauty" (1.162).

[12] Longman (2006) sees the Hebrew of Prov. 8:22–31 as alluding to Genesis 1 (207).

[13] E.g., LXX: Ps. 32:6–9; 94:3–6; 95:5b; 103:1–5.

tant to explore God's character and intention in the Before. It has also kept such interpreters close to the language and text of Genesis 1.

We must be careful how we portray "wisdom" when discussing both Proverbs 8 and its affect on subsequent readers. The "wisdom" of Proverbs 8 cannot be reduced into simply a "pre-existent mediator of creation." Many scholars assume that "wisdom" in Prov. 8:22–31, as well as "wisdom" in early Jewish texts which build upon Proverbs 8 (e.g., Sirach 1 and 24, Baruch 3–4, and Wisdom of Solomon 9; see below), provide just such an image.[14] Yet it is not universally accepted that "wisdom" in Prov. 8:22–31 should be considered a mediator of creation.[15] This is especially so in light of how the LXX treats the Hebrew. Johann Cook observes that each time the Hebrew seems to attribute creative activity to "wisdom" (and even this is debated[16]) the LXX changes the subject to God. The LXX thereby seems to remove any notion of "wisdom" herself participating as co-Creatrix.[17] And yet Philo, using the same Greek as the LXX of Prov. 8:22–23, does interpret wisdom as co-begetter of the world with God the Father (*Ebr.* 30–31). It is therefore best to conclude that while it is possible to understand "wisdom" in Proverbs 8 as creation-mediation, it also seems quite possible to employ Prov. 8:22–31 without understanding "wisdom" as creation-mediator. (Paul makes just this move in 1 Cor. 2:7; see below.)

Proverbs 8:22–31 casts the minds of readers into the Before. It does so in a manner that easily evokes the text of Genesis 1 itself. While this "wisdom" may take different forms in the writings of different readers, it is always pre-creational, existing before the events as described in Genesis 1.

We will now see that both the *presence* and the *content* of a pre-creational Before are discernable in the comments of both Philo and Paul. Philo and Paul each use a text other than Genesis to gain entrance into the Before. For Paul the text is Prov. 8:23. For Philo, while Prov. 8:23 is important (as will be mentioned below), in his commentary on Genesis 1-2 it is Plato's *Timaeus* by which Philo gains entrance into the Before. Both interpreters then use the language of Genesis' Beginning to further express and apply this Before to their audiences. It will be in light of these broad hermeneutical similarities between Paul and Philo that he depth of their different conclusions will emerge regarding what God was actually think-

---

[14] Lange, 1995, 34 regarding "wisdom" in Proverbs 8. This description of "wisdom" is given to Philo's understanding, especially in *Her.* 199 and *Virt.* 62, by Lorenzen, 2008, 102–03. For some who apply this notion of "wisdom" while discussing Paul see Reiling, 1988, 204 and Barbour, 1979, 64, 68.

[15] Fee, 2007, 606–19.

[16] Yee, 1992, 91–93; Murphy, 1985, 5.

[17] See the shift of "I" to "he" in vv. 30–31 LXX. Cook, 1997, 224, 246; cf. Jobes, 2000, 231–32.

ing *before the beginning*. And these divine thoughts in the Before carry interpretive significance for their readings of the Beginning.

1.2 Philo's "Before"
God's Pre-Creational Deliberation for Goodness' Sake

In a world where scriptural texts, early Jewish writings, and famous philosophies were presenting their thoughts on the Before,[18] Philo joins the discussion. He does so in a similar manner to Prov. 8:22–31. In fact, the manner in which many modern scholars depict God's "wisdom" in Prov. 8:22–31 could well be explanations of Philo's own creation-theology and interpretation of Genesis 1 and the Before.[19] For example, "wisdom" in Prov. 8:22–31 is described as "God's skills as Creator" which "prove the Lord's unsurpassed wisdom,"[20] as "the great plan underlying all of reality,"[21] as "God's wise blueprint,"[22] and even as God's "creation-plan, as a prototype of the world."[23] Such "wisdom" as is found in Proverbs 8 "provokes the imagination to conceive of reality as the well-designed world of a divine architect who, by means of wisdom, proportions its components into a harmonious, elegant whole."[24] Functioning as God's "companion" (ἁρμόζουσα), wisdom "guarantees creation's perfection and purposeful

---

[18] Regarding philosophy, Aristotle famously argued (according to Ps.-Plutarch [Aëtius 1.7 at 881B-C] and Philo [*Aet.* 83]) against Plato: "What did god do *before* he proceeded to create? Was he simply idle?" (see Runia, 2001, 113). Plutarch discusses the condition of matter (as disorderly, corporeal, and irrationally motive) "*before* the genesis of the cosmos" (πρὸ τῆς τοῦ κόσμου γενέσεως) (*Moralia XIII: On the Generation of the Soul in the Timaeus* 1014B.8). He also defends Plato's theory of *pre*-existence by showing that, depending on Plato's context (whether in *Phaedrus* [245C.5–246A.2] or in *Timaeus* [34b.10–35a.1]), the Soul and even certain "bodies" existed "*before* the genesis of the cosmos" (πρὸ τῆς [τοῦ] κόσμου γενέσεως) (1016C.6, 1016D.10). Plotinus discusses how the "Mind" existed "*before* the cosmos" (πρὸ κόσμου) (*On Difficulties About the Soul* [Ennead IV.3], 13.23), how the objects of "the Maker's" thoughts "must" (δεῖ) exist "*before* the cosmos" (πρὸ τοῦ κόσμου) (*On Intellect, the Forms, and Being* [Ennead V.9], 5.22), and how people's souls existed "*before* the cosmos" (πρὸ κόσμου) and had it in them, at that time, to belong to the universe (*On Providence* [Ennead III.2], 7.24).
[19] See Davis, 1984, 52–53 (see 179 n. 13–14 for more Philonic references).
[20] House, 1998, 64.
[21] Kugel, 1998, 44.
[22] Fee, 2007, 611.
[23] Rösel, 1994, 82: "Schöpfungsplan, als Urbild der Welt." Rösel claims that Proverbs 8 and the "Platonic presentation of creation" are not necessarily two mutually exclusive schemes (82).
[24] Perdue, 1994, 93. Cf. Ringe, 1999, 36.

beauty."[25] As we will see, these descriptions of "wisdom" according to Proverbs 8 are reminiscent of Philo's Before.

Philo describes God as "before all creation" (πρὸ παντὸς τοῦ γενητοῦ),[26] with nothing existing with him.[27] In *Ebr.* 30–31 he draws special attention to God's "wisdom" – God's wife – as presented in Prov. 8:22–31.[28] The cosmos is a child born through God's union with "wisdom" (ἡ σοφία) and "knowledge" (ἐπιστήμη). Quoting Prov. 8:22–23 as proof, Philo's wisdom says, "God created me first of his works, and before the age he founded me." Philo draws attention to this text's temporal aspect, "before the age," so as to show that "everything" is younger than wisdom, who is mother and nurse. The supremacy of Philo's own "wisdom" (toward sobriety here) is measured by its association with the Creator at creation and by its presence "before the age," i.e., according to Prov. 8:23a.

Throughout his corpus, Philo connects "wisdom" to creation at many points (often explicitly to the text of Genesis 1) in a similar fashion as had Proverbs 8 before him. Prov. 8:22–31 appears to be of some importance to his theology.[29] But it is according to Philo's commentary on Genesis 1 that God's "skills as Creator" are seen *en force*. As Prov. 8:22–31 had presented an ultimately theocentric reading of creation by drawing attention to God via his wisdom, Philo is likewise theocentric in his commentary. All five doctrines with which Philo will summarize Genesis 1–3 involve God's own nature and his decisions for creation (see *Op.* 172.5–9). Proverbs 8:22–31 had drawn attention to the Before when "commenting" on Genesis 1. Likewise, in Philo's commentary on Genesis 1 he delves into the divine thoughts *before* the age of the visible cosmos in order to show God's surpassing skillfulness and beauty in creation. For Philo, the existence of

---

[25] Hengel, 1974, 1.162.

[26] *Migr.* 183. Cf. *Somn.* 1.65, where Philo follows his reference to "God, who existed before the world" (§65) with a reference to both "wisdom" and "the divine word" (§66); cf. *Mut.* 27, 46.

[27] *Leg.* 2.2; cf. *Op.* 23.

[28] So Laporte, 1976, 104, 114–15; Tobin, 1983, 141.

[29] Radice (2009) observes that "wisdom" played "a role in the creation of the world" in Philo (see *Fug.* 109; *Det.* 54) (138–39), but does not mention Proverbs 8. Tobin (1983) does (141). Philo arguably connects the "wisdom" of Prov. 8:22–31 with the text of Genesis 1 in *Somn.* 2.242, in (esp.) *Virt.* 55–65 (see Laporte, 1976, 104, 115; Tobin, 1983, 141), and in (perhaps) *Fug.* 94–102. Cf. *Det.* 54. For a slightly different relationship between "wisdom" and Creator/creation in Philo (where it searches beyond creation to the Creator) see *Cong.* 79; *Abr.* 68–71 (cf. *Her.* 96–99); *Migr.* 36–42 (here he quotes Gen. 1:31); *Deus* 160; *QG* 1.11 (here he combines elements of Eden and Prov. 8:22–23). (For the connection between Wisdom and Logos – the Logos obviously having creational and pre-creational functions – see Tobin, 1983, 63–64; though see 64 n. 26). Philo's relation between wisdom and creation spans across his corpus, thus showing itself to be broadly important for Philo's theology.

God's Ideas according to which creation unfolds is "a necessary prerequisite for the genesis of the world."[30]

This section on Philo will unfold in two stages. In *Op.* 16 and 26–28 Philo discusses the necessity of a pre-creational divine mental plan. Thus I will firstly demonstrate the *presence* in Philo of an explicit theory of the Before, including its timing and purpose. In §29, Philo highlights the nature of that pre-creational plan, and by this we will secondly determine its *content*. We must keep in mind throughout that Philo is self-consciously explaining the biblical text. When explicitly discussing the relationship between the Before (God's noetic paradigm) and the Beginning (God's creation of the sense-perceptible world and of humanity) Philo confesses: "This doctrine is Moses', not mine" (§25). It will be increasingly apparent throughout Philo's treatment that his Before is an important aspect of his interpretation of the Beginning. Philo's Before begins in the actual beginning of Genesis 1 and the textual phrase "In the beginning."

*1.2.1 The Presence in Philo of a Pre-Creational Plan
and the* Timaeus *of Plato (Op. 16, 26–28)*

Philo's treatment of "In the beginning..." is at odds with many modern treatments. Some presently interpret Gen. 1:1 as a presentation of the first creative act of God. His creation of light in 1:3 is thus his second act.[31] *Jubilees*, *4 Ezra*, and Josephus would have concurred with this reading.[32] This means that the earth as described in Gen. 1:2 was the way it was initially created by God. Other modern commentators disagree. They treat the words "God created" in Gen. 1:1 as a summary of all of God's activities

---

[30] So Radice, 1989, 27: "un presupposto necessario della genesi del cosmo."

[31] E.g., Sailhamer, 1992, 82 n. 2; Kidner, 1967, 44. For other notable modern advocates of this approach see the lists in Westermann, 1984, 95 and Wenham, 1987, 13.

[32] *Jub.* 2:2 says, "For on the first day he created the heavens, which are above, and the earth," either taking בראשית as "the first day" (so Endo, 2002, 14 n. 6) or else seeing the conclusion "day one" in Gen. 1:5 as summarizing the whole of 1:1–5. Likewise *4 Ez.* 6:38 says, "O Lord, you indeed spoke from the beginning of creation, and said on the first day, 'Let heaven and earth be made,' and your word accomplished the work," thus applying aspects of 1:3ff ("Let...") to the content of 1:1. (See Endo, 2002, 27). In *Ant.* 1.27, Josephus begins his history by rewording Gen. 1:1–3: "In the beginning God created the heaven and the earth. But when this [*sc.* the earth] did not come into sight, but rather was hidden in deep darkness, and a wind moved above its surface, God commanded that there should be light." For Josephus, the "earth" in Gen. 1:2 was "created" in 1:1. (Cf. Endo, 2002, 35–6; Hartley, 2000, 42). Runia (2001) reminds that Augustine "interprets the earth in Gen 1:1 as referring to unformed matter created by God as the substrate for the subsequent creation of the physical cosmos" (153). (Cf. Philo's *Conf.* 12.5–9.) For these authors Gen. 1:1 explains God's first act.

recorded in vv. 3–31. Thus the first actual creative act is found in 1:3.[33] But if the creation of light is the very first of God's creative acts that are summarized in 1:1, then what does the text say about the origin of the dark and indistinct earth of 1:2? This construal of "God created" in 1:1 could easily imply (though not necessarily so) that the earth in 1:2 was not initiated by God but merely found and then manipulated by him.[34] In this second construal, the divine activity labeled "creating" is largely a shaping of what is already present. Plato's creation account in the *Timaeus* is similar to this second interpretation of "God created" (see below). One who knows of Philo's heavy use of the *Timaeus* might expect Philo himself to see in the beginning of Genesis 1 God "commandeering" what was already present in Gen. 1:2 and then "forming" it "out of" the chaotic state of 1:2 and "into" the ordered cosmos as it now stands (cf. *Tim.* 30a).

Speaking anachronistically, Philo has actually commandeered aspects of both of the modern interpretations of his sacred text and combined them. In *Op.* 9 Philo does describe God's act of creation in a manner similar to Plato (and to the second group of modern interpreters mentioned above): God was "setting in motion," "shaping," and "enlivening" the otherwise "passive thing." God's act of creation is thus an active "changing" (μετέβαλεν) of the passive thing – i.e., a passive mass which Philo describes, in a manner somewhat dissimilar to Plato, as "of itself lifeless and motionless"[35] – "into the most perfect work, even this world."[36] Philo then describes the "cosmos" as a city that was "constructed" (κατασκευάζον, §11.2), and it is possible that here Philo shows the influence of the description of the earth in Gen. 1:2: the earth was present yet "un-constructed"

---

[33] E.g., Westermann, 1984, 95; Delitzsch, 1894, 72–81. For other notable modern advocates see the lists in Westermann, 1984, 95 and Wenham, 1987, 12.

[34] So Gelander, 1997, 97.

[35] Timaeus says, "For God, desiring [βουληθείς] all things to be good [ἀγαθά], so far as possible, and thus commandeering [παραλαβών] everything that was visible, which was *not in a state of rest* but rather *moving discordantly and disorderly*, led it into order out of the disorder, judging that [order] is always better" (*Tim.* 30a1–6). Dillon (2005) recognizes Philo's difference with Plato, mentioning Philo's alignment with the Stoics at this point ("and very possibly with the later Academy as well," 104 n. 21), while Runia (2001) downplays the difference because in §§21–22 Philo's "disorderly" and "disharmonious" matter is closer to Plato (145). Nevertheless, §§8–9 (at least) are contrary to Plato.

[36] Dillon (2005) argues that "the active cause" is not God himself but his Logos (104 n. 20). Philo's language could tend toward either interpretation. Philo writes in *Migr.* 192 about "the mind of the universe" and then explains: "that is to say, God." Therefore, although Philo does not refer to God as "intellect" or "mind" many times (perhaps a dozen; see Runia, 2001, 116), it is better to consider "the active cause…the mind of the universe" in *Op.* 8 a reference to God himself. So too Runia, 2001, 116.

(ἀκατασκεύαστος).³⁷ Like Gen. 1:1 (on the second construal), Philo remains silent in these passages about the origin of the passive stuff that God "creates" by transforming it into the beautiful cosmos. Thus Philo shares some affinities with the second group of modern readers who take Gen. 1:1 not as God's actual origination of an undefined earth *per se* but rather as a summary of his shaping of it.

Yet although Philo uses these ideas of commandeering and shaping in his general illustration of creation, in his comments on the actual text of Gen. 1:1–2 Philo does not make such an *exegetical* move. In the precise place where the second group of modern commentators sees in Genesis 1 a method of creation comparable to what Plato envisions³⁸ Philo does not read the text as such. He does not see in Gen. 1:1–3 God's commandeering of matter. Rather, Philo's exegesis of Gen. 1:1–5 (in §§16, 26–28) is in closer harmony with the first group of modern scholars (and *Jubilees, 4 Ezra,* and Josephus), where "God made" refers to God's *first* act rather than to a summary of all later acts. More importantly for this project, however, Philo's exegesis of Gen. 1:1–5 is also a textually-based presentation of the making of (and therefore the *presence* of) a divine plan *before the beginning* of the visible cosmos.

(a) Philo's Timing of "In the Beginning":
Before the Beginning (*Op.* 26–28)

Some modern experts attribute eschatological significance to Gen. 1:1 since the text uses "In the *beginning*" (בראשית, "beginning" versus "end") instead of "At the *first*" (בתחלה or בראשנה, "first" versus "second").³⁹ In the LXX too ἀρχή is also often associated with an "end" (τέλος or

---

³⁷ In general, Philo has a "predilection for enumerating pairs of contrasted terms in order to illustrate the difference between ἀταξία and τάξις" (Runia, 1986, 147–8). The negative partner usually takes the form of alpha-privative adjectives, just like those found in Gen. 1:2: "*un*-visible and *un*-constructed" (ἀ-όρατος καὶ ἀ-κατασκεύαστος). Runia lists 10 negative adjectives used by Philo in many diverse places to describe matter before it was "created." A few terms are taken from Plato himself, who makes more simply distinguishes between τάξις and ἀταξία (*Tim.* 30a5), and some from Middle Platonists (Runia, 1986, 147). But Philo's adjectival practice does have as many similarities with Gen. 1:2 as with Plato. Yet it could simply be a piece of Philo's "rhetorical flair" (Runia, 1986, 148).

³⁸ Cf. Sacks, 1990, 4; Wenham, 1987, 15–16; Waltke, 1975, 327–42. For a more radical view of the dangers present in Gen. 1:2 ("the nihilistic powers of chaos," "the chaos dragon") which need to be conquered and quelled by God, see Batto, 1992, 16–38, 33. (Yet the association of "deep" with the Akkadian "Tiamat" is now typically criticized: see Tsumura, 2005, 14–57; Noort, 2000, 8).

³⁹ Mathews, 1996, 126–27; Sailhamer, 1990, 20–23.

ἔσχατος) rather than with a sequential "second," "third," etc.⁴⁰ Philo shows that an eschatological move is not an exegetically necessary one. "In the beginning [ἐν ἀρχῇ] he made [heaven]" should be taken as a statement of sequence: "First [πρῶτον] he made heaven" (§26). In light of Philo's principle of the inseparability of time-and-cosmos (someone today may say "space-time," see below),⁴¹ this sequential "first" is not a marker of chronological or temporal sequence. It connotes order and primacy. Thus Philo can reason that "even if" all things were made simultaneously (temporally speaking), Moses would still rightly label the events of creation as "first," "second," "third," etc. because of their inherent order (§28.1–2). The notion of order (ontological, not temporal) is essential for Philo's reading of Genesis' Beginning.⁴²

The text's "beginning" can be taken as a non-temporal "first" – i.e., in the first place – because of Philo's space-time theory: "Time did not exist *before* the cosmos" (χρόνος γὰρ οὐκ ἦν *πρὸ* κόσμου), he writes, because "time" is simply "the interval of the cosmos' movement." Without a "body" existing to have measured movement "time" cannot exist. Time can only "come about" (γίνομαι) either simultaneously with or subsequently to the spatial cosmos, the "body" (§26.4–5).⁴³ As Steven Hawking has more recently put it, "[T]ime is not completely separate from and independent of space, but is combined with it to form an object called spacetime,"⁴⁴ and thus "the concept of time has no meaning before the beginning of the universe."⁴⁵ Perhaps Philo was ahead of his time.

So "time" did not exist until there was a "cosmos" present and moving. If modern interpreters wrote in Greek, many would use the word "cosmos"

---

⁴⁰ For the relation of ἀρχή to τέλος see Eccl. 3:11 and Isa. 19:15 (cf. Wis. 7:17; Heb. 7:3; Rev. 21:6; 22:13). For the relation of ἀρχή to ἔσχατος see Eccl. 7:8 and 10:13. Rev. 22:13 combines all of these when the Lord self-testifies, "I am the Alpha and the Omega, the First and the Last, the Beginning and the End" (ἐγὼ τὸ ἄλφα καὶ τὸ ὦ, ὁ πρῶτος καὶ ὁ ἔσχατος, ἡ ἀρχή καὶ τὸ τέλος).

⁴¹ Hawking, 1988, 9, 27-28. Although Philo may not have talked in the language of what Hawking calls "four-dimensional space" (27), his definition of "time" as the "measured movement" of "bodies" (i.e., three-dimensional spatial objects, see below) causes him to unite space and time in a way that foreshadows what is now referred to as "space-time."

⁴² Dillon, 2005, 106.

⁴³ Cf. *Leg.* 1.2; 2.3; *Aet.* 52. Nearly 200 years before Philo, as Hengel (1974) points out, Aristobulus (Philo's Jewish "philosopher" predecessor in Alexandria, preserved in Eusebius, *Pr. Ev.* 13.12.11f) "attempted to bring the Old Testament conception of the creation of God in time in accord with the Greek idea of the timeless activity of God" (1.166).

⁴⁴ Hawking, 1988, 26.

⁴⁵ Hawking, 1988, 9 (though wrongly attributing this theory's inception to Augustine).

to refer to what is spoken of in Gen. 1:1,[46] the phrase "the heavens and the earth" being taken as a hendiadys for "the cosmos."[47] Philo would not apply the word "cosmos" to Gen. 1:1. For him "cosmos" typically refers to the completed and adorned whole,[48] and as such it first appears in Gen. 2:1.[49] But since "time" is so intimately wed with Gen. 2:1, when Philo reads what precedes Gen. 2:1 – e.g., Gen. 1:1–5 and the opening phrase "In the beginning God made" (or "In the first place God made") – the "timing" he sees is, in a way, "before" (πρό) time began. The text's "beginning," which is meant by Moses to convey not time (which did not yet exist) but order,[50] is what took place prior to the beginning of time.

Philo then introduces God's creative intentions. Even if one cannot always see God's organization of precedence when looking at "the completed things" (τοῖς ἀποτελέσμασιν; cf. Gen. 2:1),[51] order is nonetheless present in the builder's "conceptions," "thoughts," or "plans" (ταῖς ἐπινοίαις). Thus it is to further explain the necessity of the principle of order that Philo takes his readers into the extra-temporal, "pre"-creational mind of God, into the presence of a divine plan.

In fact, it is "only" if creation comes about according to such divine "conceptions" that all the elements of creation "could be precisely arranged, and not deviate from their path or be full of confusion" (§28.6–7). God's mental functions are *necessary* to Philo's idea of creation. It is important to be clear on Philo's logic: these divine thoughts certainly take place outwith the realm of the temporal and visible cosmos – so the temporal sense of the word "before" is meaningless for Philo in this context – but God's orderly "thoughts" are the precise reason that the visible cosmos is orderly. Philo's point here is not merely that God's thoughts are "before" the visible cosmos in ontological import, though Philo certainly be-

---

[46] Sacks (1990) says just this (3).
[47] See Westermann, 1984, 101; Gelander, 1997, 97.
[48] Cf. *Aet.* 4. See Adams, 2000, 59.
[49] Compare Philo's statements about "the cosmos" in *Op.* 3 (ὁ σύμπας κόσμος), 13 (ὁ κόσμος [+ ἐξ ἡμέραις]), and 89 (ὁ σύμπας κόσμος ἐτελειώθη [+ ἐξάδος]). Note especially that this last one is an intentional rephrasing of Gen. 2:1–2, which says καὶ συνετελέσθησαν ὁ οὐρανὸς καὶ ἡ γῆ καὶ πᾶς ὁ κόσμος αὐτῶν... ἐν τῇ ἡμέρᾳ τῇ ἕκτῃ. Thus in *Op.* 3, 13, and 89 (to give but a few examples) Philo considers "cosmos" as the completed universe of Gen. 2:1–2 with all its life and adornment. (Cf. Aristobulus' use of πᾶς ὁ κόσμος with "all of the animals and plants," in Eusebius' *Pr. Ev.* 13.12.13; see also Hengel, 1974, 1.166; Holladay, 1995.) By the term κόσμος, Philo is not referring to Gen. 1:1 but rather 2:1, when time began.
[50] With such timeless presuppositions, it is actually not surprising that ἀρχή, "beginning" or "chief," could be equated with a non-temporal πρῶτος, "first [in import]."
[51] Philo often uses the τελ- lexical family (with various prefixes) to refer to the cosmos as presented in Gen. 2:1: "the heavens and the earth were completed [συνετελέσθησαν]" (*Op.* 89).

lieves that. Philo's construal here is of divine thoughts that *affect* and are therefore *logically prior* to the beginning of the visible world.[52] This is their "timing" according to Philo in *Op*. 26–28. In §16, to which we will now turn, Philo reveals not only the necessity but also the purpose of God's intentions that are (logically) *pre*-creational.

(b) The Purpose of God's Pre-Creational Intentions:
For Goodness' Sake (*Op*. 16)

By the time Philo exegeted the phrase "in the beginning" in §§26–28 (see above), he had already rehearsed what took place in God's mind. As early as §13 Philo had mentioned that order was inherent in creation and had claimed that Genesis' text gave witness to this. That is, God did not need time to create the cosmos – indeed, he performed "all things simultaneously" – yet the text says that "in six days the cosmos was crafted" (cf. Gen. 2:1–3). "Six days" is mentioned to denote order. God's simultaneous but orderly performance includes, according to Philo's exegesis, both God's "commanding" (i.e., "Let there be...") and his "thinking" or "intending" (διανοούμενον). Even when generally contemplating God's creation by *fiat* in Genesis 1, Philo sees a divine mental activity that propels the creation-by-word. But it is in §16 that Philo actually fills out this cryptic allusion to God's "intentions" that are logically (not temporally) prior to his creative commands. In §16, Philo enters into his discussion of God's mental Before not by way of a mere assumption that thinking precedes acting, but through use (and modification) of Plato's creative *Timaeus*.

In Plato's creation-account, which has many similarities with Genesis (LXX),[53] Timaeus expresses the necessary pre-conditions for a physical creation to be "beautiful," καλός. Plato's Pythagorean character reasons,

Everything which 'becomes' [γιγνόμενον] must of necessity 'become' [γίγνεσθαι] owing to some Cause, for without a cause it is impossible for anything to attain a 'becoming' [γένεσιν]. But when the craftsman of any object, in forming its shape and quality, keeps his gaze fixed on that which is uniform, using just such a paradigm [παραδείγματι], the object produced [ἀπεργάζηται] in this way must of necessity be beautiful [καλόν]. But whenever he gazes at 'the thing which has become' [τὸ γεγονός] and uses a 'created' paradigm [γεννητῷ παραδείγματι], the object thus executed is not beautiful [οὐ καλόν]. (*Tim*. 28ab)

If a creation is to result in "beauty," or "goodness" (καλός), the Creator must look at an uncreated paradigm.[54]

---

[52] When summarizing Plato's Ideas, Seneca draws particular attention to the *prior existence* of the Idea of a thing in relation to its created form: a man himself (as if the Idea) exists prior to an artist's depiction of him (as if the created form) (*Ep*. 16–21, cf. 58; quoted in full in Tobin, 1983, 116).

[53] See the comparison of *Timaeus* and LXX Genesis by Rösel, 1994, 28–58.

When Philo exegetes Gen. 1:1–5 in *Op.* 16, he uses this Platonic passage to explain the logical necessity of a pre-thought out paradigm if creation is to have "beauty." He asserts that in the text of Genesis God enacted just such a creative process. For Philo, before God created anything that we see, God himself "understood beforehand" (προλαβών) the Platonic principle, which, in Philo's words, is that "a beautiful copy [μίμημα καλόν] would never come into being without a beautiful paradigm [καλοῦ παραδείγματος]" (§16.2). Plato had furthered that God set out to create by "purposing [βουληθείς] all things to be good [ἀγαθός]" (*Tim.* 30a). So also Philo writes that God, *pre*-knowing the Platonic principle regarding "beautiful paradigms," and *before* creating this visible world, did in fact "purpose [βουληθείς] to craft" it. He even "stamped out *beforehand* [προεξετύπου] the noetic world [τὸν νοητόν]."[55] In light of these divine mental actions before creation – i.e., pre-understanding, purposing, and pre-stamping out the noetic realm – God then "produced" what is corporeal by way of this pre-determined noetic paradigm (§16.5–10). According to Philo, it was *necessary* for the sake of the quality of "goodness" for God to "think up," "determine," and "plan" a detailed design "before" (προ-) creating the visible. This expectation is discernibly grounded by Philo in (although fundamentally modifying)[56] the expectation of the *Timaeus*.

Philo's explicit point is merely to assert the "beauty" or "goodness" of the cosmos. Reasoning backwards from this Platonic value judgment, Philo concludes that because the visible cosmos is, in fact, "good" there must have been a "good" paradigm. Whereas Plato had only observation from which to conclude that the visible cosmos had "beauty," Philo combined this empirical method with something more concrete and, from his perspective, less open to dispute: the authoritative text of Genesis 1. Genesis 1 (LXX) presents καλός, "goodness" or "beauty," as the frequent and prominent descriptor of the individual aspects of God's handiwork (vv. 4, 8, 10, 12, 18, 21, 25), and the entire sensory-cosmos was together stamped with God's approval as "exceedingly beautiful" (καλὰ λίαν, v. 31). The presence of the word καλός in Genesis 1 (including within "day One," v. 4) seems to have affected Philo's exegesis (§30).[57] The text's "beauty" not

---

[54] Cf. the 1st century BCE Middle Platonist "Timaeus Locrus," *On the Nature of the World and of the Soul*, 206.11–17 (Tobin, 1983, 16–17; van Kooten, 2003, 44; Cox, 2005, 25).

[55] See Leonhardt-Balzer, 2004A, 324–44, esp. 327.

[56] See below. On a number of occasions Philo clearly alludes to Plato while asserting something that actually differs with him (cf. Philo's use of *Tim.* 30a in *Op.* 9 and the "movement" versus "no movement" cited above), something that Philo never does with the biblical texts (see Leonhardt-Balzer, 2004A, 344).

[57] The repeated use of "good" throughout Genesis 1 seems to have been noticed by Philo (see chapter 2 below). The first and paradigmatic portrayal of "goodness" in Gene-

only confirms for Philo Plato's aesthetic judgment but also the sense of order within the scriptural cosmogony. As Philo concludes, "the things 'becoming' beautifully [τὰ καλῶς γινόμενα] possess order [τάξιν], for there is no beauty [καλόν οὐδέν] in disorder [ἐν ἀταξίᾳ]" (§28). But there *is* "beauty" in Genesis 1, a lot of it.

While Philo had introduced an implicit Before into his more general construal of God's creation by *fiat* (i.e., order is present in both God's "commands" and "intentions," §13), here in §16 he introduces an explicit Before, and he does so in the language of Plato. That is, the *Timaeus* gave Philo a certain *expectation* for a Before: there *must* be a paradigm at which the Creator can look and then and thereby create the sensory world. Then, in light of this expectation regarding the necessity of a "beautiful" divine paradigm or plan before the beginning of the visible cosmos, certain features of Genesis' cosmogonic text prompted Philo to further turn his readers' attention to this Before: e.g., "in the beginning," "day One,"[58] the repeated use of καλός in Genesis 1 (particularly in v. 4).

To explicitly describe this Before, Philo uses the three words mentioned above that convey divine mental intentions: "pre-understanding" (προλαβών), "purposing" (βουληθείς), and "pre-stamping out" (προεξετύπου) (§16). Although Philo's priority involves logical and ontological rather than temporal order (§13.1–5),[59] these three verbs (two with the προ-prefix) are intended to draw his readers' minds back to three closely related divine mental activities, all logically necessary preconditions for God's creation of "the visible world." God pre-reasoned (προλαβών) what was needed for "beauty" to appear, purposed (βουληθείς) to craft the visible world, and pre-made (προεξετύπου) a mental plan. Only "after" noetically pre-deliberating in such a manner did God then set about creating the visible world. In Philo's estimation, what God thought in the Before is essential for understanding how the Beginning came about, especially as this Beginning is recounted in Genesis.

The third divine activity – "stamping out beforehand" (προεξετύπου) – is what, according to Philo, Gen. 1:1–5 explicitly recounts.[60] Regardless of

---

sis 1 is in v. 4, the creation of light. When drawing out the seven items created on Day One (in Gen. 1:1–5), Philo gives "special distinction" to "spirit" and "light," the first for a textual reason (it is labeled "of God"; θεοῦ) and a philosophical/theological reason (it is "most life-giving," ζωτικώτατον), the second for a textual reason: "because [light] is pre-eminently beautiful" (ὑπερβαλλόντως καλόν) (§30).

[58] For a discussion of the import of "day one" see Tobin, 1992, 112–13.

[59] Runia (2001) says of these two προ- prefixed verbs, "Here is a case (cf. Op. 13, 27) where what seems to be temporal precedence actually indicates ontological precedence.... The intelligible cosmos is superior" (137). Cf. Dillon, 2005, 106.

[60] We must be especially clear here. From one perspective it is only the first two noetic actions that represent Philo's understanding of *before the beginning* since the third is

whether or not Plato was the first to use the imagery of the seal or stamp (τύπος) to explain the creative act,[61] it is this aspect of the *Timaeus* that Philo here borrows (and modifies). In *Tim.* 39e7 the Creator "produced" (ἀπειργάζετο) all four types of creatures: stars, birds, fish, and land-animals, by "stamping them out [ἀποτυπούμενος] after [πρός] the nature of the paradigm [τοῦ παραδείγματος]" (cf. *Tim.* 50c-d). Jutta Leonhardt-Balzer explains the typical process of stamping something out:[62]

> First, it is necessary to carve a seal; only then it can be used on the wax. The creation follows the same pattern. The intelligible world is the seal which is used on the wax of matter so that the perceptible world can be shaped.

In Plato's reckoning there is no carving of the noetic seal, for it is fundamentally important to Plato that the paradigm be *un*-created and therefore *un*-becoming. If the paradigm is "becoming," we should recall, then what is produced in accordance with it cannot be "beautiful." The demiurge simply uses the uncreated, incorporeal, and present Forms and "stamps out" into the wax of corporeal matter the sense-perceptible object (which now is in the likeness of the seal).[63] But where Plato conceives of the demiurge as "stamping out" the sense-perceptible cosmos, for Philo it is presently the *noetic* cosmos, the seal or paradigm itself, which God is "*pre-stamping out*" *before the beginning* of "the visible world"! Using a number of Platonic themes (yet modifying them to better accord with the sacred Mosaic text),[64] Philo portrays it as necessary for the sake of goodness and

---

what begins "in the beginning" of Gen. 1:1. But from the perspective of time and especially of "the *visible* cosmos," all three of these aspects of God's mental preparation did take place before *that* beginning. It is upon this second perspective that we will now focus and which I will nuance further, for Philo is here considering God's thoughts in relation to (and "before," πρό) what he calls the *visible* cosmos. It is also this relationship that is most directly comparable with Paul's interpretation of creation.

[61] Runia, 2001, 139.
[62] Leonhardt-Balzer, 2004A, 327.
[63] Leonhardt-Balzer, 2004A, 330.
[64] Although using Plato's language and part of his general principle, Philo actually here undercuts Plato's fundamental assertion. For Plato, the paradigm must be "un-becoming" (*Tim.* 28a7-b2), and the consequence of a "becoming" paradigm is a created-object that is "not beautiful" (οὐ καλόν). Since Philo's scripture is adamant that the created world and its parts are "beautiful" (καλόν), one would expect Philo, if he were being true to Plato's point, to assert the *un*-becomingness of the noetic paradigm. Philo does not, but treats it as created (rightly Radice, 2009, 131–32 [cf. 142–43 and 143 n. 30]; contra Leondardt-Balzer, 2004, 343). Philo merely says that the reason the product is "beautiful" is because the Creator looked to a "beautiful" paradigm, thereby *not* repeating Plato's explicit (fundamental) "un-becoming" detail. And according to Philo, the paradigm is created: "pre-stamped out," even "made." Even if the notion of the "eternal creation" of the ideas in Philo is correct (so Winston, 1979, 593–606; Hillar, 1998), it does not eliminate Philo's difference from Plato at this point. Though Philo cer-

order for God to mentally determine a design before beginning to create. And so God did, in fact, pre-stamp out just such a paradigm in Gen. 1:1–5.

From *Op.* 26–28 the *presence* of a pre-creational plan within Philo's reading of creation should be clear; it is, in fact, a necessary part of his interpretation of creation. From *Op.* 16 we have considered the purpose of its presence: for the "goodness" or "beauty" of the cosmos to come about, which it so obviously does in Genesis 1 (and particularly in 1:1–5), the presence of a divine mental *pre*-determination prior to his creation of the visible world cannot be done without. I will now demonstrate that in two crucial places in his commentary on Genesis 1–2 (§§29 and 129–30) Philo turns his readers to details of the text of Genesis in order to present the nature and *content* of this necessary pre-creational deliberation of God.

1.2.2 Philo's Content of God's Pre-Creational Plan:
The Invisible, Beautiful Paradigm (Op. 29 and Op. 129–30)

After covering some important philosophical and theological preliminaries via the phrase "in the beginning" (§§13–28; see above), Philo comments on the first few verses of Genesis. He sees the Before in Gen. 1:1-5, and in 1:6 he sees the visible Beginning. Yet when one works through the rest of Philo's commentary, through Genesis 1 and into Genesis 2, problems arise. Within this one commentary Philo gives two different readings of the cosmogonic material (Gen. 1:6-31), and therefore of the anthropogonic material also (1:26-28). Philo sees two sets of textual details that testify to God's pre-creational determinations: first Gen. 1:1–5 (§29), then Gen. 2:4–5 (§§129–30). To fully identify the *content* of Philo's explicit testimony to creation's Before, and also to satisfactorily recognize the hermeneutical implications of this Before for Philo's interpretation of creation, we must ask: How does he derive the Before from each set of textual features?

(a) Philo's First Reading of the Before:
An Invisible Earth and Gen. 1:1–5 (*Op.* 29)

As we saw above concerning §§16 and 26–28, so too in §29 Philo does not treat Gen. 1:1 as a summary statement with vv. 2–5 describing the pre-created physical earth and the first creative act of visible illumination. He

---

tainly believes in a "timelessness" to creation (cf. *Leg.* 1.2, 20; *Dec.* 101; *QG* 2.47; so Wedderburn, 1973B, 304, 304 n. 2), and he explicitly *qualifies* the temporal phrases of the biblical text accordingly (see above), his concept of atemporality (or eternity) nevertheless does not directly modify the biblically attested nature of the paradigm as "become" and "made." The created aspect remains even when the temporal aspect does not. Philo opts for (a slightly modified version of) the biblical language to the contradiction of the essential point of the Platonic concept.

rather unites vv. 1–5 into a joint-depiction of what he, following the LXX, calls "making" (ποιῶν). God "made" (ἐποίησεν) everything found in 1:1–5.[65] So Philo writes in §29 (words shared with Gen. 1:1–5 italicized):

First the Maker *made* [*ἐποίησεν*] the incorporeal *heaven* [*οὐρανὸν* ἀσώματον], and the *invisible earth* [*γῆν ἀόρατον*], and the idea of air [ἀέρος ἰδέαν] and of void [κενοῦ] – of which one he named '*darkness*' [*σκότος*], since air is black by nature, and the other '*abyss*' [*ἄβυσσον*], for the void is very deep and immense – then the incorporeal essence of *water* [*ὕδατος* ἀσώματον οὐσίαν], and of *spirit* [*πνεύματος*], and, above all, [the incorporeal essence] of the crown that is *light* [*φωτός*].

The *content* of God's activity that (logically) precedes his creation of the visible world is qualitatively noetic: i.e., "incorporeal" and "invisible," "idea(s)" and "incorporeal essence(s)." I will highlight two of Philo's exegetical reasons for treating vv. 1–5 as activity residing in God's thoughts, i.e., as a noetic creation.

Self-consciously considering this interpretation exegesis (as opposed to eisegesis or imposition), Philo explains that it is vv. 1–5 itself ("day One") that "reports" God's creation of "the intelligible cosmos" (§15.9). He ties v. 1 so closely to v. 2 that the adjective "invisible" from v. 2 (italicized below) finds its way into Philo's gloss of v. 1.[66] The quality of invisibility thereby shows itself to be particularly important for his reading of the beginning of Genesis as the Before:

Gen. 1:1   ἐν ἀρχῇ   ἐποίησεν ὁ θεὸς   τὸν οὐρανὸν   καὶ τὴν γῆν
Op. 29.1   πρῶτον   ὁ ποιῶν ἐποίησεν   οὐρανὸν ἀσώματον   καὶ γῆν *ἀόρατον*

Two adjectives are added to v. 1: "incorporeal" for heaven and "invisible" for earth. It is obvious that Philo gets the "invisible" from v. 2 – "the earth was invisible and unconstructed" (ἡ γῆ ἦν ἀόρατος καὶ ἀκατασκεύαστος) – and this word choice by the LXX makes Gen. 1:2 susceptible to just such a Platonic interpretation.[67] But from where does he get the "incorporeality" of heaven (and also of water, spirit, and light)?

---

[65] As Runia (1986) writes, "Philo's chief solution to the interpretation of [the ambiguity of Gen. 1:1–2 with regard to matter]...is to take the whole of Gen. 1:1–5 as referring to the intelligible world, leaving no room for mention of pre-existent matter" (156). But while this is a solution to this issue of matter with narrow regards to Gen. 1:2, by ruling out the *potential* of Gen. 1:1 to refer to the creation of matter Philo has merely shifted the question of matter to Gen. 1:6 (see below). But with this shift the text does not even have a *potential* explicit reference to any creation of matter.

[66] So also Runia, 2001, 164.

[67] Plato's Timaeus contrasts the "visible" (ὁρατόν) and "bodily" (σωματοειδές) cosmos (30a-32b; cf. 36e) with the "invisible" (ἀόρατος) soul (36e; see Rösel, 1994, 32 n. 19) and later with the "invisible" (ἀόρατον) noetic Form (52a; cf. Plato's *Rep.* 529b5 and *Soph.* 246b7, and Alcinous' *Did.* 7.4, each noted in Runia, 2001, 165). Regardless of whether the LXX itself intended it to be Platonic (so Rösel, 1994, 33; cf. 28–58 for a number of Rösel's connections between Plato and LXX) or not (Rösel's thesis is

He implies the "incorporeality" of the items created in vv. 1–5 from the beginning of what is "corporeal" in v. 6. There the text says that God created a "firmness" (στερέωμα). When commenting on this in §36, Philo reasons that because it is a "body" (σῶμα) that is "by nature firm" (φύσει στερεόν), therefore the text itself indicates that *beginning* in v. 6 God creates what is "bodily" (i.e., "corporeal," σωματικόν). Thus *before* this, i.e., in vv. 1–5, God was, obviously, making something body-*less*, or incorporeal (ἀσώματον). "Incorporeality" and "invisiblity" are therefore the textually attested qualities of that which Philo sees "in [God's] mind" before the beginning of what is visible.[68]

The "incorporeal" quality of vv. 1–5, as deduced from v. 6, and the explicit "invisibility" of the earth in vv. 1–2 place textual ground under Philo's interpretation of vv. 1–5 as the creation of the noetic realm. There certainly are now and were in Philo's day other ways to interpret these textual features.[69] But these two examples of Philo's exegetical manoeuvres, combined with his use of the wording and concept of "made" for the noetic paradigm (a concept which undercuts Plato's notion of the necessary unbecomingness of the noetic paradigm),[70] demonstrate that the biblical text is itself an important part of Philo's understanding of the Before. His expectation for the Before may have been aroused (or perhaps merely confirmed) by the Platonic expectation of a pre-creational, invisible, and good paradigm, but it would be a hermeneutical injustice to view Philo as simply imposing a previous and formed understanding of the Before onto the

---

criticized by Cook, 2001, 315–29 and Runia, 2001, 165), its description of the earth in such a way is certainly thereby prone to such a reading (so Dillon, 2005, 103 and van Kooten, 2005, 155–57, 156 n. 11 [cf. *idem,* 2008, 272–73]; Barclay, 1996A, 165; cf. Westermann, 1984, 104; Delitzsch, 1894, 78).

[68] Though Philo does not use the term "mind" in *Op.* 17–20, but rather "within himself" and "in his soul," that he means "mind" is sufficiently clear from his use of the terms "memory" (μνήμη, §18.3) and "noetic," and this is widely accepted (so Radice, 1991, 126–34; Williamson, 1989, 133; cf. Sandmel, 1983, 24).

[69] Is a "desolate" (תהו) earth, whether before it is (further) formed (as in Gen. 1:2) or after it is destroyed (as in Jer. 4:23), actually "invisible" in the way that Philo takes it? Wevers (1993) offers that the LXX's earth was "invisible" or "unseen" inasmuch as "darkness reigned" (1–2; cf. Noort, 2005, 10). This is Josephus' explanation in *Ant.* 1.27 (and one might compare Philo's *Conf.* 172). See further Endo, 2002, 35–36 and Rösel, 1994, 32 (who also adds, like the ancient Theodoret [*Quaest in Gen* 9] and the modern Runia [2001, 165], that the covering of water would also have caused the submerged earth to therefore be "invisible," 32 n. 20). Although using the word "invisible," the LXX did not have to be interpreted as referring to Platonic invisibility, even in Philo's day. But, by the same token, it easily could be.

[70] See n. 64 above.

biblical text.[71] His expectation and concept of the Before is certainly affecting his reading of Genesis' Beginning, but it is *also* being affected and shaped by his exegesis of the biblical text.

This plan or blue-print of the cosmos, pre-set in God's mind, was of order and was laid down *before the beginning* for goodness' sake.[72] The *presence* and *content* of the Before in Gen. 1:1–5 and the Beginning of the visible cosmos in v. 6 together color Philo's reading of the rest of the biblical text. Then in §§36–68 Philo explains the beginning of the *corporeal world* according to Gen. 1:6–25 (to be explored below in chapter 2), and in §§69–88 he turns to the beginning of the *corporeal humanity* according to Gen. 1:26–28 (to be explored below in chapter 3). Philo is highly consistent throughout §§36–88 to interpret Gen. 1:6–31 as the corporeal creation which follows from Gen. 1:1-5 as the incorporeal pre-creation.

But later features of the same biblical cosmogony, namely Gen. 2:4–5, cause Philo to rethink how the Before relates to the biblical text. He then *re*-interprets Genesis 1 (in *Op.* 129–30). This re-reading of the Before we will now explore, and these final comments on Philo's exegesis will confirm the *presence* as well as *content* of the Before in his interpretation of creation. It will also confirm that God's pre-deliberations clearly have hermeneutical and theological implications for Philo's reading of both the beginning of the whole world and the beginning of particular humanity.

(b) Philo's Second Reading of the Before:
Invisible Green in Gen. 2:4–5 (*Op.* 129–30)

The grammar of the LXX of Gen. 2:5 appears awkward at first, but from Philo's perspective it actually makes sense. In §129, Philo perfectly quotes the LXX of Gen. 2:4–5a, writing:

This is the book of the genesis of heaven and earth when they came about, in the day God made the heaven and the earth and every green thing of the field before it came about upon the earth and all grass of the field before it rose up. (*Op.* 129)

Although the *toledoth*-formula of the Hebrew ("These are the generations [תולדות] of...")[73] found in Gen. 2:4a functions elsewhere in Genesis as an introduction to what is about to transpire rather than as a review of what has just taken place,[74] many scholars nevertheless take Gen. 2:4a as a

---

[71] For a criticism of a simplistic hermeneutic of imposition, see Watson's presentation of the reciprocal hermeneutic (2004, 2–5), especially as it interacts with the hermeneutic of imposition of Barton (1986, 245) on pp. 128–29 and 157–58.
[72] Williamson, 1989, 132.
[73] LXX: "This is the book of the genesis of..." (αὕτη ἡ βίβλος γενέσεως...).
[74] Cf. 5:1; 6:9; 10:1; 10:32; 11:10, 27; 25:12, 13, 19; 36:1, 9; 37:2. So Cotter, 2003, 25–26; Dorsey, 1999, 49; Anderson, 1994, 54; Childs, 1992, 113; Wenham, 1987, 49,

summary of Gen. 1:1–2:3.[75] Philo also takes this approach; he treats Moses' statement as a "summary" of what has gone before. Philo introduces Gen. 2:4 in this way: "While reflecting on the account of world-creation [*sc.* Gen. 1:1–2:3][76] in a type of summary [κεφαλαιώδει τύπῳ] he says... [quotation of Gen. 2:4–5a]" (§129.1–2).[77] But Philo goes a step further. Modern interpreters who take 2:4a as a summary of what precedes it, like Philo does here, typically take 2:4b and 2:5 together as the beginning of

---

55–56; Cassuto, 1961 (ET), 96–100; Skinner, 1910, 40–41. With the possible exception of 10:32 all others function as introductory formulas.

[75] Although most scholars do not follow Wiseman (1936) that every *toledoth*-formula was a summary, recognizing that most of the formulas do, in fact, function as introductions and not conclusions, many simply make the appeal that 2:4a is different than all the rest. So Hartley, 2000, 35 n. 1, 51, esp. 55; Dahlberg, 1998, 8, 14; Westermann, 1987, 12; von Rad, 1956, 61. The point should not be missed, however, that this formula introduces *not* the character himself (e.g., Adam, the sons of Noah, Jacob, etc.) but rather the *generations* of that character. The formula is "followed by gen. of the progenitor, never of the progeny" (Skinner, 1910, 41). This detail is often overlooked by scholars who think that 2:4a cannot be an introduction, or superscription, for chs. 2–4; they think that *toledoth* refers to the "origin" of the one mentioned (e.g., von Rad, 1956, 61), or (relatedly) that "the second creation story has little to say about the creation of heavens and earth" (Watson, 1997, 268 n. 9; cf. e.g., Rösel, 1994, 57). Genesis 2–4 does not need to be about "heaven and earth" itself for the *toledoth*-formula of 2:4a to introduce it effectively. Rather, as Skinner puts it, "the phrase must describe that which is generated *by* the heavens and the earth, *not* the process by which they *themselves* are generated" (41; emphasis added). Thus for Gen. 2:4a to effectively introduce Genesis 2–4, which is the most probable function of the *toledoth*-formula, Genesis 2–4 merely needs to be about Adam's genesis from the earth (2:7), the curse on the earth because of Adam (3:17), Cain's curse "from the earth" (4:11), etc. – i.e., the story concerning the "children" of the one whose *toledoth* is introduced.

[76] Runia (1986) argues that ἡ κοσμοποιία is "used by Philo as a *terminus technicus* not so much for the creation itself, but Moses' account of the creation; cf. *Opif.* 3, 129, 170, *Fug.* 178, *Abr.* 2, 258, *QG* 1.1" (86).

[77] Philo here uses the participle ἐπιλογιζόμενος, which means either "concluding" or "reflecting upon" (so Runia, 2001, 311; cf. *idem*, 1986, 554). (He uses the noun ἐπιλόγῳ and the verb ἐπιλέγει in *Post.* 64–65 when commenting on the same passage.) Runia treats *Op.* 129 as "a reflection on the creation account *as it has been so far presented*" (310, cf. 311; contra Tobin, 1983, 123–24, 170–71). The problem with such a reading is that if Gen. 2:4–5 is a summary of Gen. 1:1–2:3 – which Philo claims it is (calling it "a type of summary heading" [κεφαλαιώδει τύπῳ]) – and if 2:4–5 is about the creation of the noetic "Before" – which Philo treats it as (see below) – then *Op.* 129 is *not* "a reflection on the creation account *as it has been so far presented*," but rather a reflection on Gen. 1:1–2:3 *in a different way than has so far been presented*, for 1:1–2:3 had manifestly *not* been only about the noetic before. However, seeing *Op.* 129 as a *re*-construal of all of Genesis 1 in a *different* way (contra Runia) is not only equally as valid as Runia's reading on semantic and syntactical grounds, but it takes better account of how Philo then (re)treats the creation of the human of 1:27 in *Op.* 134–35 (see below).

what follows. Philo reads 2:4a, 2:4b, *and* 2:5 together, but he reads them as the united *summary* of Moses' "creation account" (τὴν κοσμοποιίαν).[78]

Philo is not treating 2:4–5 as a summary merely of "day One" (1:1–5); an allusion to such a particular and distant referent at this point in his commentary would need far more specificity than this brief statement allows.[79] Rather, Philo refers to the entire "book" of creation – i.e., Gen. 1:1–2:3 – that Moses now "reflects on" and summarizes under the retrospective "heading" (κεφαλαιώδει) found in 2:4–5.[80] This heading, however, is strikingly only about what God makes "before" things have had their genesis. That is, Genesis 1 is now only about the Before.

In this summary of Genesis 1 (Gen. 2:4–5) Moses speaks briefly, Philo explains, only relaying God's "making" of four of all the items found in Genesis 1 and "not dealing with everything in detail." Yet these four items function representatively, as indications "of the nature of the whole" (§130). The first two items revisited are "the heaven" and "the earth." The third and fourth items that "God made" – i.e., "greenery" and "grass" – have important modifiers in Gen. 2:5, and it is these modifying phrases in the text itself upon which Philo rests his new interpretation.[81] As a summary of all of Gen. 1:1–2:3 the text (quoted above) says:

God made	the heaven		
	the earth		
	every green thing of the field	before [πρό] it 'became'	
	all grass of the field	before [πρό] it rose up	

Intrigued by the text's relationship between "God made" (ἐποίησεν), "before" (πρό, x2), and "becoming" (τοῦ γενέσθαι), Philo reasons: "Does [Moses] not clearly present here the incorporeal and noetic ideas [τὰς ἀσωμάτους καὶ νοητὰς ἰδέας], which have come about together as seals

---

[78] Like Philo, von Rad (1972) sees Gen. 2:4b-7 as one sentence but, contrary to Philo who takes it as the summary of 1:1–2:3, von Rad considers it to be the introduction of Genesis 2:4bff (52). Interestingly, in *QG* 1.1 Philo takes Gen. 2:4a as an introduction to the *following* part of the account. In *Leg.* 1.19–20, it appears to function as the uniting feature of the complex cosmogonic account of Genesis 1–2, referring back to the creation of the "ideas" (Genesis 1) *and* forward to the creation of the "mind...and sensations which [were] arranged according to the ideas" (Genesis 2). For a modern reading of Gen. 2:4 as a transitional link between 1:1–2:3 *and* 2:5ff see Stordalen, 1992, 163–77.

[79] The term "creation account" is also less likely to refer to only Gen. 1:1–5 than to all of Genesis 1, especially as the term comes directly after this full treatment of the whole of Genesis 1.

[80] So Tobin, 1983, 123–25, 168–71; contra Nikiprowetzky, 1965, 288–89; Runia, 1986, 554; *idem*, 2001, 310–11. Seeing *Op.* 129 as initiating a re-construal of all of Genesis 1, which I will develop below and in chapter 3, makes better sense out of Philo's subsequent comments (§§131–50), especially his comparison of the two men (§§134–35).

[81] So also Tobin, 1992, 120.

of the completed sense-perceptible things?" Gen. 2:4–5 refers to the Before. Philo argues from the text and casts it in terms of prior "existence":

For before [πρίν] the earth became green, this green itself was existing [ἦν], [Moses/the text] says, in the nature of things. And before [πρίν] grass rose up in the field, a grass was existing [ἦν] that was not visible [οὐχ ὁρατός]. (§129.9–12)

Gen. 2:4–5 is potentially awkward, but by reading it as a one-sentence statement of the *presence* and *content* of the Before it makes sense: God "made" the incorporeal ideas of grass and greenery, which are "not visible" (cf. "not visible" [οὐχ ὁρατός] here with "invisible" [ἀόρατος] in Gen. 1:2),[82] and he made them "before" the corporeal grass and greenery "became" – i.e., *before* the "genesis" of what is visible. Because of Gen. 2:4–5 Philo concludes, "It should be understood that for each of the other things which the senses judge, the elder forms and measures (by which the things that 'become' [τὰ γινόμενα] are given form and measure) also *pre-existed* [*προϋπῆρχε*]" (§130).[83]

All of Genesis 1 has now been recast as the Before, for that is what Gen. 2:4–5 explicitly says: "before." This has hermeneutical consequences for Philo: now the beginning of the corporeal world is in Gen. 2:6 (§§131–33) and the beginning of corporeal humanity is in Gen. 2:7 (§§134–50). Each follows in turn from this *readjusted* Before.[84] This also has (well-known) theological consequences: now the beginning of the visible world and humanity are able to be compared (and contrasted) with the incorporeal and invisible "ideas" of the world (in Genesis 1) and humanity (in 1:26–28). Philo's well-known anthropological complexity (his "two-men" scheme) is rooted in his complex cosmogonic interpretations, but these exegetical/theological complexities stem from Philo's expectation that God thought before he acted, having deliberated before he created. Across his commentary on Genesis 1–2, the Before is a vital element for Philo. God's pre-creational noetic intentions and pre-set invisible blue-print affect how Philo understands Genesis' texts of the beginning of the world and humanity. But the Before is also importantly described by these texts.

---

[82] Runia (2001) writes, "It seems obvious that it was not visible because it had not yet risen up. But Philo from his philosophical perspective converts it into ontological non-visibility! Compare the earth that is invisible in Gen 1:2, cited in §29" (312).

[83] Cf. *Leg.* 1.22; *QG* 1.2. See Tobin, 1983, 123–25.

[84] Tobin (1983) is right to recognize the close connection between Philo's interpretation of the world and interpretation of man (122–23), though the *direction* of influence from anthropogony to cosmogony that Tobin perceives (122–23, 130) should be questioned, not necessarily regarding the historical development that Philo may have incorporated (which is beside the present point), but with regard to Philo's own presentation. As Philo presents it in *Op.* 129–50 (and in *Leg.* 2.12–13ff.), the cosmogonic context provides the rationale for the anthropogonic interpretation, and both are cast as they are due to Philo's Before.

In summary, two aspects of Philo's interpretation of the beginning of Genesis have been our focus: 1) the *presence* of a theory of divine deliberations before the visible creation, 2) the *content* of this pre-creational plan. Philo has a Before. It is intimately wed to his reading of the Beginning. He *implicitly* refers to the Before by describing God's "pre-understanding" and "purposes" because of which he then (simultaneously) created. Such comments will be our focus throughout chapters 2 and 3; they will confirm that the Before is an important strand which is thoroughly interwoven throughout Philo's interpretation of the Beginning. Philo's *explicit* description of the Before has been our primary concern here. The content of God's pre-creational thoughts regards the noetic, invisible, incorporeal, very good blueprint of all things. Philo's theory of the Before is shaped, in part, by his Platonic expectations of such a pre-existent paradigm. This affects his reading of the biblical beginning. Yet Philo's Before also reciprocally *receives* shape and content – occasionally even clashing with Plato's Before – due to the biblical features themselves.

One cannot engage Philo's interpretation of creation in his commentary without coming into contact with his Before, for Gen. 1:1–5 *is* the Before, and then Genesis 1 *is* the Before. Philo's *pre*-protology is closely united to his protology. In light of these aspects of Philo's hermeneutic of creation – i.e., the Before, its connection with the Beginning – we will now turn to Paul's language of the Before. Paul's references to and applications of the text of the Beginning in Corinthian and Roman letters are (obviously) more sparse than Philo's in his commentary. Yet he does display a similar hermeneutic, nonetheless. Our attention will be trained on the *presence* of a divine pre-creational deliberation in Paul and on the *content* of this divine plan. As we proceed in this manner it will become clear that Paul's reading of Genesis' Beginning, like Philo's, simultaneously informs and yet also is affected by his notion of what God thought *before the beginning*.

1.3 Paul's "Before"
God's Pre-Creational Deliberation for Our Glory

According to Paul, God wisely determined where he would be known, and this was in the cross of Christ.[85] He determined this before creation. Only after such a pre-determination did the creative events transpire according to Genesis 1–2. We see this in 1 Corinthians and Romans, where, in a broadly similar manner to Philo, Paul connects God's *pre*-creational deliberations with the texts of creation.

---

[85] Bonhoeffer, 1986 (ET), 45.

In 1 Corinthians, Paul criticizes the church of Corinth for following the "wisdom" that is "of this age" (1 Cor. 2:6). Some have explained Paul's criticism in terms of the classic Jewish and Christian eschatological differentiation between "this-age/age-to-come,"[86] stating that Paul's wisdom "belongs to the new creation, not the old."[87] Though somewhat helpful, such language can also obscure the fact Paul does not here explicitly describe the wisdom he preaches as of "the new creation." Rather, the "wisdom" Paul preaches was there *before* the "old" creation. Paul claims:

> We speak God's wisdom in mystery, [a wisdom] which has been hidden, [a wisdom] which God *pre*-marked out [προώρισεν] *before* the ages [πρὸ τῶν αἰώνων] unto our glory, which none of the rulers of this age understood. For if they had understood it, they would not have crucified the Lord of glory! But rather, just as it has been written, 'What things no eye has seen and no ear has heard and into a person's heart have not entered: what God prepared [ἡτοίμασεν] for those who love him.' (2:6–9)

Many ancients used the phrase "before the age[s]" to express a "time" when God alone existed.[88] Philo drew special attention to God's self-sufficiency and goodness in the period "before the age" (πρὸ αἰῶνος),[89] and he specified that this phrase meant "before the genesis of the cosmos" (πρὸ τῆς τοῦ κόσμου γενέσεως).[90] For Paul, God was obviously present "before the ages," for according to 1 Cor. 2:7 he was actively doing something in this Before: "he pre-marked out" (προώρισεν). Paul thereby asserts more than God's pre-existence; he was active, not merely present. Other ancients attributed to God certain activity – e.g., "knowledge" of the future – that took place "before the age."[91] As we have seen in some detail, Philo had a detailed understanding of this timeless period.

Like Philo, Paul also believed God to be engaged in deliberations "before the ages," though Paul's concept of *what* God was planning contains some remarkable differences from Philo's concept. After a short discussion

---

[86] Pearson, 1975, 49; Thiselton, 2000, 165.

[87] Hays, 1997, 43. Cf. Theissen, 1987, 365; Collins, 1999, 564.

[88] Cf. LXX Ps. 54:20 (πρὸ τῶν αἰώνων) and Ps. 73:12 (πρὸ αἰῶνος – followed by God's cosmogonic power, vv. 13–18a). When Ben Sira highlighted God's creative power in language of Genesis 1 (42:15–43:33), he labeled God as the one who is "before the age [πρὸ τοῦ αἰῶνος] and unto the age [εἰς τὸν αἰῶνα]" (42:21; cf. 24:9). Cf. Ps. 89:2.

[89] *Mut.* 12.9. Here Philo, while commenting on God's revelation of his own name (his "eternal" or "age-long name," ὄνομα αἰώνιον; cf. Ex. 3:14–15), takes the cue from Moses' label αἰώνιον and divides between "our own age" (τῷ καθ' ἡμᾶς αἰῶνι) and "the [time/age] before the age" (τῷ πρὸ αἰῶνος). In the human-age God is known by names, accommodating to a purely human need. But "in the before-age" God has no name: he is simply "the Being One" (τὸ ὄν).

[90] *Mut.* 27.5; 46.2.

[91] E.g., "Even before the world was created [God] knows what is forever and what will be from generation to generation" (*1 En.* 39.11; cf. Tob. 6:18; 1QS 3:16; Plotinus, *Ennead* V.9, 5.22). See also *2 Bar.* 54:1–5, esp. v. 1 (cf. 21:8b).

concerning a method for approaching Paul's Before, we will see that he enters the Before through a combination of the text of Prov. 8:23 and his own experience of God's wisdom in Christ. It will also become clear, however, that the beginning of Genesis itself gives further shape and content to exactly what Paul believes God determined before the beginning.[92]

Concerning my present method, 1 Cor. 2:7 and its context will be the primary focus, for there Paul expresses that God not only "pre"-did something, but that this "pre-" was "before the ages." This statement, having been built on Prov. 8:23 (and therefore intimately connected to Genesis 1), is the best entrance into both Paul's Before and its relation to creation. But 1 Cor. 2:7 does not give the full picture of either. Other passages need to be considered. There are three types of "before"-passages which have been used by others in conjunction with 1 Cor. 2:7, but which I will not use.

First, one could explore every προ–prefixed verb that Paul uses.[93] While some of these express the helpful general similarity to 1 Cor. 2:7 that God thought "before" he acted – an assumption important for understanding Paul (as well as Philo) – the majority of these occurrences express a "before" that is too narrow to be helpful for our exploration of Paul's reading of creation and *the* Before.[94]

Second, there are a number of passages in Luke-Acts that may offer parallel thoughts to 1 Cor. 2:7, using ὁρίζω or even Paul's προορίζω to explain what God has "[pre-]marked out," some having other similarities as well. Many have used these passages to elucidate what God "pre-marked out" in 1 Cor. 2:7,[95] and most of these "parallels" are most likely helpful.[96]

---

[92] On this type of spiral (or reciprocal) hermeneutic in Paul and Philo see Watson, 2004, 2–5; cf. 127–29, 157–58: "The assumption that interpretation must *either* reproduce an original meaning *or* impose a meaning created by the interpreter is hermeneutically naïve" (129; emphasis original). Paul did not merely reproduce what the beginning of Genesis says, but neither did he merely import Prov. 8:23 and his experience of Christ into Genesis' creation account: each factor makes interpretive impressions on the others.

[93] Paul uses προ-prefixed verbs over 50 times in his undisputed letters (11 of these being προφητεύω, etymologically meaning "to speak beforehand," only occurring in 1 Cor. 11–14).

[94] Within these texts his most common is "I/we said before" (προλέγω; Rom. 9:29; 2 Cor. 7:3; 13:2 [2x]; Gal. 1:9; 5:21 [2x]; 1 Th. 3:4; 4:6). Cf. 2 Cor. 9:5 (3x προ-prefix). In Gal. 3:8 Paul does radicalize temporality by mentioning scripture "having known beforehand" (προϊδοῦσα) and having "preached beforehand" (προευηγγελίαστο). This, however, is also unhelpful for our purposes since the context shows the timing to be in Abraham's day rather than "before" creation.

[95] Dunn (1980) asserts that Luke 22:22, Acts 2:23, 4:27–28, 10:42, and 17:31 should be included as parallels to 1 Cor. 2:7 (234–35), and he summarizes each of these passages with this one statement: "In each case... what was determined long before in the will of God came to historical actuality in Christ – not, of course, in the sense that Jesus just happened to be the one who fitted the divine specifications, but in the sense that

Yet none of these texts specifies explicitly that the timing of this divine activity is before creation,[97] and therefore I will not employ them below.

Third, there are other passages in the disputed Pauline letters that host similar language to 1 Cor. 2:7 *and* which do explicitly refer to a time before creation (cf. Eph. 1:4–6; 2 Tim. 1:9; Tit. 1:2).[98] We are restricting our exploration to the Corinthian and Roman correspondences.

One other passage cannot remain unmentioned before we proceed. Paul's argument in Rom. 9:19–23 is similar to the Luke-Acts passages mentioned above. His statements in 9:19–23 pertain to God's creative activity of "forming" humans.[99] He casts this topic in the imagery of the Potter and clay.[100] Paul's context is thus creation of a sort, and the prophetic metaphor of the Potter itself is often rooted in Genesis 1–2.[101] Paul even

---

Christ was the one who from the beginning had been pre-ordained for this role" (235, emphasis original). Cf. Fee, 1987, 106 n. 37.

[96] E.g., Schrage (1991) has observed that like 1 Cor. 2:7 each aforementioned passage in Luke-Acts relates to Ps. 2:2 (LXX) and the conspiracy of "the rulers" against "the Christ" (1.253 n. 181).

[97] Allen (1970) sets (προ)ὁρίζω against the background of Ps. 2:7 as the "decree" of the Son of God (104–08). This opens the possibility that God's "marking" of Jesus is his resurrection and that his "pre-marking" may be the scriptural text (Psalm 2) itself. A pre-creational decree is not ruled out, however, even if the language or motif comes from Psalm 2. Without arguing the point, Allen asserts that although Paul borrows προορίζω from the thought world of Psalm 2, it is still to be seen as "a deliberation framed before the world's foundation" (108). In 1 Cor. 2:7, the pre-creational nature of προορίζω is made explicit by the other modifier πρὸ τῶν αἰώνων rather than by the verb itself. The same verb in Luke-Acts, while perhaps having the same scriptural roots and *probably* having the same temporal reference, is not *explicitly* referring to pre-creation. Without criticizing those who have used these parallels, we will not.

[98] So Kammler (2003) parallels 1 Cor. 2:7 with 2 Tim. 1:9; Tit. 1:2; John 17:24; Eph. 1:4; 1 Pet. 1:20; and John 17:5 (211, n. 115; behind all of these being πρὸ τῶν αἰώνων in Ps. 54:20). He thus concludes that "the real pre-existence of Christ and the ideal pre-existence of the community... are also implicit in the usage from 1 Cor. 2:7b" (211–12).

[99] Cf. τὸ πλάσμα, τῷ πλάσαντι, and ἐποίησας in 9:20 with ἔπλασεν in Gen. 2:7 and ἐποίησεν in Gen. 1:1, 27.

[100] Parallels often given are these: Ps. 2:9; Job 10:8–9; Isa 29:16; 41:25; 45:9; 64:8; Jer 18:1–12; Sir 33:13 (listed by Byrne, 1996, 300). See also Job 38:14; Wis. 13; 15:7; *T. Naph.* 2:2, 4; 1 QS 11:22 (listed by Moo, 1996, 602n 75). For many more Jewish texts that contrast humans (who are from clay) with the Creator, see Seifrid, 2007, 644–46.

[101] Cf. Isa. 45:4–46:13 (esp. 45:7, 12, 18, 46:9–10) with Genesis 1 (and 2:7). This does not seem to be the case in Isa. 29:16 (and Paul quotes Isa. 29:14 in 1 Cor. 1:19), in Isa. 64:8 (and Paul quotes, or shapes his thoughts on, Isa. 64:4 in 1 Cor. 2:9a), and in Jer. 18:4 (which Witherington [2004] thinks Paul is primarily using here, 257). While it is actually not necessary to make a choice from all of these texts as to which Paul is "using" (so Moo, 1996, 602), Paul's actual language in Rom. 9:18–23 is closest to Isa. 45:9, and Isaiah 45–46 is replete with references to creation in the language of Genesis 1. There are also similarities with Sir. 33:11–13 (so Byrne, 1996, 297–98), and Sirach roots the pot-

uses a προ-compound to describe God's "vessels of mercy" as "prepared beforehand" (προητοίμασεν) "unto glory" (εἰς δόξαν) (9:23). This statement looks remarkably similar to 1 Cor. 2:7–9, especially when Rom. 9:23 is seen in the wake of what Paul just wrote in 8 28–30[102]:

1 Cor. 2:7	God pre - marked out	unto our glory
1 Cor. 2:9	God prepared	for those loving him
Rom. 8:28–30	God pre - marked out	for those loving God... and glorified
Rom. 9:23	God pre - prepared	unto glory

Although the timing of God's "preparation beforehand" of his vessels "for glory" in Rom. 9:23 is almost certainly rightly comparable with God's "marking out beforehand" of wisdom "for our glory" in 1 Cor. 2:7–9, it is not *explicitly* clear that "beforehand" (προ-) in 9:23 does in fact refer to "before creation."[103] Though not as likely, it *could* simply refer to being

---

ter-imagery in the creation of Adam from the earth (v. 10; cf. Gen. 2:7). Likewise, Paul's language is close to Wis. 15:7 (although their message is quite different), and 15:7 is surrounded by the language of Gen. 2:7 (cf. 15:5, 8, 11). Regardless of the precise "background" of Paul's pottery language in Rom. 9:19–23, it is highly possible that it – like Sirach and Wisdom – is closely connected to Genesis 1–2 via the prophetic medium.

[102] Byrne (1996) also compares Rom. 9:23 with 8:29 and 1 Cor. 2:7 (303).

[103] The two related issues of exegesis and theology cause readers of Rom. 9:23 to produce differing construals of the timing of God's "pre-preparation." Yet the emphasis and language of Paul's argument show that there is no *theological* problem with understanding 9:23 as pre-creational. The larger context demonstrates this. For example, God's "purpose according to election" (ἡ κατ' ἐκλογὴν πρόθεσις; 9:11b) takes place temporally *before* (and logically without contemplation of) any ethical practice (9:11a). Thus what comes about in the life-history of these scriptural characters is *not* because of human "works" (9:12a) and *not* even due to human "willing [τοῦ θέλοντος] or running [τοῦ τρέχοντος]" (9:16), but *rather* (ἀλλά; 9:12, 16) due to God's "calling" (9:12b) and "mercy-ing" (9:16). (Paul's strong contrasts [οὐ... οὐδὲ... ἀλλά] rule out the possibility that the religious lives of these patriarchs were originated by even a *combination* of "God's call" *and* his foresight of their future "willing" or "running" – such is not Paul's concept in these verses.) It is God's purpose ("for this very thing I raised you up," εἰς αὐτὸ τοῦτο ἐξήγειρά σε; 9:17) according to his own "willing" (ὃν θέλει ἐλεεῖ, ὃν δὲ θέλει σκληρύνει; 9:18) that causes things to transpire as they do – whether for mercy or hardness. Paul's notion of divine causative intentionality, especially as he self-consciously relates God's "will" (ὃν θέλει) and "plan" (τῷ βουλήματι) to human responsibility (9:19), is what prompts Paul to introduce the prophetic concept of the Potter (i.e., Creator) and *his* freedom to do what *he* intends with *his* vessels (i.e., his creations) (9:20–23). Paul's seemingly "hypothetical" notion of divine desire (i.e., "But *if* God, wanting... [εἰ δὲ θέλων ὁ θεός]; 9:22–23) turns out to be Paul's construal of God's *actual* "willing" as Paul applies it without a break to "even us" (9:24a). Thus contextual considerations cause us to assume that, for Paul, God's intentions are prior to (and the logical cause of) his historical activity of mercy-ing and hardening, and when these intentions are related to the prophetic Potter/Creator imagery they should therefore be seen as *pre-creational* intentions.

"prepared" by faith during life for glory "before" receiving this glory in the eschaton.[104] As with the "[pre]destine" passages in Luke-Acts, so too with Paul's statement in Rom. 9:23: because it refers only probably but not definitely to God's deliberations before creation, we will therefore analyze it no further. We will restrict ourselves to two principal texts: 1 Cor. 2:7 and Rom. 8:29–30; the reasons for these will become clear as we proceed.

Though Paul was not writing a commentary on Genesis for the Corinthians and Romans, this section on Paul can naturally unfold in the same two stages as did the section above concerning Philo's commentary. Firstly, we will determine the *presence* in Paul of a theory of the Before, including its timing, purpose, and relation to the scriptural Beginning. This will be done primarily through an analysis of 1 Cor. 2:7 and Paul's allusion to Prov. 8:23 (and therefore also Genesis 1, as if in tow). Secondly, we will discern the *content* of Paul's Before. This will be done by navigating from 1 Cor. 2:7 ("pre-marked out"... "glory"), through 1 Cor. 15:49 ("glory"... "image"), and ultimately to Rom. 8:29–30 ("pre-marked out"... "image"... "glory"). Most scholars link these three passages in some manner, but our eyes will be trained specifically toward the connection between Paul's Before and the actual scriptural texts of the Beginning. As with Philo, Paul's connection between Beginning and Before will be confirmed and fleshed out in chapters 2 and 3. There we will notice that when Paul interprets both the beginning of the world (see chapter 2) and the beginning of humanity (see chapter 3) he himself points his readers to the previous and causative

---

Three things can thus be said about theology, exegesis, and Rom. 9:23. First, there is nothing *theological* in this context that would stop Paul from saying that God's vessels of mercy were "prepared before creation" for glory. Second, there is no real *philosophical* difference with regards to human responsibility whether God's intentions are placed just prior to the vessels' historical "willing and running" or are placed prior to creation itself; in this passage Paul sees God's intentions as *causative* and yet nonetheless not lessening human responsibility, regardless of their precise timing. Yet third, it remains the case *exegetically* – and this is the present methodological point – that in Rom. 9:23 Paul does not make it *explicit* that the temporal moment of God's "pre-preparation unto glory" was *before creation* (even if the prophetic-creative metaphor would encourage such a reading), but merely before it happens. Therefore, although I am not criticizing others who have used this passage as a parallel to 1 Cor. 2:7, we will not use it to consider Paul's thoughts about *before creation*.

[104] For example, according to Witherington (2004), "It is not said that the vessels of mercy are *destined* for glory beforehand, but that they are *prepared* for glory beforehand. So the subject is not some pretemporal determination, but rather what ch. 8 has referred to – namely that God did always plan for believers to be conformed to the image of his Son, and during their Christian lives, through the process of being set right and being sanctified, they have been prepared for such a glorious destiny. Thus Paul would be alluding to the process of sanctification here, which has a pretemporal plan behind it" (258–59; emphasis added; cf. Seifrid, 2007, 646).

"desire" and "purpose" of God – i.e., to an implicit Before. In this section, however, I must limit our consideration to Paul's *explicit* Before, that is, where he basically writes, "This is what God planned before creation...."

When many think of "predestination" in Paul, they initially think of Rom. 8:29–30. But when that text is read in light of both 1 Cor. 2:7 and 1 Cor. 15:49 – and below I will argue why it should be – Paul's wording in Rom. 8:29–30 more explicitly reveals the hermeneutic of creation which was previously perceptible, but only implicitly so, in 1 Cor. 2:7. That is, Paul reads Genesis' Beginning in a mutually interpretive manner with *before the beginning*.

1.3.1 The Presence in Paul of a Pre-Creational Plan and the Text of Proverbs 8 (1 Cor. 2:7)

Three observations will help us analyze the *presence* of the explicit Before in Paul, specifically in 1 Cor. 2:7. First, within 1 Cor. 1:18–2:5 (the immediate context of 2:7) Paul finds the idea of God's pre-set and causative intentions important for his interpretation of general social happenings surrounding the gospel's proclamation. Second, in 2:7 itself Paul then alludes to Prov. 8:22–31 to ground certain divine intentions before creation itself. Third, this use of Proverbs 8 connects Paul's Before closely to his interpretation of Genesis' Beginning. These observations have been either completely missed or insufficiently developed in recent scholarly discussion.

Regarding 1 Corinthians 1–4, many over the last century have searched for the proper "religio-historical background" against which Paul's Corinthian opponents and/or Paul himself should be understood.[105] Earlier contexts in Gnosticism[106] or mystery cults[107] have now been generally left behind.[108] Some attention has been paid to Graeco-Roman or Jewish rhetori-

---

[105] For helpful historical summaries see Davis, 1984, 3–5 and Sterling, 1995, 355–56.

[106] Pearson (1973) labels the placement of Gnosticism behind 1 Cor. 1–4 as "almost standard" for the first seventy years of the 20th century (1); the "Gnostic hypothesis" being first posited by Lütgert in 1908, carried forward by Dinkler and Kümmel, but moved *en force* by Wilckens, Schmithals, and Winter (1–4, 7–9; cf. Davis, 1984 153 n. 7).

[107] According to Scroggs (1967/68, 38), this was initially argued by Reitzenstein, 1927, 338–40 and further by Wilckens, 1959, 53–8. According to Stuhlmacher (1987, 331), Bultmann (1969) thought it was "certain" that Paul himself was "thinking along the lines of the mystery cults." This supposition was built especially on Paul's positive use of "mystery" (μυστήριον) and its revelation to the "mature" or "perfect" (τελείοις, i.e., the "initiates of the mystery religions"). See Barclay's critique in 1996A, 390. In another strand of the applicability of the mystery cults, Sterling (1995) has more recently argued that the Corinthian opponents, not Paul, had been influenced by the mystery cults and the initiation of the "perfect" (355–84; cf. Welborn, 2005, 215ff).

[108] Martin, 1992, 70–71. Pearson (1973) has provided one of the most foundational critiques of the Gnostic-hypothesis. Bornkamm (1967) distances Paul's message in 1 Cor.

cal practices.[109] Others have found fruitful the backdrop of Hellenistic-Jewish wisdom[110] and/or creation traditions,[111] especially as represented in the works of Wisdom of Solomon and Philo.[112] As important and illuminating as many of these discussions are,[113] the religio-historical background to 1 Corinthians 1–4 does not (and neither does whether Paul is using the language of his opponents or not[114]) have significant bearing on the fact that at a crucial juncture of his argument about "wisdom" Paul points his Corinthian opponents and friends toward God's determination "before the ages."[115] It is *that* to which we must now turn.

Most agree that Paul's reference to "predestination" in 1 Cor. 2:7 refers to the "time" before creation.[116] But Paul's understanding of the Before is more closely connected to the text of Genesis 1 than has been observed,

---

2:6–7 (and indeed in Jesus and Paul at large) from both Gnosticism and the mystery cults (4.820–824). Cf. Brown, 1958, 438, and Reiling, 1988, 200–01; Dunn, 1995, 34–41; Hays, 1997, 43; Garland, 2003, 102.

[109] For Graeco-Roman rhetorical practices see Mitchell, 1991, 20–64; Witherington, 1995, 76. For Jewish homiletic patterns see Wuellner, 1970, 199–204 and Ellis, 1978, 155 (cf. Barbour, 1979, 61–2 and Williams, 2001, 11–14 for more discussion and bibliography). Welborn (2005) sharpens the Graeco-Roman rhetorical setting to the "comic-philosophical tradition" found in the theatre. In a slightly different manner, Martin (1992) culls from Graeco-Roman sources – philosophy, plays, medical texts, etc. – a certain ideology found also among the Corinthians, i.e., a thought pattern which split the educated from the non-educated, the social elite from "the masses" (108–17).

[110] See Pearson, 1973; Horsley, 1978, 203–231. Davis (1984) furthers the efforts of Pearson and Horsley (5). Cf. Theissen, 1987, 353–67.

[111] Sterling, 1995, 355–84.

[112] See explicitly Horsley, 1978, 206–07; implicitly (but clearly) in Pearson, 1973, 11–12, 17–21. Cf. Davis, 1984, 49–62. For detailed argumentation *against* Wisdom of Solomon see Theissen, 1987, 353–67; and *against* Philo see Sterling, 1995, 355–84. Martin (1992) is careful in his critique of Horsley's use of Philonic Platonism, writing that "the sort of dualism implied [by Horsley] was not limited in the first century to Platonists, it need not imply a matter/non-matter dichotomy, and the Corinthians need not have come by it via any form of Judaism. Hellenistic Jews such as Philo expressed such dualistic notions for the same reason that many other intellectuals did: it was simply "in the air" in first-century popular philosophy" (272–73 n. 10).

[113] Cf. Williams, 2001, 10–14; Reiling, 1988, 201; Barbour, 1979, 61–2.

[114] For Paul's use of Corinthian language: Martin, 1992, 263 n. 68; Davis, 1984, 3; Dunn, 1980, 177; Pearson, 1973, 3–4, 31; Wilckens, 1971, 7.519, 522; Barrett, 1968, 60. For a criticism: Schnabel, 1985, 243.

[115] What follows may add extra support to a background found in Hellenistic-Jewish creation/wisdom traditions but is not contingent on such a "background."

[116] So, e.g., Garland, 2003, 96; Collins, 1999, 130; Hays, 1997, 45; Blomberg, 1995, 66; Witherington, 1995, 127; Ellingworth and Hatton, 1994, 54–55; Fee, 1987, 105; Morris, 1985, 54–5; Prior, 1985, 51; Conzelmann, 1975, 62; Bornkamm, 1967, 4.820 (cf. *idem*, 1985, 617). Some see this phrase in 1 Cor. 2:7 as synonymous with the more explicit Eph. 1:4, πρὸ καταβολῆς κόσμου (Best, 1998, 120; Lincoln, 1990, 23).

and this connection has hermeneutical and theological implications for his interpretation of creation. When approaching Paul's notion of "before the ages" in 1 Cor. 2:7, it is contextually significant that in his discussion about "wisdom" in 1:18–2:5 he insists that the Corinthians' own social experiences are themselves the ramifications of God's own pre-set intentions. This more general feature of Paul's thought in 1:18–2:5 lends even more import to his ultimate example in 2:7–9 of God's determinations that were, in the latter case, explicitly understood as laid out before creation itself.

(a) The Presence of God's Pre-Set Intentions (1 Cor. 1:18–2:5, 2:7)

Concrete situations are in Paul's mind by the time he introduces the Before to the Corinthians. He interprets those social interactions through the lens of divinely pre-set intentions. These hermeneutical glasses not only affect Paul's *scriptural* interpretation but also his *sociological* interpretation. When presenting the gospel, Paul has been opposed by both Jews and Greeks as they reject his message. These rejecters considered Paul's "word of the cross" moronic due to both the simple manner in which Paul presented it in Corinth and its content (1:18).[117] Yet others accepted his message in spite of its form and in light of its content. Paul thought that those who scoffed at his words (and therefore at the Christ and his cross represented in it) considered themselves to be "wise" in such a rejection.

But these types of social scenarios (mentioned in 1:18, developed in 1:22–24), the substance of which Paul thought was infecting the Corinthian church,[118] were for Paul merely manifestations of God's intentions that he had revealed through Isaiah long before (1:19; quoting Isa. 29:14). Isaiah announced that God's intention ("I will...") was to "destroy" the "wisdom" of these "wise" people, ironically proving *it* stupid. As Paul sees it, God was presently enacting within his own time and experiences this very pre-set and destructive deliberation (God's "I will") within the very act of the "wise" foolishly rejecting the best, most true, and wisest.[119] God had now,

---

[117] Horsley (1977) saw a neglect in most literature through 1977 of wisdom's *form* ("of word"), neglected for the sake of wisdom's *content* ("Christ crucified"), (224–39) and Barbour (1979) furthered the relation of "form" and "content" (60–61).

[118] Paul saw the schismatic behavior of the Corinthian Christians (1:10–17) – their "boasting" in human "wisdom" and separation from what they deemed "foolish" – as sharing important and unfortunate substance with the attitude of the non-Christians who "wisely" called the cruciform truth "foolish."

[119] A γάρ connects v. 18 ("The word of the cross is foolish to those perishing") to v. 19 ("*For* it has been written, 'I will destroy the wisdom of the wise...'"). The logic shows that for Paul God's intention revealed in Isa. 29:14 has come about precisely in the (wrong) opinions of "those perishing" in contrast to the (right) opinions of "those being saved." Thus God's pre-announced, and therefore pre-determined, salvific and destruc-

definitively in the Christ and socially in the message, made foolish the world's "wisdom,"[120] just as he pre-announced he would more than 750 years before.[121] Paul sees his present experiences – gospel acceptance or rejection – as functions of God's long-past (pre-set) determinations.

To further explain God's pre-intended humiliation of the world's wisdom,[122] Paul states in 1:21a the general principle that God had also wisely determined beforehand to not be "known" by human "wisdom,"[123] and that, conversely, it was actually "pleasing" to God (and therefore also his determination or design)[124] to save through the so-called "stupidity" of the cross those who submitted to the truth and relevance of its proclamation (1:21b). All of this was, according to Paul, desired and decided by God ("in his wisdom") long before it ever happened in history. In 1:22–24, Paul elaborates on the historical outworking of these divine pre-determinations, and he highlights two particulars of the aforementioned social scenarios:

1) 1:22–23a	Jews seek signs Greeks seek wisdom	vs.	We preach Christ crucified
2) 1:23b-24	Scandal to Jews Stupid to Greeks	vs.	God's power and God's wisdom to those called (whether Jews or Greeks)

Paul focuses first on the contrasting *content* that was desired versus delivered: "We want signs or wisdom!" versus "We give you a crucified Christ!" (1:22–23a). He then draws attention to the contrasting *responses* to that content: "This is a scandal or stupid!" versus "This is God's power

---

tive "power" – saving those who believe while destroying the wisdom of unbelievers – is manifested in the preaching of the cross and in its respective social responses.

[120] Paul's question οὐχὶ ἐμώρανεν ὁ θεός... (1:20) expects an affirmation. The aorist (ἐμώρανεν) shows that Paul is thinking of something that God has already done definitively to which the Corinthians may think: "Yes, in that event – in the cross and its declaration – God *has* rendered as stupid the world's so-called wisdom."

[121] Some more recent critical analyses of the timing of this Isaianic prophecy would, of course, place it much closer in time to Paul than 750 years. The timescale above is expressed from Paul's own perspective, which would have held that Isaiah prophesied around and during the Assyrian attack on Jerusalem (c. 722 BCE; cf. Isaiah 36–37). Since we are trying to discern Paul's opinions, the date above is more helpful than any of the modern alternative constructs.

[122] This is the logic of Paul's "For since" (ἐπειδὴ γάρ) in 1:21.

[123] The meaning of the difficult phrase ἐν τῇ σωφίᾳ τοῦ θεοῦ cannot be discerned by grammar alone. See Wedderburn, 1973A, 132–34. The reading above is a valid understanding of the grammar, and it comports well with the context of God's intentionality. Even within the diverse readings of this phrase (see Thiselton, 2000, 167–69), a common assumption is that it denotes some sort of intentionality of God. Davis (1984) rewords ἐν τῇ σωφίᾳ τοῦ θεοῦ as "the plan of God as a whole" (92).

[124] Thiselton, 2000, 167.

and wisdom!" (1:23b-24). These concrete events that Paul is remembering and describing are comparable to the social exchanges later recorded in Acts (and even in the gospels).[125] Temporally and causatively behind these social realities of seeking/presenting and rejecting/accepting Paul saw God's wise purpose and pleasure. He interprets the situations accordingly.

The remarks above are intended to make explicit Paul's implicit interpretive grid that affects even his "reading" of the social happenings that surround him and the Corinthians. Throughout 1 Cor. 1:18–25, Paul has been interpreting the entire theological issue of "wisdom," with all of its social correlates, through a lens in which a divine pre-deliberation determines certain concrete and historical happenstances. Paul continues in 1:26–31 to view contemporary circumstances in light of God's causative pre-set intentions. There he effortlessly mentions the divine intent behind the more personal circumstances of the Corinthian believers. He places even their own "calling" within the structure of divine intent. God "chose" and "called" those who were foolish and weak nothings (1:26–31). Paul avers that God *intended* these choices for a *purpose*: "in order that" (ἵνα, x3) he might shame and nullify those who were wise and strong somethings. God also *intended* his selection "so that" (ὅπως) he might silence all inappropriate boasting (v. 29). God made Christ become the benefit of those whom he himself "chose" and "called," "in order that" (ἵνα) the injunction in Jer. 9:24 would be established: "The one boasting in the Lord, let him boast" (v. 30). Thus God's "election," "calling," and Christological blessing of certain types of people were, for Paul, further concrete fulfilments of God's *previous* (and causative) intentions (1:26–31).[126] Behind

---

[125] See Matt. 12:38; John 6:30. Cf. Matt. 16:1; Mark 8:11; Luke 11:15–16; (maybe 23:8); John 2:18; (cf. Jesus' comment at John 4:48;) 12:18. Thiselton, 2000, 170. The issue in Corinth, according to 1 Cor. 1 (1:23a) and Acts 18 (cf. vv. 5, 27–28), was the identity of the Christ. Thiselton, 2000, 171; Robertson and Plummer, 1911, 22 (see the nuanced treatment of the Corinthian issue in Barbour, 1979, 60–61). Cf. Stuhlmacher, 1987, 335.

[126] It is important to notice in this context that Paul understands God's "calling" as the divine action which takes place in history while being *based upon God's previously made decisions and intentions*. Eskola (1998) states about the verb προορίζω that "the *act* of election can be found *in* the call of God" (177; emphasis added). Eskola explicitly treats "predestination" as "an historical act" (173) rather than as a "temporal predestination" (177) which occurred "before the beginning of 'history'" (173). Eskola's construal is clearly at odds with my argument concerning the *timing* of Paul's "predestination" and the *causative* nature of what *preceded* God's historical "call." (Eskola's treatment of "predestination" and "calling" directly concern Rom. 8:29–30 [173–77], but he explicitly reads this into "election" in 1 Cor. 2:7 [179], which makes this discussion applicable and necessary here.) Restricting "predestination" to an event *within gospel proclamation* enables Eskola to say that according to Paul "all people" – i.e., "the descendants of Adam" – "have been predestined" (176). Eskola deduces this from the fact that Paul wants all

each of these social and personal moments, Paul saw a complex and wise divine intent, part of which was announced by Isaiah, part by Jeremiah, but all pre-established by God.

With this hermeneutical structure in the foreground of our minds, discerned as it is from 1:18–2:5, we can analyze 2:7. In 2:7 Paul uncovers the roots of "God's wisdom," planted before creation. Philo had used terms such as "*pre*-understood," "purposed," "*pre*-stamped out," and "before" to express God's deliberative actions *before* the beginning.[127] Paul also uses the prefix "pre-" (προ-) and the preposition "before" (πρό) to describe something that God previously did.[128] God "marked out *beforehand*" (*προώρισεν*, "*pre*-destined") a wisdom; he did this "*before* the ages" (πρὸ τῶν αἰώνων). God also did this for a purpose, or toward a certain end: "*unto*" or "*for* our glory" (εἰς δόξαν ἡμῶν, v. 7).[129] As Paul then claims in v. 9: God "prepared things for those who love him."[130] For Paul, God "marked out" and "prepared" before he historically enacted these purposes.

Throughout all of 1:18–2:5, and then especially in 2:7, Paul "reads" the concrete social interactions as functions of God's pre-set intentionality. From this passage itself we cannot say that God's pre-set "I will" in 1:18–

---

descendants of Adam to *hear* the gospel proclaimed (177). But in Eskola's desire to be "universal," as he calls it, he actually flattens Paul's use of the important terms – "calling," "election," "predestination" – and his logic falls short of Paul's actual wording. In 1 Cor. 1:26–31, Paul considers it important that God does *not* "elect" and "call" *all* the descendants of Adam, but only certain types of people. Paul shows (implicitly in 1:18, 22–24) that he certainly *proclaims* the gospel to all – universally and indiscriminately – while yet in the same breath still insisting that God is *not* thereby "electing" or "calling" everyone universally or indiscriminately. Paul's language and concept of "election" and "calling" in 1 Cor. 1–2 does not comport with Eskola's use of Paul's words.

[127] Cf. προλαβών, βουληθείς, προεξετύπου, and πρό/πρίν (above).

[128] In line with what we saw in n. 109 above, Eskola (1998) downplays the temporality of the προ- prefix in Rom. 8:29–30 (170–71, 173 n. 29). We will come to Rom. 8:29–30 below. Such a supposition certainly cannot be maintained in an analysis of 1 Cor. 2:7, in which Paul reinforces his προ-prefixed verb with the additional phrase πρὸ τῶν αἰώνων. In a more sound methodological move than Eskola demonstrates, the clear temporality of 1 Cor. 2:7 helps shed light on the potential of the προ-prefix in Rom. 8:29–30 (repeated 3x) to retain an assumed temporality. Discussing the importance of God's "purpose" for Paul, and its determinative effect in Paul's life, Dunn (1998B) notes, "Note the frequency of *pro-* ("before") words attributed to God in [Rom. 8–11] – Rom. 8.28–29; 9.11, 23; 11.2; also 1 Cor. 2.7; Gal. 2.8; Eph. 1.5, 11; 2.10; 3.11" (40 n. 64).

[129] The eschatological nature of the phrase εἰς δόξαν ἡμῶν is brought out well by Robertson and Plummer (1911, 38–39). Cf. Kammler, 2003, 212; Orr and Walther, 1976, 156; Pearson, 1973, 34–5. Contra Feuillet, 1966, 39–40 (also quoted and discussed favorably in Davis, 1984, 95–96).

[130] Brown, 1958, 437. Ben Sira also says that it is only "by [God's] gift" that God "supplies" wisdom "to those who love him" (τοῖς ἀγαπῶσιν αὐτόν, 1:10); cf. 1 Cor. 2:9d, 12, and 4:7.

2:5 was set down before creation, for our only glimpse at its timing is its announcement in the prophets.[131] But regardless of its timing, the same basic principle is at play in 2:7: God pre-sets his intentions and then manifests them in a future time and space. In 2:7 this divine pattern is brought to an explicit and radical point of temporality: God marked out his "wisdom" not merely "beforehand" generally, nor even in the prophets' time specifically, but actually "before the ages." But when exactly is this "before"? Does it relate to the actual creation-texts? And how?

(b) The Timing and Text(s) of "Before the Ages":
Prov. 8:23, Genesis 1, and Before (1 Cor. 2:7)

Most scholars simply assume that by "before the ages" Paul means something like "before the foundation of the world" or "before creation."[132] This is certainly a true assumption. But questions regarding where Paul got this idea of a predestined wisdom and how this fact of pre-creationally ordained wisdom might be related to his reading of the creation-text of Genesis emerge virtually untouched. Many have paralleled various aspects of 1 Cor. 2:6–8 with scriptural or other texts,[133] but few link the precise

---

[131] In Rom. 16:25–27 Paul ascribes glory to "the only wise God" who strengthens Christians "according to the revelation of the mystery [μυστηρίου] that was kept hidden for long ages [χρόνοις αἰωνίοις σεσιγημένου] but which has now been disclosed and through the prophetic writings has been made known to all nations according to the command of the eternal God [τοῦ αἰωνίου θεοῦ]." Out of the many verbal and conceptual parallels this statement shares with 1 Cor. 2:7 (e.g., wise God, mystery, hidden, ages, revealed), the one particular feature to which attention may be drawn now is that Paul thinks that the "prophetic writings" (γραφῶν προφητικῶν) make known a *previously* established mystery. Thus it is possible that in 1 Cor. 1:18–2:5 God's "I will" disclosed in Isa. 29:14 was, in Paul's understanding, a *revelation* of God's desire which had been marked out *beforehand* – before the ages, perhaps – and thus hidden for long ages, and therefore an aspect of Paul's more radical (pre-creational) Before. Yet because it is not as explicit as 1 Cor. 2:7 we will pursue it no further.

[132] E.g., Collins (1999) writes, "'Before the ages' (cf. Gal. 1:4) places the divine initiative before creation itself" (130). Contra Eskola, 1998, 173, 177, 185.

[133] For example, one can compare προορίζω in 2:7 and its antithesis to "the rulers" in 2:6–8 with the anointing of the Christ and the raging "rulers" in Psalm 2 (Allen, 1970, 107; cf. Schrage, 1991, 1.253 n. 181); the title "Lord of glory" in 2:8 with the same title throughout *1 Enoch* and with the question and answer posed to "the rulers" in Psalm 23 (LXX), "Who is the King of glory, the Lord" (a psalm that Paul will quote in 10:26). See the many references in Kammler, 2003, 214, n. 130; cf. Williams, 2001, 166, n. 52. One can compare the ignorance of "the rulers" in 2:8 with their lack of wisdom in Bar. 3:16 (Williams, 2001, 166, n. 53); the revelation of "wisdom" and "mystery" by the "Spirit" in 2:6–8, 10–11 with the revelation of "wisdom" and "mystery" in Dan. 2:19–23 (Williams, 2001, 166–68; see the qualification of this "possible echo" in Ciampa and Rosner, 2007, 701–02) and this revelation by the "Holy Spirit" in Wis. 9:17 (Theissen, 1987, 353 n. 1). While each of these may provide some insightful parallels for certain aspects of Paul's

phrase "before the ages" to an actual scriptural text.[134] Some posit a more general "(Hellenistic) Jewish wisdom tradition" behind 1 Corinthians 1–4.[135] Proverbs 8:22–31 is then usually recognized as foundational and influential in such a "wisdom tradition,"[136] but it has only seldom been noticed that Paul most likely has Prov. 8:22–31 itself in mind in 2:7. Where recognized, this has been traced out either insufficiently[137] or in the wrong direction.[138] G. Theissen notices a "mythical being" in Proverbs 8, but he

---

thinking in 2:6–16 and beyond, I am narrowing our attention to the temporal, conceptual, and textual framework of Paul's phrase "before the ages."

[134] Kammler (2003) connects Paul's phrase πρὸ τῶν αἰώνων to the identical phrase in Ps. 54:20 (211, n. 115), but Paul is writing in 1 Cor. 2:7 of something more precise than the "Gottesprädikation" in Ps. 54:20 will in itself warrant, i.e., Paul is not merely claiming that God pre-existed.

[135] For example, some see a Hellenistic Jewish wisdom tradition behind the Corinthians (Horsley, 1977, 225), some see it behind Paul himself (Pearson, 1973, 27, 101 n. 4; Theissen, 1987, 353–67), and others see it as more broadly present (Sterling, 1995, 355–84; without mention of Prov. 8:22–31 [et par.] at 367–76, esp. 371).

[136] According to Hengel (1974, quoting von Rad), "that 'powerful conception of world and salvation history'," which was begun by Prov. 8:22–31 (and Job 28) and developed by Sirach 24, "tenaciously influenced not only the Palestinian *haggada* but also the Alexandrian philosophy of religion" – the latter beginning with Aristobulus (c.170 BCE) and "culminat[ing] in Philo" (1.163, 166) – "and was itself of decisive significance for the development of christology" (1.162). Cf. Whybray, 1965, 12; Skehan, 1979, 365–79; Murphy, 1985, 3–11 (esp. 10–11); Harrington, 1996; Alexander, 2002, 236–38 (though, contra Alexander concerning a tension between Job 28 and Prov. 8; they are in tension with each other inasmuch as two sides of one coin could be considered such).

[137] E.g., Kremer, 1997, 58 and Eskola, 1998, 179. Pearson (1973) sees "wisdom" as a "personified hypostasis" in Hellenistic Judaism, and cites Wisdom of Solomon, Aristobulus, and Philo as sources with nuanced versions of such wisdom. These are also in the "background," Pearson claims, of "the Corinthian doctrine of the Spirit." But he does not notice Prov. 8:23 itself behind 2:7 (35–37; cf. n. 155 below for Aristobulus' use of it).

[138] Barbour (1979) thinks that Paul "no doubt draws to some extent on Jewish wisdom-traditions" (62) and says that "there is then at least an indirect reference [in 1 Cor. 1:21] to the wisdom of God in creation portrayed in differing ways by Job 28; Prov 8; Sir 1,24; Baruch 3–4 and Sap Sal" (64). Barbour is careful to nuance that "wisdom is not being hypostatized here" (64). Barbour then argues concerning 2:6–16, "We have accepted as indubitable the general hypothesis that Paul identified Jesus, at least in some measure and for certain purposes, with the wisdom of God present with him or active alongside him or on his behalf in creation and in history, as we see her especially in Prov, Sir, Baruch and Sap Sal" – Barbour has in mind 1 Cor. 8:6 and Col. 1:15–20; Phil. 2:6–11; and "possibly" 1 Cor. 10:4 and Rom. 10:6–8, but *not* 1 Cor. 2:7 (68) – but quickly qualifies: "but it is not clear that this identification has played any very large part in 1 Cor 1 and 2, although it undoubtedly lies in the background" (68). The reason for this virtual denial of Prov. 8 playing a "very large part" in 1 Cor. 1–2 is due to the fact that Barbour has directly and necessarily correlated "wisdom" as found in Prov. 8:22ff with a "wisdom-christology" that speaks of Christ as co-Creator. Granted, such was and is a typical way to interpret "wisdom" in Prov. 8:22–31 – as the "pre-existent mediator of

argues that it is the more developed "Jewish wisdom tradition" on which Paul draws. He describes correspondences (and divergences) between 1 Cor. 1:18–2:16 and Wisdom of Solomon at large,[139] and Wisdom of Solomon 8–10 specifically,[140] but does not further mention Prov. 8:22–31.[141] According to Theissen, although Paul "restructure[ed the] traditional framework of interpretation"[142] he nevertheless "unmistakenly presupposes wisdom traditions of the type of Wisdom of Solomon."[143] While there are points of contact, both negative and positive, between 1 Corinthians 1–4 and Wisdom of Solomon,[144] and while it is helpful to recognize that Wis-

---

creation" (Lange, 1995, 34) – though it is not universally accepted that "wisdom" in Prov. 8:22–31 is such a mediator of creation (Murphy, 1985, 5; Yee, 1992, 91–93). This is especially doubted when considering how "wisdom" is presented in the LXX of Prov. 8:22–31 (see Cook, 1997, 224, 246; applied to wisdom-christology in Jobes, 2000, 226–50, 231–32).

In a manner similar to Barbour, Reiling (1988) questions whether "we have to understand this wisdom [*sc.* in 1 Cor. 2:6–16] as a σοφία-christology," that is, "a christology after the model of the personified wisdom of Prov. 8,22–25; 9,1–6; 4,6–9 and its elaboration in Wis and Sir" (204). He thinks not, but he is still functioning with an unnecessary one-to-one relationship (such as Barbour's) between the type of "personified wisdom" in much contemporary "wisdom-christology" and the "wisdom" personified in Prov. 8:22–25. Reiling is rightly critical of a "personified wisdom" Christology in 1 Cor. 2:7, yet he has wrongly dropped Prov. 8:22ff from discussion altogether. Confirming Prov. 8:22–31 behind Paul's statement about wisdom in 2:7 needs not imply a complete acceptance of the type of "σοφία-christology" in modern discussions. The mere fact that Jesus is not portrayed as the mediator of creation in 2:7 in no way weakens the supposition that Prov. 8:23 is present behind 2:7. While I am not denying to wisdom a role in creation in Prov. 8:22–31, and while I am certainly not denying to Paul the notion of Jesus as mediator of creation (e.g., 1 Cor. 8:6; cf. Col. 1:15–16), I am claiming that one can refer to wisdom *as it is presented in Prov. 8:22–31* without referring to it as a "pre-existent mediator of creation." And I am claiming that Paul has done just this in 1 Cor. 2:7.

[139] Theissen, 1987, 355–67. Scroggs (1967/68) argues: "The teaching in 1 Cor. 2:6–16 is derived directly from the context of Jewish and Christian apocalyptic-wisdom theology," and he argues at length for Paul's direct dependence on Wis. 9:9–18 (48–54) and other "apocalyptic-wisdom" texts (37–48). He does not mention Prov. 8:22–31. Granted, Proverbs 8 would not be classified under the sub-category of "apocalyptic" in the wisdom genre, but Paul's blending of wisdom language with apocalyptic language surely does not disqualify Prov. 8:22–31 from the possibility of having a direct and authoritative influence on Paul.

[140] Theissen, 1987, 353 n. 1.

[141] Theissen (1987) does later use similar language to describe 1 Cor. 2:7 as he had Proverbs 8. That is, in 2:7 Paul shows a connection between "the historical cross" and "the *mythically* conceived pre-existence of divine wisdom" (376; emphasis added), but Proverbs 8 is not actually mentioned again.

[142] Theissen, 1987, 360.

[143] Theissen, 1987, 358.

[144] Cf. Wis. 6:22 and 1 Cor. 2:6–8a for a parallel not mentioned by Theissen but which could have strengthened his argument.

dom 9 itself blends together Genesis 1 and Proverbs 8 (see below), it is significant that Wisdom of Solomon lacks the phrase from Prov. 8:23 "before the age" (πρὸ τοῦ αἰῶνος).[145] From where did Paul get the particular idea that wisdom was "before the ages"? Paul's contemplation of the character of God's "wisdom" somehow brought him into contact with this temporal expression. This is most readily explicable as the influence of Prov. 8:23 itself.[146] When we compare Prov. 8:22–23 and 1 Cor. 2:7 (for clarity's sake replacing the referents to wisdom in both passages – "me," "which" – with "wisdom") we see important similarities:

Prov. 8:22	Lord	created	[wisdom]	beginning of his ways	for his works
8:23	he	founded	[wisdom]	before the age (in the beginning)	
1 Cor. 2:7	God	pre-marked out	[wisdom]	before the ages	for our glory

Both Proverbs and Paul are discussing what God actively did to "wisdom." Both describe this act as taking place "before the age(s)."[147] Both present "wisdom" as directed "for" (εἰς) a beneficial purpose. Both present wisdom as such so as to make their particular form of "wisdom" more attractive and desirable to their readers. Paul appears to have had Prov. 8:23 in mind when he wrote 1 Cor. 2:7.

To develop this claim more helpfully, let us briefly recount how Prov. 8:22–31 is itself evocative of Genesis 1. Then, by adding how a few ancient Jewish interpreters explicitly linked these two passages, I will demonstrate that the textual and conceptual correspondences just mentioned between 1 Cor. 2:7 and Prov. 8:23 *strongly imply* that Paul's notion of

---

[145] The author of Wisdom of Solomon certainly bases much of his explanation of wisdom on Prov. 8:22–31 (e.g., cf. Wis. 6:22 with Prov. 8:22–23), but he does not use the phrase "before the age(s)." That is significant for our present discussion.

[146] Contra Whybray (1965) who, for no specified reason, sees a connection between Paul and Proverbs 8 only as mediated through later wisdom writings (12).

[147] Why did Paul use the plural "ages" while Prov. 8:23 (and others who quoted/glossed it) used the singular "age"? Plural "ages" was certainly used in the OT, occasionally of God's pre-existence (Ps. 54:20; cf. Sir. 36:17), and in one of the typical phrases for (future) "eternity": "unto the ages" (εἰς τοὺς αἰῶνας or εἰς τὸν αἰῶνα τῶν αἰώνων; cf. over 40x in the longer Greek of Daniel). In Eccl. 1:10 there are plural past "ages." When one compares Philo's use of "before the age" from Prov. 8:23 in, e.g., *Ebr.* 31 or *Mut.* 12, one sees only "our age" (τῷ καθ' ἡμᾶς αἰῶνι) and "the [age] before the age" (τῷ πρὸ αἰῶνος) (*Mut.* 12; *Ebr.* 31), and thus a fundamental difference with Paul, for whom exist "this [present evil] age" (τοῦ αἰῶνος τούτου; cf. Gal. 1:4), "the ages" (τῶν αἰώνων; 1 Cor. 10:11), ["the ages to come" (τοῖς αἰῶσιν τοῖς ἐπερχομένοις), cf. Eph. 2:7], and "before the ages" (πρὸ τῶν αἰώνων). Philo's and Paul's similar handling of this phrase (each taking it from Prov. 8:23) to prove the validity of the "wisdom" that they themselves teach, yet with different numbered "age(s)" therein, indicates that Paul's plurality is most likely tied to his apocalypticism, i.e., his understanding of the dramatic in-breaking of the new creation proleptically in Christ (and thus the overlap of the two creations/ages). This is most likely what affected his gloss of the "age" in Prov. 8:23.

God's pre-determination and destination of "wisdom" is connected closely to the actual text of Genesis 1. This implied connection will be confirmed when we finally see how in Rom. 8:29 Paul combines the same language of the Before – "pre-marked out" – with the "image" language from the beginning of Genesis itself. This case will now begin to build more surely by briefly rehearsing the bond between Prov. 8:22–31 and Genesis 1.

Through the phrase "before the age" (πρὸ τοῦ αἰῶνος), Prov. 8:23 expressed that God's wisdom was firmly established and present with him "before" (πρό, 6x in vv. 23–25) the earth or anything else was made. What is more, Proverbs 8 is evocative of the text of Genesis 1.[148] Recalling a few examples will suffice. The temporal description "in the beginning" (ἐν ἀρχῇ) is immediately obvious (cf. v. 23 and Gen. 1:1). The enigmatic temporal marker "before the age" is immediately explained in v. 24 as "before" (πρό) the "making" of "the earth" (cf. Gen. 1:1), πρό the "making" of "the abysses" (cf. Gen. 1:2a), and πρό the proceeding of the fountains of "the waters" (cf. Gen. 1:2c). Verses 27–29 discuss God's "preparation" (ἑτοιμάζω) of "the heaven" (cf. Gen. 1:1, 6–8, 14–19) and his "making" the foundations of "the earth" strong (cf. Gen. 1:1, 9–10). When having Prov. 8:22–31 in mind, it is highly possible that Paul, or any such interpreter, would also have had in mind the text of Genesis 1. But this possibility is not merely a logical supposition. The blending of Prov. 8:22–31 (particularly v. 23) and Genesis 1 was common before and during Paul's time.

In Sirach 24, wisdom is placed in her cosmic and cosmogonic setting, having "come from the mouth of the Most High" and having "covered the earth" as a mist (24:3). This description reminds many of the speech of God in Genesis 1 and of the Spirit of God hovering over the face of the waters in 1:2 (cf. also Gen. 2:6).[149] Wisdom explores "the circle of heaven" and "the depth of abysses" (24:5), recalling two of the realms of Gen. 1:1–2 that were also mentioned in Proverbs 8. After finally finding a home "in Jacob," "in Israel" (24:8), the pre-eminence (and desirability) of this wisdom is expressed in the language of Prov. 8:23 where she says about her relationship to "the Creator of all things": "Before the age [πρὸ τοῦ αἰῶνος], from the beginning [ἀπ' ἀρχῆς] he created me [ἔκτισέν με], and until the age [ἕως αἰῶνος] I will surely not cease" (24:9).[150] Not creation in general, and not "wisdom" in general, but specifically the texts of Genesis 1 and Proverbs 8 are brought together as mutually interpretive.[151]

---

[148] Longman, 2006, 207.

[149] So Collins, 1997, 50–1; Skehan and Di Lella, 1987, 332; Sheppard, 1980, 21–27. Cf. Fee, 2007, 613; Witherington, 1994, 95.

[150] Skehan, 1979, 377.

[151] Despite the reticence of Conzelmann (1971 [ET], 235, n. 27 [= 1964, 228, n. 27]) to see Genesis 1 behind Sirach 24, it is now typically agreed that there are indeed "strong

In a similar manner, Wisdom of Solomon conveys the desirability of the wisdom taught by "Solomon" by inserting a reference to Proverbs 8 into a discussion of creation in the language of Genesis 1. In the prayer in Wisdom 9, God is the one "who made [ποιήσας] all things by your word [ἐν λόγῳ σου]" (v. 1; cf. Gen. 1:3ff) and who "constructed man [κατασκευάσας ἄνθρωπον] in your wisdom [τῇ σοφίᾳ σου] in order that he might rule [δεσπόζῃ] over the creatures you made" (v. 2; cf. Gen. 1:26–28). Solomon's contemplation of his task of making the temple in correspondence with the "holy tabernacle" that was "prepared beforehand [προητοίμασας] from the beginning [ἀπ' ἀρχῆς]" (v. 8; cf. ἐν ἀρχῇ in Gen. 1:1)[152] leads him to desire the "wisdom" that "was with [God]" (μετὰ σοῦ), that "knew [God's] works," and that was "beside [God] when [he] made the cosmos [ὅτε ἐποίεις τὸν κόσμον]" (v. 9; cf. Prov. 8:22–31). After considering his desperate need for such wisdom (and for God to grant wisdom by the Holy Spirit) (vv. 10–18), his mind immediately goes to (or remains in) the beginning of Genesis, thinking of wisdom's work in restoring Adam from his fall (10:1). The text of Genesis is in the author's mind. Wisdom of Solomon inserts clear allusions to the text of Prov. 8:22–31 into a scenario built upon God's creative designs, not merely in creation in general, but specifically according to the text of Genesis 1. Proverbs 8 and Genesis 1 are, again, brought together as mutually interpretive.

Likewise, Baruch makes his "wisdom" more desirable by relating God's "finding" of it to the timing of creation and the text of Genesis 1. In Baruch 3, Israel has abandoned "wisdom" (vv. 9–13) and is commanded to find her (vv. 14–15). But no one knows wisdom (vv. 16–23), and the giants

---

echoes" of Genesis 1 there (Skehan, 1979, 376–7; Skehan and Di Lella, 1987, 333). Sirach also presents a reading of Genesis 1 in 42:15–43:33. This reading has numerous lexical correspondences with Genesis 1 (particularly with Gen. 1:14–19 in Sir. 43:1–10; see Tigchelaar, 2005, 37, 37–39; Thiselton, 2000, 1268–69), and it is a theocentric reading: God's "making" (ἐποίησεν) of all things presents God's "glory" (42:17, 25; 43:28), "great is the Lord who made it" (μέγας κύριος ὁ ποιήσας αὐτόν, 43:5), and "in summary: He is all" (συντέλεια λόγων τὸ πᾶν ἐστιν αὐτός). It should also be noted, especially in preparation for what we will see in Paul, that in Sir. 42:21 we find the mention of God's "wisdom" (τῆς σοφίας αὐτοῦ). God's wisdom does not have as active a role in chs. 42–43 as it did in ch. 24, and neither is it here personified, but a phrase that had been used of wisdom in 24:9 (πρὸ τοῦ αἰῶνος... [καὶ ἕως αἰῶνος]), there intentionally taken from Prov. 8:22–23, is applied in 42:21 to God himself: "he is before the age and unto the age" (ἐστὶ πρὸ τοῦ αἰῶνος καὶ εἰς τὸν αἰῶνα). As do Philo and Paul, so also Ben Sira presents a theologically-focussed reading of Genesis 1, and Prov. 8:23 is closely allied with this reading.

[152] Also cf. Wisdom's "pre-prepared" (προητοίμασας) above with "prepared" (ἡτοίμαζεν) in Prov. 8:27, "prepared" (ἡτοίμασεν) in 1 Cor. 2:9, and "pre-prepared" (προητοίμασεν) in Rom. 9:23.

(from Genesis 6) were destroyed for not having it (vv. 24–28). All appears hopeless (vv. 29–31)[153] until Baruch says:

> The one knowing all things knows [wisdom]; *he found her with his understanding* [ἐξεῦρεν αὐτὴν τῇ συνέσει αὐτοῦ]. The one constructing the earth [ὁ κατασκευάσας τὴν γῆν] unto the eternal time [εἰς τὸν αἰῶνα χρόνων] filled it with four-footed beasts [κτηνῶν τετραπόδων]. The one sending the light [τὸ φῶς] and it goes, he called it and it listened to him in trembling. (vv. 32–34)

This passage is less explicit than the other passages. Yet like the others, Baruch's contemplation of "wisdom" and of God's "knowledge" of it – and especially of God's "finding" or "discovery" of it (cf. Prov. 8:22–23) – is what prompts his discussion of God's good creation as expressed in the language of Genesis 1. The two texts, Proverbs 8 and Genesis 1, appear to walk hand-in-hand through the mind of yet another interpreter.

Aristobulus, Philo's Alexandrian predecessor in "Jewish-philosophy" (c. 170 BCE), in whom are "intermingled" certain "Jewish-Palestinian and Pythagorean-Platonic and Stoic conceptions,"[154] inserts "wisdom" into a discussion of creation. Neither wisdom in general nor creation in general, Aristobulus refers to wisdom and creation as they are found in Prov. 8:22–25 and Genesis 1. While discussing God's gift of rest on the seventh day and God's "genesis of light" on the first day – two obvious references to Genesis 1 – he links "wisdom" with light. He cites "some members of the Peripatetic school," but claims that Solomon had more beautifully presented the creation of wisdom "before heaven and earth," i.e., in Prov. 8:22–31. Solomon's account corresponds to that of Genesis 1, for light came about before sky and earth.[155] The combination of Prov. 8:22–31 and Genesis 1 serves to show the surpassing worth of Aristobulus' wisdom.

Likewise, and as we have already seen, Philo himself blends Genesis 1 with Proverbs 8.[156] His language of creation in *Ebr.* 30–31, into which he introduces Prov. 8:22–23, is similar to his typical cosmogonic expression in *De Opificio Mundi*, which is a formal and intentional commentary on Genesis 1. He there quotes 8:22–23a and the phrase "before the age" (πρὸ τοῦ αἰῶνος). Yet again, this association between Proverbs 8, the phrase "before the age," and creation according to Genesis 1 functions to present God and his wisdom (represented in Philo's own wise perspective on so-

---

[153] Here Baruch quotes Deut. 30:11–14. Cf. Rom. 10:6–8.

[154] Hengel, 1974, 1.166–67; cf. Barclay, 1996A, 150–58; Tobin, 1983, 10, 50–55; Radice, 2009, 135.

[155] See the fragment preserved in Eusebius, *Pr. Ev.* 13.12.9–11. Cf. Holladay, 1995; Hengel, 1974, 1.167. Pearson (1973) also mentions the impact of Prov. 8:22ff on Aristobulus (36, 108 n. 74).

[156] For comparisons between Aristobulus' interpretation of the creation narrative and Philo's interpretation see Tobin, 1983, 50–55.

briety) as validated and surpassing all else in desirability precisely because of this wisdom's cohabitation with God at (before and in) creation.

Within Paul's atmosphere of scriptural interpretation there was both a natural and well-worn link between Prov. 8:22–31 and Genesis 1. In each writer observed above it was the specific text of Prov. 8:22–31 and the specific text of Genesis 1 that were mutually evocative. The actual phrase "before the age" (8:23) was not only the frequent textual focal point, but was also virtually synonymous with "before creation *as described by Genesis 1*." Proverbs 8:23 had hermeneutical implications for Genesis 1.

Paul's concept and language in 1 Cor. 2:6-10 (v. 7) closely correspond with Prov. 8:22–23. Like his contemporaries, and like Proverbs 8 itself, Paul's *purpose* is to show the surpassing greatness of "God's wisdom" over against the wisdom of "the rulers," "humans," and "the world." Paul does this by claiming that God in some way delineated (cf. "founded," "begat," "created," "found," "pre-marked out") his own wisdom "before the ages." In light of Paul's own language and purpose in 2:7, and in light of the general hermeneutical practice of Paul's contemporary scripture-interpreters, two conclusions are appropriate. One, Paul has Prov. 8:22–31 in mind. Two, Paul's interpretation of Genesis 1 will have been affected.

At this point it is merely an assumption, albeit a strong one, that Paul's Before is connected to his reading of Genesis' creation texts. We will now see confirmation that this is indeed the case. But while continuing to display *that* Paul has a Before and *that* Paul's Before is hermeneutically related to his Beginning, we also must delineate precisely what elements are contained in Paul's Before. We will now define the *content* of Paul's Before more specifically than merely "God's wisdom." We can do this because Paul himself does, and he ultimately uses the beginning of Genesis to help him express what God "pre-marked out" *before* the beginning.

1.3.2 Paul's Content of God's Pre-Creational Wisdom: Christ, His Cross, and a Plurality of Preparations (1 Cor. 1–2, 15, and Rom. 8:29–30)

Paul understands God to have "marked out" and "prepared" Christ, his crucifixion, and a plurality of benefits before the beginning for those who love God. This is to be gleaned from Paul's presentation of the Before in 1 Cor. 2:7–9 and its context. That this Before was connected to Paul's interpretation of Genesis' Beginning has, for now, been left as a strong plausibility. When we turn below to Paul's other explicit presentation of the Before – Rom. 8:29–30, especially as this is seen in light of Paul's argument in 1 Cor. 15:49 – two things will become evident: 1) the Before has affected his reading of the Beginning, and 2) the text of the Beginning has mutually granted content to his Before. To accurately see this aspect of Paul's hermeneutic of creation we must now draw attention to the more specific content of the Before in 1 Corinthians 1–2, then move through 1 Corinthians 15, finally to dwell in Romans 8 with our eye focused both on the content of Paul's Before and its relation to creation.

(a) Paul's First Presentation of the Before:
Mediator, Means, and Goal of Glory (1 Cor. 1:24, 30, and 2:7, 9)

An interpreter of 1 Corinthians faces an exegetical challenge when posing the question, "What is the *content* of God's pre-determined wisdom?"[157] For in the very pericope where Paul explains that he and his companions do teach wisdom (2:6–16), his references to what this wisdom actually is are elusive. What *is* the wisdom that God "pre-determined unto our glory" (v. 7)? What exactly *was* unknown to the rulers (v. 8) and unknowable to general humanity (v. 9a-b), while "prepared for those who love God" (v. 9c) and made known to believers by the Spirit (v. 10)? What "things" have been "freely given to us" (v. 12)? Paul continuously refers to this plurality of "things" which have their referent back in "God's wisdom" in 2:6–7,[158] but after announcing there that he does in fact speak a pre-creationally determined wisdom, Paul does not define its *content* more specifically. Paul's lack of explicitness in 2:6–16 has frustrated some.[159] But explaining the content of God's wisdom is not in Paul's scope in 2:6–16.[160] This does not mean, however, that we are at the proverbial impasse. At the heart of Paul's silence in 2:6–16 is the fact that he has already made clear what "God's wisdom" is. This he did in 1:18–2:5.[161]

We have already discerned a unified theme, or approach, underlying both 1:18–2:5 and 2:6–16: God's pre-set and "wise" intentions have his-

---

[157] So Barbour, 1979, 66.

[158] Davis, 1984, 95–96; Hamerton-Kelly, 1973, 115–16.

[159] Cf. Wilckens, 1959, 60 with *idem,* 1979, 508. Theissen (1987) pointedly asks, "What is the relationship of the preaching of the cross [i.e., 1 Cor. 1:18–2:5] to the wisdom teaching [i.e., 2:6–3:23]?" (343). See his helpful and balanced treatment of the relationship between "God's wisdom" in 1:18–2:5 and "God's wisdom" in 2:6–16 (345–52).

[160] Contra Davis (1984) who argues that Paul's task in 2:6–9 is to "define carefully the wisdom which he speaks" (88). Paul's narrow purpose in 2:6–7 is to assert that he does teach a wisdom, and his general purpose in 2:6–16 is to establish the unknowability of this wisdom apart from God's Spirit. Neither of these purposes necessitate specifying its content, and he does not so specify.

[161] So Kammler, 2003, 89–91, 211, 246; Theissen, 1987, 343–52; Fee, 1987, 105; Davis, 1984, 92; Pearson, 1975, 51 (cf. Eskola, 1998, 179). Contra e.g., Bultmann, Käsemann, early Wilckens. See the historical surveys in Stuhlmacher, 1987, 328–32; Davis, 1984, 85–87; Barbour, 1979, 61–62; Pearson, 1975, 50–51. For Wilckens' "about-face" from seeing 2:6–16 as contradictory to 1:18–2:5 to seeing them in closer harmony cf. Wilckens, 1959, 60 with *idem,* 1979, 508 (see also Stuhlmacher, 1987, 351; Theissen, 1987, 350 n. 9).

torical and social ramifications. Both of Paul's references to "God's wisdom" are further unified,[162] not least in that in each sub-section of his argument Paul draws an intimate connection between "God's wisdom" and the "crucifixion."[163] Underlying the whole discussion in 1:18–2:16 Paul understands "God's wisdom" (whether in 1:18–2:5 or in 2:6–16) and its benefits as having its source in God and its destination in the benefit of believers (cf. 1:30 with 2:7 and 9–10). As he was writing 2:6–16, Paul seems convinced that he had already conveyed the *content* of God's wisdom successfully enough to allow himself mere references back to it without further explanation. This divinely pre-marked out wisdom is this: "Christ Jesus" (1:30), "a Christ who was crucified" (1:24),[164] the Christ-event.[165]

---

[162] The precise nature of the unity between the two references to "God's wisdom" remains vague enough to allow for differences between the details of Paul's teaching to general Christians and to the "mature" (as if the differences between an introduction to theology and a higher level class). If there is any difference it should be conceived of quantitatively (the detail shared), not qualitatively (the subject matter – e.g., Christ).

[163] The precise nature of the connection between "God's wisdom" and "crucified the Lord of glory" in 2:7–8 is more difficult to pin down than the mere fact that they are connected. The difference in title between "Christ" in 1 Cor. 1:23–24 and "Lord of glory" in 2:7–8 may be significant, yet this neither negates nor even dulls the fact that there is a connection between "God's wisdom" and the "crucifixion" in both 1:23–24 and 2:7–8.

[164] In both 1:24 and 1:30, the two passages where Paul explicitly relates "Christ" and "wisdom," it is not a pre-existence that Paul has in mind but the historical manifestation in the man Jesus. This is especially the force of "became" in 1:30. A few chapters later, in 1 Cor. 8:6, Paul certainly attributes creative agency to Christ. Although others were doing something like this with "Wisdom" or "Word," and it is possible that Paul had in mind "wisdom" as creation-mediator in 8:6, Paul does not *explicitly* relate "wisdom" to this pre-existent and creative Christ in 8:6. In the only place in 1 Corinthians where Paul *explicitly* discusses "wisdom" as pre-existing and relates it to Christ in some way – i.e., 1 Cor. 2:7 and context – he does not have a co-creative hypostasis or personification in mind. The relation of 1 Cor. 2:7 to Prov. 8:23 developed above (especially as this relates so closely to 1:24, 30) thus adds another (different) dimension to the continuing debate about Paul's "wisdom-Christology."

[165] Barbour, 1979, 71. The apparent difference between two "wisdoms" – one presented to all Christians and another to the "mature" – has kept some scholars from importing the content of "God's wisdom" in 1:18ff (Christ crucified) into "God's wisdom" in 2:6ff (predestined) (so Agourides, 1980, 102 in response to Wilckens' change of opinion in 1980, 501–37). Barbour (1979) warns that either "a premature fusion or confusion of the different types of language with one another [*sc.* 'God's wisdom' in 1 Cor. 1:18–2:5 and 'God's wisdom' in 2:6–16] or with utterances of Pauline theology in general will fail to reveal the complex nature of the language-event which they jointly constitute and of the Christ-event to which they refer. Either the cross [*sc.* 'God's wisdom' in 1:18–2:5] will be submerged in the universality of the myth or the cosmic significance of the myth [*sc.* 'God's wisdom' in 2:6–16] will be lost in a concentration on the strange foolishness of God which the word of the cross proclaims" (71). This warning is helpful by preserving important nuances in each of Paul's sections. Yet it is still possible to acknowledge that "God's wisdom" in both stages of Paul's "language-event" refers to *Christ-crucified-*

Most scholars therefore believe that "God's wisdom" in 2:7 is equivalent to "God's wisdom" in "Christ crucified" from 1:24, 30.[166] The Christ being crucified historically enacts – "realizes" – God's pre-creational, wise intention to destroy the "wisdom" of those who boast in non-cruciform human cleverness as well as to save those who boast only in the once-crucified Lord of glory. H.-C. Kammler, identifying "God's wisdom" in 1:18–2:5 with "God's wisdom" in 2:6–16, concludes that 2:7 itself "implies" that the cross-event, with its destination in the glorification of believers, was God's *eternal* and *original* purpose of salvation.[167] B. Witherington simply asserts: "Christ crucified was what God planned before the foundation of the world."[168] In 2:7 Paul claims that God "pre-marked out" the Christ and his crucifixion both "before the ages" and "unto our glory."

One more detail in this passage has implications for properly understanding Paul's relation of the Before to the texts of the Beginning: the shift from the singularity of "wisdom" in 2:2–8 to the plurality of "things" in 2:9–16.[169] Part of this shift may be due to the text Paul quotes here

---

for-our-salvation-and-glory while in the first Paul focuses on its apparent foolishness and in the second Paul focuses upon its cosmic and pre-temporal origin.

[166] Witherington, 1995, 127 (cf. *idem*, 1994, 302). Robertson and Plummer (1911) say, "The 'wisdom' is 'Christ crucified' (i.18–24), fore-ordained by God (Acts iv.28; Eph. iii.11) for the salvation of men. It was no afterthought or change of plan, as Theodoret remarks, but was fore-ordained ἄνωθεν καὶ ἐξ ἀρχῆς" (38–39). Bornkamm (1967) calls this "pre-temporal council" of God "the divine will to save fulfilled in the crucifixion of Christ" (4.819–20). Hays (1997) writes, "The *content* of the wisdom of God, which makes human wisdom look ridiculous, is precisely the cross" (40; cf. Welborn, 2005, 215). Kremer (1997) explains, "Jesus' death on the cross is not about the epitome of Christ's or God's powerlessness," as the non-Christian Corinthians believed and as the Christian Corinthians were demonstrating, but rather it was about what God had decided "before the beginning of the aeons" (58; translation mine). Wilckens (1971) was not convinced even though "[a]lmost all exegetes take the σοφία of 2:6f to refer to God's plan of salvation" (7.519 n. 382). He criticizes this treatment of σοφία by saying it is out of place in the Jewish apocalyptic use of σοφία (7.503ff) and in the use of σοφία in "the Greek sphere" (7.467–76). Since in 1 Corinthians 1–2 Paul is in the process of challenging the notions of σοφία among both "the Jews" and "the Greeks," it might be even more surprising if his view had fit comfortably into their schemes!

[167] Kammler, 2003, 246 (cf. "God's *original* will" [211]; 89–91). Cf. Fee's careful wording (1987, 105).

[168] Witherington, 1995, 127.

[169] Garland (2003) sees ἑτοιμάζω in v. 9 as explanatory of προορίζω in v. 7 (98). Below is a chart begun by Fee, 1987, 107, and slightly modified and elaborated:

v. 8	None of the rulers of this age understood [God's wisdom]	= v. 9a	What eye did not see and ear did not hear and did not enter into man's heart
v. 7	a wisdom which God pre-marked out before the ages for our glory	= v. 9b	What God prepared for those who love him

(whatever the text may be; cf. Isa. 64:3 [LXX]).[170] Regardless of the reason for his pluralizing, Paul does not see a conflict between the plural and the singular "wisdom." He even continues to use plurals throughout 2:10–16, even though the revelation by the Spirit continues to refer back to the "wisdom" which "has been hidden." It seems as though it is not merely "Christ" or "Christ crucified" that God "prepared" for those who love him, but something of a plurality of benefits.[171] Whatever the exact referents – perhaps righteousness, sanctification, and redemption,[172] though Paul does not find it imperative to disclose these details in 2:6–16 – it is important to observe this plurality, for in his later letter to the Romans Paul will make explicit a plurality of things which he refers to as "pre-marked out" by God which end in the glory of those who love God. It may be impossible to connect these plural preparations with absolute certainty, but it is perhaps the benefits later mentioned to the Romans which Paul foreshadows in the plurality of preparations here mentioned to the Corinthians.

God had intentions before the beginning and these were not simple but manifold. Regarding the *content* of God's pre-creational wisdom – which, in a manner similar to Prov. 8:22, Paul sees as beneficial "for" God's works[173] – the aspects of God's deliberation involve 1) the *death* of his *Christ* "for us" at its center, and 2) the equally pre-creational *benefits* and ultimate *glory* of the community of God-lovers.

In summary, we have now seen in Paul's first presentation of the Before (1 Cor. 2:7) both the *presence* and *timing* of God's pre-creational deliberations, as well as (part of) the *content* of this pre-marked out plan. The part of the *content* of the Before that Paul reveals in 1 Cor. 2:7 has to do with the end or *telos* of God's pre-determination: glory and benefit for believers, as well as with the particular pre-determined *mediator* and *means* of this glory: Christ and him crucified. The pre-creational timing and wise character of Paul's Before in 1 Cor. 2:7 were largely derived from Prov.

---

[170] See the treatment of the citation in Williams, 2001, 157–65.

[171] Pearson, 1973, 34–35; Barbour, 1979, 66; Davis, 1984, 96.

[172] The three benefits of Christ – righteousness, sanctification, redemption – can be described as a plurality of benefits coming from the Christ and his crucifixion regardless of precisely how they relate to "wisdom," whether appositional to "wisdom" (so Fee, 2007, 106 n. 63), appositional to "you" (so Witherington, 1994, 310–11; criticized by Fee, 2007, 106 n. 63), or additional to "wisdom."

[173] Though Paul's statement that God's predestined "wisdom" is "for" the benefit of those who love God (1 Cor. 2:7) is conceptually (and even syntactically) similar to the statement in Prov. 8:22 that God's "wisdom" is "for" the benefit of all of creation (and in Rom. 8 Paul clearly sees the predestined glorification of those who love God as beneficial for all of creation), it is not as clear that Paul actually *derived* the cosmic benefits from Prov. 8:22 as it is that he derived the concept of God's "pre-marking out" and the language of "before the age(s)" from Prov. 8:23.

8:23. The well-defensible implication of this allusion to Proverbs 8 is that Paul's Before is connected to his interpretation of the beginning of Genesis. We have not yet confirmed that this is indeed the case with Paul as it is with others of his contemporary scripture-interpreters, not least with Philo. However, Paul's second presentation of the Before, i.e., in Rom. 8:29–30, reveals an even greater robustness to Paul's theory of God's pre-creational determinations. What is more, Paul ties this second presentation of the Before directly to the textual Beginning according to Genesis. This hermeneutical move was expected based on his use of Prov. 8:23 and its clear and popular connection with Genesis 1. As we will now see, in Rom. 8:29–30 Paul combines his own reading of Prov. 8:23 from 1 Cor. 2:7 with his own reading of Gen. 5:3 from 1 Cor. 15:49. In Rom. 8:29–30 Paul describes the eschatological enactment of the protological principle of "image"-bearing, and he claims that this is something that God "marked out" *before* the protological enactment.

(b) Paul's Second Presentation of the Before:
Method and Members from Image to Glory (1 Cor. 15:49; Rom. 8:29–30)

Paul uncovered the pre-creational roots of God's wisdom in 1 Cor. 2:7; he unveils its eschatological fruit in 1 Cor. 15:35–49.[174] In 1 Cor. 2:7, Paul does not explain how the pre-set "glory" will actually come to those for whom Christ was crucified according to the pre-creational desire and wisdom of God. In 1 Cor. 15:35–49, however, though not explicitly mentioning the Before Paul does explain the eschatological reception of the pre-set telos,[175] i.e., "glory" (along with a plurality of other benefits[176]). He explains this in the language of Genesis' Beginning. My hypothesis above, based on Paul's use of Prov. 8:23 in 1 Cor. 2:7, has been that his interpretation of creation will have been affected by his Before in a similar hermeneutical manner that we found in Philo (and others). Paul's use of Genesis' protological texts in 1 Cor. 15:35–49, and particularly his use of Gen. 5:3 in v. 49, will add more credence to this already probable assumption. In Rom. 8:29 this assumption will be confirmed; Paul's Before is connected to his interpretation of Genesis' Beginning.

1 Corinthians 15 and Romans 8 are themselves connected to 1 Cor. 2:7 by most commentators. This association typically revolves around the

---

[174] So Héring, 1962, 18. Cf. Bruce, 1971, 38; Senft, 1979, 49–50; Garland, 2003, 95.
[175] Beker, 1980, 365; Collins, 1999, 130.
[176] E.g., resurrection in incorruptibility, glory, power (1 Cor. 15:42–43), a Spiritual and heavenly body (vv. 44–49), a change into incorruptibility and immortality (vv. 52–54), and victory (vv. 54–57).

word "glory"[177] as well as Paul's re-use of the term "pre-marked out" (προορίζω).[178] In fact, in Rom. 8:29–30 Paul appears to be bringing together the concepts, wording, and scriptural argumentation of 1 Cor. 2:7 and 1 Cor. 15:42–49 into one statement[179]:

	Origin		Goal		Means of Attainment
1 Cor. 2:7 discusses	προορίζω	for	(eschat.) δόξα		–
1 Cor. 15 discusses	–		(eschat.) δόξα	via	εἰκών (Gen. 5:3)
Rom. 8:29–30 unites	προορίζω	for	(eschat.) δοξάζω	via	εἰκών (Gen. 5:3)

In all three passages "glory" is one of a plurality of benefits received in the end.[180] In all three Jesus' followers are described in similar terms to how Jesus himself is described.[181] In all three Paul employs creation motifs. We have explored the creation motif in 1 Cor. 2:7: pre-Genesis 1 based on Prov. 8:23. What about the protological motifs in 1 Corinthians 15 and Romans 8? A brief look at these themes in 1 Corinthians 15 and Romans 8 will effectively set the context for our understanding of Paul's re-use of the Before in Rom. 8:29–30. (A fuller treatment of creation in these two passages is reserved for chapters 2 and 3 below.)

---

[177] So Robertson and Plummer, 1911, 38; Héring, 1962, 18; Barrett, 1968, 71; Pearson, 1973, 34; Schrage, 1991, 1.252 and n. 171; Kremer, 1997, 58; Thiselton, 2000, 243, 245; Kammler, 2003, 212, n. 118; Garland, 2003, 95–96 (Senft, 1979, 49–50 connects the nullification of the "rulers"; Bornkamm, 1967, 4.819–20 connects "mystery"). Also, creation's problem of "corruption" (φθορά, Rom. 8:21; 1 Cor. 15:42) is remedied by the appearance of "glory" (δόξα, Rom. 8:21; 1 Cor. 15:43), specifically the δόξαν ἀποκαλυφθῆναι εἰς ἡμᾶς (Rom. 8:18), i.e., εἰς δόξαν ἡμῶν (1 Cor. 2:7), [ἡ] δόξ[α] τῶν τέκνων τοῦ θεοῦ (8:21), who ἐγείρ[ον]ται ἐν δόξῃ (1 Cor. 15:43), who are "changed" from τὸ φθάρτον into ἀφθαρσίαν (1 Cor. 15:52–54). As Beker (1980) puts it, "The future glory will wipe out the contradictions of the present" (365).

[178] So Schrage, 1991, 1.252; Fee, 1987, 106 (cf.106 n. 33); Reiling, 1988, 204, n. 17; Eskola, 1998, 179 (cf. 170 n. 17).

[179] Similarly Bruce, 1971, 38; Dunn, 1988, 1.483.

[180] Käsemann (1980) does not see "glorified" in Rom. 8:30 as referring to what is received in the future (244). Lorenzen does (2008, 210–11). Jewett (2004) considers the aorist in Rom. 8:30 to convey "the initial evidence of this glory that will one day fill the creation (cf. 2 Cor. 3:18)" (34). Paul certainly has eschatological "glory" in mind in 8:17–21, and his language there of "co-inheriting," "co-suffering," and being "co-glorified" have a special family resemblance with his use of "co-forms" and "image" in 8:29, a process which is begun with God's "pre-knowing" and "pre-marking out" and completed with "glorification."

[181] Paul's description of the *method* of glory-attainment (i.e., bearing/being conformed to the εἰκών of Jesus, 1 Cor. 15:49; Rom. 8:29) has affinities with Paul's *description* in 1 Cor. 2:7–8 of "us" and "the Lord" with the modifier "glory" (cf. Welborn, 2005, 216; Fee, 1987, 106; Conzelmann, 1975, 63 n. 63; Scroggs, 1967/68, 46, n. 3).

In 1 Cor. 15:35–49, Paul's argument unfolds in two parts. The first is based upon the beginning of the world according to Genesis 1 where Paul highlights God's original desire for diverse bodily structures (15:38–41). The second is based upon allusions to and a quotation from the beginning of humanity according to Genesis 2 and 5 (15:42–49) and a comparison between these and Jesus' resurrection. Paul develops the protology and its eschatological re-enactment in vv. 37–47 and makes them applicable to contemporary people in vv. 48–49. To make these extensions from Adam and Christ to those "in" them Paul employs the protological principle inaugurated in Gen. 5:3:

Gen. 5:3   *Adam* lived 230 years and gave birth according to his appearance [κατὰ τὴν ἰδέαν αὐτοῦ] and according to *his image* [κατὰ τὴν εἰκόνα αὐτοῦ], and he called his name Seth.

1 Cor. 15:49   And just as we bore *the image* [τὴν εἰκόνα] of the dust-one [*sc.* 'the first man *Adam*'], also we will bear *the image* [τὴν εἰκόνα] of the heaven-one [*sc.* 'the last *Adam*,' 'the second man'].

In v. 49a Paul summarizes Gen. 5:3 (cf. v. 48a), and in v. 49b he recapitulates it for the eschaton (cf. v. 48b). The eschatological "glory" (and other benefits, in vv. 42–44) that belongs to the resurrected "heavenly" nature of the last Adam is made applicable to this last Adam's family through the re-enactment of the protological principle first enacted in Gen. 5:3. This connection between protology and eschatology is relatively straightforward: the latter (the new beginning) takes place according to the pattern of the former (the original beginning).

In Romans 8 Paul maintains his previous understanding just mentioned, but he reveals another dimension. The eschatological "glory" is again "for those who love God" (8:28; cf. 1 Cor. 2:9[182]), and, drawing a conclusion similar to what Prov. 8:22 had done, the ultimate aim of God's activity is "for" the whole of God's created works (Rom. 8:18–22). This "glory" (and other benefits) is attained by Christ's family through the method of "image"-conformation (borrowed from 1 Cor. 15:49b):

Rom. 8:29–30   Whom he foreknew [προέγνω] [for them] he also pre-marked out [προώρισεν] to be conformed to [συμμόρφους] *the image* [τῆς εἰκόνος] of his Son so that he might be the firstborn among many siblings. And whom he pre-marked out [προώρισεν] these he also called... and justified... and glorified [ἐδόξασεν].

---

[182] Conzelmann, 1975, 64. Cf. Kammler, 2003, 212 (and n. 118); Schrage, 1991, 1.252; cf. Dunn, 1988, 483; Bruce, 1971, 38.

Paul claims in 8:29 that the *method* of "image"-sharing found in the text of the beginning (i.e., Gen. 5:3) was itself "pre-marked out" (προώρισεν).¹⁸³ Neither of Paul's statements of "pre-marking" in Rom. 8:29–30 are identical with his statement of "pre-marking" in 1 Cor. 2:7–9.¹⁸⁴ The differences, which I will briefly note regarding Rom. 8:30 and then 8:29, add to our understanding of the *content* of Paul's Before.

In Rom. 8:30, what is "pre-marked out" is not Jesus himself. It is not his cross. It is not even God's "wisdom." It is people: "*whom* [plural] God marked out beforehand" (οὓς προώρισεν). Paul is not arguing merely that those who accepted God's previously marked out *way* to glory (i.e., Jesus crucified) he then called, but rather that "*those whom* he pre-marked out he also called...."¹⁸⁵ Paul's Before contains not only the *mediator* (Christ) and *means* (crucified) of "our glory" (1 Cor. 2:7), but also the *members* or participants of this glory whom God will subsequently call, justify, and "glorify" (Rom. 8:30).

Lastly, in Rom. 8:29 God brings the pre-destined glory from the pre-set cross of the pre-determined Christ to the pre-delineated members through a "pre-marked out" *method* or *mode*. Using a series of προ-prefixed verbs, Paul presents what God was doing *before* the beginning: God "*pre*-knew" (*προ*-έγνω), and God "*pre*-marked out" (*προ*-ώρισεν). Whereas the direct object of God's foreknowledge are people (οὓς, 8:29a), in a similar manner as in Rom. 11:2,¹⁸⁶ the direct object in v. 29b that God "marked out"

---

¹⁸³ For Gen. 5:3 behind Rom. 8:29 see Eskola, 1998, 171–72 and Heil, 2005, 234. For the more general recognition of "the Adam story" behind Paul's "image" language in Rom. 8:29 cf. e.g., Cranfield, 1975, 1.432; Käsemann, 1980, 244–45; Ziesler, 1989, 227; Byrne, 1996, 272–73; Witherington, 2004, 230. Collins (1999) writes: "The exhortation [*sc.* in 1 Cor. 15:49] harks back to the biblical tradition according to which the descendants of Adam bear his image (Gen. 5:3). This is combined with the notion that humans are created in the image of God (Gen. 1:27)" (572). For a similar passing reference to Gen. 5:3 but then a reversion back to Gen. 1:27 see Sterling, 2004, 42. Paul's language is closer to Gen. 5:3 than 1:27, and this is important, but the main implications of this observation will be reserved for chapter 3.

¹⁸⁴ Schrage, 1991, 1.252. Cf. Eskola, 1998, 170 n. 17.

¹⁸⁵ Thiselton (2000) warns against importing "two thousand years of philosophical tradition" into God's "predestination," thereby "impos[ing] a supposed fixity on the *mode* by which the goal is reached" (242). In 1 Cor. 2:7 not only is the goal of glory fixed but so is "Christ crucified." In Rom. 8:29–30 Paul adds the fixed *mode* of "image"-sharing, even fixing "those" who would receive this glorious goal. There is still room to debate what Paul sees as the *reason* or even *criteria* for God's pre-creational marking of "those whom" he so marks – but that discussion falls outwith my present purposes.

¹⁸⁶ Both Witherington (2004) and Eskola (1998) refer προγινώσκω in 8:29 to its use in 11:2, but they both miss different aspects of the impact of this relationship. Witherington denies that relational (i.e., covenantal) "knowing" could be part of προγινώσκω in 8:29 on philosophical grounds, i.e., because of the pre-temporal nature of the word: it is not possible, Witherington reasons, to have a relationship with someone who does not yet

for these people is actually the quality of "co-formity" (σύμμορφος), i.e. sharing the form of "the image" (ἡ εἰκών) of God's Son.[187]

This point should not be missed: it is the *eschatological enacting* of the protological principle that actually pre-dates the original Beginning. That is, Paul claims that the "co-formity" with *Jesus'* "image" were what God

---

exist (228 n. 25). Therefore "fore-know" must refer to God's knowledge not of *them* but of a future fact *about* these not-yet-existent people: "*that* they would respond to the call of God in love" (229 n. 28; emphasis added). Therefore, according to Witherington, in Rom. 11:2 God can "foreknow" Israel without this guaranteeing any individual salvation (229–30). Yet Paul does not merely believe that God knew certain facts *about* Israel beforehand, as if merely (fore-)knowing what they would become, but that he actually made Israel to be what it is out of "nothing" (so Rom. 4:17). From Paul's point of view of the inception of Israel, to say that God "*fore*-knew" Israel (11:2) is undoubtedly more than saying that God knew some fact *about* their future (which is actually true about any people – not just Israel). Why not interpret "fore-know" in 8:30 in such a robust manner?

Eskola, on the other hand, recognizes in Rom. 8:29 (and 11:2) the more robust "covenantal" nuance of the Hebraic concept of "know" (170; cf. Dunn, 1988, 482). But Eskola does not consider the temporal prefix of προ-γινώσκω (or of προ-ορίζω) to be of importance. This equation of προ-γινώσκω with γινώσκω (contra Witherington, who sees significance in the prefix) works well for Eskola's theology, but he thereby flattens Paul's way of relating Israel to God. As Eskola acknowledges, Paul's use of "foreknow" is based on the OT, especially Gen. 18:15 and Jer. 1:5 (170 n. 15). Yet both of those passages have important *temporal* and even *causal* connotations. See the MT's perfect: "I knew him" [ידעתיו], and the LXX's pluperfect: "I had known" [ᾔδειν] in Gen. 18:19. See the explicitly telling temporal nature of God's relational "knowledge" of Jeremiah in MT 1:5: "*before* I formed you in the womb I *knew* you" (אצרך] בבטן ידעתיך] *בטרם*), and the especially striking temporal interplay in LXX Jer. 1:5 between the aorist "formed" (cf. Gen. 2:7) and the *pre*-"formed" *present* "I know": "*before* I formed you in the womb I *know* you" (πρὸ τοῦ με πλάσαι σε ἐν κοιλίᾳ ἐπίσταμαί σε). One could neglect the robust concept of "[pre-]know" against the evidence of Rom. 11:2 (as Witherington does), and one could neglect the (pre-)temporal nature of the προ-prefix against the evidence of Gen., Jer., and 1 Cor. 2:7 (as Eskola does), and he or she would thus end up at Witherington's and Eskola's theological construct. But it is exegetically better to see that Eskola helpfully recognizes the OT conceptual background of Paul's use of (προ)γινώσκω in Rom. 8:29 and 11:2 (although not realizing the full weight of his own insight), and that Witherington helpfully recognizes the (pre-)temporal nature of this "knowledge" (though not realizing the OT ability of God to relate to creatures, such as Jeremiah, that do not yet exist).

[187] Considering "form" and "image" to be mutually interpretive, Lorenzen (2008) sees Paul referring to "the outward" (i.e., "bodily") "appearance of Christ" (207–08; cf. Michaelis, 1968, VI.877 n. 37). This criticizes an epexegetical rendering of 8:29 as regarding "the image of [*God, which is*] his Son" (as in Dunn, 1988, 1.483; Hughes, 1989, 27). Though Lorenzen does not think that the "Adam-Christ-typology" is in Paul's mind in Rom. 8:29–30, she not only acknowledges it as a possibility but helpfully adds that "*if* the thought of Adam-Christ-typology is present, it would be – as in 1 Corinthians 15 – not primarily Gen. 1:26f but 5:1–3 that is in the background" (210 n. 54; translation mine). This is a helpful recognition, and I will defend and develop it in chapter 3.

determined – "pre-marked out" – before the beginning.[188] With this statement in v. 29, the reasonable assumption above concerning a connection between Paul's Before and his interpretation of the Beginning is truly confirmed. Paul has re-employed the protological principle of Gen. 5:3 from 1 Cor. 15:49 – Adam's family sharing his "image" – but neither to explain protology (as in 15:49a) nor even mere eschatology (as in 15:49b). He uses one of Genesis' creation-texts to explain more of the *content* of what God had determined *before* the creation of Adam's "image" or even the world.

In summary, when Paul reads the Beginning of his scriptures he sees a Before. This ultimate Before consists of a wise and divine "preparation," a pre-delineation that is intended to result in the "glory" of God's Son's family who "love God." Through their pre-determined glory an incorruptible freedom will come to the whole creation itself (Rom. 8:21). Paul's notion of the Before is thoroughly Christocentric.[189] This does not mean that Christ himself was the only object of God's pre-determination, but rather that the plurality of God's determinations before the beginning each are related to the pre-determined Christ.[190] The *content* of Paul's Before includes as of first importance the *mediator* and *means* of a pre-delineated glory: the Christ and his crucifixion. It is also the *members* of the glory and the actual *method* of its attainment that Paul considers to be "pre-marked out" by God before the beginning of the ages. The pre-determined *method* toward glorification is conformation to the very "image" of God's Son (Rom. 8:29), the "heavenly man" and "last Adam" (1 Cor. 15:49), the "Lord of glory" (1 Cor. 2:8). With this multiplicity of divine pre-deliberations in mind we can boldly affirm the claim that should now be obvious: Paul indeed had a notion of the Before. But there is more.

1 Corinthians 2, 15, and Romans 8 together unveil in Paul not only a particular way of thinking about the Before, but also a way of interpreting scripture. Paul has woven together a tapestry of thoughts including protology, eschatology, Christology, doxology, the telos of believers, and our likeness with Jesus in glory. Each of these are connected to what Paul considers to have been "marked out" by God before the creation of the world. But these considerations about the beginning, the end, Christ, and believers are not disconnected from the texts of Paul's scripture. He connects these aspects of the Before to the creation texts of Prov. 8:22–31 and Gen. 5:3.

---

[188] Cranfield, 1975, 1.432.

[189] So Eskola, 1998, 180.

[190] P. Jewett (1985) asks, "Does the problem consist in the fact that many have misunderstood the *object* of predestination, that when they should have thought of the object of election as Christ, the Chosen Servant of the Lord, they have instead thought of a fixed number of individuals...?" (2). Though all objects of "predestination" *are* somehow related to Christ, we can see from only 1 Corinthians and Romans that Paul saw a complex of "objects" marked out by God before creation, not only Christ himself.

As we will explore further in the remainder of this study, just as Philo displays a reading of the Beginning and of the Before in which both function in dynamic reciprocal relation to each other, so does Paul.

1.4 Comparisons and Conclusions
Philo and Paul on Before the Beginning

There are a number of similarities in Philo's and Paul's interpretations of creation. Both took aspects of texts outwith Genesis but similar to it – Philo using the *Timaeus*, Paul using Proverbs 8 – to begin to fix their eyes on God's mental and causative *pre*-protology. Both took empirical observation – Philo seeing the world's beauty around him, Paul seeing the risen Christ who had been crucified – and then further developed their respective Befores by combining the texts and these experiences. Thus both connected the Before to Genesis itself, reading the Beginning in light of their perceived Before. Philo thus exegeted the necessity of a "good" and noetic paradigm of the cosmos' structure that would result in like "goodness" in the visible creation; Paul thus exegeted the "wise" intentions of God that would result in both "good" and "glory" (and "freedom") for God-lovers and the whole creation. Neither Philo nor Paul, however, simply imposed a fully pre-defined pre-protology onto Genesis' protological texts. Their interpretations of Genesis also shaped their understandings of precisely what God set out in the Before. There exists a broad similarity between Paul's and Philo's interpretation of creation.

Both interpreters also display a theocentric emphasis to the Before. (We will see this emphasis continue throughout both of their treatments of the beginning of the world [chapter 2, below] and of humanity [chapter 3, below].) It is God's skillfulness as Creator that Philo highlights by drawing attention to God's pre-set intentions and pre-deliberations. Philo boasts in God for his creative genius. For Paul also, God is the pre-Intender who deserves our boasts. God is the one who marked out in the Before not only the ultimate goal of goodness and freedom for creation, but also a whole host of salvific benefits for people who love God in Christ. In one way, this theocentric emphasis of both interpreters is to be expected, for the textual object of each man's exegesis – the beginning of Genesis – is itself theologically oriented, emphasizing the God who creates the cosmos and humanity. Their shared text itself stresses the superior word of God and enforces that things continue to happen "in this manner" in which he decided. As we will see in chapters 2 and 3, both Philo and Paul continue to re-enforce such themes.

Within these broad hermeneutical and theological similarities, however, we must also acknowledge differences between Philo and Paul. It is precisely in light of their similarities that these differences can be refined appropriately. In both men's schemes God's preparatory deliberations are *causative* – another similarity – but for Philo God's plan causes a beautiful architectural and structural triumph in humans and the world, while for Paul God's plan causes a historical and cruciform triumph for humans and the world. Both emphases can be seen in Genesis 1ff in that there God causally initiates both ontic structure and historic direction. Each of these facets of the beginning of Genesis comes out especially clearly when read in light of either Plato's "paradigmatic" structure or Proverbs" destiny of "for his works." We should be careful, however, not to relegate structure to only Philo's interpretation of creation, for as we will see in chapter 2 it is the differentiated ontological structure of bodies on which Paul focuses in 1 Cor. 15:38–41. It would be equally inappropriate to relegate historical-enactment to only Paul's interpretation of creation, for it is of chief theological import for Philo that God's creativity is intimately wed to his providential and continuous caring for his creation.[191] Nevertheless, regarding their explicit Befores, the type of effect enacted in creation because of God's pre-deliberations does have this different focus for each interpreter: Philo's ontic structural focus, Paul's historical redemptive focus.

Many people in Paul's and Philo's day were gazing into the Before. While Philo is confident that due to God's intentions *before* creation the physical world would turn out structurally "good," Paul is confident that due to God's intentions *before* creation all things in history (even suffering) will turn out "for good" and "for glory" for those who love God and whom God purposefully called in Jesus. While for Philo God's pre-determination did not directly affect historical moments, it did affect the outcome of the physical creative process. It made it beautiful and made possible a goal toward which to aspire and to which people could attain. Paul saw in God's Before God's Son coming in a flesh that was to be crucified for the benefits of believers, and he saw a pre-determined people receiving pre-determined glory through a pre-determined conformation to God's Son's image. Lest we forget the primary argument of this chapter, however, it should be reasserted that Paul's *language* and *conceptuality* of the Before, just like with this first strand of Philo's hermeneutic of creation, has been seamlessly intertwined with his reading of the Beginning. This hermeneutical similarity does not deny their difference. The core to each Before is still aeons apart, and these Befores will affect the remainder of their readings of Genesis' texts concerning the beginning of the world and the beginning of humanity.

---

[191] See, e.g., *Op.* 9–11 and 171–72.

1.4 Comparisons and Conclusions

Our understanding of Paul's theology of the Before has been sharpened by comparison with Philo's, especially as each "theology" is analyzed as a reading of shared texts. Paul's Before understands God's wise pre-creational plan as a revelational and redemptive purposing of what God would *do* with this creation once it had been created (and after it had been subjected to the slavery of sin, death, and corruption). For Paul, God revealed something of his nature (his eternal power and divinity) through the things that he created in Genesis (Rom. 1:20). But *before* he created such things, God had already wisely determined that a more full knowledge of himself would be found only in his Son. God pre-determined that his wise self would be found most clearly in the crucifixion of this Lord of glory as well as in the shared-glory given to those whom he had marked for conformity with what would become – in time, space, history, and resurrection – the "image" of this last Adam. *Then* God created the world, Adam and Eve, and the propagation of Adam's "image" to humanity as recorded in the beginning of Genesis.

Chapter 2

The Beginning of the World

God said, "Let there become...," and the universe became. In the beginning of Genesis, God's voice and word quickly commands attention.[1] Other themes are certainly important in Genesis 1,[2] but the fact that "every day begins with God speaking"[3] can imply that creation "is about [God] first of all,"[4] even about his powerful and effective intentions.[5] God's imperatives abound in the text, and imperatives naturally imply his desire.[6] God's "intelligence and volition"[7] prompt his effective word; the word is the "outward expression" or "realization" of his "deliberately formed purpose."[8]

In chapter 1 I sought to demonstrate how Paul's understanding of God's mental activity in the Before was, like Philo's, intimately related to his interpretation of the textual Beginning. Though their Befores had roots in texts outwith Genesis, neither interpreter's Before was merely imposed onto the text from previously held and disassociated metaphysical speculations. Rather, both interpreters' Befores were reciprocally affecting and affected by their interpretations of the textual features themselves. Yet since our focus was on Philo's and Paul's understandings of the Before, we only received a few glimpses of *how* these reciprocal affects took shape.

Here in chapter 2, the focus will be on the beginning of the world. One aspect of Paul's and Philo's interpretations of this cosmic Beginning is still a Before, albeit an implicit one: i.e., God's desire and purpose according to which he then creates. This chapter therefore has two purposes. One, it will bring to light more details than are typically observed about Paul's interpretation of the creation of the world in comparison with Philo's. Two, it will also further confirm and explore the interrelatedness of the Beginning (of the world) and the Before in the interpretations of both ancient writers.

---

[1] Cf. Ps. 32:8–9 (LXX), which uses language of Genesis 1 to highlight God's effective and trustworthy word. See Currid, 1997, 61 (he also compares with Genesis 1 "the logos doctrine" of ancient Egyptian cosmogonies, 60–61; 61 n. 58, 62–63).

[2] E.g., order, blessing, and land: so Sailhamer, 1992, 81–2.

[3] Van Wolde, 1996A, 22.

[4] Kidner, 1967, 43.

[5] Westermann, 1984, 110–12; Wenham, 1987, 17–18.

[6] Currid, 1997, 63; Childs, 1992, 385; Scroggs, 1966, 4.

[7] Skinner, 1910, 7.

[8] Driver, 1926, 5; Garr, 2003, 181. Cf. Watson, 1994, 145.

Let us approach Philo's and Paul's treatments of the beginning of the world in two stages: first, their understandings of the creation of light on day one (Gen. 1:2–5), second, of the creation of everything else within heaven and earth on the second–sixth days (Gen. 1:6–31). I will introduce both of these stages together with a few comments on Genesis 1 itself.

2.1 Genesis 1, God's Desire, the World's Goodness

The first divine words in the Bible are elegant in simplicity and powerful in effect: "God said, 'Let there be light,' and there was light" (1:3). God's voice pierces the darkness; light appears *ex nihilo*.[9] Genesis 1 does not present creation in only one way. It is neither only from nothing (*ex nihilo*) nor merely by God's word. Creation is performed by a combination of 1) God's bare "commands," which themselves "immediately produce the desired effect,"[10] 2) God's craftsmanship as "Maker,"[11] and 3) God's employment of "mediators" such as the water or earth.[12] This complex of creative methods occurs irregularly, but harmoniously.[13] These different models of divine creativity are distinct, yet they are unified by the grammatical similarity which precedes and introduces them all, beginning in 1:3: "And God said...."[14]

---

[9] Cf. Mathews, 1996, 129 and Haffner, 1995, 47. Though Sacks (1990) is critical of the doctrine of *creatio ex nihilo* in Genesis 1, he recognizes it in 1:3 (4).

[10] E.g., light, dry land. Watson, 1994, 140–41. Noort (2005) remarks that in Genesis 1 the phrase ויהי כן "claims that the word of Elohim is carried out in such a way that the result is in conformity with that word" (8).

[11] E.g., firmament, luminaries, humankind. Watson, 1994, 141. The MT hosts seven enactments in which God is the specified actor. (Watson calls these "fabrications" since God "makes" or "fabricates" the object instead of merely speaking it into existence.) The LXX adds a perfective statement after God's volition in v. 9a thereby producing a perfect balance of God speaking and of things happening just as God speaks them (see Cook, 1982, 25–36, esp. 28–30). (Concerning the possible hermeneutical motivations for the LXX's changes to the Hebrew, see Rösel, 1994; critiqued by Cook, 2001, 322–28).

[12] E.g., vegetation, sea creatures, living creatures. Watson, 1994, 142.

[13] For example, in Gen. 1:24 God commands "the earth" to participate in "bringing up" animals, but in v. 25 God is himself the one who "makes" the animals with no mention of the earth's participation. This can be called an "irregularity" since regularity would have the earth participate after God called it to. Between these two statements, however, the text records that what God said in v. 24 did, in fact, "happen in this manner." Thus the text (as it stands for Philo and Paul) presents irregularity without tension: God doing it himself is harmonious in "manner" with him calling the earth to participate.

[14] Watson (1994) writes, "Grammatical similarity ('Let there be...') conceals the presence of different models of divine action" (141). My statement above, intentionally borrowing Watson's language, is focusing on a different (mutually inclusive) issue. The di-

The resultant phrase, "And it came about, light" (ויהי אור, καὶ ἐγένετο φῶς), is paradigmatic for the repeated phrase throughout the rest of the account: "and it came about in this manner" (ויהי כן, καὶ ἐγένετο οὕτως).[15] The grammatical pattern begun in v. 3, where the thing summoned by God ("light") is exactly what comes into being ("light"),[16] remains structurally the same in the successive statements:

"And God said,   'Let light...'   →   and it came about,   light"
"And God said,   'Let [X,Y,Z]...'   →   and it came about   in this manner"

The only change is that the fulfillment clause becomes general, i.e., "it came about," to allow for exact repetition regardless of its precise created referent (whether firmament, plants/seeds, luminaries, etc.). Throughout the narrative, starting in v. 3 and shaped by v. 3, what came about was exactly what God desired.

The same type of programmatic and paradigmatic significance is also evident between God's value-judgment in v. 4: "And God saw [וירא אלהים, καὶ εἶδεν ὁ θεός] the light, that it was good [כי טוב, ὅτι καλόν]," and the oft-repeated but shorter phrase: "And God saw [וירא אלהים, καὶ εἶδεν ὁ θεός] that it was good [כי טוב, ὅτι καλόν]."[17] This aesthetic pattern is finally and climactically repeated in the conclusion: "And God saw [וירא אלהים, καὶ εἶδεν ὁ θεός] all that he had made, and behold, it was exceedingly good [והנה טוב מאד, καὶ ἰδοὺ καλὰ λίαν]" (v. 31).[18]

And God saw   the light   →   that it was   good
And God saw   –   →   that it was   good
And God saw   all that he had made   →   and look,   good exceedingly

The wording of Gen. 1:3–4 is significant for the rest of the cosmogony. What "came about" on *day one* was exactly what God commanded and was ontologically "good." Likewise, each time the phrases established on day one are repeated throughout the *second to sixth days* the reader is reminded of the initial claim and therefore of the exact, immediate, and good fulfill-

---

versity remains, as Watson observed, while it is *also* true (as Watson himself writes) that "the coming into being of an entity is always preceded by a divine word" (141).

[15] Cf. MT 6x and LXX 7x: v. 3 is grammatically (and thus thematically) paradigmatic for vv. 6–7, 9, 11, 14–15, [LXX 20,] 24, 29–30. The six-fold repetition of the first ויהי-phrase suggests that the MT meant for the latter six to be interpreted in light of v. 3, thus making an "even" seven ויהי-phrases. Noort (2005) helpfully highlights the thematic comparison (11), but the equivalence is more profound than a mere comparison. Wenham (1987) thus hits the mark when he calls the subsequent fulfillment formulas an "exact echo" of the one in v. 3 and concludes that this "emphasizes the total fulfillment of the divine word" (18).

[16] Westermann, 1984, 41.

[17] Cf. v. 4 with vv. [LXX 8,] 10, 12, 18, 21, 25.

[18] V. 31 does use the direct object in the way of v. 4 (contra Noort, 2005, 8).

ment of God's will and word.[19] These two statements in "day one" thus stand out from the rest (as a paradigm stands out from its model), and yet at the same time are integrally inseparable from the remaining cosmogony (also as a paradigm is with its model). Genesis 1:3–4 opens to the reader two of the major themes which are repetitively confirmed and developed throughout Genesis 1 as a whole: 1) the sovereignty of the Creator's action and desire, and 2) the ontic goodness of his creation which perfectly accords with God's desire. Paul, like Philo in his contemporary and formal commentary on Genesis 1–2, makes much of both of these themes as he interprets the same beginning of light according to Gen. 1:2–5 and the same beginning of the rest of the world according to Gen. 1:6–31.

2.2 Philo and Paul on Genesis 1:2–5
The God Who Spoke Light

Philo and Paul treat God's creation of light as something special. It seems to have stood out to them both. As testified to in their shared scripture and among their fellow scripture interpreters, light plays an important part in Jewish history,[20] cultic practice,[21] and lawful piety.[22] God's being and ac-

---

[19] So Westermann, 1984, 41; Gelander, 1997, 95; Watson, 1994, 140–41. Contra Parker (2005), who interprets כן (445–47; contrary to its typical use as an adverb of manner [BDB, 4573]: cf. Judg. 6:38, 40; οὕτως in LXX 2 Ki. 7:20; 15:12) and its irregular use in Genesis 1 (443–45, 447) as presenting a god whose will and words are not perfectly obeyed. For Parker, ontology is "more differentiated than [God had] planned" (451). (Noort, 2000, 12 and 18 draws similar theological conclusions from the narrative of Genesis 2). As we will see below, Parker's reading of Genesis 1 has less affinities with Paul's and Philo's interpretations of Genesis 1 than it does with certain third century gnostic tractates, with the early second-century heretic Saturninus (as described in Irenaeus' *Adversus haereses* 1.24.1–2), and with Menander (as described in Irenaeus *Haer.* 1.23.1, 5) – all three of whom, according to Thielman (2005), "apparently believed that the created world was essentially an imperfect place, mired in the inept fabrications of the god described in the early chapters of Genesis" (411; see 410–11). F. Watson's interpretation of "good" as "a conformity between the final product and the original intention" (1994, 145–46) is much closer to the reading of both Paul and Philo, in which God willed and spoke and all things happened exactly in that manner (see below).

[20] E.g., Ex. 10:23; Est. 8:16; cf. 2 Mac. 1:32.

[21] E.g., Ex. 27:20; 35:14; 39:16; Lev. 24:2; Num. 4:16; 2 Chr. 4:20; Eze. 42:7; cf. 1 Mac. 1:21; 2 Mac. 1:32.

[22] For the law as a light and personal piety as light, e.g., LXX Ps. 118:105; Prov. 4:18; 6:23; Isa. 26:9; 58:8, 10; cf. Sir. 24:27 (and 24:32, both in the context of 24:23ff); Wis. 18:4; Bar. 4:1–2 (see also 1 John 1:7; 2:9–10).

tions are often associated with or characterized by light.[23] "Light" and "glory" shine from the Lord's face.[24] The association between light and God certainly has a cosmogonic dimension – i.e., he created the light[25] – but it often also describes his historical accomplishments on behalf of people.[26] Light was associated with the illumination of "knowledge" or "wisdom,"[27] itself occasionally salvific.[28] This last feature of the light-motif – its link to knowledge and wisdom – had correlates within both formal and popular philosophical discussions of the Graeco-Roman world.[29]

Not surprisingly, light became invaluable for communicating the nature of *God's* understanding, his "wisdom."[30] For example, in Wisdom of Solomon God's "wisdom" has "untiring brightness" (7:10). This "worker of all things"[31] is the "eternal light." As such it is cosmic (7:27; 8:1), salvific (7:27),[32] and even had been revealed to Israel during the Egyptian plagues (Ex. 10:21–23) as a forerunner to "the incorruptible light of the law" (τὸ ἄφθαρτον νόμου φῶς) for eternity (Wis. 18:4b).[33]

Within such a context where so many scriptural, religious, and philosophical concepts shared the significance of light, both Philo (in *Op.* 30–35) and Paul (in 2 Cor. 4:6) turn their audiences to God's creation of light, particularly as it is described in Gen. 1:2–5. I will now demonstrate that

---

[23] E.g., 2 Sam. 23:4; LXX Ps. 35:10; 103:2; Job 37:3, 11, 21–22; Isa. 2:5; 51:5; 60:1–3, 19–20; Dan. 2:22; Hos. 6:5; Hab. 3:4, 11; cf. Sir. 50:29; Bar. 5:9 (see also Jam. 1:17; 1 Tim. 6:16; 1 John 1:5).

[24] See especially Num. 6:25; cf. LXX Ps. 4:7; 30:17; 66:1; 79:4, 8, 20; 88:16; 118:135. The facial shining is connected to "mercy" in Num. 6:25 and to "salvation" in LXX Ps. 30:17; 79:4, 8, 20.

[25] For God's creation of light: LXX Ps. 135:7; 148:3 (cf. vv. 5–6); Job 37:15 (φῶς ποιήσας ἐκ σκότους); Isa. 45:7 (ὁ κατασκευάσας φῶς καὶ ποιήσας σκότος); Jer. 10:12–13; 28:15–16 (= 51:15–16 MT); 38:36 (= 31:35 MT); cf. Bar. 3:33. For God's new creation of light see Isa. 42:16 (ποιήσω αὐτοῖς τὸ σκότος εἰς φῶς).

[26] For "salvific" acts characterized by light: 2 Sam. 22:29; LXX Ps. 17:29; 36:6; 42:3; 96:11; 111:4; 138:11–12; Prov. 13:9; 20:27; Job 29:3; Isa. 9:1; 30:26; 42:6, 16; 49:6; 50:10; 51:4–5; 53:11; 58:10; 62:1; Mic. 7:8–9; cf. Pss.Sol. 3:12 (see also Luke 1:79; Eph. 5:8; Col. 1:12–13; 1 Pet. 2:9).

[27] So LXX Ps. 88:16; 118:130. Cf. Philo: *Op.* 53–54; *Plant.* 40; Paul: Rom. 2:17–20.

[28] See Isa. 53:11; Hos. 10:12. (Cf. Eph. 1:18).

[29] E.g., Van Kooten (2005) demonstrates the broad impact of Plato's allegory of the cave (see book 7 of Plato's *Republic*), not only among philosophers but also within Diaspora and Palestinian Judaism (151–62, 168–91). Cf. Berchman, 2000, 63ff.

[30] "Light" and "wisdom" are not explicitly connected much within Philo's and Paul's scripture, but compare Eccl. 2:13, 8:1, and Dan. 2:22: God "knows" (γινώσκω) both what is in darkness and what is "in the light" (τὰ ἐν τῷ φωτί) (cf. Luke 8:17). Philo writes (in a cosmogonic context) that "wisdom itself is splendor and light" (*QG.* 1.7).

[31] Cf. Prov. 8:22–31 and Genesis 1.

[32] On Wis. 7:25–31 see Goodenough, 1935, 268–76.

[33] See Davis, 1984, 49–62.

Paul, like Philo, emphasizes God's creative voice, connects God's initial cosmogonic shining to God's subsequent salvific illumination, and displays a hermeneutical manoeuvre that emphasizes God himself within these two all-important activities. Within these similarities, Paul and Philo show different understandings of the light of Gen. 1:2–5, not least in how it relates to its bodily encapsulation.

2.2.1 Philo's Reading of Genesis 1:2–5: A Special Light and its Bodily Dimming (Op. 30–35)

God himself is the transcendent light, unsurpassable in essence.[34] But he also created light. Within Philo's commentary on Genesis 1, God spoke his wisdom and thereby "made" the incorporeal paradigm of light in Gen. 1:3–5. This was an invisible light that would serve as a paradigm for all light-bearing bodies in Gen. 1:14–19. Throughout his corpus, when Philo dwells on the nature of created light, he often turns to Genesis 1 to do so. Within many of these discussions, Philo transitions easily from various aspects of Genesis 1, and particularly Gen. 1:2–5, to personal experience and ethics.[35] Although God's light is cosmic and cosmogonic, it is not thereby only transcendent and distant.[36] It can be experienced by divine gift.[37] For example, Philo explains his own experience of personal study in terms of God giving (or even withholding) "light" and "sight" (*Migr.* 34–35).[38] God is a personally sovereign Illuminator as well as a cosmically sovereign one. We will now investigate Philo's exegesis of Gen. 1:3–5 in *Op.* 30–35, and

---

[34] Philo often characterizes God as light, and he typically uses light to illustrate God's unsurpassableness: *Ebr.* 37–45, esp. 44 (surpassing other gods); *Somn.* 1.72; cf. 65–71, 83–84 (surpassing his assistants); *Spec.* 1.36–37 (surpassing all other light).

[35] Philo often moves from the cosmogonic text to personal experience, especially via the motif of "light." In *Abr.* 156–63, Philo connects God's purpose in Gen. 1:3–5 and 1:14–19 as being "for sight" with the human ability to cosmically contemplate through "wisdom." In *Migr.* 38–42, Philo moves from God's "wisdom" in Gen. 1:31 to personal experience of the "light" of "wisdom." And in *Spec.* 4.186–96, which is not only relatable to *Tim.* 53ab (so Dillon, 2005, 99) and *Tim.* 30a (so Runia, 2001, 117; idem, 1986, 140–48, 451–52) but has also been affected by Genesis 1 (so Runia, 2001, 145–46; Leonhardt-Balzer, 2004A, 335, 343) more profoundly than is typically realized, Philo moves from God's activity of bringing "light out of darkness" in Gen. 1:2–3 to the desired activity of rulers in bringing good out of bad situations (cf. van Kooten, 2008, 195–96; Runia, 1986, 146).

[36] Cf. *Op.* 31; *Migr.* 40–42; *Plant.* 27 (light as divine revelation). So Radice, 2009, 139; see Lorenzen (2008) for more on Philo's links between "light" and "understanding" and "wisdom" (77–80, 97–100).

[37] Barclay, 1996A, 165 (cf. 165 n. 90).

[38] For Philo's combination of "light" and "sight" see, e.g., *Spec.* 1.54 (cf. LXX Ps. 35:10; 2 Cor. 4:4); van Kooten, 2005, 160–61.

we will particularly note his hermeneutical move from this text and its transcendent light to the personal experience of illumination.

Four textual features were decisive in Philo's reading of Gen. 1:1–5 as God's noetic Before, and they set the stage for Philo's exegesis of the light of vv. 3–5 in §§30–35. One, the textual label "day one" (Gen. 1:5) – the day within which light is produced (vv. 3–5) – testifies to uniqueness ("one-ness") and therefore to the ideal realm (§15).[39] Two, an ideal realm is expected anyway, for only modeled upon a "beautiful" Before can the product itself be "beautiful" (§16), which the world clearly is in Genesis 1, and light clearly is in v. 4.[40] Three, only an incorporeal paradigm is "invisible," which the "earth" of day one is (v. 2) (§29).[41] And four, only a corporeal product is "firm," which all things subsequent to light are (vv. 6–31) (cf. §§36, 51). Within this construal of day one, the "light" of Gen. 1:3 is obviously "the incorporeal essence of light" (§29).

Out of the seven incorporeal elements that God "made" in vv. 1–3, Moses set "special distinction" on "spirit" in v. 2, calling it "of God," and on "light" in v. 4, specifying that it was "surpassingly beautiful" (ὑπερβαλλόντως καλόν) (§30). For Philo, this textual light "out-shines [λαμπρότερον] and out-radiates [αὐγοειδέστερον] the visible."

Combining details of v. 2 ("invisible") and v. 3 (God's creative command), Philo explains: "that 'invisible' [ἀόρατον] and noetic light has become an image [εἰκών] of the divine word [θείου λόγου] which communicated [διερμηνεύσαντος] its genesis" (§31). Plato would probably not have appreciated Philo's description of this noetic light as having "become" (γέγονεν) and as having a "genesis" (τὴν γένεσιν). But Philo's sacred text compels him to consider it so. What it "became" was an "image" of God's causative word, a word which "communicated its genesis." This communication of light's beginning, as elsewhere in Philo's writings, is derived from the paradigmatic phrase "And God said…" in Gen. 1:3.[42]

A slightly different nuance is presented in *Somn.* 1.75. There Philo describes God himself as "light" (quoting LXX Ps. 26:1). Thus he himself is

---

[39] In *Spec.* 3.180 Philo explains this in slightly more detail: the "unit" is the "image" of "the first Cause"; the number two, however, being divisible, is an image of "the divisible matter that is worked upon" (cf. *Leg.* 1.3). See Radice, 2009, 132; Leonhardt-Balzer, 2004A, 343; Tobin, 1983, 60, 97–98.

[40] See *Abr.* 156; Leonhardt-Balzer, 2004A, 343.

[41] Radice, 2009, 132.

[42] Radice (2009) writes that the repeated phrase, "And God said… and there was" led "Alexandrian exegetes" "to give particular emphasis to the relationship that exists between the word of God (*logos*) and the act of creation" (137). Other scholars also connect "Word" with "And God said": cf. van Kooten, 2005, 154; Cox, 2005, 18; Leonhardt-Balzer, 2004A, 343; Runia, 2001, 143. More generally on Philo's Logos see also Tobin, 1992, 117–19 and Runia, 1986, 438–51.

the divine "paradigm" for light. Philo qualifies this, however. He explains that God is actually the "paradigm of the paradigm" since the direct paradigm for the corporeal lights mentioned in Gen. 1:14–19 (a passage cited a few sections later in *Somn.* 1.85–86) is actually the incorporeal light of Gen. 1:3.[43] But Philo then *identifies* this incorporeal light with God's own "most perfect word."[44] This is a slightly different nuance to his interpretation of Gen. 1:3 found in *Op.* 31, the main passage of our consideration, for there the noetic light is *not identical* with God's word but is rather its "image." However, due to the fluidity of Philo's language and concepts (which we will see more in chapter 3 regarding "image" in Gen. 1:27), the difference in these two relationships between "light" and "word" is actually more perceived than real.[45] The same "tension" is found within *Op.* itself in a very similar manner. That is, in *Op.* 17–20 the noetic cosmos (the Before) is located *in* God's "word" just as a mental blueprint of a city is *in* the architect's mind, but in *Op.* 24–25 the noetic cosmos *is* God's "word" (λόγος) just as the mental city-plan *is* (ἐστιν) the architect's mental activity (λογισμός).[46] Philo also does not use "image" uniformily either within *Op.* 15–25 or in his broader corpus.[47]

Likewise, the text of Gen. 1:3 itself can stimulate either interpretation: word as light (so *Somn.* 1.75) *and* light as "image" of word (so *Op.* 31). That is, one could ask: When God opened his mouth in Gen. 1:3, what was produced? Some may answer "light" while others "word," for God spoke and light happened. There is a common theme of both of Philo's readings

---

[43] That in *Somn.* 1.75 Philo has the specific text of Gen. 1:3–5 in mind should be clear from his combination of "word," "light," and "created." This is confirmed when Philo then quotes Gen. 1:4. Concerning the likeness of the sun to God, Philo may have in the back of his mind, e.g., Plato's *Rep.* 509a (so van Kooten, 2008, 183), Proclus' *Hymn to Helios* 1.33–35 (van Kooten, 2008, 94–95), and/or something like Plutarch's *To an Uneducated Ruler* 780e-f (van Kooten, 2008, 97). Yet even if these texts are behind him, Philo himself explicitly traces out the symbolism *scripturally* and cosmogonically, actually citing Psalm 26 and Genesis 1.

[44] Runia, 2001, 168; cf. *Somn.* 1.85.

[45] Runia (2001) offers that *Op.* 31 may be corrupt (168). This is probably unnecessary in light of the fluidity of some of Philo's concepts. Leonhardt-Balzer's description of Philo's use of metaphor and simile in *Op.* 15–25 warns against pressing Philo's language too far (2004A, 324–44).

[46] See Radice, 2009, 143.

[47] In *Op.* 17 εἰκών is unphilosophical; in the broader context εἰκών and its conceptual partners (ἀπεικόνισμα [§16]; ἄγαλμα [ἀγαλματοφορέω] [§18]; εἴδωλα [§18]; εἰκών x4 [§25]) are philosophical. Compare how in *Abr.* 153 Philo does not use "image" in the manner of paradigm-product, but merely to convey that someone knows the soul's emotions by looking at the eyes (e.g., tears = sadness, etc.). See Siegert, 2009, 184 (cf. *Leg.* 3.101; *Dec.* 105); Berchman, 2000, 62 (though Plato's notion of a mirror in *Tim.* 45b-46b is unhelpful here).

of Gen. 1:3 above, despite their seeming tensions: light is produced by none other than God's own word. Claus Westermann posits that Genesis 1 "is colored and determined by the words 'and God spoke...and it was so'."[48] The whole text of Genesis 1, but particularly 1:3, had drawn special attention to the sovereignty of God's word in the paradigmatic creation of light. So too does Philo.

Philo's purpose in *Op.* 30–35, however, is not actually to elucidate the relationship between light and word. His main task is to relate Gen. 1:3–5 to 1:14–19.[49] This textual relationship, and thus the philosophical and scientific quandary of how light can exist apart from light-bearing bodies, can be (and has been) explored from different perspectives: scientific, semantic, etc.[50] Philo reasons that the "light" of 1:3 is "a bodiless and noetic paradigm" for the sun and other heavenly luminaries. It is a "superheavenly star" (ὑπερουράνιος ἀστήρ), the "all-radiance" (παναυγή) (§31).[51] It is "before" (πρό) the sun (§33) and the "fountain" of all sense-perceptible stars (§31).[52]

Philo furthers this paradigmatic relationship with a slight elaboration: "That unmixed and pure radiance [τῆς ἀμιγοῦς καὶ καθαρᾶς αὐγῆς] is dimmed when it begins to change according to the transition from the noetic to the sense-perceptible" (§31.8–10). Philo's reason, that the noetic light accomodated "according to each [luminary's] ability" (§31), recalls one of his earlier statements concerning God: God himself lessened his gifts and graces "toward the abilities of the beneficiaries" (§23).[53] The greater is naturally diminished so as to accommodate the lesser. Yet Philo's accommodation of the noetic light to the inability of the sensory realm goes one step further than does God's accommodation of himself even to the noetic realm. The "dimming" of light happens "since none of the objects in the sense-perceptible realm is absolutely pure [εἰλικρινές]" (§31.11).[54] While Philo could speak of the ontic differentiation between

---

[48] Westermann, 1984, 41.

[49] He relates "light" to "word" only in §31.1–3, while he mentions the paradigmatic relationship between light and luminaries in §30.5–8, §31.3–11, §33.1–2, and §34.6–10. Cf. *Spec.* 1.279.

[50] Van Till, 1986, 90; Westermann, 1987, 10; Sailhamer, 1992, 87, 92–93.

[51] Cf. Wis. 7:26. On the comparison of Philo and Wisdom generally see Winston, 1979, 59–63, and particularly on this word "radiance" see Tobin, 1983, 85–86.

[52] In Plato, the incorporeal soul contemplates and ascends to "the super-heavenly place" (ὑπερουράνιος τόπος) "in pure radiance" (ἐν αὐγῇ καθαρᾷ) (*Phdr.* 250c4; also presented by Runia, 2001, 169). Philo has just used the adjective "super-heavenly" (ὑπερουράνιος) and is also about to use the phrase "pure radiance" (καθαρᾶς αὐγῆς).

[53] See Runia, 2001, 169.

[54] Cf. Wis. 7:25. "Absolutely pure" (εἰλικρινές) is often used of motives and morals that are unmixed with anything false (Louw and Nida, 1988, 88.41–42 [p. 747]; cf. 1 Cor. 5:8; 2 Cor. 1:12, 17; Phil. 1:10; 2 Pet. 3:1).

God and the noetic realm without treating the noetic as being thereby less than absolutely pure (cf. *Aet.* 1), Philo can only speak of light as an "unmixed and clean radiance" and as "absolutely pure" before its unavoidable "dimming" through the taking on of bodily form.[55]

In *Op.* 33, Philo then calls the darkness of 1:4b-5 light's "adversary" (τὸ ἀντίπαλον). Though Philo does not always treat darkness as negative,[56] he often does see it as contrary to God, whether the darkness is cosmological and pre-creational (e.g., in *Spec.* 4.187) or anthropological and ethical (e.g., in *Spec.* 1.54 and *Deus* 3).[57] In contexts where darkness is negative – and Gen. 1:3–5 and 1:14–19 are often not far away in these contexts – Philo sees God's "light" as helpful for a person's virtuous living.[58] It is even a remedy to the darkness of sin.[59] At this point in his commentary, too, while explaining the "darkness" of Gen. 1:4–5 as light's adversary, Philo treats God's light as salvific (though this treatment takes shape in a slightly different manner than one typically assumes from the word "salvific"). That is, fortunately for the creation God "knew well" (εὖ εἰδότος) the "natural contrariety" between light and darkness, and in light of this knowledge God's "separation" of light from darkness in Gen. 1:4b is a kind of pre-emptive rescue of the cosmos. God moderated light and darkness (§33) by causing them to peacefully introduce each other through the boundaries "evening" and "morning" (Gen. 1:5b) (§§33–34). A theological implication of this reading of Gen. 1:3–5 is that for Philo both light and darkness are, as David Runia writes, "firmly under the control of the creator."[60] This is Philo's hermeneutical pattern: the manner in which God created light is interpreted in light of God's *pre*-understanding. God cre-

---

[55] Cf. *Deus* 3. For Philo's general denigration of (cosmic) matter see *Spec.* 1.329. Radice (2009) speaks of the Logos as being "able to redeem the world itself from the negativity that association with matter inflicts upon it" (138). For Philo, the negativity of anthropological flesh is set within the broader cosmological context of the negativity of matter. As we will see below regarding Paul's difference with Philo at this point, this is also one broad difference between Philo and the Gospel of John, again regarding light (van Kooten, 2005, 151–56); in John, as in Paul but not Philo, there is no hint of dimming when "the true light" (also associated with Genesis 1) "became flesh" (cf. John 1:1–5, 14; 3:19; 8:12; 9:5; 12:46).

[56] Compare *Mos.* 1.158 and 2.70, which are both on Ex. 34:29 (cf. the "darkness" covering the mountain in Ex. 19:16, 20:21, and Deut. 4:11; see Thrall, 1973, 149), and *Post.* 14–15 with Philo's treatment of the invisibility and darkness of Gen. 1:1–2 in *Op.* 29–32.

[57] Waltke (1975) treats the "darkness" of Gen. 1:2 as "contrary to God" (327–42). For "darkness" as negative see Eccl. 2:13; Amos 5:18–20; Jer. 4:23; 13:16; Eze. 32:7–8; cf. Acts 26:18; 2 Cor. 6:14; 1 Th. 5:5; Eph. 5:8–9; Col. 1:12–13. Plutarch (*Table-talk* 670B) says Egyptians considered darkness superior to light (see van Kooten, 2005, 161).

[58] E.g., *Somn.* 1.85–86.

[59] Cf. *Somn.* 1.82, 91; *Virt.* 164; *Deus* 131–35.

[60] Runia, 2001, 170.

ated as he did for a purpose. What is more, due to God's pre- or foreknowledge creation itself is, in a manner, a form of salvation.[61]

To complete his reading of Gen. 1:3–5, Philo lastly forms an *inclusio* with his introduction to the incorporeal and noetic "day one" from §§15–16. That is, he reminds his readers that the light, darkness, evening, and morning about which he had just been writing are incorporeal and noetic realities (§34.6–9; cf. §16). He points out again that in the text itself "the Maker 'called' [ὁ ποιῶν ἐκάλεσε]" the new measure of time "day One." To round off his treatment of vv. 1–5 Philo has brought back into the foreground the nature of the Before, and he especially emphasizes the God who pre-knows, acts accordingly, and pre-emptively rescues. The "incorporeal cosmos" – the Before – "now has a conclusion" (ἤδη πέρας εἶχεν), being settled or established "in the divine word." The "sense-perceptible" cosmos is "ready for birth" according to this completed "paradigm" (§36.1–3). Philo has set the stage nicely for a discussion of the corporeal creation in Gen. 1:6–31.

In summary, Philo sees God's creation of light as not only the perfect paradigm but also as a beneficent precaution. In many of Philo's discussions on light, one can find an engagement with Gen. 1:3–5 (and 1:14–19) on either an implicit or explicit level. Hermeneutically, Philo moves naturally from text to experience, from the beginning of light to personal illumination. Two recurring hermeneutical manoeuvres can be highlighted, both within Philo's exegesis of Gen. 1:3–5 itself and also as he moves from this text to human experience. (These happen to correspond to the two principles mentioned above regarding Gen. 1:2–5 itself: God spoke and it happened accordingly, and it was good.) One of Philo's recurring moves regards theocentricity.[62] From Philo's exegesis it emerges that God is the unifying factor in each "shining." The God who spoke into existence the cosmic light of Gen. 1:3–5 (creating Light, the paradigm) is the same God who anthropically illuminated at creation (creating the human mind) and who still illuminates in present experience (granting understanding). The second recurring move involves Philo's tri-level ontology. God is the model of the noetic and the noetic is the model of the corporeal. God surpasses the noetic in ontic essence even more than the noetic ontologically surpasses the corporeal. Yet while both God and the noetic light remain "absolutely pure," the bodily containment of light necessary dims its noetic source in impurity.

We will now observe how Paul makes a similar hermeneutical move from text to personal experience. He even bases this transition on a similar

---

[61] As Barclay (2006) points out, for Philo "creation and salvation are not clearly distinguishable categories" (143 n. 11).

[62] Frick, 1999, 4.

theocentricity concerning the one God who is active in both creative and salvific shinings. Yet for Paul, the light of God's glory has in no way been dimmed when radiating from the face of one particular corporeal body.

2.2.2 Paul's Reading of Genesis 1:2–5: A Special Light and its Facial Glory (2 Cor. 4:6)

For Paul, as for Philo, God's "shining" of light in Gen. 1:2–5 is something special. It is also paradigmatic for subsequent shinings that God will accomplish. As Philo had found important a combination of God's creation of light and God's personal illumination, so too Paul in 2 Cor. 4:6 finds in God's creative shining of light a ready motif for describing the experience in which God "shone" his glory into believers' hearts.[63] In Paul's scripture not only is God himself often described by "light,"[64] but light often portrays specifically "the glory of the Lord" (e.g., Isa. 60:1; Eze. 1:26–28), especially located in his face (Num. 6:25). When Moses stood face-to-face with this Lord (Ex. 33:11), his own human "face" would visibly display the reflected divine glory as if a mirror of it (Ex. 34:29–35). Moses became a "light-bearer" himself.[65] But for Paul, the "glory" which Moses displayed, though truly glorious, had been eclipsed by a surpassing glory in the "face" of another (2 Cor. 3:7–4:6).[66] As Philo had compared the beginning of light (Gen. 1:3) to its embodiment (1:14–19) and then to the inward personal experience of divine illumintation, so too Paul moves from the text of light's beginning (Gen. 1:2–3) to an embodied display of glorious illumination (Christ's face) and then to the divine shine of personal and inward experience.

In 2 Cor. 4:6 Paul writes, "The God who said out of darkness, 'Light will shine,' himself shone in our hearts to give the illumination of the

---

[63] 2 Cor. 4:6 is probably Paul's "theological reflection" on his conversion (so Witherington, 1994, 233; cf. Vorholt, 2008, 211–24; Segal, 1990, 61–67), yet generalized to encompass "our" hearts. In 1 Corinthians, Paul highlights "seeing" Jesus: "I have seen [ἑόρακα] Jesus" (1 Cor. 9:1), "Jesus was seen [ὤφθη] by me" (1 Cor. 15:8 [cf. vv. 5–7]), and in 2 Cor. 4:6 itself Paul combines: "light," "shining," and "glory." In Acts Paul combines (according to Luke): "light," "shining," and "glory" as he "saw" (εἶδον) the Lord (cf. 9:3; 22:11; 26:13; see Vorholt, 2008, 215; Harris, 2005, 336–37; Watson, 1997, 283–84; Kim, 1980, 5ff, 229). Hubbard (2002) observes that Paul's language of darkness-to-light is "typical transfer symbolism" for conversion found in various rites of passage, and that such symbolism is also typically conjoined with cosmogonic imagery (159–60).

[64] See note 23 above. Noort, 2005, 17; Wenham, 1987, 18.

[65] Noort, 2005, 17; Watson, 2004, 293; Thrall, 1994, 1.243; Richardson, 1994, 158.

[66] See Nguyen, 2008, 158–65, 174–94. On the shock that Christ's eclipse of Moses would have held for many of Paul's fellow diaspora Jews see Barclay, 1996A, 386–87, 426–28. Cf. Acts 21:21.

knowledge of God's glory in the face of Jesus Christ." One can compare the more overt similarities between Gen. 1:2–3 and 2 Cor. 4:6 as follows:

Gen. 1:2–3	2 Cor. 4:6
Darkness [σκότος] was over the deep	It is the God who said [ὁ θεὸς ὁ εἰπών]
And God said [εἶπεν ὁ θεός]	out of darkness [ἐκ σκότους]
Let light come about [γενηθήτω φῶς]	Light will shine [φῶς λάμψει]
And light came about [ἐγένετο φῶς]	he shone... light [ὃς ἔλαμψεν... φωτισμὸν]

Paul's wording is evocative of Genesis.[67] At the same time, the divine word which Paul records – "Light will shine" (4:6a) – has a more prophetic tone than seems obvious in the divine imperative of Genesis. It is therefore tempting to see Paul's statement of divine activity, "he shone... light" (4:6b), as the direct fulfilment of "Light *will* shine." Yet while between the last two clauses of Gen. 1:3 there is immediate fulfilment, between Paul's last two clauses there is a lengthy historical gap. The best way for us to avoid the opposite errors of denying the clear allusion to Gen. 1:3 and of treating it as an allusion to *only* Gen. 1:3 (i.e., without recognizing its other layer of complexity) is to briefly comment on each of Paul's phrases in 4:6 in the order in which he wrote them.

"The God who said...." Although many OT texts speak of God's causation (or promise) of light out of darkness, not all draw attention to the sovereignty of God's *word* as does Gen. 1:3.[68] This effective word was also central to Philo's interpretation of Gen. 1:3. For Paul too, his theocentric introduction, "The God who said... 'Light'" (ὁ θεὸς ὁ εἰπών... φῶς), is the clearest indication that Paul is intentionally casting the minds of his readers back to the beginning where "God said... 'Light'" (εἶπεν ὁ

---

[67] As Minear (1994) writes, "Paul viewed the moment of a person's conversion as marking the first day of creation, when God commanded light to shine out of darkness" (74; cf. Balla, 2007, 762–64).

[68] Concerning the original creation of light cf. Job 37:15 and Isa. 45:7. Concerning the light-motif subsequent to the original creation: judgment is often seen as God's *de*-creation of light – e.g., removing the sun and moon of Gen. 1:14–19, even the light of Gen. 1:3 itself (Jer. 4:23; 13:16; Eze. 32:7–8; cf. Mark 13:24–25) – while salvation is then often *re*-creation – e.g., re-entering light and life into darkness and death. So, although people walk "in darkness" (ἐν σκότει) and dwell "in the shadow of death" (σκιᾷ θανάτου), the prophet announces that "light will shine [φῶς λάμψει] upon them" (Isa. 9:1). God promises, "I will make [ποιήσω] for them the darkness into light [τὸ σκότος εἰς φῶς]" (Isa. 42:16). This re-creation of light can even be non-solar and non-lunar, reflecting the situation in Gen. 1:3–13 where light existed before and without luminaries. In Isaiah 59–60, God's people will themselves be "enlightened" (φωτίζου), not by sun or moon but by "the light" (τὸ φῶς), i.e., "the glory of the Lord" (ἡ δόξα κυρίου), the Lord himself being their "everlasting light" (φῶς αἰώνιον) through the presence of his Spirit (see Isa. 59:21–60:21; cf. Rev. 20:22–25).

θεός... φῶς),⁶⁹ thus evoking Gen. 1:2–3.⁷⁰ This is especially the case as it closely follows Paul's application of Gen. 1:27 in v. 4.⁷¹ Recognizing the power of the divine speech will help us avoid the error of "abandoning" Gen. 1:3 as Paul's referent and turning to an *alternative* text, such as Isa. 9:1 (in which God is not the speaker).⁷²

"...out of darkness...." Many texts in Paul's scripture, whether referring to God's original creation of light or to a re-creation of light as salvation, reflect a scenario like that in Gen. 1:2–3: there was or is a darkness over which God proved and proves to be sovereign.⁷³ Paul does likewise, for it is "out of darkness" that God's voice sounds toward light.⁷⁴ This cosmic scenario of a present darkness that is assumed by Paul's picture of God's voice should grant hope to his contemporary Corinthians since not even the power of "the god of this age," who presently exerts this power by bringing dark blindness onto the minds of unbelievers (4:4), can prevent the God who created light out of the original darkness from granting illumination to such minds and hearts now (4:6).⁷⁵ Paul knows from the text of

---

⁶⁹ Meyer (2009) calls this verbal correspondence between "said" in Gen. 1:3 and 2 Cor. 4:6 "too close to be coincidental" (109 n. 161; cf. Hubbard, 2002, 160).

⁷⁰ The list of scholars who see Gen. 1:3 behind 2 Cor. 4:6 is a long one: e.g., Vorholt, 2008, 214–15, 214 n. 58, 218–19; Watson, 2004, 312–13 (*idem*, 1997, 282); Matera, 2003, 103–04; Thrall, 1994, 315 (*eadem*, 1973, 145); Minear, 1994, 74; Witherington, 1994, 233; Hays, 1993, 152–53; Newman, 1992, 221; Scroggs, 1966, 96–97.

⁷¹ See Nguyen, 2008, 178; Scroggs, 1966, 97. See chapter 3 below on Paul's interprettation of Gen. 1:27 in 2 Cor. 4:4.

⁷² Contra Collange, 1972, 138–39. Isa. 9:1 (LXX), often offered as another source for Paul's wording here (e.g., esp. Collange, 1972, 138–39; cf. Meyer, 2009, 108–09; Harris, 2005, 334 n. 95; Matera, 2003, 104; Hubbard, 2002, 160; Hays, 1993, 152–53; Stockhausen, 1989, 160n 21), does not in itself provide the divine speech motif in the way that Genesis 1 does. In Isaiah 9 it is the prophet's own words which promise the people who were in darkness that "A light will shine upon you!" The addressees of Isa. 9:1–6 LXX are difficult to follow, but it is Isaiah himself speaking throughout: announcing the light to "the people" in v. 1, then speaking *to* God in v. 2, then speaking in general (i.e., *about* the people and *about* the Lord – both in third person) in vv. 3–4, and then *among* the people as one of the "us" in vv. 5–6: "A child has been born *to us*...," thereby obviously not representing God's own speech. Although it is certainly possible that Paul could cast any scripture as God's speech (e.g., as "God's word"), a connection with God's overt speaking in relation to light and darkness in Gen. 1:3 is a more ready conceptual link with Paul's statement, "the God who said" in 4:6a than is Isa. 9:1. This is *not* an argument that Isa. 9:1 is *not* part of what is behind Paul's statement in 2 Cor. 4:6a, especially in view of the wording "light will shine" (φῶς λάμψει). Below I will also note that Isa. 9:1 was probably influential. But this observation of divine speech is the strongest argument against Collange's "abandonment" of Gen. 1:3 as being behind 2 Cor. 4:6a.

⁷³ See note 68 above.

⁷⁴ So Meyer, 2009, 108.

⁷⁵ Matera, 2003, 103.

creation that it is precisely out of the heart of darkness that the Creator's glorious light can shine.

"...'Light will shine'...." When turning the Corinthians (yet again) to the text of the Beginning, why did Paul not simply quote God as recorded: "Let light come about"? Some will use this wording to distance Paul's statement from the text of Genesis, as if the word "shine" is too unlike what Genesis describes for Gen. 1:3 to be behind Paul's account.[76] Yet the word "shine" (λάμπω) itself can naturally and accurately capture what light did in Genesis 1. For example, one might notice how Ben Sira refers to Gen. 1:14–19 by using the language of "glory... *shining*... illuminating" (δόξα... ἐκλάμπων... φωτίζων, 43:8–9) and compare this with Paul's language of "*shone*... illumination... glory" (ἔλαμψεν... φωτισμόν... τῆς δόξης) in 2 Cor. 4:6.[77] Also, as we have seen in his formal commentary on Genesis 1, Philo himself glosses the specific text of Gen. 1:3 with light "out-*shining*" (λαμπρότερον) and "out-*radiating*" (αὐγοειδέστερον) (*Op.* 30), and one could compare Paul's combination of terms in 2 Cor. 4:6 where light "*shines*" (λάμψει, v. 6) and "*radiates*" (αὐγάσαι, v. 4). On the level of word-choice, Paul's terms in 2 Cor. 4:6 are perfectly apt and were already used formally as descriptors for what happened in Gen. 1:2–3.

Paul does seem to reword God's speech with a slightly prophetic nuance, however.[78] It rings like a promise for the future rather than as a sim-

---

[76] See Collange, 1972, 138–39.

[77] This comment in Sirach 43 is clearly a reference to Gen. 1:14–19 (see vv. 1–10; Tigchelaar, 2005, 37, 37–39; cf. Thiselton, 2000, 1268–69).

[78] Concerning the prophetic ring to Paul's record of God's word, Isaiah speaks in 9:1 (LXX) of how "light will shine upon you" (φῶς λάμψει ἐφ' ὑμᾶς), and this seems to be connected to the arrival of the person of the Messiah in vv. 5–6. The light motif itself is dropped after v. 1, and thus "light" is not directly connected to the actual mention of the Messiah, but Paul shares Isaiah's focus on "the Christ." Unlike Isa. 9:1–6, Paul does directly (verbally, not merely conceptually) connect "the Christ" to the light shining in human hearts. Yet as mentioned above, Isa. 9:1 does not offer the motif of divine speech that is central to Paul's statement in 4:6a and that is so evocative of Gen. 1:3.

We should be wary of attempts to set Isaiah and Genesis against each other as mutually exclusive "sources" of Paul's thought (well said in Meyer, 2009, 109 n. 161), especially due to the seemingly widespread hermeneutic in ancient Judaism (and certainly in Paul) which assumed the accord of all scriptures (van der Horst, 2006, 114–27; Kugel, 1998, 14–19). Genesis and Isaiah both show profound influence on Paul's thought, especially in his debates with the Corinthians. Our first assumption should be that Paul has a "mutually interpretive" hermeneutic (so Stockhausen, 1989, 60), especially where words and phrases are exchanged such as here (161; cf. Hays, 1993, 152–53). Thus without denying their original origin and assumed fulfillment in the beginning (in Genesis), Paul nevertheless sets the creative words of God in a slightly enhanced prophetic (Isaianic) tone. The combination of a primarily cosmogonic reference (Gen. 1:2–3) with a prophetic nuance toward salvation in the Messiah (Isa. 9:1) answers the difficulty that each side of the debate has faced. That is, why does Paul use Isaiah's wording if he is really referring

ple pronouncement, though this distinction is itself somewhat inappropriate, even for Gen. 1:3.[79] It is as if Paul treats the creative word as pending until its enactment in Christian hearts. The initial fulfilment of God's voiced desire occurred in the beginning when light originally shone. The same effect would have been accomplished had Paul said something like: "God said, 'Let there be light,' and there was light in our hearts." The latter *appears* to directly fulfil the former, but by evoking the creation account it is clear that this is not exactly the case. Paul has created, however, an intimate connection between God's speech in the beginning and the Christian experience in the end.

For both Genesis 1 and Paul, God's desired action is followed by an enactment that mirrors God's desire:

		God's Desired Action		Enactment
Gen. 1:3	God said	"Become light"	→	Light became
2 Cor. 4:6	The God who said	"Light will shine"	→	He shone light

As in Genesis itself, for Paul there is a direct correlation between what God speaks and what comes about. Perhaps encouraged by Isaiah, who not only links darkness and light in 9:1 but who elsewhere announces salvation in the language and conceptuality of Genesis 1–2,[80] Paul presents God's creative shining as a paradigm for the subsequent salvific shining. The theme of creation gives meaning, emphasis, and a theocentric source to the Christ-follower's experience of heart-illumination.[81]

---

to Genesis, yet why does Paul focus on the divine speech (as in Genesis) if he is really referring to Isaiah (which does not have God speaking)? With this construal of Paul's logic we may also maintain Paul's own emphasis on divine speech (and thus *primarily* Gen. 1:3) and Paul's subtle nod towards the promise of the Messiah (and thus a *nuance* of Isa. 9:1).

[79] Future indicatives (such as in 2 Cor. 4:6a) can function as imperatives (cf. Lev. 19:18; so Harris, 2005, 334), and this in itself blurs the line between a "futuristic" statement such as prophecy and an effective imperative such as in God's creation. In fact, within the Pentateuch the aorist imperatives of γίνομαι in Gen. 1:3 (γενηθήτω), 6 (γενηθήτω), and 14 (γενηθήτωσαν) are comparable with other records of prophetic pronouncments (all recorded by Moses, according to Paul): e.g., Gen. 9:27 (γενηθήτω), 49:17 (γενηθήτω), and Ex. 9:9 (γενηθήτω) (for interest cf. Ex. 10:21–22 [γενηθήτω σκότος... καὶ ἐγένετο σκότος] with Gen. 1:3 [γενηθήτω φῶς καὶ ἐγένετο φῶς]). According to Paul's view of Mosaic authorship of the whole Pentateuch, the language of Genesis 1 and the prophetic language mentioned above would likely cohere much more closely for him than for many modern scholars. These observations limit the assumption of Collange (1972, 139) that the change of aorist imperative to a future indicative in 2 Cor. 4:6a somehow distances Paul's statement from Gen. 1:3.

[80] E.g., Isa. 45:7–8 (cf. Isa. 43:1a and 44:2: ὁ θεὸς ὁ ποιήσας... ὁ πλάσας).

[81] So Becker, 1993, 77 ("the calling experienced is the repetition of the beginning of creation"); Hubbard, 2002, 160.

Yet even this construal of *creation* as paradigmatic for *salvation* does not quite take full account of Paul's language. As already noted, Paul also seems to use the *salvifically* charged words from Isaiah to express God's *creation* of light (v. 6a). Before we therefore construe Paul's understanding of Gen. 1:3 as itself "salvific" or "redemptive,"[82] however, we should recognize that the "Isaianic" phrase in Paul – "light will shine" – is only salvific by association. That is, there is nothing inherently "salvific" about the actual words "light will shine." Yet such a choice gloss of Gen. 1:3 does seem to hint that this very God of the original shining of light *also* had something to do with the Isaianic promise of salvation by light. This complex relationship between creation and salvation as distinct acts which are yet related actions would be confirmed if Paul's focus were actually on the actor himself rather than directly on the actions. And this is precisely the case. Paul's explicit emphasis is on "the God who," the *God* who both spoke and shone light. *That* Creator has now again shone (re-creationally, salvifically) in our dark and blinded hearts, just as Isaiah foretold.

This explanation of Paul's choice of wording sharpens our focus on the central element of Paul's reading of Gen. 1:2–3. What unites creation and salvation for Paul, here centered around the motif of light, is not the nature of *both* events as creational-salvific (for 2 Cor. 4:6 does not really convey creation itself as redemptive) but rather the fact that *both* are acts of *the same God*.[83] Paul demonstrated the connection between creation and salvation in 4:6a by his use of a theocentric substantival participle, "the God who said" (ὁ θεὸς ὁ εἰπών), a practice done by many others.[84] Paul con-

---

[82] As Stockhausen (1989) does (161), though her notion of "mutual interpretation" is a good first stage in understanding Paul's hermeneutical dynamics here (and elsewhere) (160n 21, 161 [cf. p. 60]; cf. Meyer, 2009, 109).

[83] Harris, 2005, 335; Childs, 1992, 392. This emphasis on the God and Lord of both creation and redemption as the tie that binds them together is a major thesis of Gibbs, 1971, though he approaches the issue through an analysis of different texts: Rom. 8:19–23, 38–39; Rom. 5:12–21; 1 Cor. 8:6; Phil. 2:6–11; Col. 1:15–20; and Eph. 1:3–14.

[84] Psalm 145 (LXX) uses the language of Genesis 1 to set covenant/salvation in creation-language, and it uses substantival participles to explain the God of both activities: "the God of Jacob" (v. 5 = election/salvation) is *"the one who* made [τὸν ποιήσαντα] the heaven and the earth, the sea and all that is in them" (v. 6 = creation; cf. Gen. 1:1, 6–10, 20–24) and is *"the one who* makes [ποιοῦντα] justice for those wronged," etc. (vv. 7–9 = salvation). The later divine event of personal covenantal aid is cast in the language of the former divine event of creation – "the one who made…makes" – thus granting a better understanding of the salvific event as well as the God who accomplished it. This is the same method Isaiah 45 (LXX) takes to emphasize God in both creation and salvation/election: although "darkness" (σκότος) was engulfing "the unconstructed earth" (ἡ γῆ… ἀκατασκεύαστος) in Gen. 1:2, nonetheless God is *"the one who* constructed light [ὁ κατασκευάσας φῶς] and *who* made darkness [καὶ ποιήσας σκότος]" (v. 7 = creation), and is *"the one who* created" Israel (ὁ κτίσας σε, v. 8 = cove-

firms his emphasis on God himself by his use of the relative pronoun "who" (ὅς: "he," "himself") in 4:6b. Even when referring to the inward and anthropic illumination Paul does not speak of a light abstractly shining on people (as does Isa. 9:1), but rather of the Creator himself who actively caused it to shine (as in Gen. 1:3): "the *God* who said... *himself* [ὅς] shone." In this sense it is not even actually God's *word* upon which Paul has brought focus, though the speech of God is an explicit and prominent part of Paul's reading of Gen. 1:3. In Paul's construal of the creation of light there is no hint of God's word taking on a quasi-disconnected identity from God, a conclusion toward which some of Philo's language can tend. God's word is vital, but it is precisely because it is from "the *God* who said" it that it holds significance.

Within the situation of darkness and blindness (4:4, 6a; as in Gen. 1:2; as in Isa. 9:1a), for Paul the important thing is "the God who...." God's character as Creator had been of central importance to Philo, having enabled him to apply God's actions in creation to contemporary experience and even salvation.[85] In 2 Cor. 4:6, Paul moves from the same starting point and in a similar direction. It is the God of creation whose being, word, and act give structure and heightened significance to the communication of this same God's subsequent redemptive actions in Christ. Below we will notice a similar trend in Paul's reading of Gen. 1:6–31 in 1 Cor. 15:37–41 where he uses the text's protological conceptuality – the "word-field of creation"[86] – to apply the fundamental concept of God as Creator in the beginning to a description of the resurrection of the dead in the end.

A few items may be drawn out in summary of Paul's reading of Gen. 1:2–5, especially in comparison with Philo's formal commentary on these verses. For Paul, as for Philo, God's "shining" of light in Gen. 1:2–5 is something special. Gen. 1:3 itself provides a creative paradigm wherein the beginning of the created thing – light, in the paradigmatic instance, and

---

nant/salvation; cf. Isa. 43:1a; 44:2; 2 Mac. 1:24–25 [see Childs, 1992, 387–88]). This participial presentation of "the God who" expresses both his creative and salvific acts through creational terms. Likewise, other early Christians (as recorded by Luke) used substantival participles to focus their prayer upon "the God who," and they began with creation: "*the one who* made [ὁ ποιήσας] the heaven and the earth [cf. Gen. 1:1] and the sea [cf. Gen. 1:9–10] and all that is in them [cf. Gen. 1:11–13, 14–19, 20–27], *the one who* said [ὁ... εἰπών] through the mouth of our father David by the Holy Spirit..." (vv. 24–25; see Noort on this feature of other prayers, 2000, 2; cf. Job 10:8–9). 2 Cor. 4:6 is comparable.

[85] In *Aet.* 1 Philo writes, "In every uncertain and important business it is proper to invoke God, because he is the good Creator of the world, and because nothing is uncertain with him who is possessed of the most accurate knowledge of all things" (Yonge's translation); cf. Frick, 1999, 1–4.

[86] Usami, 1976, 480 n. 45.

then the rest of the world – perfectly accords with God's sovereign will and word. As it had been in Philo's treatment of Gen. 1:2–5, in Paul's as well this beginning of light is paradigmatic for subsequent shinings that God will accomplish in like manner. Philo related the shining of Gen. 1:2–3 to the subsequent textual shining of heavenly bodies in Gen. 1:14–19. The beginning of light was the ontological paradigm for similar, though necessarily dimmer, luminaries. Paul related Gen. 1:2–3 to a subsequent shining, but Paul's was the historical shining in the hearts of believers who recognized God's glory in the risen body of Jesus. For Paul, the beginning of light was the conceptual paradigm for glorious Christian illumination.

Thus for Paul, as for Philo, there is an intimate relationship between the text of Gen. 1:2–5 and personal illumination. For both interpreters the connection between text and experience was primarily theological: *God* is the actor in both events. In the beginning of light, God's word is both prominent and sovereign for Paul as it had been for Philo. For Philo, this theocentricity primarily involved God's fore-knowledge and wisdom, and it was according to these that he created light beautifully in the beginning. By this creation God pre-emptively saved humanity from darkness as well as by his anthropogonic gift (i.e., at the creation of humans) of mental illumination. By God's fore-knowledge and wisdom he also continues to save by shining on those who repent. For Paul, his theocentricity involves "the God who" both created light by word and saves by light through Paul's preaching (which Paul also relates to "God's word," 2 Cor. 4:2) about the glorious face of Jesus Christ, the Lord.

In spite of (and in light of) all these hermeneutical similarities between Philo and Paul, two fundamental differences have emerged. First, for Philo God's salvation by light was sometimes (though not always) God's ontological-intellectual gift to humans at creation itself. For Paul, although God's salvation by light similarly took place within humans (in their hearts, toward knowledge), it was divinely performed not ontologically at creation but in a subsequent (explicitly post-Mosaic) historical act. These hermeneutical bents in each interpreter are reminiscent of what we saw in chapter 1, where Philo saw the Before as an ontologically perfect blueprint of the universe while Paul saw it as pre-marked out historically salvific events.[87]

---

[87] Barclay (1996A) and Leonhardt-Balzer (2009) make observations on other aspects of Philo's thinking that nevertheless confirm his hermeneutical tendency mentioned above. Barclay points out Philo's tendency to "dehistoricize," e.g., the patriarchal narratives (170) and even characters (170 n. 98). Leonhardt-Balzer demonstrates Philo's tendency to replace the historical and eschatological aspects of the "doctrine of the two Spirits" (of which, she argues, Philo seems to be aware) with anthropological aspects toward present and personal morality (129–47).

Second, for Philo the pure ontological radiance of Gen. 1:3 – i.e., the "image" of God's word – began to dim when it descended into bodily form (in sun, moon, and stars) just as God's "salvific" luminescence is dimmed to the extent that it is blended with flesh and its bodily desires. For Paul there is no trace of dimming when the God who spoke light into being in Gen. 1:3 shines another light through the face of Jesus – i.e., the "image" of God – even though this "face" is corporeal. For Paul, the Jesus in whom the Creator of light shines his glory is not a faceless reflector of eternal light. Paul is not referring to a radiation from an un-embodied glory unsullied by this physical world. This physical (even crucified, though resurrected) embodiment of God's glory is so *un*-dimming of the original light that Paul can portray his dawning in human hearts *almost* as if it is the actual divine enactment of the initial divine word in the beginning.

In 2 Cor. 4:6, as well as in 1 Cor. 15:35–49 (see below), we receive a glimpse of the general principle to which scholars often refer, that eschatology mirrors protology.[88] Some have seen eschatology (or at least teleology) within Genesis 1 itself.[89] By analyzing in some detail how Paul actually interprets the Beginning (in connection with the Before), especially in light of how his interpretation is similar to and different from that of his contemporary commentator Philo, a greater clarity should be dawning as to how exactly the Beginning gives to Paul his "framework,"[90] "format,"[91] or "model"[92] for contemplating and understanding something about the End. Though it would certainly be fruitful for another study to explore what might cause Paul to highlight the particular aspects of the Beginning that he does – since he does not highlight every aspect – it is most important for this present study to recognize that, so far, the primary hermeneutical direction of Paul's thought is that "the original creation provides the conceptuality for describing the new creation,"[93] not the other way around. Many scholars focus on Paul's description of the new creation. But without a proper understanding of how Paul understands the "model" or "framework" for the new creation – i.e., the original creation – the research on the new creation is highly susceptible, to say the least, to misunderstanding the New. The present study is sharpening our understanding of the first half of Paul's dynamic: his interpretation of the "original creation." As will be further confirmed and filled out in what follows in the second half of this

---

[88] Watson, 1997, 282; Minear, 1994, 74. Cf. also 1 Cor. 11:12c with 2 Cor. 5:17–18.
[89] E.g., Sailhamer, 1990, 23; Mathews, 1996, 126–27; Watson, 1994, 138; Childs, 1992, 385–86.
[90] Westermann, 1987, 13.
[91] Hardy, 1997, 110–11.
[92] Collins, 1999, 25–26.
[93] Watson, 1997, 282; cf. Moffatt, 1938, 261; Adams, 2002, 35.

chapter (and then even moreso in chapter 3), for Paul the original is not left behind because of the new; the original actually provides a maintained conceptuality for the new.

2.3 Philo and Paul on Genesis 1:6–31
Six Days of Ontic Order and Divine Design

As we saw above, Gen. 1:3 and 4 opened to the reader two of the major themes of Genesis 1 as a whole. One, the Creator is sovereign in his actions and desires as he summons and makes what he wants. Two, his creation is ontologically good due to its exact correspondence with his desire. Genesis 1:3 had established a direct (and syntactically paradigmatic) connection between God's word and its fulfilment, and this is followed in the second to sixth days. For example, God's second voiced volition, "Let there be a firmness" (v. 6a), is followed by a fulfilment clause, "And it happened in this manner" (v. 6c). This is then followed by God's own enactment, "And God made the firmness" (v. 7). This portrayal of God's first post-light creation (and the rest of his creative works are similar) strongly reinforces the notion established in vv. 3–4: God's action does indeed directly fulfil his word and therefore desire.

As we now turn to Philo's and then Paul's treatments of this record of the beginning of the world, it will become evident that both interpreters draw out each of these major creational themes. In chapter 1 we analyzed Philo's and Paul's explicit statements about what God was thinking "before" he created, and I drew attention to a few of the ways that their theories of the Before affected (and yet were also affected by) their readings of the Beginning. As we now focus on each interpreter's reading of the post-light beginning of the world, I will point out how both the commentator and the apostle continue to draw attention to God's purposes and desires because of which he created the world as he did. It will also be evident that both interpreters see within Genesis 1 a theocentrically grounded and therefore good ontology. A major aspect of this theocentrism, for both readers, is the divine Before that initiates the world in the Beginning.

2.3.1 Philo's Reading of Genesis 1:6–31 (Op. 36–68)

The "transition from intelligible to sense-perceptible," as Philo explains, necessarily causes a "dimming" in the incorporeal light. Thus one might expect Philo to present a somewhat dark reading of Gen. 1:6–31, the creation of the ontologically less pure corporeality. Yet his interpretation of

vv. 6–31 is very positive.⁹⁴ Though Philo certainly has an anthropocentric slant to creation, he nevertheless reads the corporeal creation positively primarily because it is *God's* creation.⁹⁵ Throughout vv. 6–31, Philo focuses upon God: his character, fore-sight, decision-making perfection; in short, God's wisdom. God knows what he is doing, and that makes all of the peculiarities of Genesis 1 "good."

(a) The Second Day, Philo on Genesis 1:6–8 (*Op.* 36–37)

It was very important to Philo, as we have seen, that on the second day God created a "firmament," or "firmness." While the Hebrew word "expanse" (רקיע v. 6) may have portrayed God as something like a divine "metal-worker,"⁹⁶ "solidity" is not necessarily inherent in the term.⁹⁷ But the LXX's use of "firmament" (στερέωμα) solidifies the "heaven" of vv. 6–8 as something "firm."⁹⁸ Philo finds in the word "firmness" the initiation of the world of sense perception (found in vv. 6–31, according to his first reading in §§13–128), as opposed to the noetic, incorporeal world of the Ideas (found in vv. 1–5).⁹⁹ Looking "toward" (πρός) that incorporeal paradigm of vv. 1–5,¹⁰⁰ "the Craftsman" begins the sense-perceptible

---

⁹⁴ Radice, 2009, 145.
⁹⁵ On Philo's "fundamental anthropocentric approach" to creation in *Op.* see Runia, 2001, 204, 211. On his "strong anthropocentric emphasis" on luminaries in particular see Runia, 2001, 197, 204, 206. Though Runia nuances this anthropocentricity with theocentricity at p. 199, this is mainly in reference to Philo's explicit theocentric statement in *Op.* 61 (see below) and is not functionally an acknowledgment of a more general theocentric hermeneutic. I will highlight Philo's more general theocentric reading.
⁹⁶ Currid, 1997, 67.
⁹⁷ Delitzsch, 1894, 85–86; Rösel, 1994, 36. Harris, 1980, 2217b.
⁹⁸ The LXX's choice "firmness" could be due to influence of Egyptian cosmogony (Currid, 1997, 64), or perhaps to that of Platonism (cf. *Tim.* 31b; Rösel, 1994, 36, 82), though since Plato sees "earth" as inherent in "firmness" (στερεόν, *Tim.* 31b7–8) while Gen. 1:6–8 refers specifically to "heaven," the latter option is not as viable.
⁹⁹ In chapter 1 I pointed out how Philo's exegesis of Gen. 2:4–5 (in *Op.* 129–30) causes him to backtrack over his own previous interpretation of Genesis 1 and to re-read Genesis 1 *as a whole* to be the incorporeal paradigm. Unfortunately for us, he does not then re-comment on the "firmness" of 1:6.
¹⁰⁰ The phrase "toward the paradigm" is Platonic (cf. *Tim.* 28a-29a), but seems to be part of a larger (and later) philosophic system of prepositional metaphysics (see Cox, 2005, 49–51, 49 n. 49, 51 n. 54). On Philo's own prepositional metaphysic see *Cher.* 124–27 (no mention of "toward which") and *Prov.* 1.23 (replaces "because of which" with "toward which"); *Leg.* 3.96, *Fug.* 12, and *Somn.* 2.45 where the Logos is both paradigm and instrument; cf. *Cher.* 28; *Sacr.* 8; *Deus* 57; *Conf.* 62; *Migr.* 6; *Fug.* 95; *Spec.* 1.81. On the key texts on prepositional metaphysics compare Aristotle (e.g., *Met.* 7.7; *Phys.* 2.3–9; cf. *Met.* A 3, 983b 7, as cited in Norden, 1923, 242 n. 2; cf. Tobin, 1983, 68–69 n. 39), Middle Platonism (cf. Sterling, 1997, 220–21; Siegert, 2009, 184,

cosmos in v. 6 by making the corporeal heaven (§36.1–3). The "firmness" (στερέωμα) is obviously corporeal (σωματικόν) because the body (τὸ σῶμα) is "by nature firm" (φύσει στερεόν).[101] Some modern scholars have difficulty relating "heaven" in 1:1 to "heaven" in 1:6–8 and thus treat v. 1 as an overarching summary and vv. 6–8 as the actual creation.[102] Philo also differentiates the two textual "heavens," but his resolution is ontological rather than literary: bodiless vs. body rather than introduction vs. body.

In §36, the Craftsman's title "Firmness" for heaven is "correct" and "suitable" (§36.6, 11; cf. Gen. 1:8), because it is bodily and distinguished from the noetic.[103] Likewise, God's label of this firmness as "heaven" is "a highly appropriate title" (§37), for οὐρανός accurately conveys the thing's character. This divine quality of knowing and acting in perfect propriety, here only subtly presented, becomes more hermeneutically prominent in Philo's exegesis of the third day of creation in vv. 9–13.

(b) The Third Day, Philo on Genesis 1:9–13 (*Op.* 38–44)

The third day contains two creative acts. In vv. 9–10 God forms dry land. In vv. 11–13 God summons plants, fruit, and seeds. We will look at each.

(i) On vv. 9–10: Primordial Ooze, Good Land (*Op.* 38–39)

When the sacred text says, "Let the waters be gathered...and let the dry land be seen" (v. 9), it may seem natural to picture a primeval ocean. In fact, many ancient cosmogonies did understand the primordial earth to have been enveloped in or characterized by water: Mesopotamian (e.g.,

---

184 n. 23; Runia, 1986, 171–74; Tobin, 1983, 67–71), and Seneca (van Kooten, 2003, 123–24; Tobin, 1983, 68 n. 37; Cox, 2005, 51–52).

[101] In *Tim.* 31b, "the becoming thing" is necessarily (δεῖ) "body-like" (σωματοειδές), "visible" (ὁρατόν), and "tangible" (ἁπτόν) (31b5), but nothing is "tangible" without "firmness" (στερεοῦ), and "firmness" (στερεόν) must have "earth" (31b7–8). This relationship between "firmness" and the "body-like" cosmos may be behind Philo's ontological assumption that "this sense-perceptible and body-like [σωματιοειδῆ] thing" is appropriately "called 'firmness' [στερέωμα]" (36.10–11). Yet, as noted above, Plato assumes "earth" is a necessary constituent of "firmness," while Philo here deals with "heaven." Also, as we look ahead to Paul's use of "dusty" versus "heavenly" in 1 Cor. 15:45–49, in light of Philo's labels of "corporeal" for "heaven," one would need to be careful indeed to legitimately use a material-immaterial dichotomy when differentiating "earth"/"earthly" from "heaven"/"heavenly" (so Martin, 1992, 3–15, esp. 13–14).

[102] E.g., Skinner, 1910, 4, 13–14; von Rad, 1956, 47; Westermann, 1984, 96–97.

[103] It is sometimes difficult to know whether Philo commends God for using a particular word or Moses for recording it in such a way. Here, however, the Demiurge is the subject of "made," and there is no reason to assume a switch of subjects. (So also Runia, 2001, 175; though cf. 176).

Tiamat and Apsu in the Babylonian *Enuma Elish*),[104] Egyptian (e.g., Ptah, who is Nun [primordial waters], in the Shabakah Stone of Memphite theology),[105] Canaanite (e.g., Yamm in the Ugaritic Baal cycle),[106] and Grecian (e.g., Okeanos in Homer's *Iliad*).[107] Whether Genesis 1 borrowed from any of these has long been debated in modern scholarship.[108] In his commentary on Genesis 1, Philo somewhat distances Genesis from such conceptions. He was certainly aware of such construals. For example, he related how certain Stoics considered primordial "chaos" as water (*Aet.* 18; see below), some reasoning that the name "Chaos" (χάος) derived from χύσις, "what is poured out" (χέω, "to pour").

In *Op.* 38, Philo does not treat the pre-formed state as simply water, but more as a mass of paste-like mud. Since the text specifies that *dry* land (ἡ ξηρά) was to appear, perhaps some sort of *wet* land – like mud or paste – was already visible. Philo calls this biblical situation "indistinct" (ἀδιάκριτον) and "formless" (ἄμορφον) (§38.7). These two α-privative descriptors of the "primal ooze or mud"[109] are reminiscent of Philo's description of the "pre-cosmic chaos"[110] in §§8–9 and 21–22, which are themselves reminiscent of some Greek cosmogonic accounts, Plato himself, and Genesis 1.[111] Such Philonic descriptions of creation as found in *Op.* 8–9 and 21–22 have prompted debates contrasting creation from pre-

---

[104] Bremmer, 2005, 76; Currid, 1997, 55 n. 13; Batto, 1992, 32–34.
[105] Currid, 1997, 60–61.
[106] Currid, 1997, 54 n. 8.
[107] Bremmer, 2005, 76.
[108] So Gunkel, 1984 (reprint of 1895), 26; von Rad, 1956, 48; Bremmer, 2005, 76; Batto, 1992, 32–34; critiqued in Tsumura, 2005, 14–15, 43, 56–57; Noort, 2000, 8; Clifford, 1994, 140–41; Wenham, 1987, 16; Westermann, 1984, 105–6; Kidner, 1967, 45.
[109] Runia, 2001, 181.
[110] Dillon, 2005, 99.
[111] Note Philo's cosmogonic alpha-privative descriptors in §9: "the passive thing" is "soul-less" (ἄψυχον) and "un-moving" (ἀκίνητον), and in §22: the "substance which of itself had no beauty" is "un-ordered" (ἄτακτος), "quality-less" (ἄποιος), "soul-less" (ἄψυχος), <"dis-similar" (ἀνόμοιος)>, "inconsistent" (ἑτεροιότητος), "non-adjusted" (ἀναρμοστίας), "dis-harmonious" (ἀσυμφωνίας). Cf. Plato's use of cosmogonic alpha-privatives in *Tim.* 30a: "disorderly motion" (κινούμενον... ἀτάκτως) and "disorder" (ἀταξίας), and in 53ab: "the dissimilar things" (τὰ ἀνομοιότατα) (Dillon, 2005, 99). Cf. the use of cosmogonic alpha-privatives in Gen. 1:2: "in-visible" (ἀόρατος) and "un-organized" (ἀκατασκεύαστος) (cf. Philo's cosmogonic statement in *Spec.* 4.187, which is closer to Genesis 1 [creation by word, "light out of darkness," "likeness"] than is often realized). Runia (2001) relates Philo's comment to "many Greek cosmogonic accounts" (181). Creation therefore often takes the form of "division." The beginning of Diodorus Siculus' cosmogonic account, *Universal History* (quoted in Runia, 181), is in this way strikingly similar to an ancient Chinese cosmogony called *Huai Nan Tzu* (quoted in Lee, 1993, 191, n. 6). Cf. also Philo's *Her.* 134–35, where the "divisions" are reminiscent of Genesis 1 (Radice, 2009, 139).

existent matter and *ex nihilo*. Such debates in Philonic studies have parallels among studies on Genesis 1, other early Jewish writings, and early Christianity.[112] For example, some think Genesis 1 explains the origin of the watery mass[113] while others do not.[114] Some see a similar debate among ancient Jews themselves: e.g., between Wis. 11:17, which claims that God's hand "created [κτίσασα] the world *out of formless matter* [ἐξ ἀμόρφου ὕλης]," and 2 Mac. 7:28, which asserts that "it was *out of non-being* [ἐξ οὐκ ὄντων] that God made [ἐποίησεν] these things."[115]

This context is relevant not least because in *Op.* 38 Philo writes that in Gen. 1:9 "the entire [body of] water *had been poured out* [ἀνεκέχυτο] into all the earth." Was there a time when the water was not? One might wonder if the Stoic equivalence (as Philo himself recorded it) between "chaos" (χάος) and water (χύσις, i.e., that which is poured out) might in some way lie behind Philo's use of the same basic verb (-χέω) for what God did in v. 9: i.e., the chaotic waters of the beginning were not always there as such but "had been poured out" into all the earth. In this connection, it is helpful to note that in *Aet.* 17–18 Philo uses a combination of Hesiod's *Theogony* 116–17 and Gen. 1:1–2 to prove that the water of "Chaos" had itself been "created." (Philo there equates his own γενητός with Hesiod's γένετ'.)[116] Although in *Op.* 38 Philo does not treat the water of Gen. 1:1–2 itself in

---

[112] Some assert a general absence of *creatio ex nihilo* in Genesis 1, early Judaism, or early Christianity: e.g., Schwarz, 2002, 173; Fergusson, 1998, 12; May, 1994; Clifford and Collins, 1992, 13 (cf. Clifford, 1994, 141); Sacks, 1990, 4; Goldstein, 1983, 307; Winston, 1979, 38–40. For Philonic studies: cf. Radice, 2009, 144–45; Runia, 2001, 152–53 (cf. *idem*, 1986, 289); May, 1994, 9–21; Wolfson, 1947, 1.300–10. *Op.* 38, however, is not typically featured in these discussions.

[113] E.g., Sailhamer, 1992, 82 n. 2; Wenham, 1987, 13; Kidner 1967, 44. For other advocates see the lists in Westermann, 1984, 95 and Wenham, 1987, 13.

[114] E.g., Alter, 1996, 3; van Wolde, 1996A, 15; Westermann, 1984, 96–97; von Rad, 1956, 47; Clarke, 1952, 341; Skinner, 1910, 13–14. For other notable advocates see Westermann, 1984, 95.

[115] On Wis. 11:17 as referring to pre-existent matter see, e.g., Clifford/Collins, 1992, 13; Goldstein, 1983, 307; Winston, 1979, 38. On 2 Mac. 7:28a as referring to *creatio ex nihilo* see e.g., Schwarz, 2002, 172; Mathews, 1996, 141 n. 117; Moo, 1996, 282; Haffner, 1995, 45–46; Jordan, 1979, 122–28; Skinner, 1910, 15; Origen, *Commentarius in Johannem* I.17.103 and *De principiis* ii.1.5. Yet 2 Mac. 7:28a is probably not referring to *creatio ex nihilo* in its full sense. When one notices how in 7:28b "the race of humans" (τὸ τῶν ἀνθρώπων γένος) came about "in the manner" (οὕτω) of v. 28a (i.e., "out of non-being" [ἐξ οὐκ ὄντων]), and then compares that with how in v. 23 God "formed" (ὁ πλάσας) "the genesis of man" (ἀνθρώπου γένεσιν) (cf. Gen. 2:7), then this is highly probable: "non-being" in v. 28a is conceptually synonymous with "dust of the earth."

[116] Whitaker's translation of Hesiod ("First Chaos *was*") and Yonge's translation ("First Chaos did *rule*") both obscure the textual detail on which Philo bases his point: Hesiod asserted that chaos "became" (γένετ'), and was therefore, as Philo puts it, "created" (γενητός).

the same way as he did in *Aet.* 17–18 (for in *Op.* he sees the water of 1:1–2 as the "incorporeal essence of water," see §29), by glossing God's action toward corporeal water in Gen. 1:9 with the pluperfect, "had been poured out" (ἀνεκέχυτο), Philo implies that in *Op.* he can picture such primordial (corporeal) "water"/mud as not always existing as such.

This passage certainly does not resolve all questions regarding Philo's attitude toward primordial matter. *When* the "pouring" happened is unanswerable from what Philo says. It is more important (and discernible) to ask Philo these questions: *By whom* is this "pouring" done? and What was *the result*? The answer to the first is obvious: God. Philo uses a "divine passive" to convey this.[117] Regarding the second, the "becoming" of the "indistinct" and "formless" ooze (§38) was the *result* of the divine "outpouring."[118] Not only is this indistinct and amorphous (chaos-esque) passive mass no challenge to God's ontic uniqueness,[119] but in §38 divine action has actually preceded and caused it.

Although Philo's elaborations sometimes stray from the text, he is here more atuned to the nuances of the sacred text than may at first meet the eye. Throughout §§38–39, Philo incorporates words and phrases from the LXX into his comments,[120] for example:

LXX 1:9	And God said, εἶπεν ὁ θεός	Let the water be gathered συναχθήτω τὸ ὕδωρ	Let the dry land be seen ὀφθήτω ἡ ξηρά
Op. 38	God commands προστάττει ὁ θεός	the water to be gathered τὸ ὕδωρ ἐπισυναχθῆναι	the dry land to appear τὴν ξηρὰν ἀναφανῆναι

Even Philo's specification of "the water" of v. 9 as "salt water," "sweet moisture," "veins," "rivers," and "springs" – which is so obviously an elaboration on the biblical text – is itself prompted by v. 10 where the singu-

---

[117] Runia (2001) compares Philo's verb, "poured out" (ἀναχέω), with his description of the flood in *Abr.* 42–44; *Mos.* 2.63; *QG* 2.18, 19 (181). Philo uses a similar passive in each of these parallels to show that each "pouring out" is done by God; hence they are "divine passives." The biblical account itself uses two passives in Gen. 7:11 to explain the flood (quoted by Philo in *QG* 2.18). Especially interesting for our project is this: behind Philo's passives (noted explicitly in *Abr.* 42–44) lie God's pre-determinations.

[118] In *Op.* 38, the entire water "had been poured out… so as to be" (ἀνεκέχυτο… ὡς εἶναι) swamps and mud. In §§8–9 and 21–22 (cf. *Spec.* 1.327–29) Philo's illustrations merely assume an already present mass that God commandeered so as to "make" it into order. Based on §38 (and *Aet.* 18–19) one may wonder whether Philo envisioned divine action in the background in the other passages as well.

[119] Immediately following Philo's description of the pre-shaped mass in *Op.* 21–22, Philo specifically draws attention to God's status as the One unequivicated Being: "With no one as counselor – for who else was there? – relying only on himself…" (see Leonhardt-Balzer, 2004A, 336–37).

[120] So Runia, 2001, 182.

lar "water" of v. 9 (x2 LXX) is extended into the plural "systems of the waters" (τὰ συστήματα τῶν ὑδάτων). Within this textually stimulated and shaped set of comments, Philo portrays God as the active cause who both fore-knows and preventatively protects his work.

In Genesis 1, the creation is almost totally passive. The only activity attributed to the earth (i.e., "produce," v. 12) is solely in response to God's command (v. 11).[121] Philo downplays the participation of the earth in vv. 10–12 so that even the earth's sprouting in v. 12 he takes as something that God himself does: "*God* caused to grow [ὁ θεὸς... ἀνέφυεν] all kinds of trees" (*Op.* 40.6; cf. 42.2).[122] In §§8–9, Philo had offered what is typically referred to as the doctrine of the two principles: "the active" or "efficacious cause" (τὸ δραστήριον αἴτιον) and "the passive object" (τὸ παθητόν). While implicitly (but undoubtedly) connecting these principles with contemporary "philosophy,"[123] in §8 Philo is explicit that the two principles derive from Moses, specifically from Genesis 1. Thus the biblical creation account can be read, basically, as the interaction of two things: "God" and "the heavens and the earth" (cf. Gen. 1:1). At vv. 9–10, Philo heightens the activeness of God and the passiveness of the earth by downplaying what little activity the text had attributed to the earth.

Yet it is not only God's *activeness* that is important to Philo, but God's pre-active *purposefulness* as well. In his comments on vv. 9–10, Philo expresses God's purpose or "telos" in at least six ways. First, salt water was "about to cause barrenness to crops and trees," yet God "commanded" it to be "gathered." This is not explicitly purposive, but Philo presents the creative act as God curbing any potential damage in a kind of pre-emptive rescue that enables fruitfulness. Second, sweet moisture "was left behind," and this was "*for the sake of* [εἰς] preservation." Through the "glue" that

---

[121] For a balanced description of the earth as "co-creatrix" and yet as subservient to God and his word see Noort, 2000, 8–9; Seebaß, 1996, 71–72.

[122] Despite this discrepancy, Philo remains close to the text in a number of ways. 1) He soon concedes an active participation of the earth as she "gives birth to" (τίκτει) all the things sown (§43). (This confirms that in §§40 and 42 Philo has a particular bent toward theocentric interpretation). 2) He has God "command" (κελεύω) the earth, mimicking the imperative of v. 11. 3) In v. 12 the earth "produced" (ἐξήνεγκεν; aorist of ἐκφέρω), and Philo writes that the earth was "to bear greenery" (χλοηφορεῖν) and "to bear grain" (σταχυηφορεῖν), possibly basing his φορέω-compounds on ἐκφέρω from v. 12. 4) Philo explicitly uses the LXX's βοτάνη and χόρτος: God sent "pastures [βοτάνας]" and "well-grassed [εὔχορτα] plains." See Runia, 2001, 183.

[123] Radice (2009) considers this doctrine of two-principles Stoic in origin (130). After reviewing the scholarly evidence from the Stoics, Aristotelians, and Platonists, Runia (2001) concludes that because Philo emphasizes "the transcendence of the active cause," emphasizes creation, and alludes to Plato's *Timaeus*, we should assume about Philo's doctrine that "the basic thought here is Platonist," though "formulated with some reference to Stoic and Aristotelian terminology" (115; cf. 122).

came about from God's out-pouring,[124] Philo then draws attention to the third and fourth interrelated divine purposes: he left moisture *"for the sake of"* (ὑπέρ + genitive) the land not becoming dried up (and thus unproductive), *"so that"* (ὅπως) like a mother the earth could provide food and drink for the coming plants. Fifth, *"for this reason"* (διό, i.e., the maternal reason just mentioned) God "flooded [the earth's] veins like breasts."[125] Sixth, God also "extended invisible moisture-bearing capillaries throughout the rich and fertile soil" (i.e., "the systems of waters" in Gen. 1:10), each creatively enacted *"toward"* (πρός) the *end-goal* of "unreserved plenitude" for the crops. Divine purpose (or, rather, many purposes) lies behind God's manner of creation in vv. 9–10. In this way God "ordered" (διαταξάμενος) what he then labels "earth" and "sea" (cf. Gen. 1:10ab). For Philo, what God thought *before* this specific creative act is inherent to the text which relates its beginning.

(ii) On vv. 11–13: Illustration of the Seed (*Op.* 40–44)

God now "begins to ornament" (διακοσμεῖν ἄρχεται) the earth (§40).[126] Philo elaborates on v. 12 in three ways. The trees were immediately and fully laden with mature fruit (§40.8–10; cf. "mature" [τελείαν] in §42.3). This is miraculous, for it is contrary to the natural and observable botanical process (§41.1–20).[127] Behind this miraculous process it is as though there were present a "painter's knowledge" (§41.21–22).[128] Then in §42, Philo returns to the text to emphasize the "maturity" of the fruit and the presence of the "seeds."

The LXX of vv. 11–12 places more emphasis on "the seeds" than did the MT. It draws noticable attention to their activity of "seeding" (σπεῖρον σπέρμα),[129] and it focuses upon their nature as "according to kind and according to likeness" (κατὰ γένος καὶ καθ' ὁμοιότητα). Philo demon-

---

[124] This idea of "glue" was a "fairly typical scientific idea" (Runia, 2001, 182).

[125] Cf. the "teleological approach" to cosmogony taken by Pliny in *Natural History* 2.166: "The intention of the artificer of nature must have been to unite earth and water in a mutual embrace, earth opening her bosom and water penetrating her entire frame by means of a network of veins..." (quoted in Runia, 2001, 182). Cf. *Op.* 131 (see below p. 178 and n. 41); *Plant.* 10.

[126] Philo's term διακοσμέω probably not only comes from philosophical cosmogonies (cf. Plato's *Tim.* 37d5; Ps.-Aristotle's *Mund.* 2, 392b12) but also from the influence of Gen. 2:1 (so also Runia, 2001, 183).

[127] Philo's "scientific" elaboration on the botanical processes (cast as exegesis) compares with e.g., Pearce, 1969, 85–93, who presents a modern scientific interpretation of Genesis 1. Pearce and Philo both seek to demonstrate accurate correspondences between Genesis 1 and contemporary theory.

[128] Berchman (2000) argues aestheticism is central to Philo's "philosophy" (49–70).

[129] On the strange grammar see Wevers, 1993, 6 and 6 n. 21.

strates in two basic ways that the realized teleology (τελείαν, i.e., "maturity") of the fruit of v. 12 is divinely purposeful. One, it is "for" (εἰς) the immediate use/enjoyment of the forthcoming living beings (§42.4–6).[130] Two, it is "toward [πρός] the eternal genesis of what is similar [τῶν ὁμοίων]" (§43.6–7); that is, these mature fruit immediately contained "the seed-substances" (τὰς σπερματικὰς οὐσίας) in which exists the potential for endless self-propagation. Concerning this latter spermatic principle, Philo reasons:

> For God purposed [ἐβουλήθη] nature to run a course, immortalizing [ἀπαζανατίζων] the kinds [τὰ γένη], and granting to them eternity [ἀιδιότητος]. Therefore he also led and spurred on the beginning [ἀρχήν] toward the end [πρὸς τέλος], and he made the end [τέλος] to bend back around upon the beginning [ἐπ' ἀρχήν]. For out of the plant comes the fruit just as [ὡς] out of the beginning [ἐξ ἀρχῆς] comes the end [τέλος], and out of fruit comes the seed which contains the plant in itself again just as [ὡς] out of the end [ἐκ τέλους] comes the beginning [ἀρχή]. (Op. 44)

Philo uses an ontological principle of reality, one which appears to have been well enough known for him to not defend or explain it, to elucidate what God did in the text. Nature contains a beginning and an end that are mutually perpetual. There exists in nature "the eternal genesis of likenesses" (§43), and that is precisely what Moses meant by the repeated phrases "according to kind" (4x in vv. 11–12) and "according to likeness" (2x). On the third day of creation God established this principle; he thereby fixed an "immortalizing" and "eternity" of "the kinds" (§44).[131]

But as much as making a general ontological claim about the nature of beginning (ἀρχή) and end (τέλος), and as much as making a textual claim about seeds, fruit, and kinds, Philo is making a theological claim.[132] "God purposed [ἐβουλήθη]... and therefore *he* led [ἦγε] and *he* spurred on [ἐπέσπευδε]... and *he* made [ἐποίει] to bend back around."[133] This is reminiscent of Philo's point in *Aet.* 13–19. There he bases the indestructibility (ἀφθαρσία) of the cosmos upon God's "providence" (πρόνοια).[134]

---

[130] Cf. *Aet.* 63.

[131] Cf. *Her.* 113–22, where Philo again uses seeds and plants to exalt the primary causal work of God in "natural" agriculture over the secondary cause of the one who sows (cf. §§115, 117, 119; *Leg.* 1.5–7). This theocentric understanding of agriculture will find a correlate in Paul (cf. 1 Cor. 3:6–7 and 15:37–38; see below).

[132] For a similar reading of Genesis 1 (in this aspect) see Batto, 1992, 32.

[133] Plato had emphasized God's cosmic "purpose": the demiurge "purposed" (ἐβουλήθη) the cosmos to be like himself (*Tim.* 29e), "purposing" (βουληθείς) all things to be good and useful (*Tim.* 30a), "purposing" (βουληθείς) to make the cosmos resemble (ὁμοιῶσαι) the most beautiful (καλλίστῳ) and most perfect (τελέῳ) thing, the intelligible paradigm (*Tim.* 30d [the cosmos being "most like" (ὁμοιότατον) the noetic realm both as a whole and also "according to its parts/kind" (κατὰ γένος), *Tim.* 30c]).

[134] Frick, 1999, 91–94, 102–08; Runia, 1986, 152, 241–42. Cf. *Dec.* 58.

He argues this by quoting *Tim.* 41ab, where Plato guarantees the cosmos' (and the gods') indestructibility solely on the basis of God's "will" and "purpose" (ἐθέλοντος... ἐθέλειν... τῆς ἐμῆς βουλήσεως). Philo then simultaneously proves the antiquity of Plato's "indestructibility" theory and of Hesiod's "creation" theory (mentioned above) by quoting Gen. 1:1, alluding to Gen. 1:14–19, and glossing Gen. 8:22. The last of these biblical references guarantees cosmic eternality due to God's promise.

Within his commentary on Genesis 1 itself, Philo had already written about the Before that God "purposed" (βουληθείς) the construction of this visible world and therefore pre-stamped out the noetic world (*Op.* 16; see above). Now, in his direct comments on Gen. 1:11–13 in §44, Philo reintroduces the creative "purpose" of God. This time seeing them in God's ontological structuring of the botanical processes in the beginning of the *visible* world too.

For Philo, God knew beforehand exactly what the world would need. The individual decisions he then made on the third day (as on the second) testify to his surpassing wisdom and intentionality. Because of this wisdom, God again pre-emptively saved the cosmos (as he had done through light on day one), this time from death and dissolution. As we see in days two and three, from the Beginning onward (and based, both explicitly and implicitly, on his intentions before the beginning) God granted an ontologically self-perpetuating "immortality" to the world.

(c) The Fourth Day, Philo on Genesis 1:14–19 (*Op.* 45–61)

God created the luminaries. The fact that light itself (and plants) preceded heavenly luminaries in Genesis 1 easily stimulates various attempts to relate the text's truth-claims to whatever are the present scientific standards.[135] Some are not bothered by the text's order. U. Cassuto writes, "The existence of light before the creation of luminaries does not, of course, present any difficulty, for we are all familiar with light that does not emanate from the heavenly bodies, e.g., lightning."[136] Or, from an implicitly theological angle, Gerhard von Rad reasons,[137]

Perhaps the remarkable distinction between the creation of light and the creation of the stars has something to do with this emphasis on their creatureliness. The stars are in no

---

[135] Cf. the treatments in Poythress, 2006; Sailhamer, 1992, 87, 92–93; Van Till, 1986, 90. See Westermann, 1987, 10 and Watson, 1994, 148 for more general comments.

[136] Cassuto, 1961, 26. Cf. Wenham, 1987, 18. Currid (1997) merely refers to the light of day one as "supernatural," and notes a parallel with some Egyptian cosmogonies which recount the creation of light and only subsequently "gave birth to the sun-god" (66).

[137] Von Rad, 1956, 54.

way creators of light, but only mediating bearers of a light that was there without them and before them.

S. Gelander gives an explicitly theological explanation: "God is altogether independent in His relations with nature and its laws."[138]

Philo knows the oddity of pre-solar plants (cf. *Op.* 45, 47), but neither sun-less plants nor bodiless light truly concerns him regarding the seeming disorder of vv. 14–19.[139] While he recognizes it as a potential signal of disorder, at least on a surface level, to Philo this order actually makes good theological sense. In §§45–46, at which we will now look, Philo presents his theological reason for the textual delay in presenting heaven's adornment. In §§53–61, to which we will then turn, he presents God's teleological purposes for the luminaries.[140]

(i) The Theological Delay of the Luminaries (*Op.* 45–46)

To validate the perceived discrepancy in the concept of proper order, Philo yet again builds his cosmogonic reading on God's fore-thought, perfect knowledge, and supreme ability. By making stars after plants, God pre-emptively facilitates trust in and awe for his independent and all-powerful Self. Elsewhere Philo does speculate on both the intellectual and essential nature of celestial bodies,[141] the latter of which he is particularly unsure.[142] Here, however, Philo sets aside all such speculation for the sake of making evident the Mosaic emphasis on theocentric dominion. The delay of heaven's adornments was textually established "for proof" (εἰς ἔνδειξιν) of God's "most evident power of rulership" (§45.5–6). Humans were going to tend toward idolatry of the created order by attributing the "causes"

---

[138] Gelander, 1997, 98.

[139] Because Philo presents Gen. 1:1–5 as the paradigmatic Before, there actually *is* no corporeal light that precedes its embodiment. And, because all creative acts are actually occurring simultaneously (§§13–14, 67), plants do not technically precede the sun.

[140] Because §§47–52 is an arithmological excursus that is relatively disconnected from the biblical text (other than being about the number 4 and the text calls this the "fourth" day), it is unhelpful for our present purpose of analyzing what Philo does with the textual details. On it see Runia, 2001, 187–88.

[141] Sometimes Philo calls stars "rational" (*Plant.* 7, 12; cf. *Gig.* 8; *Somn.* 1.135; so Conzelmann, 1975, 282 n. 23; Runia, 2001, 240). According to Runia (2001): "Some early Greek philosophers such as Anaxagoras and Democritus regarded the heavenly bodies as masses of solid matter, but from Plato and Aristotle onwards it was generally accepted that they were living beings whose superior intelligence could be deduced from their perfect movements" (240). In *Spec.* 1.66 (as here in *Op.* 55), however, it is interesting that Philo associates the heavens with the sanctuary of the temple, regarding the angels as (obviously rational) priests and the stars as (seemingly a-rational?) "dedicatory objects."

[142] See *Spec.* 1.39. He records a vast array of opinions in *Somn.* 1.21–24, 53–54.

(αἰτίας) of seasonal plant-growth to the heavenly bodies themselves. Although Philo admits that attributing causation to stars is somewhat "reasonable,"[143] the danger is that people will show too much admiration for the phenomena and thus "believe in" or "put their trust in" (πιστεύσουσι) them rather than God. God's "sovereignty" as Creator, Cause, and primary object of trust is at stake.

But just as God had "understood in advance" (προλαβών) the (semi-)Platonic principle that "a good copy would never come into being without a good paradigm" (§16; see chapter 1), so too now God "understood in advance" (προλαβών) this coming human trend.[144] Just as on the third day God had fore-seen the potential infertility of the earth, and so creation there took the shape of a kind of pre-emptive rescue from natural disaster, so too in this fourth day God's fore-knowledge incorporates even future human impiety. Creation thus transpires according to Gen. 1:14–19 because of God's pre-established intent of pre-empting false trust. On the fourth day, the all-powerful God intentionally demonstrated that he does not *need* "his heavenly offspring"; they are "not autonomous in their rule" (οὐ αὐτοκρατεῖς). It is God himself who, like a charioteer, "leads [all natural processes] however he wants [ἐθέλῃ], each according to law and justice" (§46.10–11; cf. §46.6 [ὅταν αὐτῷ δοκῇ]).[145] All things are "possible for God."[146] According to Philo, the dignity of God's rule is "the reason on account of which the earth sprouted first," i.e., before heavenly lights were made (§47.1–2).

---

[143] For Philo's use of "reasonable" (εὔλογον), as well as "persuasive" (πιθανά) and "likely" (εἰκότα), cf. Dillon, 1977, 52–69 and Runia, 2001, 189. Philo can see some validity in attributing some sort of causation to stars. He labels stars as visible "gods" (*Spec.* 1.19; cf. *Op.* 27; *Spec.* 1.209; 2.165; see Radice, 2009, 129; Runia, 2001, 160, 208) and attributes to them predictive nature (see van Kooten, 2003, 28, though note that Philo's statements subsequently quoted by van Kooten [*Op.* 56–57, 58–59, 59–60; *Aet.* 19; *Spec.* 1.92] merely show that the events are *pre-announced* rather than, as van Kooten explains, being actually "influenced" or "determined" by the movement of the stars). Von Rad (1956) is emphatic that the notion that "time was determined by the cyclical course of the stars" was "ancient Oriental," and "not Old Testament!" (54), but cf. Philo's treatment in *Leg.* 1.8. Regardless of Philo's often heightened language for stars, for him they must be relegated to secondary causes (*Spec.* 1.16–19; *Migr.* 178–94). God alone is primary cause (*Spec.* 3.180). God alone is to be worshiped, even in the context of astronomy (*Op.* 45–46; *Spec.* 1.13–20; *Prov.* 1.77–88; cf. *Spec.* 1.59–63; *Her.* 97; *Migr.* 181; see Runia, 2001, 160, 205).

[144] See Runia, 2001, 189.

[145] Cf. *Conf.* 174, where stars and angels follow their "leader," God, "in obedience to the principles of law and justice." Radice (2009) posits that God is not himself bound to "law and justice," for miracles break just such laws (130).

[146] "All things" does not include evil (*Agr.* 129; *Mut.* 30), so Radice, 2009, 130.

(ii) The Teleological Ends of the Luminaries (*Op.* 53–61)

Philo's grounding of ontology on theology continues (although more subtly) through the remainder of the fourth day. After his arithmological excursus whereby "four" is considered perfect for "the Maker to adorn [διεκόσμει] the heaven" with "the most God-like adornment [κόσμῳ]" (§§47–52),[147] Philo reminds his readers of light's ontic perfection (§53.4) by relating God's fore-knowledge to God's creative act. "Knowing [εἰδώς]," Philo reasons, that "of existing things light is best," God "was shining" it (ἀπέφαινεν; cf. Gen. 1:14–15 [ὥστε φαίνειν]) as the instrument of sight, the best of the senses (§53.5–7).[148] This knowledgeable shining has blessed mankind with many "good things." The greatest is "philosophy," the love of wisdom (§53.23–24), through which humans "feast" on the majestic "dance" of the luminaries, asking unanswerable questions of existence (§54).[149]

When Philo begins to explain the luminaries' purpose – their *telos* – he portrays them mainly from the perspective of their "benefits" to and "usefulness" for humans.[150] This earns Philo what David Runia calls his "fundamental anthropocentric approach" to the fourth day.[151] The luminaries are for humans. Yet Philo's teleological approach incorporates a source as well as a goal, and both the source and goal Philo subsumes under purpose.

Concerning the (anthropocentric) goal, Philo lists three aspects (each of which follow the LXX): 1) to be for illumination (τοῦ φωσφορεῖν), 2) for times (καιρῶν), 3) for days, months, and years (ἡμερῶν, μηνῶν, ἐνιαυτῶν) (§55.7–11; cf. Gen. 1:14–15 and Philo's consecutive exposition in §§58–59). Each of these are anthropocentric, but Philo introduces these

---

[147] Again it is possible that Gen. 2:1, and its use of "cosmos" in the phrase "heaven and earth and all their adornment [πᾶς ὁ κόσμος αὐτῶν]," has influenced Philo's concept of creation.

[148] Cf. *Abr.* 156–63, where Philo again glorifies "sight" through exegetical points from Gen. 1:4 (§156) and Gen. 1:14 (§158).

[149] For Philo, *philosophia* is "the preparatory science for *sophia*, which includes the contemplation of the cosmos and God's theoretical and moral revelation to Israel" (Berchman, 2000, 58 [cf. 51, 51 n. 6]; following and summarizing Malingrey, 1961). Cf. *Somn.* 1.21–24, 53–54; *Spec.* 1.39.

[150] Cf. χρείαν τε καὶ ὠφέλειαν in §56.2, τὸ χρησιμώτατον in §60.4, and ὠφελείας in §61.2.

[151] Runia (2001) points out Philo's "anthropocentric bias of the treatise" generally (204, 211), as well as his "strong anthropocentric emphasis" and "fundamental anthropocentric approach" to the fourth day specifically (197, 204, 206). He qualifies this: "Philo does not fully take over Plato's strong anthropocentric emphasis"; he rather "prefers to emphasize the magnificence and munificence of God as creator," thereby keeping such affinities with Hellenism "within strict bounds because of Philo's prevailing Jewish theocentrism" (199). But Philo's theocentrism has even more profoundly affected (and been affted by) his exegesis of Genesis 1 than Runia exhibits.

goals by way of their (theocentric) source (and inherent purpose): God "crafted the sensory heavenly bodies... for the sake of many things [πολλῶν χάριν]" (§55.4, 7–9), i.e., those listed in the text (for light, signs, times, etc.). Likewise, the sun's role as "a great king" is due to the fact that "the Father gave [ἀνεδίδου] [to it] the power over the day" (§56.7). Thus Philo sees within the specific textual statement in 1:16, that "God made" the "great" light for "rulership" over the day, the meta-theme that cosmological structure is due to the Creator's cosmogonic gift. Even the stars, which Genesis 1 hardly mentions[152] but which play such an important role in the cosmic religion of the Chaldeans and Greeks (particularly the Alexandrians),[153] Philo subordinates to God's sovereign allotment.

Although Philo has read the astronomical benefits as mainly oriented toward coming humanity, he concludes the fourth day with both a cosmic and theocentric emphasis:

I am sure that there are many others [*sc.* benefits, ὠφελείας] which are unclear to us – for not everything is known to the mortal race – but which contribute to the preservation of the whole [τοῦ ὅλου]. These, along with the ordinances and laws [θεσμοῖς καὶ νόμοις] that God immovably marked out [ὥρισεν] in the universe, are certainly and in every way manifested together as having been completed [ἐπιτελεῖσθαι]. (§61)

As Runia notes, Philo's summary has been influenced by both "the command structure of Genesis 1" and "the Greek philosophical notion of a rational order which is embodied in the cosmos as the product of a divine intelligence."[154] Philo places the rational and moral order of the universe as well as its benefits for humans immovably in the hands of God.

According to the LXX itself, the fourth day reveals more purpose clauses than any other day. There are eight repetitions of the teleological εἰς ("for"), two of the purposive ὥστε ("so that"), and five infinitives of intent ("to..."). Following suit, for Philo the heavens "have come about" (γεγόνασι)[155] for many purposes: "in order that" (ἵνα, §58.1–2), "so that" (ὅπως, §58.3), "for" (εἰς, §59.5), and "toward" (πρός, §60.1) benefits for both humans and the world. Sun, moon, and stars may have appeared to many of Philo's contemporaries as controlling the destiny of life. But Philo stands upon the text of the fourth day, and particularly on the notion of di-

---

[152] Gen. 1:16 is ambiguous whether God merely made the stars "also" (καί), thus only assigning "rule" to the two "greater lights," or whether God made the stars *unto rulership* "also." Philo clarifies the textual ambiguity: they share the moon's dominion (§56; cf. *Spec.* 1.13–14). This is empirically evident to Philo and connects Genesis 1 more closely to the cosmic religion(s) of Philo's contemporaries.

[153] Frick, 1999, 119.

[154] Runia, 2001, 207. See Philo's use of the astronomy in Plato's *Timaeus* (esp. *Tim.* 37e1; 39c1–5) in Runia, 2001, 198–99, 202, 206 (cf. *idem*, 1986, 222–23).

[155] See γεγόνασι in *Op.* 58, 59, 60; cf. γενηθήτωσαν in Gen. 1:14 (Runia, 2001, 205).

vine intent found therein, and he proclaims that it is God himself who "marked out" (ὥρισεν) the natural and immovable laws,[156] along with their teleological benefits.

(d) The Fifth Day, Philo on Genesis 1:20–23 (*Op.* 62–63)

Since earth and heaven "have been arrayed" (διακοσμηθέντων) with appropriate "ornaments" (κόσμοις), God then "undertook to form the lives of the mortal beings" (§62.1–4). God began by "making" (ποιούμενος) aquatic beings (cf. ἐποίησεν, Gen. 1:21), but only "after deeming" (νομίσας) "five" to be perfect for living beings (§62.4–6). Yet again, God "considered" *before* he "made."[157]

Although Philo's comments on the fifth day are brief, he nevertheless draws out a few important features of the text. Philo sees that "*living* things" and "en*soul*ed things" (cf. "living souls," ψυχῶν ζωσῶν, Gen. 1:20–21), which have "five" senses, were made on the "fifth" day. By this correspondence Philo demonstrates a divinely established ontological principle of sense-perception: "The Maker distributed [προσένειμεν] to each [ἑκάστῃ] of the senses its own [ἴδιον] special material and criterion by which to judge what it notices" (§62.9–11), e.g., colors for sight, sounds for hearing. Other than the number five, this seems to have no textual basis. Nevertheless, what is clear is that Philo again sees in the text that ontology is based on theocentric sovereignty. That is, Philo's principle is not merely "to each [ἑκάστῃ] their own [ἴδιον]," although this is ontologically true, but is more particularly "*God distributes* to each their own." Philo's principle captures both the general emphasis in Genesis 1 of God's causation as well as the particular principle in vv. 20–23 of order through categorization: "according to kind."[158]

In the MT of Gen. 1:20 God says, "Let *the waters* swarm…," and v. 21 responds, "And *God* created…." Thus the MT of v. 21 does what Philo had done with v. 12, dimishing the water's participation by highlighting God's own enactment. In the LXX of v. 20, however, after God says, "Let the waters lead forth…," v. 21 responds, "And God made… which the waters led forth." The LXX followed the MT's emphasis on God's own enactment (v. 21a), but then added the water's participation as well (v. 21b). Interest-

---

[156] Cf. *Plant.* 8: "It is the eternal law of the everlasting God which is the most supporting and firm foundation of the universe" (cf. §10). (*Plant.* 2–4 had explained creation in phrases similar to those in *Op.*, and are thus evocative of Genesis 1 itself).

[157] We must keep in mind that, for Philo, God's "thinking" and his "acting" are "simultaneous" (*Op.* 13; see Wedderburn, 1973B, 305; Lorenzen, 2008, 161–62 n. 77), and therefore my constant use of "before" is, like Philo's, meant logically, even causatively, and not temporally.

[158] Van Wolde, 1996B, 148.

ingly, in §63.1–2 Philo resembles the MT (not intentionally) when he writes that God "commands [κελεύει] all kinds of fish and sea-creatures to be constituted...," and adds that God "proceeded to form [διεπλάττετο]..." (cf. §63.16). Philo again emphasizes God's activity, even to the neglect of v. 21b (LXX).

Genesis 1:21 specifies "according to kinds" about both water creatures and birds. As with the seeds, Philo concentrates on the "kinds" and the similarity/diversity which this entails. The "kinds" (γένη) of fish and sea-monsters involve "differing" (διαφέροντα) sizes and structures (§63.2–3).[159] For example, fish differ from fish since "in various [ἐν ἄλλοις] seas various types [ἄλλα] are found." (Paul uses similar language to describe God's desired diversity within the cosmos; see below.) According to Philo's reading of day five, all "kinds" of fish and birds are suitably different from eachother; to each thing God gives its particularly suited qualities (cf. *Plant.* 11–15). So God's actions are "reasonable" (εἰκότως).

(e) The Sixth Day, Philo on Genesis 1:24–26 (*Op.* 64–68)

"Now that water and air had received the kinds [τὰ γένη] of living beings that were appropriate to them," God again "was calling [ἐκάλει] the earth unto the production [εἰς τὴν γένεσιν] of the parts that had been left outstanding" (§64.3).[160] Philo quotes Gen. 1:24 ("Let the earth lead out..."), substituting "beasts" (κτήνη) for the text's "living beings" (ψυχὴν ζῶσαν) and the more specific "according to *each* kind" (καθ' ἕκαστον γένος) for the text's "according to kind" (κατὰ γένος) (§64.6–7). Although Philo only uses the word γένος once in this section, he accurately reflects the text's further emphasis on diversification (which the text conveys through repeating κατὰ γένος 5x).

Philo now fully presents the earth's active response to God's imperative: "And the earth immediately released what it had been commanded," that is, creatures "differing" (διαφέροντα) in build, strength, and purpose (§64.7–10). Intriguingly, while Philo had downplayed the previous places in the text where the water or earth were bid to action, this time it is actually his emphasis on the active and immediate response of the earth that has no correlate in the text. In vv. 24–25, "God made" (v. 25) in response to his own imperative (v. 24), yet Philo records the earth's obedience. Despite such minor divergences, the general pattern of Philo's exegesis of this type of textual feature seems to be to treat God's call and activity as primary,

---

[159] These creatures "differed" in their ποιότησιν, "qualities." Runia, 2001, 214: "Philo has noted the zoological term γένος (kind or genus) in the biblical text... [which] allows him to relate the Mosaic account to philosophical discussions on the distribution of genera of living beings in the cosmos."

[160] For the cosmogonic "call" see *Spec.* 4.187; cf. Bar. 3:32–35.

and the response of the stuff as secondary, if active at all. When the passive thing does act, as here, it is merely following the orders of its sovereign, the wise and all-knowledgeable God.

Philo is now almost to 1:26, the creation of humanity. But before commenting on the beginning of humanity, Philo wishes to recapitulate the "zoogony" (ζῳογονίαν),[161] showing its "all-beautiful" (πάγκαλος) "chain of sequence." Thus he organizes it by levels of "ensoulment" (ἐμψύχη) (§65). Concerning fish: "of the ensouled beings" fish are least, having "more bodily [σωματικῆς] than soulish substance [ψυχικῆς οὐσίας]," thus being "in a manner somewhat living [ζῷα] yet not living [οὐ ζῷα]," as "moving soul-less beings" (κινητὰ ἄψυχα). In truth, whatever "soul-like thing" (τοῦ ψυχοειδοῦς) there is has merely been "sown" (παρασπαρέντος) in them to preserve their bodies, acting like salt to slow down their "decay" (φθείροιντο) (§66.1–7). Concerning birds and land-animals: they have "better sense-perception" than fish, and "through their construction they manifest more clearly the distinctive quality of being soulish [τῆς ψυχώσεως ἰδίτητας]" (§66.8–10). Concerning "the human": God "made [ἐποίει] the human [τὸν ἄνθρωπον] over all [ἐπὶ πᾶσιν]" (§66.11; cf. §65.1). Whitaker (*Loeb*) translates "over all" as "to crown all," justified by Runia as reflecting the "ascending" nature of the sequence. Humans are the ontological "climax of the creative acts."[162] Humanity received "mind" (νοῦν) as a choice gift, "a sort of soul [ψυχὴν] of the soul [ψυχῆς]" (§66.11–15).

The Craftsman employed the process of order and ascension in "the genesis of everything." He developed life from foam-like "seed" (τὸ σπέρμα), then to firmness (στηρίσῃ = στέρεον/στερέωμα), then to movement (κίνησιν), then to life-formation (ζῳοπλαστεῖ; cf. Gen. 2:19), then to the distribution of "moist substance" into the body-parts and "spiritual [substance]" (τὴν πνευματικήν) into the soul. The last gives nourishment and sense perception (§67).[163] The order of creation transpired as it did simply because God "deemed to form [διαπλάττειν ἔδοξε]" fish to

---

[161] I.e., the "origin of life" or "birth of the animal realm" (Runia, 2001, 62).

[162] Runia, 2001, 216. Philo's language of "over all" (ἐπὶ πᾶσιν) may also reflect the influence of Ps. 8:6b-7, where God "placed [κατέστησας]" humanity "over [ἐπί]" the works of his hands, and God "subjected all things [πάντα ὑπέταξας] under his feet." Philo seems to read Ps. 8:6–7 into Gen. 1:28 at *Op.* 84–85 (so Borgen, 1995, 369–89; cf. Runia, 2001, 256).

[163] "Reason" [ὁ λογισμός], which is linked to moral capacity, Philo defers until §§69–75. In *Deus* 47–48, God's gift of mind to the otherwise animal human is a gift of liberation, i.e., freedom from the "necessity" to which mindless lower animals are bound. With liberation comes moral responsibility to act in such a way – to choose to move in such a way – that "does honor to its Liberator" as if a "grateful freedman" (see Winston, 1983, 181–195, 182; cf. Runia, 2001, 240).

humans, least to greatest, with birds and land-creatures in between (§68). Philo has now shown the zoogonic (indeed the whole cosmogonic) account to be according to God's logically prior "consideration" of order, differentiation, and propriety. His treatment of the world's Beginning has within it an implicit Before. And now that he has set the cosmic scene satisfactorily, Philo is ready to turn to Genesis' first anthropogonic text, Gen. 1:26–28 (§§69–88), to which we shall turn in the next chapter.

(f) Summary: Philo's Beginning of the World

Throughout his reading of the beginning of the world, Philo repeatedly draws attention to two things: God's sovereign activity (both in "call" and in enactment), and God's "pre"-creational understanding because of which he created as he did. Because he sees creation as based upon God's forethought, Philo repeatedly portrays creation as a kind of pre-emptive rescue, whether from natural dissolution or from coming human wickedness. As we have seen in brief above and as we will see further in the next chapter, Philo interprets the beginning of "all things in the cosmos' from a limited but nonetheless present anthropocentricity; the cosmos is what God "pre-prepared" (προητοιμάσατο) for humanity according to his previous "purpose" (βουληθείς) (§§77–78).

The three strands of creation at which we are looking (world, human, and Before) are interwoven in what we have seen thus far in Philo's treatment of Genesis 1. As we will see further in chapter 3, even this human-oriented aim of the creation of the world Philo sets within the context of its ultimately theocentric cause and prior purpose. Though this Before has been exhibited in a slightly more implicit form than what I analyzed in chapter 1, it is still the case that what God thought and purposed *before* the beginning propels and shapes Philo's actual interpretation of the beginning of the world (Gen. 1:6–31). Yet at the same time, it is the text of the cosmic Beginning that itself stimulates in Philo's mind this implicit Before. The Beginning of the world (with its pointers toward the Beginning of humanity) and the Before are reciprocal hermeneutical partners within Philo's interpretation of creation. I will now demonstrate a broadly similar hermeneutical pattern in Paul's reading of the Beginning of the world.

2.3.2 Paul's Reading of Genesis 1:6–31 (1 Cor. 15:35–41)

Within the Corinthian church some said, "Resurrection of corpses does not exist" (v. 12). More particular queries involved: "How are the corpses raised?" and "In what bodies do they come?" (v. 35).[164] Paul thinks that

---

[164] The second question seems to narrow the first, bringing more specificity to the central issue: the body (Morissette, 1972B, 227; Fee, 1987, 780).

these questions can be answered satisfactorily, at least, if not exhaustively. He gives a partial answer in v. 37 to the latter question, saying, "In the coming body." He lays out a more direct answer in v. 44: "a Spiritual body is raised."[165] To elucidate his short answer concerning the resurrection Paul introduces in vv. 36–49 numerous themes and words from the beginning of Genesis, both from the creation of the world generally (see below) and from the creation of humanity specifically (see chapter 3).

Most scholars recognize that Paul's use of creation in this argument is important.[166] Somewhat amusingly, opposite conclusions concerning his theology of resurrection are put forward precisely due to what is perceived to be Paul's understanding of creation in these verses. For example, J. Becker and N.T. Wright both consider Paul's references to creation fundamental to 1 Cor. 15:36–49.[167] Both even consider Paul's general view of creation to be *ex nihilo* (and both largely base this on Rom. 4:17).[168] Yet Becker and Wright draw opposite conclusions from Paul's creation-language. Becker understands Paul's *creatio* to be *ex nihilo*, and this is an important reason why he considers Paul's view of resurrection to be *ex nihilo* as well. God needs no "left-overs" to initiate resurrection. Rather, God leaves the corpses – i.e., "Adam's entourage" – in the grave while crafting

---

[165] See Collins, 1999, 564; Lambrecht, 1981, 512; Usami, 1076, 483. De Boer (1988) helpfully adds that Paul gives a "double answer" to his questions from v. 35: "'The dead will be raised *incorruptible*' (v. 52) with 'a *spiritual* body' (v. 44a)" (128). I will be focusing on the answer in v. 44 for this one is tied more closely to Paul's interpretation of Genesis.

My capitalization of "Spiritual" above reflects a deliberate exegetical decision (and therefore theological position) contrary to, e.g., D. Martin (1992). Martin assumes that πνεῦμα and πνευματικόν in 1 Cor. 15 refer to the anthropological "compos[ition] of pneuma with sarx and psyche having been sloughed off along the way" (126). Because Paul believes that Christians have become "one πνεῦμα" with Christ (1 Cor. 6:17), it is difficult to always discern when he refers to the anthropological ethereal substance – i.e., the human πνεῦμα (e.g., 2:11a; 14:14) – and when to the working and character of the divine πνεῦμα (e.g., 2:11b; 12:4). As I will argue more fully in chapter 3, in 1 Cor. 15 πνεῦμα and πνευματικόν refer to the theological "presence, power, and transforming activity of the Holy Spirit" (so Thiselton, 2006B, 342–43 [*idem*, 2006A, 283; *idem*, 2000, 1276–77]; Wright, 2003, 350, 352; Schreiner, 2001, 458; Moffatt, 1938, 259–60; Vos, 1930, 166–67; Robertson and Plummer, 1911, 372).

[166] This includes scholars who disagree substantially on what Paul says concerning the resurrection, but who still consider creation a fundamental aspect of his argument: e.g., Becker, 2007, 165; Wright, 2003, 313, 340; *idem*, 2006, 28; Collins, 1999, 537; Muddiman, 1994, 135; Conzelmann, 1975, 281.

[167] See Becker, 2007, 167; Wright, 2003, 313.

[168] Becker, 2007, 165, 167, 168; Wright, 2002, 498. For a brief critique of this use of Rom. 4:17 see above pp. 4–6 and notes.

new bodies from nothing.¹⁶⁹ Wright's view of Paul's *creatio* includes but extends past its *ex nihilo* quality, focusing upon the "goodness" of the physical creation. Thus it is "simply unthinkable" that Paul would have conceived of the graves remaining full.¹⁷⁰ Merely recognizing *that* creation is an important ingredient in Paul's argument about resurrected bodies obviously does not solve every issue! The fact that this recognition is so common while simultaneously understood and theologically applied toward such divergent ends certainly confirms the importance of what follows, i.e., *how* Paul interprets creation, particularly in 1 Corinthians 15.

By criticizing the Corinthian denial as "ignorance [ἀγνωσίαν] of God" (v. 34), Paul implies that the answer to the question concerning eschatological ontology (i.e., "In what body do they come?") is closely associated with the proper understanding of God himself.¹⁷¹ They ignorantly rejected the idea of resurrection for they could not fathom its "how" and "in what body," but they failed to take into account the God of Genesis 1.¹⁷² Deniers are unthinkingly "foolish" (ἄφρων) (v. 35). This label, ἄφρων, was "generally associated with one who fails to recognize the creative power of God."¹⁷³ It would simultaneously cut to the heart of a community obsessed with "wisdom."¹⁷⁴ In response to this ignorance of the divine ability and technique, Paul presents God's cosmic creativity as prolegomena to resurrected bodily ontology.¹⁷⁵ The Beginning proves to be a major influence on Paul's understanding of salvation and the End, in this instance of the "how" and "in what body" of the new life.¹⁷⁶

In vv. 36–43, Paul presents cosmic and cosmogonic prolegomena, "preparing the way" for his fuller anthropological answer in v. 44 and for its own anthropogonic explanation in vv. 45–49.¹⁷⁷ Presented below in outline form is Paul's logic:

---

¹⁶⁹ Becker, 2007, 165–168 (cf. Conzelmann, 1975, 281; Martin, 1992, 130; Thiselton, 2000, 1267; and see Moiser's discussion of earlier scholars holding similar views [1992, 10–30, esp. 22]).
¹⁷⁰ Wright, 2003, 314, 335 (cf. Sider, 1975, 428–39).
¹⁷¹ Garland, 2003, 722; Schreiner, 2001, 458; Thiselton, 1978, 525.
¹⁷² Cf. Rom. 1:21–22. So Fee, 1987, 779–80. Cf. Garland, 2003, 727; Schrage, 2001, 280–81; Moiser, 1992, 15, 19; Barrett, 1968, 370.
¹⁷³ Asher, 2000, 78. Asher writes that Paul's use of ἄφρων "operates on two levels: the first level is the rhetorical use of the appellative to dismiss the objection of a foolish and uni[n]formed [*sic*] student, and the second is to anticipate his argument from creation in vv. 36b–38" (78).
¹⁷⁴ Horsley, 1998, 209; Kistemaker, 1993, 567; Harrisville, 1987, 274.
¹⁷⁵ Morissette (1972B) sees in 1 Cor. 15:38a ("God gives") "the intervention of the Creator" (220), though the term "intervention" is not quite strong enough for Paul's argumentation.
¹⁷⁶ Watson, 1997, 282; Probst, 1991, 344; Moffatt, 1938, 261.
¹⁷⁷ Héring, 1962, 173.

v. 35   Question(s):   How are the dead raised? In what bodies do they come?
vv. 36–43   Prolegomena: Consider God's cosmic structuring based on Genesis 1.
v. 44a   Answer: A *psychikon* body is sown, a *pneumatikon* body raised.
vv. 44b–49   Explanation: Cf. Adam in Gen. 2:7/5:3 and Jesus' resurrection/application.

Concerning the prolegomena itself, Paul begins with an appeal in vv. 36–41 to the present structure of the cosmos based on God's activity and on his intentions at creation. In vv. 42–43 Paul then draws God's creative power into direct relationship with his resurrecting power: "in this manner is the resurrection."[178] (Because vv. 42–43 has shifted from the general world to particular humanity I will defer discussion of it to chapter 3).

We will now see how Paul's "argument from creation"[179] in vv. 36–41 is based on his interpretation of the initial text of Genesis. Although my primary purpose is not to settle the (deep-rooted) debate concerning the resurrection body mentioned above, what follows may produce the secondary benefit of ruling out certain arguments that arise from improper readings of Paul's present understanding of creation. Primarily what will emerge from the following investigation is a similar two-sided treatment of God's creation of the world in Paul as we found in Philo: cosmic ontology is good, and this is because of the action and desire of the Creator. In vv. 36–38a Paul sows the seed of this theocentrically beautiful ontology. In vv. 38b–41 he draws out its cosmic scope and preparatory implications for resurrection. He does both of these through the themes and language of Genesis 1.

(a) "Sowing the Seed" of God's Creative Power (1 Cor. 15:36–38a)

After quoting the Corinthian queries regarding the coming of resurrected "bodies" (v. 35), Paul writes,

Foolish person! What you yourself sow is not made alive unless it dies. And what you sow, it is not the body that will come about that you sow, but rather a naked kernel (perhaps of wheat or of something else). And God gives to it a body just as he wanted, and to each of the seeds its own body. (vv. 36–38)

The "sowing" of a "seed" helps Paul posit in vv. 36–37 two present ontological principles. Both of these ontological principles he then roots in divine action in v. 38a and divine intent in v. 38b. In light of this theocentric construal of nature, he then refines his main ontological point in v. 38c.

Concerning the two ontological principles in vv. 36–37, the nature of the "thing" (ὅ) sown is to be "made alive" after it has "died" (v. 36), and its nature is to have a different "body" when it comes back to life (v. 37). Thus far Paul has not specified the cause of either ontological principle,

---

[178] So also Asher, 2001, 107–08; *idem*, 2000, 78.
[179] Senft, 1979, 204–10.

whether life-from-death or bodily change. Both are obviously from God (especially in light of 1 Cor. 3:6–7), but theology is not his point in these two opening statements of the analogy. In vv. 36–37, Paul's principal point is ontological.[180] This makes sense since he is answering an ontological question: "in what *body*" do raised corpses come? But Paul does not stop at the ontological, but readily shifts into the theological.

In v. 38a, Paul introduces the theological foundation of these two ontic realities. J. Asher labels the overall point of vv. 36–38 "the will and activity of God in creation."[181] This is partly ture. Paul's point is actually double-edged: 1) ontological differentiation of bodies (vv. 37, 38c), 2) by the will and activity of God in creation (as well as in providence, see below) (v. 38ab).[182] For Paul, the structure of nature with its ontological differentiations and theological causation functions as prolegomena to a proper understanding of the final resurrection.

Verse 38 is of pivotal importance for Paul's prolegomena in vv. 36–41,[183] and in that pivot Paul's timing is important. In v. 38a, Paul shifts from the ontology of v. 37 to theology proper; from seed to giver. He turns from the nature of the seed's body (as it is set in contrast to the [plant-]

---

[180] Some have been led by Paul's emphatic positioning of the "you" (σύ) in v. 36 to conclude that Paul is primarily contrasting agencies (as he had in 3:6–7): "*you* sow... but *God* gives the body" (so Asher, 2001, 108 n. 9; Morissette, 1972B, 221, 228; Simon, 1959, 149). Yet this is not the best reading. First, the emphasis on "you" is adequately accounted for as Paul's appeal to their own common (and obvious) knowledge: "*Your own* knowledge of something as common as agricultural demonstrates a thing going from death to life" (Lockwood, 2000, 585–86; Morris, 1985, 219). Second, although the "you" is the subject of the introductory (though subordinate) clause ("what you yourself sow"), the actual subject (and point) of the main clause is the "what"/"it": "*What* you yourself sow – *it* is not made alive unless *it* dies." Therefore, while it is true that Paul is not *ultimately* intending to base the ontological principle of life-from-death on "the innate capacity of the seed" (rightly Asher, 2001, 108 n. 9), and though it is true that the passive in v. 36 is a "*divine* passive" (rightly Asher, 2001, *ad loc.*; Minear, 1994, 73; Kistemaker, 1993, 567; Morris, 1985, 219), and although it is true that Paul's statement has nothing to do with some "necessity" of death as a "precondition" for eschatological life (contra Morissette, 1972B, 221) since not all will die (v. 51; rightly Garland, 2003, 728; Asher, 2001, 107; Thiselton, 2000, 1264; Conzelmann, 1975, 281 n. 12), it is nevertheless still the case that Paul's point in vv. 36–37 concerns ontology (two facts about the "what") and not causation/agency. Paul *will* introduce agency in v. 38. (For an example of someone who *is* contrasting the causation of the divine sower to that of the human sower in agriculture, see Philo's *Post.* 170–71; cf. §175b).

[181] Asher, 2000, 78–79.

[182] Thiselton (2000) judges: "The use of ἴδιον σῶμα, 'its own particular body'..., ranks almost equally in emphasis with 'God'. The key phrase remains 'God gives to it a body just as he purposed,' but the second principle is that of *contrast, differentiation, and variety* which simultaneously promotes a *continuity of identity*" (1265).

[183] Morissette, 1972B, 221.

body of the future) to what one might call the creative activity of God, i.e., "God gives to it a body."[184] I use the careful phrase "one might call" because Paul is technically referring to activity which God does *presently*: "he gives" (δίδωσιν). Thus he is not in this instance directly referring to what God did in the beginning. God's "giving" is, however, a creative act inasmuch as it involves the causing of growth, life, and change within nature. It is therefore *of one character* with God's "making" in Genesis 1, particularly in vv. 11–12, except that in Paul's reference the recipient of the "body" is a "seed" which already exists. God's "giving" is not his creation of the seed itself, but rather the seasonal gift of what Paul called in v. 37 "the body that will come about" (τὸ σῶμα τὸ γενησόμενον).[185] This is a divinely caused present-day agricultural event rather than the third-day creational event itself.[186]

Paul's sowing-analogy from vv. 36–38a demonstrates three things: 1) an ontological principle similar to resurrection (v. 36), 2) the ontological principle of body differentiation (v. 37), and 3) God's causative agency in present-day providential creativity (v. 38a). In the remainder of v. 38, however, Paul bases *all* of this, especially numbers two (present body-differentiation) and three (present divine causation), on the original creation.[187] He does so by rooting it in God's past *intention* as found in Genesis 1 (v. 38b) and by expressing this theocentric ontology as if writing a commentary on Gen. 1:11–12 (v. 38c). As we will now see, in v. 38bc Paul subtly relates the *future* (the body that will be, v. 37) and *present* (God's continual cosmic providence, v. 38a) to God's *past* intentions in the creation of all things.[188] In vv. 36–38 Paul has sown the seed of creation into

---

[184] So N. Watson, 1992, 175; Simon, 1959, 149.
[185] Fee, 1987, 782.
[186] Cf. God's present agricultural "causing growth" in 1 Cor. 3:6–7.
[187] Some scholars overemphasize v. 36 and neglect v. 37 (e.g., Y.S. Kim, 2008, 94; cf. 92–95), when v. 37 is what Paul actually develops (so Fee, 1987, 781; Lockwood, 2000, 586, 588). V. 36 introduces agriculture in the language of resurrection, and Paul will again use "making alive" (ζῳοποιέω) in v. 45 (a verb which can "call to mind the original creation" [Collins, 1999, 551; cf. 2 Ki. 5:7 and Neh. 9:6] and which is typical Pauline language for the divine gift of eschatological life, particularly through resurrection: see 1 Cor. 15:22; 2 Cor. 3:6; Gal. 3:21; Rom. 4:17; 8:11; cf. Ps. 70:20b; John 5:21, 1 Pet. 3:18 [de Boer, 1988, 113]). (For more complexities in the use of ζῳοποιέω, see Judg. 21:14; Eccl. 7:12; Job 36:6; cf. Ps. 70:20a; John 6:63–65 [de Boer, 1988, 221 n. 88]). Though it is tempting to highlight v. 36 due to its close connection with resurrection language and concept, Paul's main ontological point that is developed in vv. 35–41 is from v. 37 (rightly Vos, 1930, 180).
[188] Paul's unification of providence and creation as both "God giving" has a broad affinity with Philo's unification of creation and providence as God always "making" (*Leg.* 1.5; *Mut.* 27–28; see Radice, 2009, 130, 139). This is not to say that Paul believes in *creatio continua*, but that Paul sees correspondence (not identity) between God's activity

his argument, and in vv. 38bc-41 he begins to word it all – both theology and ontology – in accordance with the themes and language of Genesis 1.

(b) Days 2–6: Paul's Cosmology and Genesis 1 (1 Cor. 15:38b–41)

In vv. 38–41 Paul alludes to Genesis 1 in two ways: he conveys its themes and he employs its language. In v. 38bc, Paul condenses and conveys two dominant *themes* of Genesis 1: a) theological intentions are enacted, and therefore b) ontological differentiation comes about. Even there some of his language sounds like a commentary on the biblical text. In vv. 39–41, Paul uses the *language* of Genesis 1 to broaden this ontological comment about seeds/plants into a fully cosmic perspective about the bodily adornments of heaven and earth. His focus is present ontology, but his expressions make clear that under it all he is still assuming the creative activity and desire of God as set out in the beginning of Genesis.

(i) The Third Day (Gen. 1:11–13): Two Themes of Genesis 1 (v. 38bc)

As we just observed, in v. 38ab Paul's timing is important: "God *gives* to [the seed] a body just as *he wanted*." In contrast to the present "giving" in v. 38a, the aorist "wanted" (ἠθέλησεν) in v. 38b refers to what God "willed," "purposed," "determined," or "chose" to do in the past, and it is right to consider this as being at creation as recorded in Genesis 1.[189] Paul refers in v. 38b and v. 38c to two of the major *themes* found in Genesis 1,

---

in the beginning and God's continued rule over nature. (Cf. Philo's notion of God as the architect of the human mind originally *and* at every birth: *Plant.* 31). What Paul reveals here in v. 38 is that he sees a close connection between God's providential activity in nature and God's creational design as displayed in Genesis 1.

[189] Fee, 1987, 782. Cf. Sider, 1975, 432; Morris, 1985, 220. Thiselton (2000), favorably quoting Kennedy's *St Paul's Conceptions of the Last Things*, writes: "the aorist denotes the final [i.e., purpose] act of God's will, determining the constitution of nature," and, favorably quoting Findlay's *Expositor's Greek Testament*, writes: "The aorist in this context denotes 'not "as he wills" (according to his choice or liking) but in accordance with his past decree in creation, by which the propagation of life on earth was determined from the beginning (Gen 1:11, 12)'" (1264–65). Cf. Robertson and Plummer, 1911, 370; Kistemaker, 1993, 568; Lockwood, 2000, 583–84, 586. Some English translations miss the significance of the aorist: e.g., NAB, NKJV, NLT; cf. TEV, as do some commentators: e.g., explicitly Ellingworth and Hatton, 1994, at 15.38; implicitly Moffatt, 1938, 257. Vos (1930) objects to the reading I put forward above, saying, "The Past Tense in the Greek 'as it pleased Him,' might seem to suggest a reference to the creative appointment of the 'bodies' of things. But in connection with the Present Tense 'gives' this is little likely" (179 n. 4). However, as I will develop below, a present tense "gives" can naturally indicate God's present providential activity while still being based upon God's past tense "desired" – i.e., his desire at creation – and this is very likely.

and his *wording* shares certain affinities with Gen. 1:11–12 itself and with existing treatments of Genesis 1 in general and vv. 11–12 in particular.

Concerning the themes Paul shares with the biblical text, the exact ontological correspondence with God's voiced desires and the ontic differentiation of seeds can be easily drawn from Gen. 1:11–12. In Paul's statement, the exact item that God "desired" before his "gift" of creation ("God gives *to the seed a body* just as he desired...") is particularized by his ontological phrase in v. 38c: "to each [ἑκάστῳ] of the seeds its own [ἴδιον] body." Paul's reflection of major themes of Gen. 1:11 can be seen below:

Gen. 1:11 reads:		In 1 Cor. 15:38bc Paul writes:
God said...	→	God gives...
...and in happened in this manner		... just as he desired

seeding seeds
  according to kind and
  according to likeness
	→	to each of the seeds
		  its own body
		  (whether wheat, etc.)

Paul refers to *kinds* of seeds: "whether of wheat or something else" (v. 37c).[190] God grants to each seed its own body according to kind. Scholars often note that Paul has Gen. 1:11–12 in mind,[191] though this reference is not developed as much as it could be.

For a careful reader of the LXX (but perhaps especially for one who also knows the Hebrew), the additions, modifications, and awkward wording of the Greek of Gen. 1:11–12 would likely cause both "seeds" and the theme of similarity/differentiation of "kinds" to stand out.[192] Philo displayed such exegetical focus in *Op.* 44 (cf. §§62, 64; see above and further

---

[190] The plural helps confirm this: Thiselton (2000) writes (quoting Grimm-Thayer, 583), "It is important to note that 'the singular [of σπέρμα] is used collectively' of grains or kernels sown; hence when the plural occurs (as here) it often denotes *kinds* of seeds. English offers parallels in such words as *cheese* or *fruit* where novelists will often write of *cheeses* or *fruits* to denote a bountiful provision of *kinds of fruit* and *types of cheese*" (1265; emphasis mixed original and added).

[191] See especially the careful reasoning of Collins, 1999, 563–64. Cf. Thiselton, 2006A, 280; Lockwood, 2000, 583–84, 586; Kistemaker, 1993, 569; Usami, 1976, 479, 479 n. 43; Sider, 1975, 432; Conzelmann, 1975, 281; Héring, 1962, 174.

[192] Three of the LXX's modifications of the Hebrew of vv. 11–12 would make it probable that these verses would stand out in an interpreter's mind. 1) The LXX adds the phrase "and according to likeness" to "according to kind," repeating it in both verses. 2) The LXX assimilates v. 11 to v. 12 (see Cook, 2001, 321, 324; Rösel, 1994, 42) so that the phrase "according to kind and according to likeness" modifies the "seeding seed" rather than the fruit in both verses (see Wevers, 1993, 7). 3) The LXX uses the "unusual construction" σπεῖρον σπέρμα, "seeding seed" (Wevers, 1993, 6), which later translators, such as Aquila, attempted to "smooth out" (Wevers, 6 n. 21; cf. Rösel, 1994, 41). Because of its awkward nature it would have been easy for an interpreter's attention to be drawn to the seeds.

below). Paul not only writes of the present-day "sowing" (σπείρεις) of "seeds" (τῶν σπερμάτων; cf. σπεῖρον σπέρμα in Gen. 1:11–12),[193] but he presses upon the Corinthians that it is God who makes the future [plant-] body, giving to "*each* of the [kinds of] seeds" (ἑκάστῳ τῶν σπερμάτων) "its *own* body" (ἴδιον σῶμα). There are slight differences, however, between Paul's point regarding seeds and plants, Philo's point regarding the "seeds" of Gen. 1:11–12, and the point of vv. 11–12 itself. In the biblical text one finds "plants yielding seeds." In Philo one finds "plants yielding fruit [the end] which yield seeds [the beginning] which yield plants [etc.]," i.e., the divinely purposed (ἐβουλήθη) and granted cyclical self-preservation unto "immortality" (ἀπαθανατίζων) (*Op.* 44). In Paul one finds "seeds yielding plants," i.e., the divinely desired (ἐθέλησεν) and granted end-body coming out of the beginning-body. Paul is ultimately employing the analogy of God's creation of plants from seeds so as to arrive at "immortality" (ἀθανασίαν) and "incorruptibility" (ἀφθαρσίαν) (vv. 52–54), in this manner having a reading broadly similar to Philo. But for Paul this telos of immortality is due not to ontological self-perpetuation effected by God at the beginning (Philo's point), but is rather due to the ontic "change" effected by God in the end.[194]

Such ontology comes about in perfect accord with God's desires, and this is the other major theme in which Paul (in v. 38) and Genesis 1 accord. We have already seen how such a theme can be easily drawn from Genesis 1 itself.[195] Through an example in a psalm and one in Philo we will now see that such an interpretive move – whether regarding creation in general (the psalm) or a commentary on Genesis 1 in particular (Philo) – was being made both before and contemporarily with Paul. Speaking of creation in general, Ps. 134:6 LXX makes explicit what is obvious but implicit in Genesis 1: "All things – as much as he desired [ὅσα ἠθέλησεν] – the Lord made [ἐποίησεν] in heaven and in earth."[196] From Paul's perspective, this statement itself could be seen as a later commentary on Genesis 1. It pre-

---

[193] Collins, 1999, 563–64; cf. 566 n. 38.

[194] Philo can also attribute the perpetual "incorruptibility" (ἀφθαρσία; cf. 1 Cor. 15:52–54) of the cosmos not to God's initial ontic structuring but to his perpetual "providence" (*Aet.* 13–19; *Dec.* 58; Frick, 1999, 91–94, 102–08; Runia, 1986, 152, 241–42; though cf. *Plant.* 8–10). But in this particular reading of Gen. 1:11–12 (*Op.* 44) (the textual point of contact with Paul), when Philo expresses a pattern of plants-seeds that mirrors broader reality (as Paul also does), the difference summarized above between Philo's and Paul's approaches emerges as a *true* (if not *full*) picture of one of their differences.

[195] So Westermann, 1984, 41; Delitzsch, 1894, 71. As I noted at the outset of this chapter, Parker (2005) takes a different approach to the phrase "and it happened in this manner" (443–51), and thus ends up at a different interpretation of Genesis 1 than both Philo and Paul, where creation is "more differentiated than (God had) planned" (451).

[196] Lockwood, 2000, 586; Kistemaker, 1993, 568–69.

sents the same notion that Paul develops in 1 Cor. 15:38–41 of a previous "desire" according to which God makes the cosmos. Likewise, as we saw above, in Philo's commentary he saw in God's creation of the "seed" in Gen. 1:11–12 that God "purposed" (ἐβουλήθη) seeds, plants, and general reality to be structured in a specific way (*Op.* 44). Philo extended this theme and wording to Gen. 1:20–23 wherein God granted "to each" (ἑκάστῃ) kind of being "its own" (ἴδιον) qualities and characteristics (§62), and they became structured in that manner. For Paul, God "desired" (ἠθέλησεν) seeds, plants, and general reality to be structured in a specific way (1 Cor. 15:38), "granting" "to each" (ἑκάστῳ) seed "its own" (ἴδιον) body. Paul will also extend this theme to the existence of various types of flesh and glory in heaven and earth (vv. 39–41; see below). Paul's point is that God created particular bodies in Genesis 1 just as he wanted, and the resurrection of corpses happens "in this manner" (οὕτως).[197]

Lying under and driving Paul's seed-analogy in 1 Cor. 15:37–38 is an interpretation of Gen. 1:11–13. It emphasizes ontic difference based on divine desire and causation. Using this analogy, Paul begins to build this principle: bodies, whether present (like a seed) or future (like a plant), can easily be different, for this has been God's creative desire and action since the beginning. This ontology, shaped by Gen. 1:11–12, is *not* applicable to the Corinthians' queries about the somatic ontology of the resurrection by expressing that something inherent in the natural order organically grows new human bodies out of the "seed" of the old, as if God had built immortality and resurrection into the nature of created bodies. Though easy to derive from a seed-analogy, that is not Paul's point. Genesis 1:11–12 is applicable to the resurrection because God's creative pattern, established in Genesis 1 but constantly enacted in his present providential activity, is that *he himself* "gives" bodies according to his own purpose. Therefore these bodies are appropriate according to their (divinely determined) kinds.

Yet Paul does not move directly from this creative seed-analogy to its application in the resurrection. In the next stage of his creative prolegomena to the resurrection, vv. 39–41, Paul extends this ontological point about body-differentiation from botany to cosmology. And he does this in the language of the second – sixth days of Genesis 1.

(ii) The Other Days: The Language of Genesis 1 (vv. 39–41)

Paul transitions, almost abruptly (i.e., with no "and," "but," etc.), from explaining an ontic diversity which God gives among plants to explaining an ontic diversity throughout the entire cosmos. He asserts:

---

[197] Harrisville (1987) marks well the importance of the direct correspondence between creation and resurrection according to Paul's concept of the divine "will" (275–76).

Not all flesh is the same flesh, but rather one for humans, and another flesh for beasts, and another flesh for birds, and another for fish. And there are bodies that are in heaven and bodies that are on earth. But there is one glory for the ones in heaven, and there is another for the ones on earth. There is one glory for the sun, and another glory for the moon, and another glory for the stars; for a star differs from a star in glory. (15:39–41)

It would be difficult to argue that Paul is not still assuming that God's "giving" and "desire" are behind these various diversities as they were behind Paul's botanical theory. Indeed, his entire use of cosmological ontic diversity (vv. 39–41) as the setting for God's undeniable ability to raise the dead in changed bodies and glories (vv. 42ff) rests on the assumption that v. 38 governs vv. 39–41. It is God who "gives" diverse bodies – indeed, now the even more particular "fleshes" and "glories" – not only to seeds and plants but to all of these "bodies" throughout the cosmos, each according to his previous "desire."[198] Now *all* bodies "in heaven" and "on earth" are distinguished from each other, each according to their own kind, whether in "flesh" or in "glory."

Although there are recognizable similarities between Paul's cosmological expression in vv. 39–41 and what was "philosophical[ly] commonplace" in his day,[199] and these could be fruitfully explored, it is the case that the text of Genesis 1 *also*, perhaps even primarily, lies behind this particular cosmological description.[200] Paul not only often supports his arguments with scripture, but he has already used and will continue to use texts

---

[198] For v. 38 lying underneath vv. 39–41 see e.g., Thiselton, 2000, 1265; Harrisville, 1987, 275; Morris, 1985, 220; Vos, 1930, 181.

[199] Martin, 1992, 125.

[200] So Collins, 1999, 563–64. The key features of the "philosophical commonplace" that Martin (1992) sees in 1 Cor. 15:39–41 are 1) "different kinds of creatures exist in different cosmic realms," 2) "each occupying a body appropriate to its own realm," and 3) each "composed of substances derived from that realm" (125). The Genesis-text itself can be arguably presented as God creating realms (i.e., heaven, water and air, earth) on days two and three (1:6–13) and then filling those realms with realm-appropriate beings or bodies (i.e., stars for the heavens, fish and birds for the water and air, beasts and humans for the earth). It even presents (in a limited way) that the various beings are produced out of their respective realms (fish [and birds] from water, beasts and humans from earth). Radice (1989) argues that this is precisely Philo's structure in *Op.*: creating realms, filling them with appropriate bodies (117–23, esp. 120, 122). Thus two points need to be made. 1) The "philosophical commonplace" described by Martin above (1992, 125) has affinities with the structural and essential presentation in Genesis 1 itself. 2) This structure to Genesis 1 seems to have been recognized by Philo in such a manner that he could employ technical philosophical language and motifs (moreso than Paul) within a commentary that had as its *primary goal* the explanation of *the biblical text*. Therefore, is it not probable that Paul, though expressing his cosmology in terms and ideas consistent with "philosophical commonplace," nevertheless had (even primarily) the text of Genesis 1 facilitating his communication? (See the following note.)

from Genesis 1–5 in this specific argument in 1 Corinthians 15.[201] There is an impressive array of recent scholars who recognize not merely that Paul refers to creation in general, but that Paul's cosmology in vv. 39–41 is connected to the text of Genesis 1.[202] But as was the case with v. 38 specifically, so too with vv. 39–41 this simple recognition *that* Paul is here influenced by the text of Genesis could be aided by a more detailed exploration of *how* Paul reads the text.

I have already observed that in v. 38 Paul wrote of God's *present* activity (δίδωσιν) which caused ontology to come about in exact accord with (κάθως) God's *past* intentions and desires (ἠθέλησεν). It became clear that Paul was explaining God's present botanical providence in a manner that was not only built upon God's past creational desire but that also shared affinities with both Gen. 1:11–12 itself and with a few comments on the biblical account that had been made before or contemporarily with Paul. In vv. 39–41, Paul again has his eyes in the present, describing the bodily differentiations that he *presently* sees on earth and in the heavens. His direct point is still ontological, expanding his own botanical statement from v. 38c to the cosmos. But the inseparable correlate of "to each their own" is still God's past desire and then activity. Now, although Paul's mention of present "fleshes" (v. 39) may still refer to God's present providential causation (as with plants, so with animals), his mention of the heavenly bodies (v. 41) assumes that his concept of God's "giving" is not exclusively providential, but rather includes what took place in the beginning itself (Gen. 1:14–19). For it was in the beginning, not in the present, that the sun, moon, and stars had their glorious origin in God's gift. In vv. 38-41, therefore, Paul's concept of God's "giving" encompasses both God's present providential activity in plants, animals, and humans as well as God's past creational activity in sun, moon, and stars.

---

[201] In 1 Corinthians 15, Paul has already referenced Genesis 3 in vv. 21–22 and Ps. 8:7 LXX (cf. Gen. 1:26–28) in vv. 24–28. He will shortly quote and expound Gen. 2:7 in vv. 45–47. He will then allude to Gen. 5:3 in vv. 48–49. The text of the beginning of Genesis is on Paul's mind. See Wright, 2003, 313. In a slightly different but related manner, Scott (1997) argues: "Like most Jews of his day, Paul derived his conception of the world [the *imago mundi*] from the Table-of-Nations tradition based on Genesis 10" (381). Even if this is untrue, my point remains; but if this is true then there is another concrete example of an aspect of Paul's cosmology derived from Genesis' formative chapters.

[202] Among those recognizing creation in general (but not necessarily the text of Genesis 1) in vv. 39–41 cf. N. Watson, 1992, 175; Senft, 1979, 204–05; Simon, 1959, 149; Moffatt, 1938, 258. Among those recognizing the specific text of Genesis 1 behind Paul's cosmology in vv. 38–41 see Becker, 2007, 164; Heil, 2005, 232–33, 233 nn. 5–6; Wright, 2003, 313, 340–41; Padgett, 2002, 159; Asher, 2001, 109 (cf. *idem*, 2000, 78–79); Collins, 1999, 564–67, 569; Furnish, 1999, 113; Horsley, 1998, 209; Kremer, 1997, 355; Stanley, 1992, 208; Fee, 1987, 782–83, 782 n. 32; Sellin, 1986, 219 n. 22; Lambrecht, 1981, 524 n. 68; Usami, 1976, 481–82; Conzelmann, 1975, 282 n. 18.

Regardless of Paul's exact timing of God's "giving" of the fleshes and glories in vv. 39–41, however, underlying *all* of God's cosmic body-giving is the theocentric principle that God caused this differentiated ontology to come about in exact accord with (κάθως) his *past* intentions and desires (ἠθέλησεν), i.e., from Genesis 1. This discussion is an implicit reminder that for Paul, as for Philo in his commentary on Genesis 1, what God thought and desired *before* the beginning is a crucial and interwoven aspect of Paul's interpretation of the text of the Beginning. We will now analyze in greater detail Paul's cosmic theological ontology in light of his language as it corresponds to each of the remaining days of Genesis 1.

1. The Fifth and Sixth Days: Paul's Zoology and Gen. 1:20–27 (v. 39)

According to Genesis 1, God's organization of his creatures according to their own kinds did not stop with the seeds. It is repeated many times over that the different creatures – fish (ἰχθύς), birds (πετεινόν), beasts (κτῆνος), and creeping things (ἑρπετόν) – are each "according to kind" (κατὰ γένος).[203] As I will demonstrate in further detail in chapter 3, even humanity (ἄνθρωπος) is set apart from these other animals according to a different kind: i.e., "according to the image and likeness of God." The oft-repeated phrase in Genesis 1, "according to kind," in itself emphasizes similarity, but when read in the context wherein *each* matches its *own* kind the implicit cumulative force is differentiation as well. Paul writes,

God gives to it [*sc.* a seed] a [plant-]body just as he wanted, and to each [ἑκάστῳ] of the [kinds of] seeds its own body [ἴδιον σῶμα]. Not all flesh is the same flesh; rather: one for humans [ἄλλη ἀνθρώπων], another flesh for beasts [ἄλλη σὰρξ κτηνῶν], another flesh for birds [ἄλλη σὰρξ πτηνῶν], and another for fish [ἄλλη ἰχθύων]. (vv. 38–39)

Paul's language and point are reminiscent of Philo's as he had read Gen. 1:20–25. In *Op.* 63–64, Philo interpreted God's command to the "kinds" (γένη) of animals as involving "differing" (διαφέροντα, x2) habitats, sizes, structural qualities, strengths, and capacities. Philo highlighted ontological differences. Paul not only reads Gen. 1:20–25 using similar words as Philo for the animals (cf. Paul's κτῆνος, πτηνός, ἰχθύς with Philo's ἰχθύς, πτηνός, κτῆνος), but he even "differentiates" similarly: compare Paul's διαφέρω (v. 41) with Philo's διαφέρω, and Paul's "one [ἄλλη]... another [ἄλλη]" (v. 39) with Philo's "one [ἄλλα]... another [ἄλλα]." Also like Philo, Paul's explicit claim in v. 39 is ontological.

By the parallels mentioned above I am by no means asserting that Paul was in any way dependent on Philo. Rather, due to the strong correlations

---

[203] After "according to kind" (and "according to likeness") occurs 4x on day three, it occurs 2x on day five and 5x on day six (not including "according to image" and "according to likeness" in 1:26).

of language and theme, one cannot differentiate Paul's cosmological expressions in vv. 39–41 from those of a formal commentary on Genesis 1 from an interpreter from the same time-period and scriptural background.

Paul's "descending hierarchy"[204] of creatures in v. 39 carries forward Paul's prolegomena to his answer about the ontology of resurrection-bodies. It does by making the same double-edged point as Genesis 1: ontology (to each body its own flesh, according to kind) based on theology (God's action according to his "freely willed determination").[205] In v. 40 Paul extends these earthy examples to the heavens.

2. The Second Day: Paul's Cosmology and Gen. 1:6–8, 9–10 (v. 40)

While still focusing on "bodies" in v. 40, Paul now differentiates between those "in heaven" and those "on earth."[206] Paul writes:

And there are bodies in heaven [σώματα ἐπουράνια] and bodies on earth [σώματα ἐπίγεια]. But the glory of those in heaven [τῶν ἐπουρανίων] is of one kind [ἑτέρα], while that of those on earth [τῶν ἐπιγείων] is of another kind [ἑτέρα]. (v. 40)

Genesis 1 opens with God's creation of "heaven and earth" (v. 1). It continues with God making "the heaven" firm (vv. 6–8) and "the earth" dry (vv. 9–10). God then fills the heaven with distinguishable lights (vv. 14–19) and fills the earth with kind-specific beings (vv. 20–27). By the end of the account, "the heaven" and "the earth" had been "completed" along with "all their adornment" (πᾶς ὁ κόσμος αὐτῶν) (2:1). Paul looks up and sees "bodies" in the two cosmic realms: in heaven and on earth (v. 40a). This implies that for Paul the two realms are not only distinguishable but also appropriate for their own kinds of bodies.[207]

In v. 40b Paul makes it explicit that the realm-specific bodies are different (ἕτερος) from each other, this time not in substance (such as "flesh") but in "glory." It should not be missed that Paul considers the *"earthly bodies"* (i.e., those of Gen. 1:20–27) to have "glory," and this is so as they are *presently* observable. In chapter 3 I will draw out some important implications from Paul's concept here, particularly regarding how he applies the word "glory" to "humans" among the rest. Here I will focus more generally on this label which Paul grants to all of the "bodies" in the cosmos.

---

[204] Martin, 1992, 125; cf. Kistemaker, 1993, 570; Usami, 1976, 482 n. 50; Robertson and Plummer, 1911, 370. This presents the opposite order (descending rather than ascending) but similar structure (hierarchy of complexities) to the biblical text's order (see also Philo's *Op.* 64–68; Radice, 1989, 122).

[205] Lockwood, 2000, 586.

[206] Fee (1987) presents in a chiastic structuring of vv. 39–41 that this particular contrast is very important to Paul's prolegomena (783; cf. Collins, 1999, 565).

[207] Barclay, 1954, 176. Cf. Martin, 1992, 125.

Of those commentators who do more than merely reword Paul's statement,[208] there is disagreement concerning its implications for Paul's thought. J. Héring judges Paul's choice of *doxa* for "heavenly bodies" in v. 40 to have been "unfortunate," for it "accidentally carries with it (15:40b) the use of '*doxa*' for earthly bodies too."[209] Héring does not think the term "glory" is appropriate for earthly bodies. He considers Paul to have agreed, but to have been too focused on pithy parallelisms to have realized (or cared) just how "unfortunate" such a concept was to bring into the earthly realm. But was Paul so bound by parallelisms that he would write something with which he himself actually disagreed? Anthony Thiselton considers that "any supposed difficulty about ascribing splendor or glory to the bodies of those who live on the earth" is "overcome" by understanding "glory" as what is "wonderful," "full of splendor," "what makes something weighty or impressive," a "source of elation," a "source of delight."[210] Simon Kistemaker writes, "The brilliance of the celestial luminaries is awe-inspiring, yet the majesty of the mountains and forests cannot be underestimated. Each has a luster of its own."[211] N.T. Wright construes "glory" as the "proper dignity, reputation and honor" of the created bodies as they fulfil their appropriate functions.[212] Regardless of the exact nuance of the word "glory," Paul demonstrates in v. 40b that he has a very positive image of the created world.

Part of the tension with finding in v. 40b a comparison of bodies in heaven and on earth where *both* have "glory," is that almost within the next breath Paul compares the body that "is sown" (clearly those mentioned in v. 39, though focusing specifically on "humans") with the body that "is raised." There he finds only the latter to be "in glory" while the former are "in dishonor" (vv. 42b-43)! Both comparisons concern bodily ontology, and one might think that such an earthly body can *either* have "glory" (v. 40) *or* be "in dishonor" (v. 43). Yet while the first comparison between "bodies" on earth and in heaven (v. 40b) is done within the context of this present "first" creation, the second comparison (vv. 42b-43 [through v. 49]) is done across an eschatological divide. Within the first comparison (v. 40), the bodies within both cosmic realms have "glory," though "different." Within the second comparison (vv. 42–49), the bodies

---

[208] Some merely reword Paul: e.g., Fee (1987) writes, "in this argument, even though the earthly body must die, it is not without its own glory" (783–84; cf. Morris, 1985, 221; Sellin, 1986, 220)

[209] Héring, 1962, 174–75.

[210] Thiselton, 2000, 1270.

[211] Kistemaker, 1993, 571. Vos (1930) speaks of "flesh" and "glory" in vv. 39–41 in terms of "quality" and "appearance" (179).

[212] Wright, 2003, 345.

of the age initiated by Genesis 1 have no honor compared to the glory of the new creation age initiated by the resurrection.

We will further pursue these contrasts in chapter 3 since they bear directly on what we can determine Paul thinks of the first Adam and what he thinks of the last. For now I will simply point out that Paul employs a similar hermeneutic of comparisons in 2 Cor. 3:10–4:6 (see chapter 3 for further analysis). Though Ex. 34:29 recorded that Moses' face "has been glorified" (δεδόξασται), in 2 Cor. 3:10 Paul writes that Moses' face (as well as his ministry of Law) "has *not* been glorified" (οὐ δεδόξασται). This is only apparently contradictory, however, since Paul's statement is functioning within a hermeneutic of comparison similar to that in 1 Cor. 15:42–49. That is, when referring to Ex. 34:29 on its own, Paul actually writes clearly that Moses and his ministry *did* come "in glory" (ἐν δόξῃ) (2 Cor. 3:7) and that he (and it) actually "*had* been glorified" (δεδοξασμένον) (v. 10).[213] Within a comparison between Moses' ministry and the ministry of the new covenant in Jesus, however, Paul writes the otherwise internally contradictory statement that "the thing which *had* been glorified *has not* been glorifed [οὐ δεδόξασται τὸ δεδοξασμένον] on account of this: the surpassing glory [τῆς ὑπερβαλλούσης δόξης]." Paul can – again to the Corinthians – legitimately attribute something positive (even "glory") to one thing based on what God had done in the past (the law through Moses, the creation of the world and humanity) and yet immediately *also* deprive the same thing of its quality ("it has not been glorified," "it is sown in dishonor") *when comparing it* with the thing that is greater still.

We return now to 1 Cor. 15:40 and Paul's depiction of the diverse "glories" within heaven and earth and all their adorning "bodies." Paul's eschatological polarity is greater than his cosmic divide between heaven and earth. When thinking about cosmology based on Genesis 1 itself, Paul sees a "glory," a beauty, an exceeding goodness among all of the God-determined and God-given bodies in heaven *and* earth. Even the bodies on earth have such a glory in Paul's eyes that, although different from those in heaven, they nevertheless retain their honor even when compared to the brilliance of the heavenly luminaries. Yet when Paul considers these same "bodies" in comparison with what will "be raised," then suddenly the God-given glory becomes no glory. The present bodies cannot be favorably compared to the surpassing glory of the coming body.

These hermeneutical observations are significant for understanding Paul's reading of Genesis 1 as well as his broader theology. Ontology created by God in Genesis 1 is very good, and it remains good despite the groaning of creation under human sin. But it has no honor in comparison with the ontology initiated by God in Jesus' resurrection. The main point

---

[213] See Watson, 2004, 287–91, 295; cf. 287 n. 32; Harris, 2005, 300, 300 n. 30.

that Paul is making in v. 40 itself, however, simply concerns differentiation: "bodies" in heaven and earth are different. Though both have "glory," their glories are "different." Differentiation of God-given "glories" is a significant part of Paul's cosmic prolegomena to the resurrection, for the corpses will themselves be raised by the Creator with a *different* "glory."

3. The Fourth Day: Paul's Astronomy and Gen. 1:14–19 (v. 41)

In v. 41, Paul turns his eyes solely to the heavens and describes the present diversified "glories" of the various "bodies" therein. The sun, moon, and stars "differ" (διαφέρει) from each other. Philo himself had catalogued the diverse brightnesses of sun, moon, and stars.[214] He knew that many contemporaries speculated about the substances and functions of heaven and the heavenly bodies,[215] some considering them as "masses of solid matter," but more (following Plato and Aristotle) regarding them as "living beings whose superior intellect could be derived from their perfect movements."[216] Philo sometimes (though hesitantly) demonstrated this second perspecitive.[217] By his and Paul's day, lovers of a particular type of wisdom still wondered whether there were only five elements from which the entire cosmos was composed, or whether "heaven and the heavenly bodies" had a "peculiar and separate nature of their own," "differing from the rest of the world" through kinship with the divine.[218] Philo considered there to be no consensus.[219]

Compared to the contemporary astronomical speculation, Paul's own rather simple statement about the sun, moon, and stars "differing" in "glory" seems to share little likeness. He may have had an opinion on the substance of stars, but this is inaccessible from what he writes here, foreign to his present intent.[220] Paul writes,

The glory of those [bodies] in heaven is of one kind, while that of those on earth is different. There is one glory of the sun [ἡλίου], and another glory of the moon [σελήνης], and another glory of the stars [ἀστέρων]; for star [ἀστήρ] differs from star [ἀστέρος] in glory. In this manner also is the resurrection of the corpses. (vv. 40b-42a)

While Paul had differentiated between the structural "substances" of the earthly bodies according to their kinds (to each their own "flesh"), and so a differentiation between substances of the "heavenly bodies" could have fit

---

[214] E.g., *Somn.* 1.116.
[215] *Somn.* 1.21–24, 53–54.
[216] Runia, 2001, 240.
[217] See *Plant.* 7, 12; cf. *Gig.* 8; *Somn.* 1.135 (Conzelmann, 1975, 282 n. 23; Runia, 2001, 240); though see *Spec.* 1.66.
[218] *Abr.* 162–63.
[219] *Somn.* 1.21–24, 53–54.
[220] Contra Martin, 1992, 125–26.

well into his present goal, he decided to shift attention from "substance" to "form."[221] Because Paul considers the category of "glory" to be so important to his concept of the resurrected life of the Christ and (in the future) of Jesus' followers – even considering "our glory" to have been pre-marked out "for" believers *before* the creation of the sun, moon, and stars! – thus the Creator's ability to grant any form of "glory" he so desired is also an important principle to institute alongside that of God's differentiation of fleshly substances.[222]

Though Paul's presentation of the heavenly bodies could have arisen merely from popular understanding and/or simple observation,[223] it is difficult to conclude that his understanding is thereby disconnected from his interpretation of the sacred text of the Beginning. It is probable that here too Paul's wording has been shaped by Genesis 1.[224] Genesis 1:14–19 relates God speaking, making, and setting "the luminaries in the firmness of heaven [τοῦ οὐρανοῦ]." Perhaps originally for polemical reasons, Genesis 1 does not give these the names "sun" or "moon."[225] Paul names the sun,

---

[221] Thiselton, 2000, 1269.

[222] Sellin, 1986, 220 n. 26.

[223] Martin (1992) is "impressed" with "how similar Paul's arguments" in vv. 40–41 are to "the assumptions underwriting 'astral soul' theory in popular philosophy" (126). In that theory, "What human beings have in common with heavenly bodies [sc. stars] is, in Paul's system, incorporation as a 'pneumatic body' – that is, a body composed only of pneuma with sarx and psyche having been sloughed off along the way" (126). To arrive at this conclusion, Martin makes at least two types of exegetical errors. First, he wrongly compares "Hellenistic folklore" with the resurrection idea of Dan. 12:3 (cf. *2 Bar.* 51:10; Wis. 3:7) (118, 274 n. 57). In Hellenistic folklore people "become" stars while it appears that Daniel (*et par.*) uses a simile to say that people will rise to "shine *like*" lights" rather than, as Martin construes it, "becoming" stars (rightly Nickelsburg, 1981, 89, 285; wrongly Johnston, 2002, 231 [who makes Martin's mistake, but about Egyptian astral anthropology]). (Paul appears to use Danielic language with the simile in Phil. 2:15.) The Danielic text(s) and Paul (Phil. 2:15; 1 Cor. 15:41) speak of form/function ("shining like") while Martin and Johnston (and their Graeco-Roman/Egyptian star "parallels") speak of substance ("becoming stars"). Thiselton (2000) gives a helpful critique of Martin (1269). Second, it is *pneuma*-as-substance that Martin sees in common between "the bodies in heaven" in vv. 40–41 and the resurrected bodies in 15:44–46 (the resurrected bodies also being "from heaven" in vv. 47–49) (126). But Paul never calls the sun, moon, and stars *pneumatic*, and if *pneuma* is divine presence and activity rather than substance in vv. 44–46 (so Thiselton, 2000, 1276–77; *et al.*, see above n. 165) then Martin's theory cannot stand at this point either.

[224] So Becker, 2007, 164; Wright, 2003, 341; Furnish, 1999, 113; Sellin, 1986, 220 n. 26; Lambrecht, 1981, 524 n. 68.

[225] So some suggest this is an implicit critique of the astral-worship of surrounding peoples: e.g., von Rad, 1956, 53–54; Westermann, 1984, 127; Carmichael, 1996, 3–4; Noort, 2000, 9 (and 9 nn. 47–48). Gelander (1997) is skeptical (98). Cf. Tigchelaar, 2005, 31–32, 32 nn. 3–6. Such astral worship was a real concern in Philo's day as well (*Conf.* 173).

moon, and stars (as had Sir. 43:1–10 when commenting on Gen. 1:14–19, see below), and he then compares them by their different "glories." The manner in which Genesis itself does name them relates the luminaries to each other as well, for it calls them "the greater light," "the lesser light," and then only passingly references God's creation of "also the stars." Thus the text differentiates between these bodies according to form (size) and/or function or appearance (brightness), not substance. Paul's assumed relationship between "glory" and "light" (which he employs in the context of a comment on Gen. 1:2–3 in 2 Cor. 4:6) is transparent here as he describes the greater light, lesser light, and also the stars as differing not according to substance, but according to form or function, i.e., "glory."[226]

Paul's astronomical conclusion says little more than what would be obvious to any Corinthians who might look up into the heavens on a clear night. And yet his comments are not thereby less related to his reading of Gen. 1:14–19.[227] For example, Sirach 43 seamlessly stitches together what is plainly visible "in the firmament of heaven" concerning "sun," "moon," and "stars" with words and concepts clearly drawn from Gen. 1:14–19.[228] Ben Sira does this to convey the stars as the "glory" of heaven: the heavenly bodies display "glory" (δόξα) both through their "shining" (i.e., their

---

[226] Paul often employs (as do others) the concept of "glory" in a more weighty manner than mere brightness, as in 2 Cor. 3:7–4:6, though it is also important that he does associate (as do others) "glory" with light and brightness (cf. Sir. 43:8–9). So Thiselton, 2000, 1270; cf. Wright, 2003, 345. Against Wright, concerning 1 Cor. 15:40–41 there is no need to choose "'honor,' 'reputation,' 'proper dignity'" *rather than* "luminosity, brightness," or splendor simply because the latter do not fit Paul's statement about "earthly bodies" (v. 40b). The word δόξα can contain each nuance without needing to differentiate sharply and can be used rhetorically with different nuances in the same context. Paul does both. Wright is right, however, that "it is of course the proper dignity, reputation and honor of the sun that it should shine brightly, and of the stars that they should twinkle in their own appropriate manner" (345). But in light of the blending in Sirach 43 of "glory," "shining," "illuminating," *and* the appropriate *function* of the heavenly bodies according to God's word/command – especially as this is found within an application of Gen. 1:14–19 (see below) – we should be careful about separating the nuances of glory-as-function from glory-as-brightness in Paul's discussion, which is also built on Gen. 1:14–19.

[227] Collins, 1999, 567 nn. 40–41.

[228] Certain affinities between Sirach 43 and Gen. 1:14–19 are noticed by Tigchelaar, 2005, 37, 37–39 (concerning the Hebrew) and Thiselton, 2000, 1268–69. The affinities in the Greek of 43:1–10 are extensive. E.g., within Ben Sira's discussion of the function of the "sun" (vv. 2–5), "moon" (vv. 6–8), and "stars" (vv. 9–10) in "the firmness of heaven" (στερεώματι οὐρανοῦ, vv. 2, 8), each of which the Lord "made" (ποιήσας) and then directed with his "words" (cf. vv. 5, 10), Ben Sira speaks of this adorned heavenly realm offering "a vision of glory," where "the beauty of heaven [κάλλος οὐρανοῦ] is the glory of the stars [δόξα ἄστρων], an adornment giving light [κόσμος φωτίζων] in the highest places of the Lord" (v. 9).

form) and through their proper obedience to God's "words" in Genesis 1 (i.e., their function). By Paul's day it was feasible (to say the least) to speak of the "glory" of the sun, moon, and stars in a way that was in line with empirical observation and yet simultaneously to also craft this description of astronomical "glory" around Gen. 1:14–19.[229]

In 1 Cor. 15:37–41, Paul presents his cosmological theory of body-differentiation. He focuses on the ontological qualities of these bodies under the categories of flesh and glory. He shaped this "reading" of the cosmos around his reading of the beginning of the world according to Genesis. For Paul the existence of the diverse bodies in heaven and on earth – discerned by sight and described according to Genesis 1 – is based on God's action which itself perfectly accords with his own previous desire. After laying such a creative foundation, Paul writes, "In *this* manner is the resurrection of the corpses" (v. 42a). This prolegomenon of the Beginning of the world according to Genesis has prepared the way for Paul's answer to the questions regarding resurrection-ontology. Yet Paul does not leave Genesis behind when he moves from this prolegomena to his direct answer. Paul will explain even the resurrection-ontology by turning the Corinthians again to the Beginning, more specifically to the Beginning of humanity, still according to Genesis.

(c) Summary: Paul's Beginning of the World

To answer the objection to the resurrection of dead bodies, Paul does not present a general credo of creation,[230] but rather the specific examples of body-construction in Genesis 1. Paul's interpretation of the Beginning of the world as presented above has certain implications. I will draw concluding attention to one, the matter with which I introduced this section: the debate between J. Becker and N.T. Wright. To import *creatio ex nihilo* into 1 Cor. 15:35–49 simply because Paul employs "creation" in his argument, and then to deduce a resurrection *ex nihilo* which leaves the old bodies in the tombs and starts from scratch,[231] is to misunderstand how Paul himself

---

[229] Hays (1997) writes, "The reference to heavenly bodies might also have helped the philosophically inclined Corinthians make better sense of the concept of a resurrection body. It was a common belief in the ancient world that the human soul and/or mind was made of the same ethereal stuff as the celestial bodies and that the soul would return to the stars after death" (271; see Martin, 1992, 118, 126 and Johnston, 2002, 231, critiqued above). Hays continues, however: "Paul, of course, did not share this view, but his description of heavenly 'bodies' that possess varying degrees of glory could help his readers conceptualize a future glorified body unlike the bodies we now know" (271; cf. Lockwood, 2000, 587, 587 n. 8).

[230] Such general statements ("creeds") of creation can be found in 1 Cor. 8:6 and Rom. 11:36 (and cf. 1 Cor. 11:12c with 2 Cor. 5:18a).

[231] So Becker, 2007, 165, 167, 168.

reads and applies "creation" to the Corinthian query of resurrection. Becker (among others) is right that the "bridge of continuity" (or the *primary* bridge of continuity, I would nuance) between the first and last bodies is "the power of the Creator."[232] This is seen explicitly in v. 38 and implicitly undergirding vv. 39–41: it is God who gives as he desired. But for Paul this power manifested in different ways. It was displayed in the creation of heavenly bodies (v. 41) (which was *ex nihilo*, see Gen. 1:14–19). It came in the creation of earthly animals (v. 39) (which was not *ex nihilo* but out of water and dust, see Gen. 1:20–27). God's power continues in his repeated gift of plant-bodies out of seeds (vv. 37–38) (not *ex nihilo* in Gen. 1:11–12 or providence). Paul's understanding of creation in 1 Cor. 15:37–41 (and 42–49) cannot be simply construed as *creatio ex nihilo* (as Genesis 1 cannot). Consequently, what can be concluded or ruled out regarding the parallel action of the Creator in the resurrection of corpses?

That question will remain merely posed, for our present purpose is limited to interpreting the Beginning and Before in Paul. For Paul, the ontological characteristics of the original creation – i.e., their diverse fleshy substances and forms, appearances, and/or functions as glorious – were set in place by God's own activity in Genesis 1 (and beyond), in perfect accord with his desires. And in *that* manner is the resurrection of the corpses and the "change" of still-living bodies into what will come about.[233]

In 1 Corinthians 15, Paul does not seem to think that one can fully understand even the anthropology of the End without first understanding the ontology of the entire cosmos in the Beginning. This is particularly so since the resurrection has been (for Jesus) and will be (for Jesus' followers) accomplished by the God whose activity and fore-desire were presented in Gen. 1:6–31. Now the Corinthians are primed to understand the humanity of the End. Yet as we will see in the final chapter, Paul's End still does not leave behind either the Beginning or the Before, for Paul casts the End in the language and conceptuality of *both*.

2.4 Comparisons and Conclusions
Philo and Paul on the Beginning of the World

In Genesis 1 the creation of light is of a special sort. It is paradigmatic for the other creative events through its theocentric emphasis on the fulfilment of God's word (v. 3), and through its "beautiful" portrayal of the product's

---

[232] Becker, 2007, 167; cf. Thiselton, 2000, 1271 (*idem*, 1978, 525); Collins, 1999, 564; Bonhoeffer, 1959 (ET), 19.

[233] Garland, 2003, 732; Thiselton, 2000, 1265–66; Lockwood, 2000, 588; N. Watson, 1992, 175–76.

ontic character (v. 4). In the light of Gen. 1:2–5, vv. 6–31 carry forward this dual project. They present an ontology of goodness that accords with the sovereign and divine word, act, and (assumed) previous intentions. Philo and Paul set apart the light of Gen. 1:2–5 for particular use. Both men retain the text's theocentricity by focussing the God who shined light in both creation and salvation. Philo sometimes sees the ontological-intellectual gift of light at creation as itself being a pre-emptive salvation. He also presents the ontological structure of corporeality as necessarily dimming the incorporeal light through its less-pure embodiment of it. Paul also relates the light of God's creative *fiat* on day one to salvific illumination. He does so by highlighting not what is inherent in creation but the subsequent historical activity of the same Creator. For Paul, the Creator's light is not dimmed by alliance with a body, or more particularly a face.

The two interpreters share mainly similarities regarding their interpretations of the rest of the world's Beginning (Gen. 1:6–31). Throughout his reading of these creative acts, Philo draws attention to two themes: 1) God's sovereign activity (his "call," his own enactments, sometimes despite God's use of created mediators in Genesis 1), and 2) the propriety of the ontic order (wherein each being has its own particular qualities). By encompassing both themes in an implicit Before, Philo repeatedly highlights God's previous fore-knowledge, understanding, and "purpose." Philo's Before – i.e., God's mental determinations and purposes *before* the beginning – affects his interpretation of creation. The beginning of the world, however, has also affected Philo's Before: the text of Genesis 1 itself, not only vv. 1–5 (the explicit Before) but vv. 6–31 too, is precisely what shows Philo God's fore-sight, knowledge, and wisdom because of which he created as he did. Philo's treatment of the creation of the world continues to have a reciprocal interplay between the Beginning and Before.

Paul draws attention to the same two themes of Gen. 1:6–31: 1) God's sovereign activity ("giving" bodies), and 2) the ontic diversity of these bodies (wherein each body has its own particular qualities of flesh and glory). By stressing God's previous "desire" according to which ontic structure and glory had their genesis, Paul undergirds and unites both themes with his implicit Before. Paul's Before – i.e., God's desires *before* the beginning – affects his interpretation of creation. Yet for Paul, as for Philo, the beginning of the world also affects his understanding of the Before: the text of Genesis 1 itself is exactly what shows Paul God's "desire" because of which he gave and "gives" heaven and earth their bodily adornments just as he did. Like Philo, Paul's treatment of the creation of the world continues a mutual interplay between the Beginning and Before.

The hermeneutic of both interpreters involves theocentric ontology. Both interpreters glory in the particularities of cosmic structure while having an overarching and undergirding faith in the sovereign Creator's creational purposes and desires. Before turning to humanity's beginning, Philo and Paul find it necessary (or at least helpful) to move through the genesis of the world. This observation is perhaps even more profound regarding Paul's understanding of the Beginning. Unlike Philo, Paul was not bound by a technical commentary to follow the text's order, which itself travels through cosmos to arrive at humanity. It is significant that at points Paul's comments remarkably resemble a formal commentary on Genesis 1. Yet such movement from broader cosmos to more particular humanity arose from his own impulse, one might say, rather than from any necessity to follow the order of the text.

Regardless of literary constraints and freedoms, however, Paul and Philo both read Genesis' Beginning theocentrically. Their comments revolve around the divine pre-creational intentions. Their understanding of the beginning of the world focused on God's sovereign call, word, and previous purpose (the Before). And for Paul, as for Philo, this interpretation of the beginning of the world sets the scene for his reading of the beginning of humanity in Gen. 1:26–28, 2:7, and 5:3.

Chapter 3

The Beginning of Humanity

"When I look at the heavens, the works of your fingers – the moon and stars which you founded – what is a human that you would remember him or the son of a human that you care for him? ... You crowned him with glory and honor and placed him over the works of your hands, subjecting all things under his feet!" (Ps. 8:3–6). The creation of humanity according to Genesis was immeasurably important for the anthropology of both Philo and Paul. But the particular texts which focus on humans are not isolated texts, either in Genesis itself or in Philo's or Paul's interpretations and applications of them. Even in the quotation from Psalm 8 above, the contemplation of God's creation of humanity – with its royal "glory and honor" – is set within the larger framework of God's creation of the heavens, the earth, and all that is in them. This is the same in both Paul and Philo, perhaps better known in Philo's writings[1] but nonetheless present and important in Paul's as well. Psalm 8 even assumes behind God's creation of humanity a certain divine consideration and thought. For Paul and Philo also, God's intentions, purposes, and desires because of which he created humanity as he did in the Beginning are an integral part of each of their interpretations of human origins.

There is a peculiar complexity regarding the beginning(s) of humanity, and it will quickly become clear how complex the hermeneutic of creation really is for both Philo and Paul. As I have been arguing, Paul's interpretation of creation, like Philo's in his formal commentary, contains three interwoven aspects. We have already analyzed the beginning of the world (chapter 2) and God's intentions in the Before (chapter 1), taking special notice of how Paul, like Philo, sees these as intimately woven together like two strands of one cord. But there is also a beginning of humanity, and it is difficult to overestimate its importance for both interpreters. According to their shared scripture, humankind begins according to "the image of God"

---

[1] As Tobin (1992) observes, "each of these two interpretations of the creation of the world [in Philo] has a parallel interpretation of the creation of man" (122), and he furthers that "these two interpretations of the creation of man are intimately interwoven with the two interpretations of the creation of the world" (125). Below I will flesh out the interwoven nature of Philo's Beginning, and I will add the third (or first) strand – i.e., the Before – to the "interwoven" cord which Tobin helpfully observes.

(Gen. 1:27) and with Adam formed as a "living soul" out of dust (Gen. 2:7). Humanity is then propelled forward according to the "image" of Adam (Gen. 5:3). We will now explore this three-part final aspect – this third strand – of Philo's and Paul's interpretations of creation.

3.1 The Image of God: Genesis 1:27

God's creative activity climaxes when he crafts a creature like himself. Humanity is begun, and it is "according to God's image." God's causative and voiced volition ("Let us make humanity") is again prominent. The prior world and the particular humanity are together "made" according to God's spoken will. With humanity as the crowning touch and ruler of creation, the beauty of God's former products has become "exceedingly good" (v. 31).Though the precise phrase "image of God" is limited in Philo's and Paul's scripture (Gen. 1:26 and 27, 5:1, and 9:6), the idea is anthropologically fundamental. It provides the first description of humanity, and only in its wake do all other depictions occur.

Throughout Philo's and Paul's scripture the word "image" (whether צלם or εἰκών) was certainly repeated. It typically referred to an artistic depiction of someone's or something's appearance.[2] There was a mirror-like relationship between an "image" and the one imaged,[3] and thus a nuance of manifestation or revelation is related to the concept of "image," minimally in that by looking at an "image" something was known about the one portrayed.

Throughout the ancient Near East, "image" was also often connected to the dominion of a god or king who would place his statue ("image") in a

---

[2] The word צלם occurs 17 times in the Hebrew scriptures, is most often translated by the LXX as εἰκών, but is translated in Num. 33:52 and 2 Chr. 23:17 by "the idols" (τὰ εἴδωλα) and in 1 Sam. 6:5 by "likeness" (ὁμοίωμα). צלם and εἰκών refer to metal figures (Num. 33:52), cast models of tumors and mice (1 Sam. 6:5, 11), physical representations of the otherwise invisible Baal (2 Ki. 11:18; 2 Chr. 23:17), "images of abomination" (Eze. 7:20), physical (gold and silver) representations of males (Eze. 16:17; Hos. 13:2), pictorial presentations of Chaldeans (Eze. 23:14), and pagan gods (Amos 5:26). In the Psalms, צלם is somewhat different, like "shadows" or dreams (e.g., Ps. 73 [72 LXX]:20). In Daniel 2–3, εἰκών is used at least ten times to refer to a statue, whether in Nebuchadnezzar's dream or of Nebuchadnezzar's golden self to which all were to bow and worship. The legitimate common denominator understands "image" as a physical and/or visible representation of someone/-thing which (in some way) stands in for the actual being (cf. Wis. 14:15).

[3] Schüle, 2005, 4–5, 9–11; Thiselton, 2000, 834–37; Mathews, 1996, 168–69 (169 n. 206); Wenham, 1987, 29–32; Westermann, 1984, 147–55; Conzelmann, 1975, 187–88. For the use of "mirror" with "image" see e.g., Wis. 7:26 and 2 Cor. 3:18 (Watson, 1997, 301 n. 7); cf. Philo's *Leg.* 3.95–99 with 3.100–01 (Siegert, 2009, 184).

city so as to remind those beholding it of his absent self yet present dominion (Wis. 14:17).[4] The "image" also hopefully conveyed something of the king's or god's splendour, beauty, riches, power, impressiveness: his glory.[5] Conversely, if the image looked dishonorable (e.g., was dirty), this reflected poorly on the reputation of the king or god. The "image of God" in Genesis 1 can easily be read in this manner, especially because the text explicitly expresses the function of humanity so defined in terms of dominion: "to rule" over God's works (vv. 26, 28). The creative Sovereign's "statue" in Genesis 1 was living, breathing humanity.[6] It functioned as God's vicegerents or ruling stewards in and over the earth within which he had created them.[7]

There is fluidity within the "image"-concept that is hermeneutically significant. Its openness to a variety of interpretations can be illustrated well in statues and coins which portray the face or form of a king. (These illustrations are especially helpful since both were related to Gen. 1:27 in Philo's and Paul's day.)[8] The statue itself can be conveyed *as* the king's "image," if it resembles and/or is intended to represent him. Yet the king's own appearance can be called his "image," and from this perspective the statue is merely *according to* the king's image. Likewise (though adding complexity), one might think of a coin on which is imprinted a king's face.[9] Now three potentials arise: the coin itself 1) can *be* the king's image,[10] 2) can be *according to* (thus like but distinct from) the image (which, from this perspective, is the king's own appearance), or 3) can even be related to the king through the stamp which impressed the king's

---

[4] Schüle, 2005, 6, 9–11, 19–20; cf. van Kooten, 2008, 2; Currid, 1997, 71; Wenham, 1987, 30–31; von Rad, 1956, 57–58.

[5] For such attributes as "glory" see Jewett, 2004, 33.

[6] Scroggs, 1966, 14–15.

[7] Moltmann, 1985, 224.

[8] The synoptic gospels use "image" (εἰκών) of Caesar's picture stamped on a coin and compare it with humanity's relationship with God (obviously as his "image"): cf. Matt. 22:20–21; Mark 12:16–17; Luke 20:24–25 (Nguyen, 2008, 177–78 n. 128). Likewise, Hillel was attributed with the direct comparison between the statue of a god and himself in light of Gen. 1:27 (Lv. Rabba 34 [130d] in Str.-Bil. [1922–28], 1.654–55; McCasland, 1950, 92).

[9] On the ancient process of stamping "images" on coins see Philo's *Her.* 181. For Philo's direct comparison of this to Gen. 1:27 see *Leg.* 3.95–96; *Plant.* 18–20. For "stamping out" as creation (in matter) see Plato's *Tim.* 39e7, 50c-d (Leonhardt-Balzer, 2004A, 327) and Philo's *Op.* 25. (In *Op.* 16 "stamping" creates the noetic world, in *Leg.* 1.32 the noetic human.) The example in the gospels of "image" and "coin" (noted above) adds the nuance of ownership to the concept of "image" from Gen. 1:27: the one "imaged" (Caesar, God) has a certain claim on the "image" (coin, humans).

[10] Thus Jesus says about the denarius not "whose image is this according to?" but rather "whose image *is* this [τίνος ἡ εἰκών αὕτη]?" (Matt. 22:20).

image upon it.¹¹ When the third relationship is in view, three tiers exist which accord with each other: the face, the stamp, the coin. Any could legitimately be called an "image" while any could also legitimately be distanced from the actual "image." There is great flexibility in both sacred and profane usages of the "image"-concept (εἰκών).

When Gen. 1:27 presents humanity "according to" God's "image," there may be three related but distinct tiers (human – image – God) or equally legitimately only two (human – God's appearance). As with the statue or coin, humanity could even be identified *as* God's "image" even though the text does not explicitly do such. Philo and Paul exploit or assume different nuances of the text's flexible "image" and "accord." While demonstrating this, I will concurrently explore how important it is for each reader's interpretation of humanity that this particular Beginning is contextualized within the broader Beginning of the world and even God's Before.

3.1.1 Philo's Reading of Genesis 1:27

Philo's reading of Gen. 1:26–28, his "anthropological base-text," is important for his anthropology though very complex.¹² Humanity's "likeness" with God could be considered his basic conception.¹³ This likeness is not direct, and it is certainly not a bodily one (rather a mental likeness),¹⁴

---

¹¹ As Dunn (1998A) writes: the word image "can denote both the image on the rubber stamp and the image that the stamp puts on the page" (238). I would add the third: the original appearance ("image") of the one according to whom the rubber stamp and then the page are successively made.

¹² For a good summary see Jervell, 1960, 51–53.

¹³ *Op.* 69.4, 71 (see below).

¹⁴ Likeness as indirect: *QG.* 2.62; *Somn.* 1.73–75; as non-bodily: *Op.* 69.5–7. The God-human likeness concerns the "mind" (νοῦς: *Op.* 69.8ff.), "reasoning" (λόγισμος, *Abr.* 41; *Spec.* 3.83), and "word" (λόγος, *Op.* 24–25, 139, 146; *Leg.* 3.96; *Spec.* 3.207). As Philo interprets Gen. 1:27, the anthropological "mind" (νοῦς), "rational nature" (φύσις λογική), and "reasoning" (λόγος) is a "copy" (μίμημα), "resemblance" (ἀπεικόνισμα), and "image" (εἰκών) of the archetype, i.e., God (e.g., *Det.* 83), by virtue of being not merely a "fragment" (ἀπόσπασμα) of the "soul of the universe" (e.g., *Mut.* 223a), i.e., of the divine nature (e.g., *Op.* 146; *Leg.* 3.161; *Det.* 90; *Somn.* 1.34), but even "more piously" (because it is Moses' language) being a "copy that resembles [ἐκμαγεῖον ἐμφερές] the "divine image [εἰκόνος θείου]" (e.g., *Mut.* 223b). See Hay, 2004, 137. For other ancient Jewish interpretations of divine-human likeness as "reason" cf. Sir. 17:7 and 4Q504 (according to van Kooten, 2008, 8–9, 16, 35, 37, 46–47). On Philo's impact on early Christian interpretations of Gen. 1:27 in a mental direction see Watson, 1997, 277–78; van Kooten, 2008, 9, 47 (though van Kooten, 43, also points to some early Christian reactions *against* an exclusively intellectual reading, esp. in Irenaeus and Tertullian, 38–44). Cf. Kugel, 1998, 81–82. Part and parcel with Philo's bent toward "virtue" and "practical spirituality," both of which are directly connected to his treatment of Gen. 1:27 as "reason," is his appropriation of the Platonic notion of "assimilation to God" (see

though the structure of the body was nevertheless crafted by God to be helpful in the pursuit of wisdom, contemplation, and thus virtue.[15] Philo's commentary presents his complexities in condensed form.

Philo arrives at Gen. 1:26–28 in *Op.* 69. After having finished 1:26–28 in §88 he returns to it and re-interprets it in §134. In his first reading (i.e., §§69–88), Philo treats the human in 1:27 as corporeal and composite: a "human body" and a "mind" (§69; cf. §82). The human is among those who are "earth-born" (γηγενές) (§69). He is "the beginning-born [human] of our race" (τὸν ἀρχηγέτην τοῦ γένους) (§79). Later Philo will label the human of 2:7 with these same titles: "earth-born" (γηγενής), "the beginning-born [human] of our whole race" (ὁ παντὸς τοῦ γένους ἡμῶν ἀρχηγέτης) (§§134–36).[16] Within that second context, in §134, Philo then calls the human of 1:27 "vastly different" from him of 2:7, not least because the former is "*non*-bodily"! Many scholars have noted such (corpus-wide) inconsistencies in Philo's interpretation of Gen. 1:27.[17]

While Philo's commentary illustrates well this complexity which is found across his writings, it also provides within its one fluid exposition of the text of Genesis 1–2 two applications of one basic hermeneutical move, first in §§13–128 and then in §§129–50. Noticing this twice employed single hermeneutical move will help make some sense of his two "vastly different" construals of the human of 1:27. We will now explore both of Philo's readings of 1:27 within his one commentary. We will especially note the interwoven relationship that exists between each of these construals and its respective cosmic Beginning and Before.

(a) Philo's First Reading of Genesis 1:27 (*Op.* 69–88)

Although it is unpopular in some present scholarship, it was not uncommon for Jewish interpreters to take Gen. 1:27 and 2:7 as a combined reference to the father of humanity.[18] Philo makes such a blend his own in *Op.*

Plato: *Theat.* 176b1, *Rep.* 500c5, 613b1, *Tim.* 90c8; see Philo: *Op.* 144, 151, *Abr.* 87, *Dec.* 101, *Virt.* 168, *Spec.* 4.187–88; *Deus* 48, *QG* 2.62 [so Runia, 2001, 343–44]). Van Kooten, 2008, makes much of this (see below).

[15] See *Plant.* 16–17, 20–22, and *Det.* 84–85, each passage being closely associated with his ("first") interpretation of Gen. 1:27 (and 2:7) as concerning the creation of the sense-perceptible human. Cf. *Tim.* 90–91. So Levison, 1988, 63–88, 86–88; Hay, 2004, 136–37.

[16] Both of these terms/phrases are clearly references to a composite being (Levison, 1988, 71).

[17] Tobin, 1983, 20–25; Baer, 1970, 81–83, 81–82 n. 1; Hay, 2004, 133–35; van den Hoek, 2000, 66–70.

[18] Schaller, 2004, 149. E.g., Ben Sira unites 2:7 ("created out of earth") with 1:27 ("in his own image") in 17:1–8 (see Watson, 1997, 280–81). For a similar hermeneutical move in Wisdom of Solomon see: Gen. 1:27 in Wis. 2:23 and Genesis 3 in Wis. 2:24;

69–88.[19] He can do this here (though not in §134)[20] because, as we have seen, he is interpreting the cosmic setting of Gen. 1:6–31 (and thus the anthropic text of 1:27) as the "firm," "bodily," and therefore sense-perceptible creation. Genesis 1:27 is harmoniously and consistently nestled (along with borrowed features from the clearly sensible 2:7) within Philo's larger interpretive context of the cosmic Beginning and the Before in §§13–128.[21] There are two aspects of Philo's beginning of empirical humanity in Gen. 1:27 that will be helpful to highlight here: humanity's "image" and "resemblance" with God in §§69–71, and God's pre-set purpose and forethought in §§77–82.[22]

(i) Gen. 1:27ab: "Imaging" and "Resembling" God (*Op.* 69–71)

It is "good" (καλῶς) to label "the human" as does 1:27 since "nothing earth-born [γηγενές] bears more resemblance [ἐμφερέστερον] to God than a human." It is the "earth-born," sense-perceptible person – not "the mind of man"[23] nor "the ideal man"[24] – whom Philo here corresponds with God.[25] This epithet "earth-born" is assumed from Gen. 2:7.[26] Such an as-

---

Gen. 2:7 in Wis. 7:1; and Gen. 1:28 in Wis. 9:1–2, Gen. 2:7 in Wis. 9:15, and Genesis 3 in Wis. 10:1. Cf. Tobin, 1983, 56–101; Hultgren, 2003, 346–48; Hay, 2004, 129. A different, contrastive approach to 1:27 and 2:7 is found in other ancient Jewish writers (see Tobin, 1983, 109–10; Levison, 1988, 69, 85; Bouteneff, 2008, 30).

[19] For a similar blend of Gen. 1:27 and 2:7 elsewhere in Philo cf. *Her.* 55–57; *Det.* 83; *Plant.* 18–22; *Mut.* 223; *Spec.* 1.171; *Virt.* 203–05 (see Tobin, 1992, 122–24; idem, 1983, 28–29, 87–90; Baer, 1970, 22).

[20] This parenthetical note must be qualified. In §§134–50 Philo will combine features of 1:27 and 2:7, but only in one direction. Since in that second hermeneutical context the human of Gen. 1:27 functions as the noetic and ideal paradigm of the human of Gen. 2:7, Philo can (and does) use concepts (e.g., dominion) from 1:27–28 to help elucidate 2:7. But Philo no longer reads the "earthiness" of 2:7 back onto the man of 1:27 (as he does in §§69–88), for that would be hermeneutically/theologically inappropriate in §§129–50.

[21] Radice, 1989: "In *De opificio mundi* there does not exist any precise cohesion (on the level of the allegorical framework) between cosmogenesis and anthropogenesis" (122; translation mine: "[N]el *De opificio mundi* non esista alcuna precisa sutura [a livello di struttura allegorica] fra cosmogenesi e antropogenesi."). "Level" is, of course, subjective and hard to dispute, but what will become increasingly clear in the study below is precisely that there *is* "cohesion" or "suture" between the "cosmogenesis" and "anthropogenesis" in *De opificio mundi*.

[22] For effective summaries of *Op.* 69–88 as a whole see Levison, 1988, 66–74; Runia, 2001, 223–59.

[23] Conta Wolfson, 1947, 1.310.

[24] Contra Radice, 1989, 122.

[25] Rightly Runia, 2001, 224 (cf. 254). It is easy to miss this if one (eisegetically) anticipates Philo's cosmogonic (and therefore anthropogonic) perspective in *Op.* 129–50, which is different than the perspective here in *Op.* 13–128.

[26] Runia, 2001, 224, 254.

sumption is easy to make, for the animals in 1:24–25 (cf. *Op.* 64) came out of earth, and if one knows that animals in 2:19 and the human in 2:7 also did, then to deduce that the human of 1:27 is earth-born is logical exegesis. Within Philo's hermeneutical flow, this deduction is natural.[27]

Philo's primary concern regarding humanity's Beginning surfaces immediately, when instead of initiating his treatment with v. 26, "Let us make...," he rather quotes the text as a conglomeration of v. 27 ("according to the image *of God*," κατ' εἰκόνα θεοῦ) and v. 26 ("and according to likeness," καὶ καθ' ὁμοίωσιν). Temporarily bypassing God's "us" (v. 26a),[28] Philo begins his interpretation with the "image of God" and humanity's "Becoming" as such, both technically from v. 27. The "resemblance" (ἐμφερής) Philo sees between the human and God is of first importance. But what is it?

"Resemblance" is emphatically not in the body (§69.5–7). It is rather in "the mind, which rules the soul" (§69.7–8). Though this betrays "the strong influence of Greek philosophy on Philo's thought,"[29] the text of Genesis is itself somewhat open to this emphasis, even if only through deduction. That is, while plants and animals exist "according to [their own] kind" (κατὰ γένος), humanity exists as "according to [κατ'] *God's* image" and "likeness." Philo glosses these two anthropogonic κατά-constructions with the term "kinship" or "shared-kind" (συγγενείας), which has a lexical link with "kind" (γενός) in the biblical text (γεν-). The combined fact of accord with God (i.e., being his "kind") and non-accord with plants and animals can facilitate a definition of God-likeness through human difference with other creatures. Intelligence and/or moral capacity is, then, a ready comparison.[30]

After comparing the mind (as "image") to a "statue" of a god, which our bodies parade around on our shoulders (§69.8–12), Philo shifts his analogy

---

[27] This is not the case in *Leg.* 2.12–13, where Philo distances not only the man of 1:27 from 2:7 but also the animals of 1:24 from 2:19. But there Philo's hermeneutical approach to Genesis 1–2 is identical to his perspective in *Op.* 129ff, not to his hermeneutical perspective here in *Op.* 69–128.

[28] Philo extracts the "our" because of the theological confusion it introduces. Across his work, the main feature that v. 26 draws to Philo's mind is the word "us" (Baer, 1970, 23 n. 1) and thus the need to defend not only God's monotheism (*Conf.* 170), but even more regularly God's supposed participation with evil (cf. *Conf.* 168–82; *Mut.* 27–32; *Fug.* 68–72). Cf. Plato's *Tim.* 41a-44d. See Tobin, 1983, 29–30 (29 nn. 15–16), 36–55, 58; Runia, 1986, 243–44; van Kooten, 2008, 49. Philo will return to this very type of theodicy in §§72–75, but he chooses to begin his comments with the notion of God's "image," against the order of the text.

[29] Runia, 2001, 224.

[30] For a modern equivalent see McCasland, 1950, 89–90, and for some exegetical roots of such modern readings see Jónsson, 1988, 33–43. Intellect is also a common point of distinction between human and animal in Greek philosophy (Runia, 2001, 324).

to focus on what is *alike* between God and humans.³¹ The human mind functions toward the rest of the person as God functions toward the cosmos: as its "sovereign" (ἡγεμών in §69.12; cf. §69.8). Philo then compares qualities which God and the human mind share. Both are "invisible" yet "see all things." Both have an "unclear substance" yet "perceive [καταλαμβάνων] the substances of others." (This use of the λαμβάνω-compound for "perceiving" [καταλαμβάνων] is reminiscent of his description of how God "*pre*-perceives" [προλαβών; §§16, 45], though for God this perception was *before* the beginning.) The human mind "resembles" or "images" the divine Mind as each "searches [διερευνώμενος] the things in the nature of others" (§69.14–19).³²

(ii) God's Foresight in Humanity's Tardiness (*Op.* 77–78 and 82)

Even though humans resemble God, does not being created last make them inferior to the rest of creation? Philo offers multiple reasons refuting such an assumption (§§77–88). While §§69–71 dealt largely with the ontology of the human as resembler ("image") of God, §§77–88 mainly deal with humanity's position and role in relation to the cosmos. In the latter, Philo emphasizes God's wisdom, forethought, and purpose that undergird the God-given relationship between humanity and world. Sections 77–78 and 82 host all three interwoven strands of Philo's creation-hermeneutic.

In §§77–78, Philo begins to explain man's tardiness in creation:

God, after giving a portion [μεταδούς] to man of his kinship [τῆς αὐτοῦ συγγενείας], that is, of reasoning [τῆς λογικῆς] – which was the best of gifts [δωρεῶν] – he did not begrudge him the other [gifts]. Rather, as for the living being who dwells closest and is most loved, he pre-prepared [προητοιμάσατο] all things in the cosmos, having purposed [βουληθείς] for his coming that not one thing be missing of what is for the means of living [πρὸς τὸ ζῆν] and the means of living well [τὸ εὖ ζῆν]. (§77.7–13)

Creation is for humanity. "Living" refers to "supplies" like a "feast," i.e., the food of Gen. 1:11–13 and the entertainment of the animals in 1:20–25

---

³¹ Above I mentioned how the "three-tiered" understanding of "image" (human – image – God), for which the flexibility of the image-concept allows, was how Philo understood the text. In *Op.* 69, however, Philo compares the human directly to God. But the seemingly two-tiered image-reality in *Op.* 69 (human mind – God's mind, with no mediating Word/image; cf. *Op.* 69.4, 71.11–15; *Abr.* 41; *Fug.* 63; and cf. *Op.* 146; *Det.* 86–87; *Abr.* 41; *Virt.* 204–05) is in no real tension with Philo's otherwise (and more fundamental) three-tiered image-reality in e.g., *Op.* 25 (so Radice, 1989, 122; van den Hoek, 2000, 69; Runia, 2001, 224–25; contra Tobin, 1983, 51). The man of 1:27 is not himself technically "the image of God": cf. *Her.* 231 (Tobin, 1983, 57–59, 96–97; van Kooten, 2008, 366–67); *Leg.* 3.96 (van Kooten, 2008, 50–51); *QG.* 2.62. Philo can actually use both tier-structures at once (cf. *Spec.* 3.83, 207): if B looks like A, and C looks like B, it is not illegitimate to say directly, "C looks like A," even if this likeness is not truly immediate.
³² Cf. *Det.* 87–90 with *Op.* 70–71 (cf. Plato's "flight of the soul," *Phaed.* 246a-249d).

(cf. §§77.13–18, 78). "Living well" refers to "contemplation of heavenly things" like a "spectacle," i.e., the stars of 1:14–19 that stimulate philosophy (cf. §§77.13–18, 78). As one modern scientist says, "The more I examine the universe and the details of its architecture, the more evidence I find that the universe in some sense must have known we were coming."[33]

From one perspective, Philo's reading could certainly be called an anthropocentric view of creation.[34] But Philo initiates this description with (and subordinates it under) the God who "gives" the ontological structure of things as a "gift."[35] After drawing brief attention to the chief gift, "reason," Philo reintroduces the Before. God "did not grudge" or "envy" (ἐφθόνησεν) and therefore he preemptively gave generously to humans through his acts of creation. In *Op.* 21, God made everything because, being good, "he did not grudge [ἐφθόνησεν] a share in his own excellent nature to an existence which has of itself nothing beautiful" (cf. *Tim.* 29e). For Philo, God's pre-creative motivation regarding the more specific creation of humanity (*Op.* 77) is the mirror-image of his more general construal of creation of the world (*Op.* 21).

Likewise, God acted in creation according to what he was "purposing" (βουληθείς). By this Philo unites this interpretation of 1:26–28 with the beginning of the world and with his explicit Before. In the Beginning of the world: in Gen. 1:11–13 "God purposed [ἐβουλήθη]... and therefore led... spurred on... and made" (§44). In the Before: because God was "purposing" (βουληθείς) he therefore "pre-stamped out" (προεξετύπου) what existed in the divine mind before the visible world came about (§16). In the Beginning of humanity: because "God purposed" (βουληθείς) he therefore "pre-prepared" (προητοιμάσατο) the world (cf. "pre-made ready" [προευτρεπίσατο] in §78.10) for human arrival. Here Philo's "pre-preparation" refers to God's activity *within* Genesis 1 rather than to the ultimate Before, creating all sense-perceptible things before and with a view toward humanity. Yet Philo's theological principle does accord with his ultimate Before. God creates according to his "purpose." He does so for the "good" of the one in mind, whether that be the entire world or the specific humanity, whom God then places over all.[36]

---

[33] Freeman Dyson, quoted with permission by Polkinghorne, 1994, 76.

[34] On the "anthropocentric" interpretation of creation in Ben Sira, the wisdom tradition, and "earlier biblical material" see Harrington, 1996, 263–76, esp. 270 (cf. Lampe, 1964, 449–51).

[35] Cf. Paul's language of God "giving" (δίδωσιν) cosmic ontology in 1 Cor. 15:38.

[36] Philo uses the language of humanity being "over all" (ἐπὶ πᾶσιν) in *Op.* 65.1, 66.11. In *Op.* 83–88, he will connect this with the "dominion" of Gen. 1:28. It is possible that he uses the preposition "over" based on Ps. 8:6b-7, where God "placed [κατέστησας]" humanity "over [ἐπὶ]" the works of his hands, and God "subjected all things [πάντα ὑπέταξας] under his feet." This possibility is strengthened when in §§84–

In §82, Philo gives his third explanation of why humanity was created last. As with so much of his interpretation of the creation of the world as well as humanity, Philo again begins with God's thinking:

God, after considering [διανοηθείς][37] to cause harmony as necessary and most loving, he made [ἐποίει] the beginning heaven [ἀρχὴν οὐρανόν] and the end man [τέλος ἄνθρωπον], the one the most perfect of the incorruptible things [τῶν ἀφθάρτων] among sense-perception, the other the best of the earth-born and corruptible things [τῶν γηγενῶν καὶ φθαρτῶν], a miniature heaven [βραχὺν οὐρονόν]. (§82)[38]

Philo strengthens this comparison between heaven and human by describing the human as "bearing as a statue [ἀγαλματοφοροῦντα] many star-like natures within himself, that is, art and knowledge and the famous theories that accord with each virtue." God's fore-thought and consideration caused perfect symmetry in the created world. The heaven with its astral dances is closely related to the human with its mental revolutions. The Beginning of the world is intimately related to the Beginning of humanity, even to the "earth-born" human of Gen. 1:27, and this is so because of the pre-creational divine design, i.e., the Before.

Within Philo's first hermeneutical structure (§§13–128) he has presented an interpretation of the sacred text of 1:27 that intertwines the beginning of humanity with the beginning of the world and with God's intentions before creation. When Philo returns to 1:27 in §134, he will again have the same three interwoven hermeneutical strands of creation, but his entire perspective will have shifted. This shift creates a re-reading of 1:27 that is "vastly different" than what we have just seen.

(b) Philo's Second Reading of Genesis 1:27 (*Op.* 134–35)

In §§129–30, Philo's exposition reaches Gen. 2:4b-5. As we saw in chapter 1, he labels this a "summary" of all of Genesis 1.[39] He claims that every-

---

85 Philo explains Gen. 1:28 in the language of Ps. 8:6–7: God "placed [καθίστη] him as king" of all sub-lunar living beings, "subjecting all things [πάντα ὑπέταττεν] to him" (though exempting "the heavenly beings," like Ps. 8:6a). (So Borgen, 1995, 369–89; cf. Runia, 2001, 256).

[37] This means to "think through" something, to "consider." Cf. Gen. 8:21: "The Lord God, after considering [διανοηθείς], said, 'I will not add to the curse on the earth'."

[38] Cf. *Tim.* 27a5–6: Critias says that because Timaeus is the best astronomer he will therefore speak appropriately, "beginning [ἀρξόμενον] from the genesis of the cosmos [ἀπὸ τῆς τοῦ κόσμου γενέσεως] and ending [τελευτᾶν] at the nature of man [εἰς ἀνθρώπων φύσιν]." Socrates heartily approves. Cf. *Praem.* 1 (see Runia, 2001, 253).

[39] In §129, Philo uses the participle ἐπιλογιζόμενος, meaning "concluding" or "reflecting upon" (so Runia, 2001, 311). He uses the noun ἐπιλόγῳ and the verb ἐπιλέγει in *Post.* 64–65 when commenting on the same passage. Runia distances *Op.* 129 from *Post.* 64–65, treating the former as "reflecting upon": "a reflection on the creation account *as it has been so far presented*" (310, cf. 311; contra Tobin, 1983, 123–24, 170–71). It is bet-

thing preceding 2:4–5 is summarized well in condensed form in 2:4–5. Importantly, however, Gen. 2:4–5 is all about the Before. But if this textual testimony to the Before is a summary of Genesis 1, then Genesis 1 has now been re-construed as the creation of the invisible, noetic realm, i.e., what "pre-exists" in the "Before" (πρό [2x], πρίν [2x], προ-ὑπῆρχε). Though this marks a substantial shift in his reading of Genesis 1, Philo still employs the same three-strand hermeneutic as he had in §§13–128. He sees a textually attested Before (§§129–30; cf. §§13–35), applies it to the beginning of the world (§§131–33; cf. §§36–68), then to the beginning of humanity (§§134–35; cf. §§69–88).[40] But now Philo has cosmogon*ies* and anthropogon*ies* to interpret (Genesis 1 *and* 2), which he did not have in his first read-through. These must now be related to each other, i.e., the two cosmogonies and the two anthropogonies.

(i) Philo's Re-Reading of the Beginning of the World (*Op.* 131–33)

In §§131–33, Philo shows how the beginning of the sense-perceptible world, now found in Gen. 2:6 rather than 1:6, displays the same sequence as the creation of the noetic world (i.e., now Genesis 1). Philo writes:

Keeping to the sequence of the creation and carefully observing the connection between what follows and what has gone before, [Moses] next says: 'and a spring went up out of the earth and watered all the face of the earth' (Gen. 2:6). (§131.1–4)

The sensible world (i.e., Genesis 2) begins to take shape in perfect accord with the noetic world (i.e., Genesis 1).

Many modern scholars keep Genesis 1 distant from Genesis 2, in source as well as in language and concept. Philo does not. He discusses the prominence of water in 2:6, he informs his readers of Graeco-Roman thought on the primordial element of water, and he reminds them of the earlier Mosaic thought on the systems of the primordial water in Gen. 1:9–10. By using words and motifs both from Genesis 1 itself and from his own construal of it earlier in his commentary, Philo models Gen. 2:6 on 1:9–10.[41] This pers-

---

ter to see it as a re-construal of all of Genesis 1 in a *different* way than has been presented thus far. Both this construal and Runia's are valid syntactically, but Runia's is less able to account for what Philo is about to say of the "man" of Gen. 1:27 in §134.

[40] Baer, 1970, 29 and Loader, 2004, 60 recognize these three aspects but do not trace out the implications as I am doing. Tobin (1992) asserts that a previous anthropogonic interpretation which contrasted Gen. 2:7 with 1:27 gave rise to a cosmogonic interpretation which needed to relocate the shift from noetic world to sensory world from 1:6 to 2:4–5 (126–27). My point concerns Philo's hermeneutic rather than historical development of causation. Philo's own interpretation in *Op.* moves from cosmogony to anthropogony instead of anthropogony to cosmogony.

[41] Cf. *Op.* 38–39 (on Gen. 1:10): "dry land" (τὴν ξηράν), "sweet" water (γλυκεῖα), "glue" (κόλλα) with *Op.* 131 (on Gen. 2:6): "sweet" water (γλυκείᾳ), "glue" (κόλλης),

pective of harmony is itself in agreement with Philo's own explanation in *Op.* 16.9–10 of the harmonious correspondence between noetic cosmos (the Before) and sensible cosmos (the Beginning).

With his perspective on Genesis 1 now shifted because of 2:4–5 (before the beginning) and set in motion by 2:6 (the beginning of the sensory world), Philo is nearly prepared to interpret the *second* anthropogonic text, Gen. 2:7 (the beginning of sensory humanity). But he must first deal with the re-construal of Gen. 1:27. While that text did refer to sensory humanity, now it refers to the beginning of noetic humanity in the Before.

(ii) Philo's Re-Reading of the Beginning of Humanity (*Op.* 134)

In §§134–35, Philo turns from world to human. While the (very brief) cosmogony of Genesis 2 had been in perfect harmony with that of Genesis 1, the anthropogony of Genesis 2 stands in contrast to that of Genesis 1. Within this context of contrast (§134.4–7a), where there is a "vast difference" between the two humans, we will now look at Philo's re-reading of 1:27 in §134, only later turning to his reading-in-contrast of 2:7 in §135.

Concerning the two humans Philo writes:

For the one formed [ὁ διαπλασθείς] is a sense-perceptible object [αἰσθητός], already having quality [ποιότητος], consisting of body and soul [ἐκ σώματος καὶ ψυχῆς], man or woman [ἀνὴρ ἢ γυνή], by nature mortal [φύσει θνητός]. The one according to the image [ὁ κατὰ τὴν εἰκόνα] is a kind of idea [ἰδέα τις] or genus [γένος] or seal [σφραγίς], noetic [νοητός], incorporeal [ἀσώματος], neither male nor female [οὔτ' ἄρρεν οὔτε θῆλυ], incorruptible by nature [ἄφθαρτος φύσει]. (§134.7b-11)

Philo's description of the man of 2:7 as "consisting of body and soul" resembles his description of the man of 1:27 in *Op.* 69–88 as being "earthborn" and having "a human body" and "mind," though he now says that the man of 1:27 is "incorporeal" or "without body." Philo has re-construed the human of 1:27 as the "incorporeal," "noetic" "idea" of humanity.

Philo's three-strand hermeneutic with its two outworkings from the text is most helpful at this point. Runia asks, "How does the exegesis here [*sc.* in *Op.* 134–35] relate to the explanation of Gen 1:27 in terms of the *nous* in §69–71?"[42] R.A. Baer thought that explaining the noetic man of 1:27 in §134 as the "Idea" (i.e., Platonic paradigm) of the sensory man of 2:7 was incorrect because such a construal "presupposes an interpretation of Gen. 1:27 and 2:7 inconsistent with Philo's interpretations of these verses elsewhere."[43] To remove the contradiction he treated the "man according to the

---

"dry" (ξηρά). Also the earth's "systems of water" in 1:10 and the "springs" in 2:6 are both compared to "veins" in "breasts" in §§38–39 and §133 (cf. *Plant.* 10).

[42] Runia, 2001, 322.

[43] Baer, 1970, 22.

image" in both §69 and §134 as sensory man's rational mind.[44] Though this may "remov[e] any contradiction," it equates "man" and "mind" in a way that Philo did not in §69 (who mentioned both but did not equate them),[45] and it cannot explain Philo's language of "man" (not mind) as "noetic," "incorporeal," and "seal" in §134. These terms are Philo's own language for the Before (cf. "noetic," "incorporeal," and "seal" in *Op*. 16–35).[46] Here in §134, the man of 1:27 is the "Idea," i.e., the paradigm of the empirical man of 2:7. The contradiction not only remains, but it has actually been sharpened by Philo's consistent use of terms in his respective passages concerning the Before.[47] Since the Before has shifted from 1:1–5 to Genesis 1 as a whole, it makes good sense why he would now apply his terms of the Before to the human of 1:27. Recognizing Philo's hermeneutical perspective admittedly does not remedy the "contradiction" (it is a fundamental part of it!), but it does make better sense out of each of these texts within Philo's overall commentary.[48]

As mentioned in chapter 1, the authoritative text of Gen. 1:1–5 ("And God 'made'...") provided Philo with some of the content of his Before, even causing him to claim that the *pre*-protological cosmos had "Become" (*Op*. 29). This was something Plato said could not be (*Tim*. 28ab), but Philo's text constrained him. Similarly, the text of 1:27 ("And God 'made'...") causes Philo to offer a "Becoming" idea of humanity (*Op*. 134.7), and this was something Middle Platonists could not do.[49] According to Philo, the "becoming" in the noetic beginning of the world is matched by a "becoming" in the noetic beginning of humanity.

---

[44] Baer, 1970, 30.

[45] In §69, the man's mind is imaged after God, but the man is not the mind. In §135, Philo's mention of "mind" does not allow us to equate it with the "man" of 1:27. In fact, in §135 Philo neither mentions nor alludes to 1:27, for he has turned away from the contrast between these "vastly different" men and has begun to focus attention on the two parts of "the human being," i.e., the one formed in 2:7ab.

[46] Philo's use of "seal" for the "man" of 1:27 is especially illuminating, for it is "usually a technical term for the relation between model and copy" (Runia, 2001, 323). See Tobin, 1993, 122–23. Cf. *Leg*. 1.31–32; *QG* 1.4, 8a, 2.56.

[47] Runia, 2001, 321–25.

[48] Perhaps it recognizes in Philo a higher degree of consistency on a larger scale.

[49] The notion of a noetic paradigm of humanity is technically absent in Plato's anthropogonic account in the *Timaeus* (40d-47e) (so Wolfson, 1947, 1.213, 307, 389–90; Baer, 1970, 22 n. 3; Tobin, 1983, 114). In Middle Platonic thought, however, Arius Didymus, a first century B.C.E. Alexandrian, clearly follows Plato's condemnation of any "Becoming" (γεγονός) of the noetic paradigm, but expands it to the noetic human: "there is a certain conception of man...*un-become* [ἀγένητον] and imperishable [ἄφθαρτον]" (*On the Doctrines of Plato*, preserved in Eusebius, *Pr. Ev*. 11.23; see Tobin, 1983, 114–18; *idem*, 1992, 125).

(c) Summary: Philo's Reading of Genesis 1:27

Philo presents one three-strand hermeneutic of creation, though he exhibits this in two distinct and mutually exclusive ways. (1) The Before that Philo sees in Gen. 1:1–5 sets off (2) his "first reading" of the Beginning of the empirical world accordingly, which in turn sets the context for (3) his interpretation of the Beginning of empirical humanity. Then Philo subsequently sees (1) this same Before in Gen. 2:4b-5 – causing him to retrospectively construe all of Genesis 1 as the Before – which sets off (2) his "second reading" of the cosmic Beginning in 2:6, which in turn re-sets the context for (3) his re-interpretation of Gen. 1:26–28 and then the anthropic Beginning in 2:7.

The shared starting point of this doubly-employed three-strand interpretation of creation is his expectation of the Before. Its textual presence (in two places) grants the structure to his two cosmogonic and thus anthropogonic readings. One of Philo's dominant and recurring tendencies within each strand and within both of their implementations is to give a primacy to God's activity, specifically as this creative activity is based upon God's previous purpose and forethought. And the aim of both readings is ultimately the same: theological praise and anthropological virtue.

3.1.2 Paul's Reading of Genesis 1:27

Paul explicitly refers to "God's image" only twice in 1 and 2 Corinthians and Romans: 1 Cor. 11:7 and 2 Cor. 4:4. In the former, God's "image" is neither God's Word nor the human mind, but rather simply "a man" (ἀνήρ) (11:7b). He is not "according to" another "image" but himself presently "exists" (ὑπάρχων) as "God's image and glory" (εἰκὼν καὶ δόξα θεοῦ). Paul follows this statement with multiple references to Genesis' broader human beginnings (vv. 7–12b) and with a concluding reference to the origin of all things (v. 12c).[50] In his second use of Gen. 1:27, "the image of God" presently "is" (ἐστιν) Jesus (2 Cor. 4:4), and as such he reflects "God's glory" (4:6). As in 1 Cor. 11:7–12, here too Paul transitions naturally from this reference to human beginnings (v. 4) to a reference to the broader Beginning (v. 6).

In both instances Paul, like Philo, interrelates 1:27 with the creation of the world. Like Philo, what undergirds both of Paul's uses of 1:27 is theocentric causation. Philo had read but then re-read 1:27 from the retrospective perspective of a later human (the created Adam). Similarly, Paul presents one application of 1:27 in 1 Cor. 11:7 and then a different one in 2

---

[50] 1 Cor. 11:8 is on Gen. 2:21–23 and v. 9 is on 2:18; v. 12a is on Gen. 2:21–23 again, and v. 12b on Gen. 4:1 (Watson, 2000A, 79) and commonly observed childbirth (Scroggs, 1972; Gundry-Volf, 1997, 162).

Cor. 4:4, and the second is from the retrospective perspective of a later human (the resurrected Jesus). Unlike Philo, however, Paul's retrospection does not deny his previous application. Regarding each application of 1:27, after first analyzing "image" and "glory" within the argument, I will then draw attention to the cosmic and hermeneutical perspective that shapes Paul's anthropic application within that context.

(a) Paul's First Application of Genesis 1:27:
Man, the Image and Glory of God (1 Cor. 11:7–12)

In 1 Cor. 11:7–12, Paul combines Gen. 1:27 and Genesis 2 to explain certain aspects of bi-gendered anthropology and therefore worship-practice. Paul's initial "ought" for "a man" is based on him "being the image and glory of God" (v. 7). After analyzing "glory," "image," and their relation to creation, I will demonstrate that God's intentions because of which he crafted the man and woman as he did are assumed just under the surface.

(i) Paul's Application of the Beginning of Humanity (1 Cor. 11:7–12b)

One of Paul's main threads in 1 Cor. 11:2–16 is "glory," and in vv. 7–12 this "glory" is cast as an original and inherent part of anthropology. It is first set within its protological framework as Paul inserts it into the textual designation "image of God" (v. 7b).[51] Paul is mainly concerned with what is "proper" (πρέπον) for "meaningful worship,"[52] especially with what will produce "glory" (δόξα) within this Christian context rather than "shame" (αἰσχρόν) and "dishonor" (ἀτιμία) (see vv. 4–7).[53] J. Gundry-Volf writes, "Paul's main point is that man and woman are both the *glory of another* and therefore both have an obligation not to cause shame to their 'heads'."[54] She specifies: "since they are the glory of *different* persons... they must use different means to avoid shaming their 'heads'."[55]

---

[51] Though Paul introduces the anthropogony in 11:7 with "image" from Gen. 1:27, "glory" is his more primary theme (so Gundry-Volf, 1997, 155–56; Fee, 1987, 515; Hurley, 1981, 174, 198 [cf. 171–75, 205]; Barrett, 1968, 252).

[52] Collins, 1999, 404; cf. Watson, 2000B, 528.

[53] For the setting of 1 Cor. 11:2–16 within the Graeco-Roman "shame/honor society" of Corinth see Gundry-Volf, 1997, 152–53, 157, 169.

[54] Gundry-Volf, 1997, 157.

[55] Gundry-Volf, 1997, 157. Cf. Thiselton, 2000, 837. Recognition of the difference in what each gender "should" do (ὀφείλει carrying "moral overtones" [Fee, 1987, 514 n. 8; Conzelmann, 1975, 188 n. 77]), should not veil the essential similarity of activity that Paul is encouraging (and modifying): both masculine and feminine "praying or prophesying." By positively modifying their practice, Paul is actively trying to keep both women and men participating in this divine – human communication (Watson, 2000B, 525–28), albeit in "proper" manners.

3.1 The Image of God: Genesis 1:27   153

The difference in respective "glory" is due to the Beginning of men and women according to Genesis 1–2.[56] As well as being different (vv. 7–9), and therefore needing to perform the same worship differently (vv. 4–6, 10), women and men are nevertheless also "essentially related" as a non-autonomous people (v. 11).[57] Even this Paul bases on origins (v. 12).

In v. 3 Paul sets the entire issue of "heads" within an explicitly Christian framework. Twice in vv. 4–12 he reminds them of their specifically Christian setting: e.g., "*while* praying or prophesying" (vv. 4–5), "*in* the Lord" (v. 11c). Yet when he actually argues the principles themselves (difference-of-method in vv. 7–10, non-autonomy-of-being in vv. 11–12), he writes as if simple protology satisfies his argument.[58] Even his principle of gender non-autonomy (v. 11), which is often itself labelled as "eschatological" or "new,"[59] Paul supports or illustrates *not* with "eschatological" or "new" facts, nor even with Christological realities, but with the mechanical origins of men and women which God built into the physical nature of humans in the Beginning. Thus throughout vv. 7–12, Paul applies to Christ's *eschatological* community of Corinth the explicitly *protological*

---

[56] That vv. 7–10 (about Genesis 1–2) prove vv. 4–6 (about distinction of praxis-method) see Fee, 1987, 513; Gundry-Volf, 1997, 153.

[57] Schrage, 1991, 2.512 ("essentially related"), 517–18 ("togetherness, interrelating"). The relationship between vv. 8–9 and vv. 11–12 has been variously construed. Though a major part of his overall purpose of 1 Corinthians is to bridge schisms (see 1:10–11ff), the particular argument of vv. 7–9 is meant, *within that context*, to (re)inforce particular distinctions, those based on Genesis 1–2. Thus vv. 11–12 neither correct vv. 8–9 (contra Schrage, 1991) nor repeat vv. 8–9 (contra McGinn, 1996); they counter potential false conclusions drawn from vv. 8–9 (so Stuckenbruck, 2001).

[58] Paul uses the same basic type of argumentation in vv. 11–12 as in vv. 7–10. His grammatically positive principle (what each gender "is," vv. 7–10) functions as true *within* a Christian-specific setting, but it is true *because* of how God "created" their respective physical natures (v. 8) and vocations (v. 9). His grammatically negative principle (what each gender "is not," vv. 11–12) functions as true *within* a Christian-specific setting, but it also is true *because* of how their respective physical natures were brought about (v. 12a) or reproduced (v. 12b) by God (v. 12c). Though disagreeing on how good this is, many recognize that Paul is arguing that creation affects church-activity in vv. 7–10: Watson, 2000B, 530, 532; cf. 529–33; Thiselton, 2000, 837; Gundry-Volf, 1997, 157; Hooker, 1964/65, 411. Though some also recognize that in v. 12 Paul uses creation/physical origins as a proof or "analogy" of v. 11 (so Watson, 2000A, 79; Gundry-Volf, 1997, 162; Scroggs, 1972), the full implications of such argumentation have often been missed. The principle of v. 11 itself is *consistent with* v. 12 – whether minimally as "analogy" (so Watson, 2000B, 523; Gundry-Volf, 1997, 160–64, 170; Schrage, 1991, 2.519) or maximally as "proof" (typical of γάρ) – and v. 12 is the *non*-Christian-specific principle of non-autonomy-via-physical-origins. I.e., Paul says that a non-Christian-specific principle is (still) the case "in" (not "because of") the Lord. The eschatological *setting* for the protological(ly-consistent) principle should not be confused with the *nature* of the principle itself.

[59] E.g., Watson 2000B, 532–33; Scroggs, 1972, 301; Jaubert, 1971/72, 429.

realities of gender difference yet non-autonomy, both of which, Paul shows, were established in the Beginning.

Within this context, Paul's very first use of human origins is a slightly modified form of the very first textual description of "the human": "the image and glory of God" (v. 7b; Gen. 1:27).[60] Two observations must be developed: 1) Paul does not use the text's preposition ("according to," κατά) but may have been influenced by it, and 2) by seeing glory (δόξα) in Genesis 2 and inserting it within "image of God," Paul presents contemporary "man" in a specifically Adamic manner.

Concerning the preposition, Paul does not refer explicitly to κατά.[61] It may still have influenced his portrayal of men and women in v. 7, though not in a Philonic way.[62] For example, in Genesis 2 God's expressed purpose ("I will...") was for the woman to "accord" with man (κατ' αὐτόν, Gen. 2:18), to be "like him" (ὅμοιος αὐτῷ, 2:20),[63] and to function in an explicitly man-ward way, i.e., as a "helper" who was "for him" (αὐτῷ) (2:18). Paul summarizes: the woman was "created *for* the man," i.e., she is "the glory *of man*." This "glory" is an Edenic theme. In Gen. 1:26–27 (and

---

[60] It is widely acknowledged that v. 7b is a reference to Gen. 1:27: e.g., Thiselton, 2000, 833–37; Peerbolte, 2000, 83–84; Collins, 1999, *ad loc*; Schrage, 1991, 2.509–12; Fee, 1987, 515; Hurley, 1981, 171–74; Conzelmann, 1975, 186–88; Feuillet, 1973, 159–62; McCasland, 1950, 85.

[61] Not everyone considered the preposition as important as did Philo: see Wis. 2:23 (see McCasland, 1950, 91).

[62] Rightly Hultgren, 2003, 369; Peerbolte, 2000, 84; Schrage, 1991, 2.509–10; Scroggs, 1966, 68–69. Contra van Kooten, 2008, 52, 54, 216–17 (and Cranfield, 1975, 1.432). Though van Kooten (2008) sometimes helpfully acknowledges that Paul says "man *is* the image of God" (e.g., 163, 202, 216; emphasis original), when constructing his broader Pauline anthropology regarding "God's image" he typically downplays 11:7 and moves quickly to man's assimilation to God via Christ as the *actual* image (199–218; cf. 69–81, 88–91; cf. Luz, 1969, 41–46). There is no evidence in 1–2 Corinthians (or Romans) that behind Paul's references to "image" lies a Philonic-type use of the κατά-concept whereby empirical man is distinguished from the actual (metaphysical) image, who is the pre-incarnate Jesus. This is a spurious reading of 2 Cor. 4:4 (and Rom. 8:29; see below). It also downplays Paul's two-tier presentation of "man" *as* "God's image" in 1 Cor. 11:7 (and of Christ *as* "God's image" in 2 Cor. 4:4, see below). (1 Cor. 11:3 should not be imported into vv. 7–9 as counter-evidence of a three-tiered system whereby "man" is only "image" via Christ the true image. Paul's logic of vv. 7–9 functions immediately from Genesis 1–2 and the first Adam and Eve to contemporary women and men. To import v. 3 into *this part of his argument* would be to confuse Paul's own revealed logic for the sake of a seemingly neater system.) Paul's related concept of "assimilation" (1 Cor. 15:49; 2 Cor. 3:18; Rom. 8:29), which van Kooten construes as the Philonic three-tiered "image"-concept (50–57, 217, cf. 54) and attributes (partly) to the κατά (without evidence; 216–17), is better construed as Paul's use of Gen. 5:3 (with evidence; see below on pp. 233–47).

[63] Loader, 2004, 35–38. Tob. 8:6 blends 2:18 with 2:20 (van Ruiten, 2000, 38).

Genesis 2 – for Paul they refer to the same man), God's expressed purpose ("Let us…") was for the "him" to "accord" with God (κατ' εἰκόνα θεοῦ),[64] to be "like" God (καθ' ὁμοίωσιν), and to function in a specifically God-ward way, i.e., to fulfil his appointment before his "Command"-er and without reference to a woman (who did not yet exist) (2:15–16). Paul summarizes: the man was "not created *for* the woman" (implied "but rather *for* God"), i.e., he is "the glory *of God*."

Such textual references may have affected Paul's gender-descriptions so that respective accord and vocational purpose enable and require respective "glory" (rather than "dishonor"). When Paul calls the Corinthian "man" the "image and glory of God," he refers to the specifically Adamic nature of accord/likeness with God and vocation for God as created by God in the beginning. The accord/likeness with God which Paul seems to have in mind here is not quite the moral/cognitive accord found in Eph. 4:24 and Col. 3:10 (cf. Gen. 3:22: "Adam has become *as* one of us *know*ing *good and evil*"), though it is not thereby contrary to it. His nuance in 1 Cor. 11:7 is closer to the accord, mentioned above, that is shared between a statue ("image") and its referent (a king or god). Due to accord and likeness, the image reflects to others the king's/god's qualities while also reflecting on the referent's reputation. To this imagery we will now return.

Paul's reference to God's "image" and "glory" is Adamic. He is dealing with the way men and women look regarding their heads. It is not about clothing or outward appearance *per se* which Paul cares, but about the "shame" and "dishonor" versus "glory" and "honor" with which these religio-cultural symbols were wed. For Paul, the actual appearance of the "image" could bring glory and honor or shame and dishonor to God. The reciprocal communication of attributes and reputation between the image/statue and the one portrayed is not far off from Paul's point. In one direction, an "image" manifested the one imaged, so that the qualities of the absent king (perhaps primarily his glory) were (supposed to be) reflected in his statue. Seeing the image was to know the absent (or invisible) one.[65] In the other direction, the quality of the image's appearance reflected on the king by drawing certain connotations to viewers' minds – for better (glory and honor) or worse (shame and dishonor). Paul's argument functions on the assumption that the qualities and appearance of the "image" are supposed to reflect the qualities and do inevitably reflect on the reputation of the one imaged.[66] Because of the way Paul sees the man's Begin-

---

[64] Cf. Eph. 4:24: "the man who was created according to God [κατὰ θεόν]."

[65] Nguyen, 2008, 177; Rowe, 2005, 306; Steenburg, 1990, 102; Kim, 1980, 195.

[66] Feuillet (1973) explains that when "glory of God" (and also "of man") in 1 Cor. 11:7 is taken as an objective genitive, it can convey the "power of his attributes… of [his] pomp, splendour, wealth, etc." (161; cf. Thiselton, 2000, 835). When taken as a sub-

ning having taken shape, specifically as "God's image" in Gen. 1:27 and generally as his "glory" in Genesis 2, "God's honor depends on the man's."[67] If the image's (man's) appearance is shameful during his public revelation of God ("while prophesying") or during his public communication with God ("while praying"), a certain inappropriate connotation is unavoidably cast onto the one imaged by him in that state, i.e., onto the Creator from whom are all things.

(ii) Paul's Cosmogonic Perspective (1 Cor. 11:12c)

Paul ultimately reduces the entire ontological discussion of beginnings to a theological statement of origins: "But all things are from God" (v. 12c). This statement encompasses the ontological "woman *from* man" (Gen. 2:21–23) in v. 12a and thus also v. 8. It thus also includes the purposive "woman *for* man" (Gen. 2:18) in v. 9 since vv. 8–9 together form the label "man's glory" (v. 7c). "All things" therefore also takes in the status and function of man as "God's image and glory" (Gen. 1:27 and Genesis 2) in v. 7b since this is the backdrop for woman in v. 7c-9. And it directly explains the ontological birth of "man *through* woman" (Gen. 4:1-until-now) in v. 12b. The ontological and ethical relationships within the human Beginning are important, and they have their import primarily because they are "from" the Creator.

This confession of ultimate divine causality accords with Paul's cosmogonic interpretation elsewhere. As we saw in chapter 2, he reads the beginning of the world theocentrically. God's causation is therefore applicable not merely for describing the past but also as governing our understanding of present historical events such as agriculture (1 Cor. 15:37–38) and here childbirth (11:12b). The beginning of light provides an understanding of present gospel events, for it is "the God who" did both that is primary. God gives bodies to plants from seeds, to sun, moon, and stars, to women out of men, and to men through women. God grants ontological "glory" (15:40–41) and relational glory and honor (11:7–9). For Paul, the protological texts which describe this causative God can therefore be elicited to encourage the perpetuation of relational "glory" instead of "shame." In 1 Cor. 11:7–12, Paul submits the various aspects of the textual and em-

---

jective genitive, "glory of God" (or "of man") may refer to God (or man) "receiving honor," "credit," or "pride" from the one who "is" their "glory" (Feuillet, 161; cf. Jaubert, 1971/72, 423, 425–26; cf. Prov. 11:16). Though I rarely opt for plenary readings, such may do the most justice in this context to the fluidity of both "glory" and genitive constructions, especially in light of the two-directional communication within this "image"-concept.

[67] Gundry-Volf, 1997, 158.

pirical beginning of humanity (initiated with 1:27) under this all-encompassing and theocentric confession of the Beginning.

In summary, within the Lord Jesus' worshiping community, men and women should perform their shared worship in different manners, yet not as genders autonomous from the other. For Paul both their different manners and their non-autonomous relatedness are the case *because* of Genesis' anthropogonic texts, first among which is Gen. 1:27. From this first application of 1:27, we may deduce that Paul considered the initial human, Adam, to not merely think like God, as Philo had it, but to himself be the visible reflector of God's glory to those watching. As such he also was to bring a reputation of honor rather than shame to God by worshiping him according to the Creator's intent. Not only does Paul assume behind the particular creation of Adam as "God's image and glory" God's previous intent (a kind of implicit Before), but he also sets this application of Gen. 1:27 within the broader context of God's cosmic causation – like three intertwined strands.

(b) Paul's Second Application of Genesis 1:27:
Christ, the Image of God (2 Cor. 4:4–6)

Paul presents the language of Gen. 1:27 in a second place, again to the Corinthians. "The light of the gospel of the glory of the Christ, who is the image of God [ὅς ἐστιν εἰκὼν τοῦ θεοῦ]," shines into hearts of darkness (2 Cor. 4:4). Paul and his companions preach "Jesus Christ, Lord" (v. 5). This is the crucified and risen one who has a ministry of life by his Spirit. They declare this gospel, i.e., "God's word," as servants for the Corinthians "because" it is the Creator of light who shines his "glory" in "the face of Jesus Christ" (v. 6). As the very "image of God," this "face" surpasses and therefore replaces Moses' face, which had previously (and legitimately) shone as a reflection of the Lord's glory (2 Cor. 3:7–10; cf. Ex. 34:29).[68] As in 1 Cor. 11:7, the "image" is related to God's "glory."[69] In this latter passage, as in the former, the "image of God" is a person whose actions and appear-

---

[68] Nguyen, 2008, argues, "Scholars generally have not given much attention to the magnitude of the phrase ἐν προσώπῳ Χριστοῦ in 4.6, which climactically concludes Paul's use of the Moses narrative and constitutes a high point for his πρόσωπον – καρδία contrast in 3.1–4.6" (180).

[69] In 2 Cor. 4:4–6 (as well as in 3:18) there is a "causative relationship" between "image" and "glory" (so Jaubert, 1971/72, 422). It is confusing to say that "glory" *means* "reflection" or "manifestation" (contra Scroggs, 1972, 299 n. 43; rightly Feuillet, 1973, 159–60) as if "glory" was synonymous with "image" (contra Conzelmann, 1975, 186–87, 186 n. 49; Jervell, 1960, 180; Kim, 1980, 230; Nguyen, 2008, 180, 176 n. 121; Hanson, 1980A, 7; rightly Scroggs, 1972, 299 n. 44). As Steenburg (1988) writes, "*Doxa* is not the appearance or visible form of Yahweh but the splendor that hides him and yet manifests his nature and/or presence" (80).

ance reflect on God even while also reflecting his glory. This latter use of the same biblical designation, "image of God," is again applied within the context of a broader reference to the cosmic Beginning. But this cosmic Beginning (4:6a) is paralleled to another Beginning (4:6b) that provides the hermeneutical context for understanding how Paul's *re*-application of 1:27 is not at odds with his first application.

(i) Paul's Re-Application of the Beginning of Humanity (2 Cor. 4:4)

In 2 Cor. 4:4, as in 1 Cor. 11:7, Paul does not use the biblical preposition "according to": Jesus simply "is" God's image. Based upon this feature of this text (though neglecting or downplaying the same feature of 1 Cor. 11:7), some have placed Christ in eternity *as* "God's image," even *in* Gen. 1:27 as the image "according to" whom the first Adam was created (like Philo's Word).[70] Others give a similar metaphysical reading, but relate Paul's reference less to the text of Gen. 1:27 and more generally to statements imported from outwith this pericope (e.g., 1 Cor. 8:6 and/or 11:3,[71] Col. 1:15 and/or Phil. 2:6,[72] or even Wis. 7:26[73]). But there is no textual reason, apart from the "parallels" just noted, to regard Paul's reference to Jesus as "image of God" in 2 Cor. 4:4 as a display of "metaphysical speculation" or as a reference to Christ's pre-human nature and/or function.[74] Paul is presenting Jesus as someone who is historically *after* Moses, having a human "face" that replaces Moses'. Thus not only is 4:4 like Paul's own use of "image of God" in 1 Cor. 11:7 in that he identifies the "image" with the referent directly and immediately, but the referent in both pas-

---

[70] Cf. van Kooten, 2008, 50–57 (52, 54), 216–17; Martin, 1983, 119; Cranfield, 1975, 1.432 (cf. Barth, 1957, 29–36; Käsemann, 1980, 244–45).

[71] So e.g., Conzelmann, 1975, 183–84, 187 (183 n. 27) and Collins, 1999, 405–06 (van Kooten [2008] also sees these as parallel [216–17, 274–75]). See Conzelmann's comparison between 1 Cor. 8:6 and 11:3 with "Greek philosophy (Platonism and the Stoa)" and "Hellenistic Judaism," most prominent among which is Philo (183–84), and van Kooten's language of "second God," which he borrows from Alcinous (pp. 154–58), applies to Philo's Logos (pp. 158, 181–99), and then to Paul's Christ (pp. 158, 199–218).

[72] So e.g., Harris, 2005, 330–31; Mathews, 1996, 171; Hanson, 1980A, 10, 22–23.

[73] Cf. "radiance," "light," "mirror," "image" (see chapter 2). So Matera, 2003, 102; Thrall, 1994, 31–11. For pre-1980 scholarly discussion on this see Hanson, 1980A, 6–10.

[74] So Ridderbos, 1975, 70–71; Luz, 1969, 43. Watson (1997) criticizes paralleling 2 Cor. 4:4 with such "metaphysical speculation," which is quite out of Paul's intention in 2 Cor. 3–4 (301 n. 6). Kim (1980) argues that Wisdom's "wisdom" and Philo's "word" are much more "visible" than our classification "metaphysical" might allow (219–20; cf. word as "appearance" in *Leg.* 1.43 and wisdom as the wilderness cloud/fire in Wis. 10:17). Watson's observation still holds in that Paul's Jesus, especially as portrayed in 1 Cor. 15 (as last Adam) and in 2 Cor. 4 (as the "image of God" with a "face"), is as such a much different type of "image" than are the semi-hypostacized and only somewhat "visible" images of Wisdom and Philo.

sages is a human as the image. Jesus as "image of God" is not only the "apprehensibility of God" generally,[75] but is more particularly the place where, like in Moses' face but in a far surpassing way, "God himself, the invisible, is known,"[76] even the "visibility of God."[77]

According to S. Kim, Paul saw Christ as "the image of God" in the Damascus theophany and subsequently interpreted him both as "the image of God" in pre-existent creation-mediation (like Philo's Logos and Wisdom's wisdom = "Wisdom-Christology") and as "the image of God" in human Adamic form (= "Adam-Christology").[78] This dual-sided εἰκών-Christology enables Kim to be more flexible with his language regarding when exactly Christ was "the image of God" in Paul's general theology.[79] Thus Kim also considers that "both the elements derived from Wisdom-Christology and those from Adam-Christology are often found together in the passages where Paul speaks of Christ as the εἰκών of God and of our transformation into that image."[80] He applies this to 2 Cor. 3:18–4:6:[81]

Christ as the εἰκών τοῦ θεοῦ is the revelation of God (2 Cor 4.4–6), i.e., the embodiment of Wisdom, but as such he is also the Last Adam who has recovered the divine image so that we may be transformed into his image (2 Cor 3.18) and become a new creature (2 Cor 4.6).

Kim defines Wisdom-Christology as "oriented to Christ's functions in creation and revelation" and Adam-Christology as "oriented to his functions in eschatology as the Last Adam."[82] The aspect of "Wisdom-Christology" that Kim recognizes in 2 Cor. 4:4 is thus "the revelation of God." But "revelation" is a concept equally at home in a fully anthropological notion of "image" drawn from Gen. 1:27 (so 1 Cor. 11:7): God is known (i.e., revealed) wrongly when his "image" appears inappropriately. There is thus no exegetical reason to see a combination of both aspects of Christology in 2 Cor. 4:4, for each nuance is effectively explained in an Adamic manner.

---

[75] Hanson, 1980A, 22–23.

[76] Barrett, 1993, 135; cf. Nguyen, 2008, 182.

[77] Hanson, 1980A, 22–23. Because Hanson imports Col. 1:15 and Phil. 2:6 into 2 Cor. 4:4, thereby expanding "image" in 4:4 to include Christ's eternality, he is less comfortable with Christ as "the *visibility* of God" than is Paul, who comfortably relates "image" to Christ's human "face."

[78] For the fundamental importance of both Adamic and Wisdom aspects to Paul's Christology see Dunn, 1998A, 231–38. For a plenary reading of "image" in 2 Cor. 4:4 (as both Adamic and metaphysical) – even if not fully accepting Kim's explanation of *how* it came about – see Harris, 2005, 330–31; Matera, 2003, 102; Thrall, 1994, 1.310–11 (cf. Ridderbos, 1975, 69–72; Black, 1954, 174–75, 179).

[79] Kim, 1980, 136–268.

[80] Kim, 1980, 267.

[81] Kim, 1980, 267.

[82] Kim, 1980, 144.

Thus "face" is a very important feature of Paul's understanding of "the image of God."[83] Paul's presentation of Christ as "the image of God" in 2 Cor. 4:4 has to do with the incarnate, human, risen, and glorified "Jesus Christ, Lord." Found between references to assimilation with the "image" by "the Spirit" (3:18; cf. 1 Cor. 15:45, 49) and to God's initial creation (4:6; cf. 1 Cor. 15:37–41), this passage should be compared with 1 Cor. 15:35–49 before the others which are typically imported as "parallels" (see above). For the Corinthians Paul had already linked "the image and glory of God" with Adam (1 Cor. 11:7–9) and had already described Jesus as "second human"/"last Adam" (1 Cor. 15:45–47, and "life-making Spirit") who conveys his benefits through assimilation with his own "image" (15:48–49). To them Paul now describes the Christ with the glorious face as "the image of God," and he explains the Spirit who transforms his followers into his own "image." We would need a lot of compelling evidence to define Jesus Christ the Lord in 2 Cor. 4:4 in a non-Adamic way.[84] So R. Scroggs writes,[85]

> No hesitation need exist in understanding εἰκὼν τοῦ θεοῦ to be an affirmation by Paul that his Lord *is* the regained humanity God intended to exist at creation.... Christ as image of God clearly describes eschatological humanity.

Although Paul considered Christ as an eternal being who aided in creation itself (e.g., 1 Cor. 8:6; cf. 10:4),[86] nothing in 2 Cor. 4:4 or the surrounding context gives evidence that such is Paul's meaning there. Due to the grammatical similarity of 2 Cor. 4:4 with 1 Cor. 11:7 (i.e., "is," no preposition), and due to Paul's connection between "image" and "face" (as a *post*-Mosaic face and ministry that surpasses the former Mosaic face and ministry), there is no reason to conclude that Paul is referring to Christ *as* pre-existent, metaphysical, and transcendent when calling him "the image of God." In 2 Cor. 4:4, "image of God" is a (neo-) *anthropo*gonic title such as "last Adam." The second original human, like the first original human before him, is "the image of God." As such, to know Jesus is to know God.

---

[83] See Nguyen, 2008, 173–94, esp. 179–80, 182–84: "As with the case of εἰκών, the usage of πρόσωπον in the Old Testament shows that Paul is using the phrase προσώπῳ Χριστοῦ in 4.6 to convey Christ as the visible representation of the invisible presence of God" (181). Cf. Steenburg (1990) on the connection between "face," "image," and Gen. 1:27 in *The Life of Adam and Eve* 13: "'Face' relates more specifically to physical, visual appearance" (96–97).

[84] So many do consider "image of God" in 2 Cor. 4:4 as an anthropological (Adamic) title: e.g., Nguyen, 2008, 178–79, 192; Rowe, 2005, 299–300; Moo, 1996, 534 n. 151; cf. Luz, 1969, 43; Scroggs, 1966, 98–99; Black, 1954, 171–72.

[85] Scroggs, 1966, 99 (emphasis original).

[86] So e.g., Cox, 2005, 173; Thiselton, 2000, 635–36; Dunn, 1998B, 267 (*idem*, 1989, 180–81); Witherington, 1995, 198. Contra e.g., Murphy-O'Connor (1978A and B) who distances 1 Cor. 8:6 from creation (cf. Kuschel, 1992, 285–91).

To "see" the glorious face of Christ within the spiritual darkness is to recognize the glory of the Creator of light, the glory that has surpassed that which was formerly revealed in Moses' face and ministry, the glory which has even surpassed that of the original beginning of humanity (see below).

(ii) Paul's Cosmogonic Perspectives (2 Cor. 4:6)

Paul ultimately turns attention to the God whose "image" Christ is, and this broader perspective helps us understand his hermeneutic concerning Gen. 1:27. As in the Beginning, darkness has no real power (even at the hands of "the god of this age") when the God of the Beginning decides to illuminate again in a new act of creative "shining." It is from the perspective of this *new* act that Paul mentions the facial "image of God."

In a manner broadly like Philo, Paul has *two* cosmogonic contexts within which to understand anthropology, and, like Philo, the perspective from which he is looking matters. Both creations are comparable for Paul: both have "bodies," "glories," an "Adam," "light," and even the propagation of that Adam's "image" to his family. These two comparable cosmic and anthropic perspectives enable Paul to apply the God-intended title of the first Adam from Gen. 1:27 to *both* the men in Corinth (1 Cor. 11:7–10) *and* to Christ (2 Cor. 4:4) without the two contradicting. In 2 Cor. 4:6a, Paul refers to the original creation (of light), but in v. 6b he seamlessly shifts to the new creation (of light). These two creations are similar: both are "shinings," both presuppose "darkness," both are even accomplished by God's word proclaimed in the darkness.[87] But it is from the perspective of the old that Paul labels "men" as "image of God" while from the perspective of the new that Paul mentions Christ as such.

Though in 1 Cor. 11:7–12 it was certainly the eschatological (new) community whom Paul directed, within that context he was applying to them only the original creation (Gen. 1:27, 2:7–23, 4:1, and Genesis 1–2 in general; see above). From that perspective and within that hermeneutical context he applies to men the "image and glory of God" (perhaps as Gen. 9:6 had): they should act a certain way because by nature they and God are mutually understood due to the "image" concept. This remains the case, even within the Christian community, simply because they are as human as was Adam. In 2 Corinthians 4, however, Paul has both the original creation and the new creation in mind. They are connected, but it is specifically God's *redemptive* (new) shining into blinded hearts in v. 6b that displays his glory in Christ's "face," and it is *this* face and glory which should be

---

[87] Cf. "the God who *said*" (4:6a) with "the light of the *gospel*" (4:4b) which Paul has just labeled as "God's word" (4:1–3).

recognized as God's glorious "image" (v. 4).[88] Paul is not claiming here that it was during the *original* creation of light that Christ was "God's image" (i.e., *within* Gen. 1:27 itself). Paul's application of the label from Gen. 1:27 to Christ is situated within the context of the *new* creation, the newly shone light of divine glory – post-Adam and, importantly, post-Moses. It is from *that* cosmic perspective that Paul looks at Christ as "the image of God" in 2 Cor. 4:4.

The implication of this discussion of Paul's two creational perspectives is that Paul had only one *reading* of the text. The initial man of creation was the image and glory of God. Within Paul's broadest possible context of God's all-encompassing creative causation – including protology and eschatology – he can apply the original (Adamic) God-given title/nature of "image of God," taken from Gen. 1:27, to the Corinthian man as a physical and functional man and yet also to Christ as initial human of the new creation – the last Adam.

(c) Summary: Paul's Reading of Genesis 1:27,
in Comparison with Philo's Reading

Paul's hermeneutical contexts within which each of his presentations of Gen. 1:27 are found, like Philo's, have an impact on how he applies the text. Paul considers the original creation of humanity (as recorded in the text) to carry the certain anthropological principles by which he then shapes Christian worship in 1 Cor. 11:7–10 and 11–12. Paul equates "the image of God" with the Corinthian "man" (not with mind, nor Word or Wisdom, nor even Christ), and while this may surprise some, it makes sense within Paul's broader perspective concerning creation in this pericope. Verses 8–9 and 12 make clear that Paul has the original, not new, creation in mind. He approaches this church-issue from the perspective of an aspect of this original creation (gender) that remains importantly real in the Lord.[89] Therefore his reference to the image as simply a man – a man with the same flesh, bones, and God-ward calling that Adam had in Gene-

---

[88] For the parallel between v. 4 ("image") and v. 6 ("face") see Meyer, 2009, 101 n. 138; Thrall, 1994, 283. Many scholars note the correspondence of ideas in 3:18, 4:4, and 4:6 (or explicitly just two of the three): cf. Nguyen, 2008, 176–77; Matera, 2003, 102; Watson, 1997, 301 n. 7; Fee, 1994, 317–18; Kim, 1980, 232.

[89] Paul's hermeneutical move from protological text to contemporary (Christian) practice should not be surprising. He makes the same move when explaining sex in 1 Cor. 6:16. There he stated dogmatically that "the one "clinging" to a prostitute is one body [with her]." That is simply the ontological nature of sex whether one is in the Lord or not. Paul knows this ontology because his Bible tells him so: Gen. 2:24. Certain aspects of ontology are derivable from God's creation and they continue to be applicable to modern people, even Christians.

sis 1–2, as well as with the same responsibility to reflect and reflect on God appropriately – fits well within this broader context of God's original (and intentional) creation of "all things."

For Paul, however, as for Philo, a detail which came after Gen. 1:27 caused him to re-apply Gen. 1:27 (2 Cor. 4:4). Unlike Philo, Paul's detail was not textual (though is certainly testified to and explained by many texts), but rather historical and personal: the resurrected Jesus Christ. This future "detail" caused Paul to see a new beginning to the world and to humanity. As Philo had analyzed Gen. 1:27 in retrospective relation to the man who came (textually) second, i.e., Adam, so too Paul looks back at the anthropological titles applied to the first Adam in Genesis 1–2 and he reads them in relation to the man who came (historically) second, i.e., Jesus. As Philo's two interpretations of the "human" (whether sensory or noetic) are of one accord with his two broader hermeneutical perspectives on the beginning of the world (whether sensory or noetic), so too Paul's two applications of the more specific text of the beginning of humanity (whether new or original) consistently follows on from his two perspectives on the cosmic Beginning (whether new or original).

Yet while Philo's readings are technically two different construals of the exact same text, Paul's readings are technically two different applications of the same construal. Philo is attempting in both places to explain who the actual "human" is within the text, first the sensible one and then the noetic one. But both cannot be the actual human of the text at the same time. Paul, however, is in neither place attempting to say either that the Corinthian "man" or that "Christ" actually *is* the one spoken of in Gen. 1:27 itself. For Paul, the first Adam holds that honor. Rather, Paul construes contemporary people, whether the Corinthian man or the resurrected Jesus, *in accord with* the title granted to the original human in Gen. 1:27.

From Paul's two applications of 1:27 we can construct his construal of the original text itself. Adam was created to be a kind of presentation (or mirror-image) of God, specifically of God's glory. The way Adam presented himself would also have reflected on God as the appearance (and behavior) of a statue (or even child) reflects on the honor or shame of the king (or parent). It is vital for Paul's broader theology and anthropology that the original "image of God" actually, grievously, and gravely shamed the Creator. Yet also fundamental for Paul is that Adam's offspring (men, at least), merely by virtue of being images of God like their father, continue to either display or veil God's glory, to either cast back a shameful or honorable reputation on their Creator who made Adam (and therefore them) to be his image(s). Likewise, Christ as the last Adam, second human, first person of the new creation through resurrected life-by-Spirit, is the "image of God." As such he reflects God's glory, making it known, while simultaneously reflecting on God's honor by his actions and appearance. Although the resurrected Jesus shares this basic Adamic (and even Mosaic) method of mirror-imaging God, Jesus' face images God's glory more clearly than had Moses with the glorious face, and *even* more radiantly and fully than had the divinely hand-crafted man of dust.

3.2 The Man of Dust: Genesis 2:7

Whether turning to 1:27 or 2:7 to form and refine one's anthropology, each text is preceded by and set within the broader context of "heaven and earth,"[90] and within the more particular context of an "earth" that is primed for human life.[91] This "life" is itself a dominant theme of Genesis 2–3. God's formation of "the human" as "dust from the earth" (2:7a) can be compared with the production of an ornate clay pot – beautiful in design, but not living. But God "inbreathes" into the formation's "face" (2:7b). As "image of God" had been the essential description of humanity in 1:27, in this second text the essential description of humanity is found in v. 7c: "and the human turned into *a living being*." Made possible by God's "breath of life" (πνοὴν ζωῆς), this new person is "a soul that lives" (ψυχὴν ζῶσαν). The subsequent narrative confirms the centrality of "life" (and death) for this human Beginning.[92]

There could be seen in 2:7 itself, especially in light of the drama which unfolds, a hint of potential negativity (or at least weakness) concerning the newly crafted human. When Adam is condemned to death, his "return to dust" is not portrayed as some aspect of him with which he was created being stripped away. Though death is sometimes portrayed in subsequent scripture as such, i.e., as God's sovereign removal of "Spirit," "spirit,"

---

[90] Cf. Gen. 1:1 and 2:4.

[91] Cf. Gen. 1:9–13, 20–25 with 2:5–6. Von Rad (1956) drew attention to the shared chaos-to-life motif in Genesis 1 and 2 (74). Yet he inappropriatly distinguishes between water in Gen.2 ("the assisting element of creation") and in Gen.1 ("the enemy of creation") (75), for in 1:20–21 God calls the water to assist him in creation. For our purposes it does not matter that many scholars have had difficulty relating the cosmic setting in Gen. 2:6 to that in Gen. 1:1–25. Both cosmic settings precede the anthropogony (Gen. 1:26 and 2:7), and neither Philo nor Paul struggle to relate 2:6 to Genesis 1. Philo places Gen. 2:6 in harmony with Genesis 1 (*Op.* 131–33; cf. *Op.* 38–39), while Paul sets Gen. 2:7 (in 1 Cor. 15:45–47) within a cosmic context drawn mainly from Genesis 1 (15:37–41), thus apparently seeing no tension.

[92] "The tree of life" is central (2:9), "death" is promised (2:17), and "depart into the earth" is pronounced (3:19). God bars the first man (along with his wife, and thus also any future progeny) from "the tree of life" and therefore from any possibility of "living forever" (3:22).

and/or "breath" (as de-creation),[93] in this initial narrative the nuance implies that Adam's body-as-created dies because he is deprived of the extrinsic aid of the tree of "eternal life" from which he (and his wife, and future progeny) was divinely barred due to sin.[94] *As he was constructed* in 2:7 there was an ability to corrupt or decay, for immortality would have been his not intrinsically but only had his created nature been supplemented by God-given "fruit" of eternal life.

When one considers the human of 2:7 there is room to rejoice in the God-given breath and in the God-formed body that live in united animation as "living soul,"[95] but there may also be the nagging wariness that the absence of what God provides means inevitable lifeless dust. But subsequent texts which highlight the human's de-creational return to dust (e.g., Job 34, Psalm 103 LXX) are viewing dust and life from the subsequent perspective where death is a clear and present reality. Within its creational context itself, especially in light of the divine will and word of Genesis 1 that brings everything (including humanity) into "exceeding goodness," God's formation of this particular human is most naturally understood as precisely what the Creator desired and purposed for him to be at that moment. Despite (retrospective) hints within Gen. 2:7 of weakness and potential decay, someone's interpretation of this text will probably remain in positive motion unless acted upon by an outside source. Philo and Paul demonstrate pre-

---

[93] See especially Gen. 6:3 (Yates, 2008, 25). In Job 34 cf. v. 13 with Genesis 1, vv. 14–15b with Gen. 3:19, v. 15c with Gen. 2:7. In LXX Ps. 103 cf. vv. 1–22, 24–30 with Genesis 1, v. 29 with Gen. 3:19, v. 30ab with Gen. 1:2, v. 30ac with Gen. 2:7. Many ancients saw God's "Spirit" as both cosmogonic and anthropogonic: in Eze. 37:9–10 the πνεῦμα coming from "four winds" is cosmic, and the activity of this cosmic πνεῦμα is explicitly anthropogonic (Yates, 2008, 32–34; Chester, 2001, 49–50); in Job 33:4 "the divine Spirit" (πνεῦμα θεῖος) is the anthropogonic "Maker" (τὸ ποιῆσαν); in Judith 16:14 God's "Spirit" is cosmogonic cause of "every creature" (cf. 10:13, "spirit of life" as a description of human existence) (Yates, 2008, 36–38). Cf. Wis. 15:11 (Sellin, 1986, 83–84); Josephus' *Ant.* 1.34. Numerous scriptural texts glossed the "breath" of Gen. 2:7 with "spirit": Ps. 103:29 LXX (Yates, 2008, 30–31); Eccl. 12:7; Zech. 12:1 (Yates, 27 n. 16); Eze. 37:9–10 (Yates, 32–34); cf. Ps. 32:6 LXX; Isa. 42:5. Interestingly, no manuscript listed in Göttingen (p. 84) substitutes πνεῦμα for πνοή. Other scriptural texts used "breath" (πνοή) and "spirit" (πνεῦμα) in close connection (at least): e.g., 2 Sam. 22:16; Job 27:3; 32:8; 33:4; Isa. 57:16. See Yates, 2008. 27 (who draws attention also to *Gen. Rab.* 14:10 [on Gen. 2:7]). Sellin explores "life-giving Spirit" in scriptural and ancient Jewish writing (80–81) and in Graeco-Roman (Hermetic, Stoic, Pythagorean) philosophy (81–90) (acknowledging their overlap, especially in Philo and Wisdom of Solomon). In modern times, cf. Kline, 1980, 23 and van Kooten, 2008, 269–311.

[94] Gen. 3:22: λάβῃ τοῦ ξύλου τῆς ζωῆς καὶ φάγῃ καὶ ζήσεται εἰς τὸν αἰῶνα. It is exegetically unnecessary to present death in Genesis 3 as of a different nature from death in Genesis 5 (contra Minear, 1994, 68, [and can have poor effects on an interpretation of Paul: 78–79]).

[95] Von Rad, 1956, 75. Cf. Scroggs, 1966, 4; Gunkel, 1997 (original 1901), 6.

cisely this double-edged hermeneutic. Each shows two perspectives on Gen. 2:7 – one positive, one negative – and for each the negative reading is due to comparison of it with an outside source.

3.2.1 Philo's Reading of Genesis 2:7

Gen. 2:7 gives to (and confirms within) Philo deep and dualistic convictions which are "the backbone of his anthropological views."[96] This dualism encompasses cosmology (the noetic – sensory divide), anthropology (the mind – body composition), and ethics (virtue according to mind/image – vice according to flesh/senses).[97] Within his anthropological dualism, the human mind takes the place of primacy in 2:7, just as it had in 1:27. But while Philo often merges these two texts of human beginnings and emphasizes the human mind and its divine origin,[98] in *Op.* 134–35 Philo intentionally distances 2:7 from 1:27 (as we saw above), and describes a "vast difference" between the two humans.

Within his one commentary, Philo has two construals of Gen. 2:7. One reading of this corporeal man is somewhat negative (§§134–35), while the other reading of the corporeal man is highly positive (§§136–50). Two hermeneutical perspectives prompt the differing qualities of Philo's two construals of 2:7, and this will be similar for Paul. When reading Gen. 2:7 *on its own*, Philo interprets its human positively. When reading 2:7 *in comparison* with an outside source, in Philo's case Gen. 1:27 and the human therein, he reads 2:7 negatively.

(a) Philo's Negative Reading:
"Earthly" Man in Comparison (*Op.* 134–35)

In §134, Philo reintroduces the person "according to the image of God" into his comments on Gen. 2:7. Philo's hermeneutic is one of comparison, and when compared, a "vast difference" is found between the humans:

The one 'formed' is a sense-perceptible object, already sharing in quality, consisting of body and soul, man or woman, by nature mortal [φύσει θνητός] (Gen. 2:7). The one

---

[96] Van den Hoek, 2000, 65. Cf. Runia, 1986, 262.

[97] Levison, 1988, 86. Philo uses the designation "consiting of body and soul" as a general anthropological statement in e.g., *Spec.* 2.64; *Cher.* 113; *Sacr.* 126; *Ebr.* 69; *Conf.* 62; *Gig.* 33 (Runia, 2001, 325). On ethics see *Plant.* 44–46 (Tobin, 1983, 136–37).

[98] When Philo blends 1:27 and 2:7 (e.g., *Leg.* 3.95–96; *Det.* 80–90; *Plant.* 14–27; *Her.* 230–31; *Mut.* 223; *Spec.* 1.80–81, 171; 3.83, 208; *QG* 2.62), it is typical that the "mind" or "reasoning soul" becomes a dominant feature of discussion (so Loader, 2004, 60, 64 n. 84; Jervell, 1960, 51–53; McCasland, 1950, 92–93). Thus the human mind/rationality images God's rationality (λογισμός) and Word (λόγος) (Gen. 1:27) and also receives the inbreathed "divine spirit" (2:7) (so Baer, 1970, 25–26).

3.2 The Man of Dust: Genesis 2:7

'according to the image' is a kind of idea or genus or seal, noetic, incorporeal, neither male nor female, incorruptible by nature [ἄφθαρτος φύσει] (Gen. 1:27). (§134.7b-11)

By calling the human of 2:7 "by nature mortal" (φύσει θνητός), and especially by contrasting this "mortality" with the "incorruptibility" (ἄφθαρτος) of the bodiless human of 1:27, Philo's nuance to "mortality" conveys a death that is the end of a wasting away, a decaying that is common to all material and "qualitatively" definable things.[99] Philo sees in the human body, as constructed in Gen. 2:7, an inevitable propensity to dissipate to dust since immortality and incorruptibility are not inherent to bodily structure.[100] Elsewhere Philo more explicitly describes what about the body is negative, or rather, potentially (and probably) negative.[101] Here he focuses on the corruptibility and mortality of its nature as physical.

In §135, Philo attends more particularly to the man of 2:7 himself. He no longer mentions the man of 1:27, though he is still functioning within his general hermeneutic of comparison. Philo summarizes Moses: "the structure of the individual man – the object of sense – is a composite one [σύνθετον]: both out of earthly stuff [ἐκ γεώδους οὐσίας] and of divine spirit [πνεύματος θείου]." By focusing on the human "structure" (ἡ κατασκευή) of 2:7a, Philo implies similarity with a vessel (= σκεῦος) such

---

[99] Cf. *Cong.* 20; *Cher.* 14. "Qualitatively definable" (i.e., "sharing in quality," ποιότητος) refers to having "distinguished characteristics" (van den Hoek, 2000, 68), i.e., to the "accidental properties necessarily possessed by things that are sense-perceptible and corporeal" (Runia, 2001, 325). Philo often uses the ἄποιος/ποιότης contrast for the things before and after God's creative ordering (cf. *Op.* 21–22, 63; *Spec.* 4.187).

[100] In *Leg.* 1.31–35 (hermeneutically comparable to *Op.* 129ff, not to *Op.* 13–128), the composite Adam in Gen. 2:7 is further denigrated as both body *and* mind are seen as "corruptible" (φθαρτός), yet God's breath is seen as a benevolent rescue – granting ethical "zeal for virtue" – and as a heightening of moral responsibility.

[101] Philo sometimes portrays matter as inherently tied to wickedness (*Spec.* 1.329; Radice, 2009, 138, 143), and therefore the body is too (*Plant.* 42–43; cf. *Leg.* 1.42, 88). The mind's knowledge is certainly limited simply by being tied to the mortal body (*Mut.* 219). More properly, however, a "composite" nature grants the *potential* for wickedness (van den Hoek, 2000, 66; Loader, 2004, 63; cf. *Somn.* 1.68–69 and *Leg.* 1.92, 95), the body being a "road *to* wickedness" (*Conf.* 179). Vice is not the *necessary* consequence of bodily existence. Sometimes Philo writes of God's creation of the body as positive, co-working with the mind to guide contemplation away from the earthly and perishable and into the heavenly and imperishable realm (cf. *Det.* 84–85; *Plant.* 16–17). Yet the body is full of contrary desires (*Plant.* 43), and the mind can and will go either way because of the "impressions" made on it like on wax (*Fug.* 69–70; *Mut.* 30–31). Neither bodiless nor mindless beings are morally culpable (*Conf.* 177), but humans, created in Gen. 2:7 as composite beings, have the propensity for virtue and vice (*Conf.* 176–78; *QG.* 1.5; *Leg.* 2.22–24). Yet as practice shows, vice through uncontrolled passions is the more prominent human way, enabled by the material body shaped out of dust in the beginning.

as pottery. Combined with this earthy vessel is "divine spirit."[102] This may seem more theologically loaded than the actual wording of 2:7b allows – "breath of life" (πνοὴν ζωῆς) – and elsewhere Philo does show discomfort reading "breath" *as* "spirit."[103] Yet "spirit" was an important part of Philo's anthropology, and as is proven by so many others (both ancient and modern) it is easy to see it in 2:7b.[104]

Providing further details regarding the composite nature of this first sense-perceptible human, Philo writes:

For the body [τὸ σῶμα] has Become by the Designer taking dust [χοῦν] and molding [διαπλάσαντος] a human form out of it [μορφὴν ἀνθρωπίνην ἐξ αὐτοῦ] (Gen. 2:7a). But the soul [τὴν ψυχήν] was from nothing out of all Becoming things, but rather from the Father and Ruler of all.

One could point out with von Rad that the "soul" (ψυχήν) in 2:7c refers to what the human – body (v. 7a) and breath (v. 7b) – "becomes" and not to a particular non-becoming aspect of him.[105] In other contexts Philo writes about "soul" as more general "life." Here Philo may have a somewhat polemical edge when reducing "soul" to that aspect of the human which contrasts with "body," perhaps attempting to keep the human "soul" from becoming too materialistic. It is not "Becoming"; it has divine origin.[106]

Philo takes this opportunity to elaborate on the "soul," or "that which God inbreathed":

For that which he inbreathed [ἐνεφύσησεν] was nothing other than a divine spirit [πνεῦμα θεῖον], a settlement that migrated here from that blessed and happy nature for

---

[102] A unity between cosmogony and anthropogony can be seen in Philo's Stoic-like pneumatology: cf. *Op.* 30, 131.21, 135, and *Leg.* 1.31ff with Gen. 1:2 (cosmogonic *pneuma*); see *Praem.* 144 (*pneuma* as a biological force); see *Fug.* 134 (*pneuma* as anthropogonic). Radice (2009) connects the pneumatology in Stoicism (141), Genesis 1–2 (141–42), and Philo (142 and 142 n. 28) (cf. Runia, 2001, 316–17).

[103] Philo has a difficult time nailing down exactly what God "breathed into" Adam. Cf. *Leg.* 1.36–42, 3.161, and *Spec.* 4.123 with *Leg.* 1.42 (Tobin, 1983, 77–78, 94–96; Runia, 1986, 306–07; *idem,* 2001, 336–37).

[104] Many scholars merely assert or assume *synonymity* between "breath" and "spirit" (which is saying too much, though there certainly was overlap): cf. e.g., Dupont, 1960, 172; Sellin, 1986, 92 (cf. 79–90).

[105] Von Rad, 1956, 75. Cf. Gen. 1:20, 21, 24, 30.

[106] Stoic anthropology often identified divine-breath with human-soul (Levison, 1988, 70, 210 n. 38). In *Op.* 135, Philo seems to join the Stoics by describing "breath of life" as "divine spirit" and by calling this inbreathing the human ψυχή (cf. *QG.* 1.4). Yet his non-materialistic treatment of "soul" in this anthropologically fundamental text curbs pantheistic tendencies. Cf. *Plant.* 14–27: conceding a Stoic somatology, he then uses 1:27 and 2:7 to prove the soul is not akin to "air" (which Becomes) but to God ("image *of God,*" breath *from God*). (See Tobin, 1983, 90). Due to the flexibility of the word "soul," even within the scriptures, Philo may have a broader theological legitimacy for this reading even if he has missed the particular nuance of "soul" and "living soul" in Gen. 2:7 itself.

the benefit of our race [ἐπ' ὠφελείᾳ τοῦ γένους ἡμῶν],[107] in order that [ἵνα] even if it is mortal [θνητόν] in respect of the visible part [τὴν ὁρατὴν μερίδα], it may in respect of its invisible part [τὴν ἀόρατον] be made immortal [ἀθανατίζηται]. Hence it may with propriety be said that man is the borderland between mortal and immortal nature, partaking of each so far as is needful.[108] (§135)

Philo thus construes the man of Gen. 2:7 in a composite manner: partly positive and partly negative. The good and immortal element is his God-inspired soul, and this was given for the purpose (ἵνα) and telos (ἐπί) of human blessedness despite their physical bodies.[109]

Philo sees in this tripartite text a body (v. 7a), a divine breath/spirit (v. 7b), and a soul (v. 7c), and he presents this textual human in mixed light. The mind ("invisible," like the noetic cosmos)[110] is very positive and receives the divine and creative Spirit, while the body ("visible," like the sensory cosmos)[111] is (potentially) very negative.[112] The body of 2:7 is not yet wicked, but certainly weak, mortal, corruptible, and primed for downfall. In the very next breath, however, Philo seems to change his tune and laud "this first man"[113] – i.e., this same "earthborn one, the ancestor of our entire race" – as "most excellent" (ἄριστος), as "in truth beautiful and

---

[107] The "divine spirit" is described similarly in *Op.* 146; *Det.* 90; *Spec.* 4.123 (Tobin, 1983, 110).

[108] Philo does not specify at this point why this dualism is "proper" and "needful," but elsewhere he does: 1) to preserve God's dignity as separate from evil (*Conf.* 175–79; *Fug.* 69–70, 71–72; cf. *Mut.* 30–31), 2) to ensure humanity's moral accountability (*Plant.* 45; *Conf.* 177–78).

[109] According to Pearson (1973), many ancient Jews used Gen. 2:7 (particularly 2:7b) as a "proof text" for man's immortality (20; cf. Philo [17–20], Wisdom of Solomon [20–21]), yet the opposite at Qumran (21–23).

[110] See Philo's cosmogonic use of "invisible" in *Op.* 12, 29 (Gen.1:2) and in *Op.* 129 (Gen.2:4–5).

[111] Plato uses "visible" for sensory and "invisible" for Idea: *Tim.* 30a, 31b, 32b, 36e, 52a; cf. *Rep.* 529b5 and *Soph.* 246b7 with Alcinous' *Did.* 7.4 (noted in Runia, 2001, 165). Cf. Rösel, 1994, 32 n. 19.

[112] Philo's labels "invisible" and "visible" reflect the general unity in Philo's theology between cosmos/cosmogony and *anthrōpos*/anthropogony (see e.g., *Op.* 82 [151]; *Post.* 58; *Her.* 88, 155; *Abr.* 71; *Migr.* 220; *Mos.* 2.127, 135; *Prov.* 1.40) and in his reading of Genesis 1–2 in particular (so Radice, 2009, 134; *idem,* 1989, 122). This cosmos-*anthrōpos* similarity is generally Graeco-Roman (so Martin, 1992, 3–15, 17; cf. Runia, 2001, 227, 254 [cf. *idem,* 1986, 555]; van den Hoek, 2000, 65, 67, 67 n. 12; Steenburg, 1990, 102, 104; Sandmel, 1983, 24; Tobin, 1983, 45, 45 n. 19, 49, 125; Kim, 1980, 191).

[113] Even though the man of 1:27 preceeded the man of 2:7 (in textual, logical, and ontological senses, not exactly temporal; so Wedderburn, 1973B, 303–26), Philo continuously labels the man of 2:7 "the first man" (ὁ πρῶτος ἄνθρωπος) and its equivalents: see *Op.* 136, 138, 140, 142, 145, 148, 151 (so Schaller, 2004, 149–50; Hultgren, 2003, 344–45).

good" (ὁ ἀληθείᾳ καλὸς καὶ ἀγαθός), even having such excellence in "both soul and also body."

(b) Philo's Positive Reading: "First Man" per se (*Op.* 136–50)

The ontic beauty presented in Gen. 2:7 (§§136–41) leads Philo to the contemplation of virtue (§§142–50). The "first human" represents the Stoic "world-citizen" (κοσμοπολίτης), a title granted in *Op.* 3 to the one who follows the Mosaic Law (and "the world," as the two are in harmony). As the first cosmopolitan he is both great in virtue and therefore representative of the importance of virtue.[114] But this "first man" is wonderful not only in soul but in body as well.

In §§136–38, the beauty of the man's body becomes Philo's focus, and it is attributed to God's ability. In §139, the beauty of his soul is proven by reuniting the language of 1:27 with 2:7. In §§140–44, the unsurpassableness of this man to all subsequent humans (particularly in body but also in cognitive capabilities and rulership) is demonstrated. In §§145–46, Philo deals with the theme that will become our concern later in this chapter: the likeness of subsequent humanity to the first human. In §147, Philo describes how the first man (and humanity in general) was at home in all four elements of the cosmos. Finally, in §§148–50 Philo moves to Gen. 2:19 – Adam's "naming" of the animals – where the theme of "king" and "dominion" from 1:26–28 resurfaces. I will now attend to Philo's defense of the goodness of Adam's body (§§136–138), to the beginning of Philo's defense of the goodness of Adam's soul (§139), and to how Philo, while commenting on Gen. 2:7 from his positive perspective, yet again assumes the intimate relationship between the three strands of creation: the beginning of the world, the beginning of humanity, and God's intentions before the beginning.

In §136, Philo navigates away from his description of the human of 2:7 *in comparison* with the human of 1:27. He continues his exegesis of 2:7 but now approaches its human *per se*. With this hermeneutical shift, his anthropological description takes a decidedly positive turn in §§136–47. "That" man whose body he had just described in a degrading tone (§§134–35) is "most excellent" in "body" (§136.1–3), is "in truth beautiful and good" (§136.6), and has "good form" (εὐμορφίαν) of body (§136.7).

Three textual features prove the goodness of Adam's "body," and here again we see the interwoven character of Philo's three strands of his creation-hermeneutic. First, when God separated the waters and rose up the ground (Gen. 1:9–10; cf. *Op.* 38–39 and 131–33), the result was pure and flawless clay that was ready to be molded (§136.8–13). (This highlights

---

[114] See Levison, 1988, 70–72.

Philo's connection between the Beginning of world and of humanity). Second, Philo sees the reason for God's election of the purest clay: he chose it because (γάρ) it was to be suitable as

> a dwelling-place or sacred temple... for the reasonable soul, which man was to carry as a statue [ἀγαλματοφορήσειν], of all statues the most Godlike [ἀγαλμάτων τὸ θεοειδέστατον]. (§§137.8–10)[115]

This ontic purity of the material Philo sets within the context of God's forethought. God did not rush his choice of materials, but selected what was "the best" (τὸ βέλτιστον), all the while looking "toward what was best for the structure" (πρὸς τὴν κατασκευὴν μάλιστα) (§137.5–7). (This highlights Philo's assumption that God's pre-creative intentions govern both aspects of the Beginning).

Philo's third proof of the beauty of Adam's body is self-admittedly "incomparably stronger" than the former two (§138.1–2):

> The Craftsman was good [ἀγαθός], as well as in all else, in understanding to bring it about that each of the parts of the body [ἕκαστον τῶν τοῦ σώματος μερῶν] should have in itself individually [ἰδίᾳ καθ' αὑτό] its due proportions, and should also be harmoniously fitted with accuracy toward the fellowship of the whole. And together with this symmetry [of the parts], God formed over [προσανέπλαττε] the body good-flesh [εὐσαρκίαν], and adorned it with good-color [εὔχροιαν], purposing [βουλόμενος] the first man to be the most beautiful [κάλλιστον] to behold. (§138.2–10)

The Creator's "goodness," which had motivated him to create a "beautiful" world (§21), also motivates his creation of a "beautiful" human. God's skill and "understanding" is unsurpassed in both cosmogony and anthropogony.[116] It grants both an aesthetically pleasing appearance to "the first man" and also what is mechanically proper and symmetrical. Due to God's design, body parts function harmoniously toward the whole body's "fellowship." (In 1 Cor. 12:12–30, Paul will show a similar description of God's creation of the human body; see below). Philo again subordinates ontic perfection under God's pre-creational "purposing" (βουλόμενος).

In *Op.* 139, Philo turns to the surpassing nature of Adam's soul. After having sharply separated the two humans as "vastly different" in §134, Philo now explains that "when God inbreathed [ἐμπνευσθέντα] into the man's face" (Gen. 2:7b) it was then that "the human became an image and copy of [God's own Word]."[117] We should not deduce from this statement

---

[115] For Philo, the human's "reasonable soul" was the thing that most represented God (cf. *Op.* 69), as a statue represents a god or king, and thus Philo likens the human body to a sacred temple that houses the statue(s) of God or the gods.

[116] Cf. *Virt.* 203.

[117] Cf. *Det.* 86–87. Runia (2001) calls *Op.* 139 "a clear illustration of how Philo tends to reconcile and coalesce the two creation accounts" (336).

that Philo makes 1:27 and 2:7 "the same event."[118] The noetic realm (now found in Gen. 1:1–2:5) and the sensory realm (now found in 2:6ff) are not identical, though they are compatible. In principle, the sensory realm's component parts match the noetic realm's (§§18–19). Thus the two texts (1:27 and 2:7) do correspond.[119] When God breathes into the human face the sensory human "becomes" an "image" and "copy" of God's "word"; this is a mirror-image of how the ideal human of 1:27 is "made" (incorporeally) according to God's "image" (Word). Since the Adam of 2:7 has "the ruling mind in the soul" he can here be identified as an "image" (ἀπεικόνισμα) of God's word.[120] Thus according to Philo's reading of Gen. 2:7 *per se*, the granted "soul" as well as the chosen and formed "body" are each of superior quality. This is due to the divine forethought and purpose. The "good" creation of Adam parallels God's creation of the world and mirrors God's Before.

(c) Summary: Philo's Reading of Genesis 2:7

Philo presents two readings of Gen. 2:7. In one Adam is cast negatively, in the other positively. Both presentations have textual grounding when the text is viewed from different perspectives. When viewing Gen. 2:7 *in itself* Philo's reading is very positive, the human being glorious in body and soul (mind), especially due to God's design. Yet when Philo's perspective is acted upon by an outside source – by the text of 1:27 and the human therein – his interpretation of 2:7 *as viewed in comparison* presents a human that is less than the ultimate good. Paul shows a similar trend.

3.2.2 Paul's Reading of Genesis 2:7

Paul has two portrayals of Adam as the first created human. Like Philo, one is positive and one negative. As I demonstrated in the introduction to this book, in much scholarship these portrayals of Adam-as-created are often overshadowed, even completely concealed, in the presence of Paul's primary depiction of Adam as Sinner. For example, R. Scroggs writes, "*Nowhere* in [Paul's] Epistles is Adam the perfect man before his sin. Paul knows *only* the Adam of sin and death."[121] This basic view is reflected by many Pauline scholars.

Yet Paul has a more complex reading of the man of Genesis 2 than is represented by quotations such as Scroggs'. Paul quotes Gen. 2:7 only in 1

---

[118] Contra Bouteneff, 2008, 30.

[119] Radice, 2009, 134.

[120] Cf. *Virt.* 204–05.

[121] Scroggs, 1966, 100 (emphasis added); cf. 59, 91. See also Dunn, 1973, 136 and 136 n. 28.

3.2 The Man of Dust: Genesis 2:7

Cor. 15:45, and I will analyze this "negative" reading of creation in the most depth below. But before this quotation, Paul has already and in the same letter built positive anthropological principles on God's creation of the human on three occasions: 11:7–9, 12:12–30, and 15:39–40. Comparing these three texts, especially in light of both Paul's own reading of the beginning of the world (see chapter 2) and Philo's more detailed treatment of 2:7 (see above), will help illuminate Paul's positive reading of the creation of Adam. Since Paul not only displays both his positive and negative readings within the same letter (cf. 11:7–9 and 15:45–47), but even within the same argument (cf. 15:39–40 and 15:45–47), it is necessary to explore his hermeneutic that enables and even prompts this seeming discrepancy. Paul's construal of the human of Gen. 2:7 *per se* is positive, and, like Philo's, it remains so until acted upon by an outside source.

(a) Paul's Positive Reading: A Glorious Adam *per se*
(1 Cor. 11:7–9, 12:12–30, 15:39–40)

It has been well rehearsed in Pauline studies the way in which many of Paul's contemporary Jewish interpreters attributed "glory" to Adam,[122] "portraying the 'beauty' of Adam prior to the fall."[123] Paul also writes of the "glory" of the beginning of humanity (1 Cor.11:7–9 and 15:39–40) and of the perfection of the human body as knit together according to God's desire (12:12–30).

(i) Adam as God's Original "Image and Glory" (1 Cor. 11:7–9)

The man of Genesis 2 is Paul's template according to which he can call the "man" of the Corinthian church "the image and glory of God."[124] Many scholars notice that Paul here blends the language of Genesis 1 and Genesis 2, but appropriate implications are often not drawn.[125] As we have observed, some even deny "glory" to Adam in Paul's thinking.[126] Yet his ar-

---

[122] For positive and negative construals of Adam in scripture and ancient Judaism see Scroggs, 1966, 1–58 (esp. 23–29 and 47–49 for Adam as glorious; cf *idem*, 1972, 299 n. 44). Cf. Bouteneff, 2008, 26; van Kooten, 2008, 15–26 (specifically on "Adam's glory" in Qumran); Kim, 1980, 186–93 (in a presentation of Wedderburn's research from *Adam and Christ*, 66–112); Jaubert, 1971/72, 422 and 422 nn. 3–5; Hooker, 1964/65, 411. Martin (1983) even wrote "What Paul had learned at the feet of Gamaliel about the 'glory' of the first Adam... he transferred to the last Adam" (119).
[123] Thiselton, 2000, 1288.
[124] Steenburg, 1990, 99. Cf. van Kooten, 2008, 72; Fee, 1987, 515.
[125] Collins, 1999, 409–10; Schrage, 1991, 2.509; Meier, 1978, 219; Conzelmann, 1975, 186 n. 52; McCasland, 1950, 86.
[126] As well as Scroggs and Dunn cf. Bouteneff, 2008, 45–47; Kim, 1980, 264 n. 1; Barrett, 1962, 88.

gumentation surrounding v. 7b makes little sense if he is not assuming that Adam himself was "the image and glory of God" when created. Since I have already exegeted this passage more fully above, here I will be very brief and pointed.

Paul's description of man as "God's glory" is set in comparison with woman as "man's glory." Woman is "man's glory" because of Genesis 2, and specifically because her physical nature was derived "from" man and her vocation was divinely intended "for" the man. The natural deduction is that Paul also derives man as "God's glory" from Genesis 2, perhaps even from the converse textual facts that man was "not" physically derived from woman (but was more immediately from God [and the earth]) and that man was "not" vocationally "for" woman (but was immediately for God).[127] Regardless of the exact textual stimulus for describing man as "God's glory," Paul's combination of this with the clear reference to Gen. 1:27 ("image of God") confirms that it is indeed the actual protological "man" as described by the texts of Genesis 1–2 whom Paul regards as "the image and glory of God." The implication for Paul's reading of the beginning of humanity according to Genesis 1–2 is that the "man" out of whom and for whom the woman was created – i.e., Adam – was the original "image and glory of God."[128] Paul's logic makes little sense if he, like so many who

---

[127] Fee (1987) writes that Paul's addition of "God's *glory*" to the "man" who is "God's image" is "Paul's own reflection on the creation of man" (515). Man as "God's glory" may also be fuelled by an understanding of man's "dominion" in Gen. 1:26,28 as God's "crowning him with *glory* and *honor*" from Ps. 8:6–9. Dunn (1998A) posits that Ps. 8:4–6 is "the key text for Adam christology" (232; cf. *idem*, 1980, 108ff). Many ancients blended Gen. 1:26–28 with Ps. 8:6–9: cf. Philo's *Op.* 84–85 (Borgen, 1995, 369–89; Runia, 2001, 256); 4Q418 81.1–3 (Stuckenbruck, 2002, 248); *Sib. Or.* 8.442–45 (Steenburg, 1990, 97); *2 Enoch* 31.3. Aquila, Symmachus, and Theodotian replaced κατακυριεύσατε in Gen. 1:28 with ὑποτάξατε (probably from Ps. 8:7) (Göttingen, "Genesis," 81; Runia, 2001, 256). Concerning the modern blending of Ps. 8:6–9 with Gen. 1:26–28: Kraus, 1993, 180, 183–84; cf. van Kooten, 2008, 6; Wright, 2003, 313; Adams, 2000, 144; Watson, 1997, 294–98; Mathews, 1996, 170–72; Bird, 1995, 8–9, 12; Minear, 1994, 79–80; Childs, 1992, 112–13; Wenham, 1987, 30; Westermann, 1987, 11; Harris, 1980, 2121a; Padgett, 1983, 81; Kim, 1980, 159–60; Jaubert, 1971/72, 422 n. 3; von Rad, 1956, 56. Paul himself alludes to Ps. 8:7b in an Adamic context in 1 Cor. 15:21–22, 27 (Morissette, 1972A, 327 n. 10; Lambrecht, 1981, 506–12, 514, 524 n. 68), thus making it a more concrete possibility that his understanding of Gen. 1:26–28 had actually been affected by the latter text. In this particular context (1 Cor. 11:7–9), Paul primarily connects "glory" to Genesis 2, even if he has been affected by Ps. 8.

[128] Barrett (1962) wrote that Adam himself "is never said by Paul to bear the image of God" (88; cf. Bouteneff, 2008, 45, 47). Paul virtually did in 1 Cor. 11:7–9, but not directly or by name. Why not? Genesis 2 itself twice dropped the otherwise regular name "Adam" and used "[the] man" (vv. 18, 24), both when speaking of a general principle of man *as man* (as template for all subsequent men). Paul similarly applies the anthro-

explain his thoughts, would have claimed to know *only* the Adam of sin and death and *always* as fallen man.

(ii) Adam's "Flesh" and Earthly "Body" as having "Glory"
(1 Cor. 15:39–40)

Within the immediate context of his quotation of Gen. 2:7 (1 Cor. 15:45), Paul mentions the "flesh" of "humans" as well as of animals, birds, and fish (v. 39). This is a cosmological statement about the present observable world in all of its multiplicity.[129] But these descriptions of bodily flesh are built upon God's creative activity of "giving," and this according to God's past *cosmogonic* "desire" (v. 38, see chapter 2). Even though it is primarily Genesis 1 on which Paul is grounding his cosmology in vv. 36–41, and so one might properly consider Paul's reference to "humans" in v. 39 as a reference to Gen. 1:27,[130] Paul considers 1:27 and 2:7 as two mutually interpretive references to the creation of the one first-man (cf. 1 Cor. 11:7–9, above).[131] This implies that for Paul the "flesh" of "humans" is as it is because of Gen. 2:7 as well as 1:27. Indeed, 2:7 may be even have been more informative for Paul's present expression at this point simply because it explicitly refers to God's crafting of the human's body (2:7a), with "flesh" mentioned in 2:21, 23.[132] Human flesh in 15:39 *cannot* be separated from Paul's understanding that it was precisely the first man, Adam, to whom this was "given" by God according to the divine "desire."

Paul then refers to this "flesh" of "humans" (as well as animals, birds, and fish) under the heading of "bodies on earth" (v. 40a), and to such "bodies" he attributes "glory" (v. 40b).[133] Paul does not say that the "bodies in heaven" have glory while the "bodies on earth" do not. "Glory" is the shared identity of all "bodies" in heaven and earth.[134] Paul sees "glory" in the physical forms of beasts, birds, and fish as well as in the human form. Since Paul refers to "humans" in plurality, "glory" encompasses all humans that come "out of" Adam and "through" Eve (see 1 Cor. 11:12,

---

pogony here: it is Adam as "man" that is particularly important, but it is nonetheless importantly Adam in vv. 8–9.

[129] Vos, 1930, 180.

[130] So Lorenzen, 2008, 161.

[131] Gundry-Volf (1994) writes, "Perhaps modern biblical scholarship, by disjoining Gen. 1.1–2.4a and 2.4–3.24 into separately authored accounts with distinct language, dynamics and intentions, has blocked the way to the ancients' view of creation and fall as interwoven, mutually interpreting biblical narratives" (110; thus making comments such as Collins, 1999, 570 n. 45 is unhelpful).

[132] Collins (1999) notes that Paul alludes to Gen. 2:7 in 15:39–41 (570 n. 45).

[133] Lorenzen (2008) discusses how Paul may and may not be using "glory," e.g., as light, or honor, or beauty, or brilliance (157 n. 54).

[134] So Lorenzen, 2008, 155; Asher, 2000, 105 n. 38.

where "glory" is again a dominant theme). All are fellow glory-bearers with the "heavenly bodies" by virtue of God's creative "desire." The implication of vv. 39–40: for Paul, this divine gift of "glory" to the human body and flesh was initiated at God's creation of Adam.

One final observation and implication should be made. When Paul attributes "glory" to the "earthly bodies" (v. 40b), he refers to "bodies" and "fleshes" *as* they were created but not *when* they were created. That is, Paul is writing about the present and observable cosmos: i.e., God presently "gives" bodies, there presently "are" bodies, they presently "differ" in glory. Paul considers humans (*et al.*) to *presently* have some sort of "glory" even within the present "fallen" context of death-by-sin.[135] This "glory" describes their ontic bodily and fleshly structure and substance as creations, this was set in place by God in Gen. 2:7 "just as he desired," and their quality as "creations" (and thus as "glorious") is not annulled by sin.

Paul again builds present ontological (even anthropological) principles on a positive appraisal of the beginning of humanity in Adam. This is even set within the broader context of the glory of the whole world's beginning and according to God's pre-creational desire – yet again, as if three strands of one interwoven cord. As we will now see, between the "glories" of 1 Cor. 11:7 and 15:39–40 Paul discusses God's creative arrangement of the human body (12:12–30). He does not mention "glory," but he does highlight the perfection with which God situated and composed the body and, again, this is "just as he desired."

(iii) God's "Desired" Construction of the Original Human Body and the World: Comparing 1 Cor. 11:7–12 and 15:37–42 with 12:12–30

In 12:1–30, Paul argues that "just as" there exist differences and yet also interdependence within the human body's structure, "also in the same manner" is it within the redeemed "body of Christ," i.e., "the church."[136]

---

[135] We cannot forget that underlying the entire discussion in 1 Corinthians 15 is the reality of "death" ("resurrection of *corpses*") and that the sting of this enemy is sin (so Lorenzen [2008] offers 15:17 and 56 when making the same point [148 n. 22], and I will add 15:3). This observation does not undercut our discussion of Paul's use of pre-sin creation. Even as the cosmos groans under its sin-infested tenants, it as well as the tenants still are God's creation and as such are crafted gloriously.

[136] Cf. Rom. 12:3–8. Martin (1992) demonstrates how common the body-society comparison was not only in Paul's Graeco-Roman context but "as far back as 900 B.C.E." and "through the Middle Ages" and "into modern political theory," displayed geographically "from India, Iran, and Russia, as well as from the ancient Mediterranean" (268 n. 13; see 87–96). By claiming that in 1 Cor. 12:12–30 we can discern Paul's *reading* of Gen. 2:7, I am not denying Martin's common-sense/cultural connections. As Philo demonstrates, a use of philosophical ideas (formal and popular) culled from various non-scripture sources does not diminish the influence of scripture – he is writing a commen-

This balancing of unity and diversity, or uniqueness and non-autonomy, evokes in the minds of many scholars Paul's argument regarding men and women not long before, in 1 Cor. 11:7–12.[137] In 12:12, Paul initiates both principles with a chiastic statement:

The body is one [τὸ σῶμα ἕν ἐστιν],
   and it has many members [μέλη πολλά],
   and though all the members [πάντα τὰ μέλη] of the body are many [πολλά],
it is one body [ἕν ἐστιν σῶμα].

In 12:14–20, Paul underscores the necessary differences that do and should exist among the body parts. He bases this on the fact that "God set/arranged the members [ὁ θεὸς ἔθετο τὰ μέλη], each one of them in the body [ἓν ἕκαστον αὐτῶν ἐν τῷ σώματι], just as he desired [καθὼς ἠθέλησεν]" (v. 18). In 12:21–26, he then emphasizes the interdependence of body parts. He bases this on the fact that "God blended/mixed together [ὁ θεὸς συνεκέρασεν] the body, having given [δούς] excessive honor to the [part] lacking" (v. 24).[138] In 12:27–30, Paul returns to the first principle, that of difference, this time applying it to the new "body." He bases the structure of this new body on the fact that "God set/arranged [ἔθετο ὁ θεός] in the church" the various gifted-roles (v. 28). Paul has already stressed that this arrangement of diverse gifts was due to the Spirit's "distributing" (διαιροῦν) of them within the church "to each his own" (ἰδίᾳ ἑκάστῳ) and "just as he purposes" (καθὼς βούλεται) (12:11).[139] For Paul, individual "members" or "parts" of the created individual body (and of the redeemed body) must function individually and uniquely as they were di-

---

tary specifically on scripture! If Paul were asked when the body was constructed in the fashion he is describing, and from where he gets his particularly theocentric construal of it, would he not say Gen. 2:7? The affirmative is confirmed by the language he uses for the various creative acts of God which he often explicitly connects to the textual details of Genesis' beginning (e.g., in 1 Cor. 11 and 15).

[137] For the comparison between the "interdependence" of 1 Cor. 11:11–12 and that of 12:21 (as well as of 7:3–4) see Watson, 2000B, 523–24 (cf. Peerbolte, 2000, 80). Thiselton (2000) draws a connection between 1 Cor. 11 and 12–14 and Paul's dual argumentation for both "unity and diversity" (803), the same recognition we will demonstrate in slightly different fashion.

[138] In vv. 22–26 his language is so evocative of socio-ecclesial issues on which he has already confronted the Corinthians – e.g., cf. 12:25 with 1:10 – that he may as well be explicitly applying this interdependence to the "body of Christ" (so Martin, 1992, 94–96), but it is the body-as-created to which he directly refers.

[139] Cf. Philo's "purposing" (βουλόμενος) in his comments on Gen. 2:7a (*Op.* 138, above and below).

vinely intended while simultaneously functioning as an interrelated unit toward the harmony of the whole.[140]

This construal of the created human body is strikingly similar to what Philo had written as a direct commentary on God's activity in Gen. 2:7a. For Philo, in God's knowledge he caused "each of the parts of the body [ἕκαστον τῶν τοῦ σώματος μερῶν] to have in itself individually [ἰδίᾳ καθ' αὑτό] its due proportions" while simultaneously "to also be harmoniously fitted with accuracy toward the fellowship of the whole" (*Op.* 138.2–10). Philo even subsumed this dual-sided ontic design of Adam's body under God's "purpose" (βουλόμενος). Paul not only draws express attention to the same two principles of created human ontology, but he also (repeatedly) submits this whole anthropic design to God's "desire" (ἠθέλησεν) and "purpose" (βούλεται). Paul's statements in 1 Cor. 12:12–30 about God's arrangement of the human body could be placed into a contemporary and formal commentary on Genesis, specifically at Gen. 2:7a, and no reader could tell the difference.

The deduction that Gen. 2:7a has itself impacted Paul's description of the creation of the human body is strengthened by comparing Paul's statement in, e.g., 1 Cor. 12:18 with his portrayal of the beginning of the world a few chapters later in 1 Cor. 15:38.[141]

But God arranged [ὁ θεὸς ἔθετο] the members, each [ἕκαστον] one of them in the body, just as he desired [καθὼς ἠθέλησεν] (12:18)

But God gives [ὁ θεὸς δίδωσιν] to it a body just as he desired [καθὼς ἠθέλησεν], and to each [ἑκάστῳ] of the seeds its own body (15:38).

For the creation of the human body in 12:18, Paul uses two aorists, "arranged... desired," while for the whole cosmos (most directly a seed) in 15:38 he uses a present and an aorist, "gives... desired." The significance of Paul's timing in 15:38–41 we have already seen: *present* cosmology accords with God's *past* (cosmogonic) desire. Paul's point in 15:38–41 thus appears to be slightly different than 12:18. It is similar, however, to 12:12 where Paul uses the present tense ("is," "has," "being") to describe *present* anthropology. In 12:18, however, Paul has in mind not only God's *past* "desire" according to which present anthropology exists, but actually God's *past* structuring ("he arranged," ἔθετο) of the human body according to this past intent ("just as he desired," ἠθέλησεν). The actual event of

---

[140] So Martin, 1992, 94. Penner and Vander Stichele (2005) concede a similar point with regard to Paul's argument in 1 Cor. 11:11–12, that "the 'body' as a whole stands to gain from proper 'bodily' comportment all around, both sexes included" (231).

[141] In connection with 15:38, Fee, 1987, 782 sees 12:11 and Thiselton, 2000, 126 and Moffatt, 1938, 258 see 12:28.

God's original creation of the human body, i.e., Gen. 2:7 (and 2:21–22), seem closer to Paul's mind than we typically think.

I will now set out in a chart some of the most applicable motifs found in 1 Cor. 15:37–42, 12:12–30, and 11:7–12. Paul's three strands of his creation-hermeneutic are clearly present:

1 Cor.	Created Ontology	Reason for Ontology	Textual Source
15:37–41	Cosmic: diversity of bodies/fleshes/glories – including "humans"	"God gives... just as he desired"	Gen. 1:1–31 (Gen. 2:7)
15:42	Resurrected diversity – different (changed) body – different (changed) glory	"in this manner also..."	–
12:12–20	Anthropic: diversity of body parts – as created	"God arranged... just as he desired"	Gen. 2:7 (cf. Gen. 2:21–22)
12:21–26	Anthropic: interdependence of body parts – as created (explicit) – as redeemed (implicit)	"God composed... having given"	Gen. 2:7 (cf. Gen. 2:21–22)
12:27–30 (cf. v. 11)	Anthropic: diversity of body parts – as redeemed	"God arranged... [just as he purposes]"	–
11:7–9	Anthropic: diversity of genders – man is "image and glory" – woman is "glory"	God "created" "of God" "from...for man"	Gen. 1–2 Gen. 1:27, 2:7 Gen. 2:21–23, 18
11:11–12b	Anthropic: interdependence of genders – the woman – the man	God brought/brings "out of the man" "through the woman"	Gen. 2:21–23 Gen. 4:1–now
11:12c	Cosmic and Anthropic: – interdependence and diversity	"all things are from God"	Gen. 1:27 Gen. 2:7,18, 21–23 Gen. 4:1–now

Two conclusions regarding 1 Cor. 11:7–9, 12:12–30, and 15:37–41 should be clear: Paul's three strands of creation are thoroughly interwoven, and the creation of Adam himself in Gen. 2:7 is very positive, even glorious. Paul's positive portrayals of 2:7 are functionally the mirror-image of his portrayal of God's causative "giving" and pre-creative "desire" enacted in the beginning of the whole world (1 Cor. 15:38–41). When thinking about the creation of Adam *per se*, Paul sees Adam's body as knit together by God with all parts functioning appropriately and in harmony according to

God's desires. Adam's body perfectly accorded with God's purpose. Adam was glorious, even in his flesh. Yet in 1 Cor. 15:45–47 Paul refers again to the *creation* of Adam, overtly interpreting Gen. 2:7, but this time to highlight something *negative* about him and those who bear his image.

(b) Paul's Negative Reading: The Inglorious Adam in Comparison (1 Cor. 15:44b-47)

Paul shifts from the Beginning to the End: "In this manner is the resurrection of corpses" (1 Cor. 15:42a). In vv. 42b-44, Paul initiates a *comparison* between resurrected existence – "raised" in "incorruptibility" (ἀφθαρσία), "glory" (δόξα), and "power" (δύναμις) – and pre-resurrection existence – "sown" in "corruptibility" (φθορά), "dishonor" (ἀτιμία), "weakness" (ἀσθένεια). Does Paul's view of Adam, after all, undercut the anthropology in Psalm 8, where by virtue of God's creation humanity actually and presently exists as "crowned with glory and honor [δόξῃ καὶ τιμῇ]" (Ps. 8:6)?[142] Suddenly casting in "dishonor" what Psalm 8 (and he himself!) had just attributed with "glory" and reserving "glory" instead for what is "raised," Paul would seem to be unexpectedly devaluing creation.

Even if one interprets vv. 42b-43 as *sinful* existence rather than *created* existence,[143] the tension in Paul remains felt when he describes what is "sown" as not only corruptible, dishonorable, and weak, but also as a "soulish body" (σῶμα ψυχικόν) (v. 44a). This last description Paul explicitly derives from God's creation of Adam in Gen. 2:7 as a "living soul" (ψυχὴν ζῶσαν) (v. 45a). By directly contrasting this Adamic-body-as-created with the "Spiritual body" (σῶμα πνευματικόν, v. 44b),[144] derived

---

[142] Dunn (1980) draws from Ps. 8:6 "God's purpose and intention for *adam*/man," "God's plan for man," what was "intended for man/Adam in the beginning" (109–10). These are not strong enough. In Ps. 8:6 "man" actually was existing as "crowned with glory and honor," the way Paul discusses humanity in 1 Cor. 15:39–40 (cf. 11:7b).

[143] It is notoriously difficult to tell whether corruptible-dishonorable-weak describes the body-as-created or the body-in-sin. The interpretive difficulty is felt when "sowing" in vv. 42b-43 is construed in such diverse ways by scholars: burial (de Boer, 1988, 131; Talbert, 2002, 126; Kistemaker, 1993, 567; Harrisville, 1987, 274; Lockwood, 2000, 588; criticized by Asher, 2001, 110 and Garland, 2003, 732), procreation (Moffatt, 1938, 259), existence in general (Conzelmann, 1975, *ad loc.*; Lindemann, 1997, 162; criticized by Asher, 2001, 102, 107–11 and Garland, 2003, 733), a non-creational combination of these (Fee, 1987, 784 [cf. 784 n. 39]; Minear, 1994, 70–73), or creation itself (Beker, 1980, 222; Asher, 2001, 101–02). Concerning our limited argument: Paul's perspective has changed from creation *per se* (vv. 37–41) to a *comparison* between a resurrection-state (vv. 42–43) and a pre-resurrection state which seamlessly transitions into and therefore includes (to say the least) creation in vv. 44–47.

[144] Paul uses *pneumatikon* to describe something like the "presence, power, and transforming activity of the Holy Spirit" (so Thiselton, 2006A, 283 [*idem*, 2006B, 242–43; *idem*, 2000, 1276–77]; cf. Wright, 2003, 350, 352; Schreiner, 2001, 458; Dunn, 1998B;

most likely from his own reception of this raised Jesus' "life-making Spirit" (πνεῦμα ζῳοποιοῦν) (v. 45b),[145] Paul is now fully entrenched in the *comparison* between Gen.2:7-bodies and resurrected-bodies. Paul's highly positive reading of Adam in Gen. 2:7 has been recast negatively due to his comparison of it with an outside source, with another human.[146]

Within this perspective of comparison (vv. 44–47), Paul underscores two particular features of Adam's own bodily nature due to God's formation of him in Gen. 2:7. Paul first draws attention to the fact that this first Adam "became" a "soul" (ψυχήν) (v. 45a; Gen. 2:7c).[147] Rather than contrasting "body" and "soul" (as Philo had done in *Op*. 138),[148] Paul more closely reflects the text's body + breath = "soul" by merely calling Adam's "body" itself "soulish." Paul here shows an interest in describing the whole person, particularly the person's "body," as existing according to the "becoming" of Adam in Gen. 2:7. "Soulish body" is functionally equivalent to "the Adamic body," or (more accurately) "the created-Adamic-body."

But Paul thinks that more of Gen. 2:7 can help answer "in what type of body resurrected people will come." After temporally separating the soulish body (which was first) from the Spiritual body (which followed), ra-

---

Scroggs, 1966, 66–68 [though I find Scroggs' "non-corporeal" nature of the resurrected body unpersuasive]; Moffatt, 1938, 259–60; Robertson and Plummer, 1911, 372) rather than to describe some anthropological substance which everyone has but the resurrected beings have more of or have more purely or perfectly (so e.g., Martin, 1992, 126; van Kooten, 2008, 298–312). Capitalizing "Spiritual" even as I capitalize "Spirit" helps avoid confusion (cf. Vos, 1930, 166–67).

[145] Paul does not *derive* v. 45b *from* Gen. 2:7 (see below pp. 221–23 and 222 n. 153). Rightly Fee, 2007, 118; Furnish, 1999, 114–15); Lindemann, 1997, 163; Wedderburn, 1987, 185 n. 8 (*idem*, 1971, 93). Contra Hultgren, 2003, 359–66; Collins, 1999, 568 (cf. 570 n. 45); de Boer, 1988, 129; Sellin, 1986, 76–79, 79 n. 1; Lambrecht, 1981, 525 n. 74; Wilckens, 1979, 531; Senft, 1979, 208–09, 209 n. 3; Conzelmann, 1975, 284; Pearson, 1973, 21–23; Dunn, 1973, 138–39; Morissette, 1972B, 223; Scroggs, 1966, 86–89; Black, 1954, 171 n. 1; Moffatt, 1938, 262–64. My language of "reception" comes from Paul: e.g., in Galatians Paul highlights the definitive moment at which Christians "received the Spirit" (τὸ πνεῦμα ἐλάβετε, 3:2; cf. 3:14) – the moment is neither creation nor conception/birth (nor at "works of law"), but "faith." Cf. Dunn, 1973, 131–39.

[146] Upon "closer examination," Lorenzen (2008) writes, "Paul does not negatively judge the creation in itself, but rather devalues it only in comparison with the eschatological creation" (148 n. 22; translation mine: "Untersuchung macht deutlich, dass Paulus die Schöpfung nicht an sich negativ beurteilt, sondern lediglich im Vergleich mit der eschatologischen Schöpfung abwertet"). She points to the fact that the "earthly body" in "v. 39" has "glory" to demonstrate this.

[147] On Paul's "additions" to Gen. 2:7c (i.e., "first" and "Adam") cf. Göttingen, 84; Wevers, 1993, 25 n. 20; Thiselton, 2000, 1281; Stanley, 1992, 208–09.

[148] Paul can use "soul" in a more anthropologically partite manner (e.g., 1 Th. 5:23), but that should not be imported into 15:44–49 (as Philo's broader use of "soul" as "living being" was not to be imported into his partite use of "soul" in *Op*. 138, see above).

ther than the other way around (v. 46), Paul adds: "the first man was out of the earth [ἐκ γῆς], a dusty being [χοϊκός]" (v. 47a). This clearly reiterates Gen. 2:7a.[149] Like the LXX, Paul relates the (first) human to the "earth" with a preposition ("out of") but to the "dust" without a preposition. By placing the two accusative nouns – "the human" and "dust" – in such an unspecified relationship, the text had practically identified the two as one.[150] The "human" virtually *is* "dust from the earth." Paul confirms this very identity by using the substantival adjective "dusty" (χοϊκός; cf. ὁ χοϊκός, vv. 48, 49): "the human" merely is the substance: "a dust-being."

Paul has drawn an anthropology of the created person from Gen. 2:7a and 2:7c. He emphasizes the "body," for he is answering questions concerning the "type of *bodies*" in which corpses will return. But what about the "breath of life"? Does Paul not exegete Gen. 2:7b? Differently than Philo, Paul's only reference to anything like a "spirit" or "breath" in this treatment of the text is to what makes the first Adam *different* from the last.[151] C.K. Barrett rightly writes: Jesus is "what his predecessor was not – namely, πνεῦμα."[152] The first Adam became a "soul that lives" (ψυχὴν ζῶσαν) while the last Adam became the "Spirit that life-makes" (πνεῦμα ζωοποιοῦν) (v. 45b). These two descriptions show Paul deliberately shaping his depiction of Christ's being-as-resurrected around Adam's being-as-created. He even makes Christ's ἐσχατο-logical "becoming" grammatically dependent on Adam's πρωτο-logical "becoming" (ἐγένετο):

Gen. 2:7c	ἐγένετο ὁ		ἄνθρωπος	εἰς ψυχὴν	ζῶσαν
1 Cor. 15:45a2	ἐγένετο ὁ πρῶτος	ἄνθρωπος	Ἀδάμ	εἰς ψυχὴν	ζῶσαν
1 Cor. 15:45b	["] ὁ ἔσχατος		Ἀδάμ	εἰς πνεῦμα	ζωοποιοῦν

The reference to the "Spirit that life-makes" (πνεῦμα ζωοποιοῦν) may be reminiscent of God's "breath of life" in 2:7b (πνοὴν ζωῆς) (and comparable with it in a limited way).[153] Yet Paul deliberately expressed this *not* as

---

[149] Lindemann, 1997, 164–65; Lambrecht, 1981, 513; Morissette, 1972B, 223; Barrett, 1968, 375; Scroggs, 1966, 87.

[150] "Dust" in LXX is probably an "accusative of material" (Wevers, 1993, 24).

[151] It is unnecessary to deduce that because Paul had Gen. 2:7a and 2:7c in mind he "thus" had 2:7b in mind (contra Sterling, 1995, 359).

[152] Barrett, 1962, 74.

[153] Many connect Paul's "life-giving Spirit" with the "breath of life" in Gen. 2:7b: Hultgren, 2003, 361; Fee, 1987, 789–90; Sellin, 1986, 92 (cf. 79–90); Lambrecht, 1981, 525 n. 74; Wilckens, 1979, 531; Usami, 1976, 486; Pearson, 1973, 24 (cf. 16–17); Morissette, 1972B, 223; Dupont, 1960, 172; Moffatt, 1938, 264. Mixed with this somewhat legitimate observation, however, is the false deduction that Paul saw Jesus' "becoming" *within* Gen. 2:7, or at least *announced therein*. Paul's use of πνεῦμα ζωοποιοῦν may have a nod toward the activity of the Spirit within the cosmogony (Gen. 1:2) and the anthropogony (2:7b), but this is no more than an acknowledgment that it is the same Spirit who is active in resurrection as was active in the first creation. (As such this is differ-

an actual reference to Gen. 2:7b, but rather as a contrastive comparison with what the first Adam "became" in 2:7c. While first-Adam and last-Adam both "became" something related to life, at both points (the something and the life) the Adams are different. Instead of a "soul," last-Adam became a "Spirit"; instead of "living," last-Adam became "life-making."

The implication for Paul's reading of Gen. 2:7 can be put conversely: the Adamic body-as-created was not created with the "Spiritual" (nor "heavenly") quality which Paul associates only with the "becoming" (i.e., resurrection) of the last Adam.[154] Paul considers the first Adam to have been created perfect (i.e., flawless), but Paul does not consider Adam to have been the perfect (i.e., full) human, even at his creation.[155] To use

---

ent from, though not in tension with, 1 Cor. 8:6 [contra Moffatt, 1938, 264] – in 8:6 Christ was creative, in 15:45b the Spirit, with whom Christ would "become" associated at his resurrection, was himself creative [so Sellin, 1986, 79 n. 9]). The construal of Fee (2007) is noteworthy: "Even though the content of Paul's second line [v. 45b] is neither present nor inferred in the Genesis text, it nonetheless reflects the language of the prior clause in the Septuagint, 'and [God] *breathed* into his face the *breath of life* [πνοὴν ζωῆς].' Now in speaking about Christ, Paul makes a play on this language. The one who will 'breathe' new life into these mortal bodies – with life-giving πνεῦμα (as in Eze. 37:14) – and thus make them immortal is none other than the risen Christ himself" (118). This is attractive and *may* capture a clever *nuance* in Paul's expression. But this is hardly Paul's *point* in v. 45. Paul intends to describe the parallel/contrast between Adam's bodily creation and Christ's bodily resurrection: the seed body (created in Adam, having to do with being a living soul) and the coming plant body (resurrected in Christ, having to do with the eschatological Spirit). In v. 45b Paul *overtly and intentionally* expresses the proleptic eschatological "becoming" and "body" in (contrastive) parallel to Gen. 2:7c. "Spirit that life-makes" is most directly shaped according to "soul that lives," though the Spirit whom the raised Jesus "becomes" may very well have been active in both events.

[154] Paul's reference to Christ as "life-making Spirit" in v. 45 is close to his other references to the *divine* Spirit (cf. "Spirit of God" in Rom. 8:9 and 2 Cor. 3:3 with "Spirit of Christ" in Rom. 8:9 and Phil. 1:19) which Christians "*received*" not at creation but in redemption (Gal. 3:2, 14; cf. 1 Cor. 2:12–14; 3:16; 6:11, 19–20; 12:3, 13). This "Spirit" is not to be confused with the anthropological "spirit" of Stoic and Aristotelian psychology (which Runia describes [2001, 326–37]; cf. Usami, 1976, 486). Paul's reference to the resurrected Christ who "became" the Spirit should not be reduced to a reference to Christ "possessing" the "restoration of man's *pneuma*" with which Adam had been created (contra van Kooten, 2008, 270; cf. 269–70, 279). A *by-product* of the eschatological gift of the divine Spirit may be the restoration of the human "spirit" to a wholeness that had been marred, but that would be a *deduction* that is not in Paul's purview in 1 Cor. 15:45–49. For Paul, Adam may have been created with a human spirit, and he most likely was (see 1 Th. 5:23), but he was not created with the divine Spirit of the eschaton. (Sterling's deduction of what the *Corinthians* must have believed [1995, 372] looks surprisingly similar to what van Kooten thinks *Paul* is arguing).

[155] The language of "perfection" comes from Scroggs, 1966, 100 and Dunn, 1973, 136 n. 28. Neither recognize that it should be understood in two different ways (as above). Both thus deny too much by saying that only Christ was the "perfect" realization of God's purpose. Adam was the *true* or *faultless* realization of God's "purpose" *for the*

Paul's own metaphor: as a seed is what it is intended to be for the time of its planting while also lacking the qualities of the future plant, so also due to his (God-intended) creation Adam was flawless yet lacked what God pre-intended for the eschatological age of Jesus' resurrection and Spirit.

Paul crafts his eschatological statements about resurrected human(ity) around the protological/textual language and conceptuality of created human(ity). Similarities between Original and New thereby emerge.[156] Both bodies "became" by two acts of the same Creator. Both acts bring life from non-life, whether from lifeless dust or lifeless corpses.[157] Both becomings are "bodily." Both bodies are associated with an "Adam" at their respective beginnings. Yet despite these similarities which arise from Paul's use of the beginning of humanity to explain its fulfilment in the new Adam, the dissimilarities are Paul's present main point. Within his hermeneutic of comparison, Paul sees in Gen. 2:7 God's creation of Adam's "soulish body," of his otherwise "glorious" bodily frame, being merely "dusty." It (intentionally) did not have the "Spiritual" or "heavenly" glory. The latter was reserved for the last Adam and his family that would bear his image.

(c) Summary: Paul's Reading of Genesis 2:7,
in Comparison with Philo's Reading

It is tempting to see a difference between the positive atmosphere of Gen. 2:7 within Genesis 1–2 and yet the negative construal of it by Paul in 1 Cor. 15:44–47, and to thereby distance Paul from the text.[158] Genesis 1–2 generally and 2:7 specifically present themselves as God's original design for world and humanity. But Paul agrees with and represents this in 1 Cor. 11:7–12, 12:12–30, and 15:39–40 concerning the beginning of humanity (as in 15:38–41 concerning the beginning of the world). Yet the creation of Adam, even within Genesis 2, does not necessarily claim to be the end-all of God's creative design for humans. The text presents a possibility of

---

beginning while he was not the *full* realization of God's "purpose" *for the end*. Relatedly, Scroggs argues, "The question whether the new creation is 'simply' a return to the conditions of the original creation, or whether it indicates something superior, probably would not have occurred to Paul" (62). Scroggs falsely understands that if Paul *had* argued that the End is better than the Beginning (which I argue that he does) this would be equivalent to claiming that "God's intention at creation was inferior" (62), and this is unacceptable. Indeed, Paul would not have accepted such an interpretation either – the *seed* is precisely what God "desired" it to be *for its particular role* – but he still saw the plant as better.

[156] Paul does this again with Jesus in 2 Cor. 4:4, and cf. 2 Cor. 4:6 for Paul's same hermeneutical practice with the protological light and eschatological gospel. See above.

[157] So Probst, 1991, 344.

[158] E.g., Schmid (1959) wrote: "through the contrast with πνεῦμα ζῳοποιοῦν" the biblical phrase "living soul" (ψυχὴ ζῶσα) "receives in Paul the meaning of the inferior, limited, transient, which it does not have in the Genesis corpus" (171; translation mine).

"eternal life" which is not yet possessed by Adam, extrinsic to his created nature. Genesis 2:7 is the beginning. It is a seed, just as God intended it for a beginning. From Paul's perspective, how is one to interpret the seed of the Beginning after having the plant of the End appear to him? Such a comparison between seed and plant is the hermeneutical setting for understanding Paul's "devaluing" of God's glorious creation of Adam.[159]

Regarding the exegesis of Gen. 2:7, Paul and Philo have many similarities. They view Adam positively when reading 2:7 *per se*, and negatively when in comparison with another human who exceeds him. For both the better human is associated with "immortality" and "incorruptibility," while Adam is associated with "mortality" and "corruptibility." An important difference emerges in that that Philo's human of comparison is the earlier textual one of Gen. 1:27 while Paul's is the later historical one of resurrection and Spirit. In incorporeal and ideal perfection Philo's surpassing human ontologically overshadows the composite form of Gen. 2:7. In bodiless incorruptibility and immortality he transcends mortality and corruptibility, never tasting either. Paul's surpassing human is ideal in his perfection, but this is while being corporeal. He also ontologically overshadows the dusty form of Gen. 2:7, but this is because prior to his bodily (resurrected) incorruptibility and immortality he had already taken the sting of death "for our sins" and had emerged in "victory." Philo's "divine spirit" was the intrinsic *creational* gift of mind that enabled Adam to accord with the surpassing human as an image of God's Word. The "Spirit" of Paul's second human is the extrinsic *eschatological* gift by whom the last Adam will make alive those who bear his, rather than the first Adam's, "image." This fulfills the third text of humanity's Beginning, Gen. 5:3.

3.3 The Image of Adam: Genesis 5:3

Genesis 5:1–3 evokes both the broader context of the beginning of the world and especially the more narrow beginning of humanity in both 1:26–28 and 2:7.[160] Yet it also *expands* the understanding of humanity within

---

[159] Rightly Lorenzen, 2008, 148 n. 22; cf. Dunn, 1973, 131; Schmid, 1959, 171.

[160] Concerning the evocation of the cosmogonic Gen. 1–2:3,4 in 5:1–3, cf. 5:1b with 2:4c (Wallace, 1990, 21). Concerning the evocation of the anthropogonic 1:26–28 and 2:7 in 5:1–3, cf. 5:1a with 2:4a, "image of God" in 1:26–27ab and 5:1c, "male and female" in 1:27c and 5:2a, "blessed" in 1:28 and 5:2b, and "Adam" in Genesis 2 and 5:1b (Noort, 2000, 8). Wallace sees a source-critical unification of "J and P material" in Gen. 5:1b-2, 3aβ-b (20–24; contra the source-critical bifurcation of Gen. 1 and 5 from 2–4 in e.g., Noort, 2000, 7–8; Minear, 1994, 68–69). What concerns us is less the authorship of these various pieces of Genesis 1–5 and more the mere notion that they do appear to be (intentionally) connected to each other (so Wallace). How much more may this appear

this context.[161] "When Adam had lived 230 years, he bore a child according to his appearance [κατὰ τὴν ἰδέαν αὐτοῦ] and according to his image [κατὰ τὴν εἰκόνα αὐτοῦ]" (Gen. 5:3). This statement is not about the first human, nor even about the first progeny. Rather, it further develops the "image" motif. It portrays the propagation of the newly initiated human existence as something that is, for better or worse, like Adam.

It is possible to imply from Gen. 5:1–3 a transfer of "God's image" from "Adam" (v. 1) to his descendants (v. 3).[162] As becomes clear from Gen. 9:6, the creation of the human "in God's image" is presently applicable to the subjects of a now violent (un-paradisiacal) world,[163] and this applicability is most likely available due to Gen. 5:3.[164] Genesis 5:3 can also imply the mere fact of qualitative (even physical) resemblance between Adam and his offspring. They are born according to *his* appearance and image.[165] Genesis 5:3 seems to have affected some early religious writings from Jewish, Christian, and Gnostic sources.[166]

---

the case for Paul or Philo, who assume the single authorship of Moses for Genesis 1–5? On the theological implications of seeing Gen. 5:1–3 as reflecting Gen. 1 and Gen. 2–4 see Wallace, 1990, 21 (cf. 24).

[161] Von Rad (1956) considers Gen. 5:1–3 as a "theological expan[sion]" of 1:26–28 (69); cf. Noort, 2000, 8. Gen. 5:3 retains the double-κατά method of describing humanity from 1:26, replacing "according to likeness" (καθ' ὁμοίωσιν) with "according to appearance" (κατὰ τὴν ἰδέαν) but retaining "according to [the] image" (κατὰ τὴν εἰκόνα). Gen. 5:3 also shifts these features from "the human" to "Adam," i.e., the man of Gen. 2:7ff.

[162] Mathews, 1996, 170; Wallace, 1990, 22, 24; Hanson, 1990, 2; von Rad, 1954, 69; Skinner, 1910, 130.

[163] So Hoekema, 1986, 17 (cf. Wallace, 1990, 22). Hoekema criticizes scholars such as Schilder (1947) and Berkouwer (1962) for forfeiting the logic of Gen. 9:6 by saying that man has totally lost God's image but may retrieve it again if redeemed (17–18).

[164] Von Rad (1954) writes that "the reader's interest in this testimony [*sc.* to 'the image of God' in 1:27] is assured only by this supplement [*sc.* in Gen. 5:3], for without this addition the reference to a primeval man in God's image would be a meaningless mythologumenon" (69). In *The Life of Adam and Eve* (Latin version), Eve calls Seth "the image of God" (Vita 37.3; cf. the Greek version *Apocalypse* 10.3, 12.1–2), presumably based on the implicit logic of Gen. 5:1–3 (van Kooten, 2008, 30–31; though van Kooten does not mention Gen. 5:3; cf. Levison, 1988, 185).

[165] McCasland, 1950, 89.

[166] In Pseudo-Philo's *Biblical Antiquities*, Hannah says, "I have prayed before God that I do not... die *without having my own image*" (50:7) (see van Kooten, 2008, 10, who calls this "reminiscent of Gen 5.3"). In *1 Enoch* 106, an expectation underlies Lamech's response to Noah's appearance that a son *should* be "the form" (τύπος) and "image" (εἰκών) of his father, being "like" (ὅμοιος) humans (106.5–6, 10–12). There the principle (and "image"-language) of Gen. 5:3 functions as a kind of litmus test of fatherhood (van Kooten, 2008, 11–13, though he does not mention affinities with Gen. 5:3). The "Gnostic" Valentinianism of Theodotus found in Clement of Alexandria's *Excerpta ex Theodoto* (in Book VII of *Stromateis*) calls Cain "irrational," "dusty" (χοϊκός), and "according to the image" (Gen. 1:26), calls Abel "rational and just," "psychical" (ψυχικός),

3.3 The Image of Adam: Genesis 5:3

Two questions naturally arise. Since it is Seth who bears Adam's "appearance" and "image," does this imply that Cain (and Abel) did not? In a related query, is it good or bad to be "according to" Adam's "image"? Philo raises the first question. Both Philo and Paul assume answers to the second question. Regarding the second, Gen. 5:3 provides interpretive-fodder in two directions. Looking backwards, the text connects "Adam" (whose "image" is passed along) to the pre-sin texts of Genesis 1–2, and particularly to the "image of God" that Adam bore (vv. 1–2). This creates a positive setting for understanding Adam's image in v. 3. But looking forward, a prominent resemblance between Adam himself in 5:3–5 and his subsequent progeny was the morbid conclusion "and he died" (5:5, 8, 11, 14, 17, 20, 27, 31; cf. 9:29; 11:11, 13a, 13b, 15. 17, 19, 21, 23, 25, 28, 32). As is clear from the parenthetical references, "death" in the genealogies initiated by Adam and his "image" is textually oppressive in its repetition. While "walking with God" granted escape once, this was not for Seth as the initial "image"-bearer (who had even "called on the name of the Lord"). The text does not explicitly say, "and he died *because* he was in Adam's image." But death is certainly a shared-likeness with Adam, and bearing his image is no remedy to the problem. Textual features could cast positive or negative light around the propagation of Adam's "image."

Philo opts for a positive reading, both physically and ethically. Paul, as one might now expect, also has a positive reading. He sees the *principle* of Gen. 5:3 as positive; it helps him explain the relationship between the last Adam and his eschatological family. The principle that God established in the beginning is, for Paul, informative for and importantly maintained in the new creation. It is the *actual* "image" of the first Adam that Paul sees as problematic. Thus Paul also has a negative reading of Gen. 5:3. Using something like an interwoven two-strand cord, connecting the beginning of humanity with the Before, Paul explains that the "image" found at the beginning of humanity is to be discarded as old, dusty clothing in favor of the new clothing of the last Adam, the "image" which God intended for our glory before creation! Yet Paul also weaves in the third strand, the beginning of the world: it is precisely this anthropogonic principle of bearing an Adam's "image" that results in glorious freedom for the whole cosmos.

---

and "according to the likeness of God" (Gen. 1:26), and calls Seth "spiritual" (πνευματική) and "according to the Form [κατὰ ἰδέαν]" (Gen. 5:3) (quoted, discussed, and attributed to 5:3 in Dillon, 1990, 73; cf. van Kooten, 2008, 307, 307 n. 51; Wedderburn, 1971, 85). This clearly calls to mind Paul's language and discussion in 1 Cor. 15:45–49 (van Kooten calling this "particular acquaintance with Paul," 307) and Dillon argues that it has some points of contact with Philo as well. This last text strengthens our own contention that in 1 Cor. 15:48–49 Paul was indeed employing Gen. 5:3, for this early reading of Paul appeared to take 5:3 as Paul's base-text.

3.3.1 Philo's Reading of Genesis 5:3

When not comparing Adam to the ideal human of 1:27, Philo attributes great nobility to Adam. This nobility – of both body and mind – Philo applies also to the imitator of Adam's perfection. This nobility takes two forms for Philo: ontological Adam-like nobility and ethical Adam-like nobility. The first is comparable, at least, to the principle of Gen. 5:3; the second Philo explicitly draws from this text of humanity's Beginning.

(a) Ontological Adam-like Nobility (*Op.* 145)

The general theme of like-producing-like is prominent in Genesis' cosmogony in the oft-repeated phrase "according to kind." Philo drew attention to this.[167] Meredith Kline calls Gen. 5:3 "the equivalent in human procreation of the phrase 'after its kind' which is used for plant and animal reproduction and of course refers to resemblance."[168] On a number of occasions Philo presents the general principle that parents produce children "like" them. As this "likeness" with parents is often set by Philo in the context of likeness with the *first* human/couple, the text of Gen. 5:3 itself may not be too far away.[169]

In *Op.* 145, a passage in which Philo defends the "beauty" (κάλλος) of not only Adam's soul but his "body and soul," he reasons about Adam's offspring:

The descendants (τοὺς ἀπογόνους) of that [human], necessarily sharing in appearance (ἰδέας), still preserved the marks (τοὺς τύπους), even if obscure, of the kinship (τῆς συγγενείας) with the fore-father. (§145; cf. §§136, 140–41)

"What is this kinship?" (or "shared-kind," συγγένεια), Philo then asks. He answers by describing Adam's descendants, and he does so using descriptions that reflect his earlier exegesis of the creation of Adam himself (which I will compare parenthetically in the quotation below). "Every human" (πᾶς ἄνθρωπος)

is allied to the divine word [λόγῳ θείῳ] according to [their] understanding [κατὰ τὴν διάνοιαν], having become a casting or fragment or radiance of the blessed nature (cf. §§71, 139). And also [every human is allied] to all the world [ἅπαντι τῷ κόσμῳ] according to the structure of the body [κατὰ δὲ τὴν τοῦ σώματος κατασκευήν] (cf. §135). For he [*sc.* each human] has been compounded out of the same things [as the cosmos]: earth and water and air and fire, each of the elements having contributed its due part toward the completion of a most self-sufficient material (cf. §137), which it was necessary for the Craftsman to take so that he might fashion this visible image [τὴν ὁρατὴν ταύτην εἰκόνα]. (*Op.* 145)

---

[167] Cf. *Op.* 43–44 (on Gen. 1:11–12), 63 (on Gen. 1:20–24), 64 (on Gen. 1:24–25).
[168] Kline, 1980, 23 n. 34.
[169] E.g., *Leg.* 1.10; *Her.* 164.

Philo's description of humans' "shared-kind" with Adam parallels the motif and method of Gen. 5:3. In 5:3, Adam is related to God according to God's "image" (εἰκόνα, v. 1) while Adam's descendants are then related to Adam according to Adam's "image" (εἰκόνα, v. 3). Similarly, here Philo writes of Adam's descendants as having "shared-kind" with Adam (συγγενείας, §145) after having just written of Adam as having "shared-kind" with God (συγγενής, §144). Descendants mimic Adam as Adam mimics God.

One should also not miss Philo's use of the word "appearance" (ἰδέας). Employing the word "appearance" renders it possible that Gen. 5:3 itself has stamped an impression on Philo's mind,[170] for there we not only read that Adam's child was not only "according to his image [κατὰ τὴν εἰκόνα αὐτοῦ]" but also (and first) "according to his appearance [κατὰ τὴν ἰδέαν αὐτοῦ]." By the word ἰδέα Philo may simply mean Adam's physical "appearance" (i.e., what is seen: εἶδον, ἰδεῖν).

Yet by the word "idea" Philo may be referring more technically (Platonically) to the "idea" according to which Adam became the molded cast or impression.[171] That would be the human of 1:27 who, in this context of Philo's second reading, is the noetic "idea" (ἰδέα) or "genus" or "seal" (§134). If Philo is using "idea" more technically-philosophically than about mere "appearance," then Philo is here describing Adam's descendants as "sharing in idea" (μετέχοντας ἰδέας), as still bearing "the impressions" (τοὺς τύπους), though faint. In Genesis 5 itself, Seth comes about according to Adam's "idea" and "image" (v. 3), Adam's "image" and "idea" having been in accord with "the image of God" (v. 1). Philo sees the "image" of God here as the divine Word. Upon this more philosophical reading, Adam's descendants accord with Adam's "image," which accords with God's Word. It therefore makes sense for Philo to call such subsequent human minds a "casting" (ἐκμαγεῖον, §146)[172] of the same divine Word according to which the original earth-born human's mind had already become an "image and imitation [ἀπεικόνισμα καὶ μίμημα]" (§139), an accurate "casting [ἐκμαγείου]" with a clear "impression [τύπον]" (§71).

Genesis 5:3 may itself be in the background of *Op.* 145. The theme is certainly similar. The language is even similar. Regardless of the precise origin, however, Philo judges it to be important for subsequent humanity to have ontological Adam-likeness.

---

[170] Runia (1986) posits that "a text such as Gen. 5:3 could have taught Philo to associate ἰδέα and εἰκών" (163 n. 23; following Willms, 1935, 77).

[171] Levison, 1988, 87.

[172] "Casting" as if "the imprint made in a soft material like wax by a seal or mold" (Runia, 2001, 233; cf. 344).

(b) Ethical Adam-like Nobility (*QG* 1.81)

Philo elsewhere does demonstrate a specific awareness of the features of Adam's genealogy in Genesis 5, even displaying an anthropological/ethical analysis of it.[173] Thus when in *Questions and Answers on Genesis* Philo presents an explicit interpretation of Gen. 5:3 itself, and he does so in an ethical rather than ontological manner, it is not surprising. Philo does not take 5:3 to be about a general principle of propagation but about a deeper anthropological truth. In *QG* 1.81 Philo asks, "Why, in the genealogy of Adam, does [Moses/scripture] no longer mention Cain, but Seth, who, it says, was made according to his appearance and form?" Philo answers that due to Cain's violence (which violated reason and order), he therefore is not presented by scripture as deserving to be either "successor of his earthly father" or "the beginning of later generations." Gen. 5:3 highlights for Philo the honorable status of sonship, particularly that of first-born. It dubs Seth, rather than first-born Cain, as "successor," a position of prominence concerning the one who will take over when the present person vacates the role. Being the wicked man that he is, Cain is effectively erased by Moses from having any part in Adamic humanity, and Seth becomes Adam's first-born successor.

Philo sees Seth, in contrast to Cain, as deservedly bearing the mantel from Adam in leading forth the rest of humanity, i.e., being Adam's image-bearer and successor:

> Thus it is not casually or idly that [scripture] says that he [*sc.* Seth] was made according to his father's appearance and form, in reprobation of the elder [brother] who, because of his foul homicide, bears within himself nothing of his father either in body or in soul. Thus [scripture] separated him and divided him from his kin, but to the other [*sc.* Seth] he apportioned and gave a part of the honor of the eldest.[174]

Because of Cain's gross immorality he "bears within himself nothing of his father either in body or in soul." Philo's addition of "body" is probably a rhetorical heightening of the completeness of Cain's unworthiness and unlikeness in relation to Adam, who at his creation was the most "beautiful" of all time "in both body and soul" (see above).

As Philo sees it, bearing Adam's image is good, even "honorable," and it is precisely Cain's ethics that disqualify him from receiving such an honor. Throughout his comments on Genesis 2–3, Philo continues to word anthropological realities that directly belong to the textual Adam – whether

---

[173] See Philo's ethical, even theocentric, contemplation on and application of Seth's genealogy through Abraham to Moses, culled from Gen. 4:25 and chs. 5, 11, and 1 Chr. 6, in *Post.* 170–85.

[174] Loeb's translation, with minor changes.

good or very bad – as belonging to a plurality of humans.[175] These applications of Adamic language to contemporary people assume that when we act like Adam we look like Adam.

(c) Summary: Philo's Reading of Genesis 5:3

For Philo, being "in Adam's image" is a good thing, even an honorable label to wear. Philo reads Gen. 5:3 in a positive way, and this is not without exegetical warrant. Even after Adam's and Eve's disobedience, curse, and exile (Genesis 3), and after the portrayal of their descendants spiralling violently out of control (Genesis 4), Gen. 5:1–2 asks us to remember the original design of the "Adam" (Gen. 2:7ff) of "God's image" (Gen. 1:27), and 5:3 applies *this* Adam's "image" to his progeny. For Philo, ontologically "every human" still bears the beautiful "marks" of Adam's "idea" or "appearance," but ethically not every human is in Adam's "image." Some are disqualified due to their wickedness.

3.3.2 Paul's Reading of Genesis 5:3

Paul first introduces Adam as the model for his subsequent family in 1 Cor. 15:48–49. Though its form will differ slightly due to context, he reintroduces this same basic Adamic notion in 2 Cor. 3:18 and in Rom. 8:29, in the latter passage combining it with the Before. Though there is little doubt that 1 Cor. 15:49, 2 Cor. 3:18, and Rom. 8:29 are intimately related to each other,[176] the influence of Gen. 5:3 on Paul's three statements has not received proper attention. In his recent monograph, *Paul's Anthropology in Context*, George van Kooten argues that ancient Judaism "offers no real analogy for the modeling of believers on the paradigm of Adam, in this way becoming similar to him."[177] I will argue that in 1 and 2 Corinthians and Romans it is Gen. 5:3 that gives Paul his basic concept of assimilation to the initial human, as well as his essential wording: "image." Recognizing the influence of Gen. 5:3 on Paul deepens our understanding of Paul's

---

[175] Concerning "toil" as a curse: *Op.* 167 (cf. 79–81); cf. *Virt.* 205. Concerning "slavery" to passions: *Op.* 165, 167; cf. *Deus* 111; *Spec.* 4.188. Concerning even "death" of the soul: *Leg.* 1.105–06.

[176] See e.g., Fee, 2007, 180–85; Matera, 2003, 102; Dunn, 1998A, 237–38 (*idem*, 1988, 1.483); Moo, 1996, 534–35 and nn. 152, 154; Sellin, 1986, 190–91; Michaelis, 1968, 877 n. 37; Scroggs, 1966, 69; Black, 1954, 175; McCasland, 1950, 88. The commentators who compare each of these three passages to the one on which they are commenting is legion. A notable exception is Käsemann, 1980, 244 (see below). Even though the semantic overlap between Gen. 5:3 and 1 Cor. 15:48–49, 2 Cor. 3:18, and Rom. 8:29 is only "image" (though Paul's three passages share "glory" among themselves), the conceptual parallels are strong.

[177] Van Kooten, 2008, 206. For van Kooten's supplement to this lack see below.

interpretation of conformity to Christ. Paul structures this according to another principle of the Beginning (and even the Before). Thus recognizing Gen. 5:3 in Paul also furthers our knowledge of his three-strand interpretation of creation.

(a) The "Image" of Adamic Ontology (1 Cor. 15:48–49)

When Paul mentions bearing the "image" of Adam in 1 Cor. 15:49, he has already been working within the broader context of the beginning of the world (15:37–41), and he has already been describing the beginning of humanity in "Adam," the "living soul," the "dust-being" (15:42–47). In vv. 48–49, Paul extends Adam's created nature to his descendants. They are ontologically like him: "we bore his image." This is not an allusion to Gen. 1:27, as if Paul were relating Adam's descendants to God.[178] He is describing their bodily likeness with Adam himself, as in Gen. 5:3.[179]

When treating 1 Cor. 15:49, G. van Kooten has recently offered a greater emphasis on Paul's own emphasis: assimilation to Christ himself.[180] Yet

---

[178] On the mere assumption that Paul has Gen. 1:27 in mind in 15:49 cf. Hay, 2004, 141 n. 38; Collins, 1999, 570; Furnish, 1999, 115; Horsley, 1998, 211; Fee, 1987, 794 n. 34; Lambrecht, 1981, 513–14; Conzelmann, 1975, 286; Pearson, 1973, 24–25; Jervell, 1960, 268. Senft (1979) denies Gen. 1:27 (210 n. 9), observing that v. 49 fits the notion of Adam's "lineage" or "descendants" (*lignée*) (209–10). Witherington writes of "physical/spiritual *progeny*" and "progenitor" when commenting on 1 Cor. 15:45–49 (and 15:21–23) (1998, 113–14). Usami (1976) argues that Paul is not comparing people to God but to "their ancestor, Adam," and he (unlike Senft and Witherington) offers Gen. 5:3 as Paul's source (488; cf. Luz, 1969, 45).

[179] Rightly Lorenzen, 2008, 161; Schaller, 2004, 148 n. 26; Collins, 1999, 572 n. 49; Lambrecht, 1981, 512–14; Usami, 1976, 488. See Fee's note about N.T. Wright's observation in an oral presentation, that "a second Adam became necessary in part because the first Adam gave birth to a son 'in his own image' (Gen. 5:1 [*sic*])" (2006, 487 n. 14). Lindemann (1997) posits the possibility of v. 49 being a reference to Gen. 5:3 or 1:27, and his own comments on v. 48 should have allowed him to be more confident that it is primarily 5:3 with which Paul was working (165). One implication of recognizing 5:3 and not 1:27 behind v. 49 is, as Lorenzen (2008) has shown, there is no reason to think that Paul is contrasting Gen. 2:7 to 1:27 (in whichever sequence he might place them): contra Theissen, 1987, 361–62 (criticized by Lindemann, 1997, 156); contra Sellin, 1986, 94 (criticized by Lorenzen, 2008, 161 n. 75). Schaller (2004) points out that even if Paul is alluding to Gen. 1:27 in v. 49, since he applies "image" to both Adam and Christ this in itself renders Sellin's direct comparison between Philo's two-men and Paul's two-men unfounded (148). We have already seen in 1 Cor. 11:7–9 that Paul treats 1:27 and 2:7 as references to the same creation of Adam. That observation combined with his use of Gen. 5:3 in 1 Cor. 15:49 render discussion about the relationship between 2:7 and 1:27 in 1 Cor. 15:45–49 unfounded.

[180] Sometimes van Kooten (2008) maintains Paul's language of *Adam's* image (e.g., 71–72, 86, 113), though more often he conflates it with *God's* (cf. 92, 114, 200, 202–03,

3.3 The Image of Adam: Genesis 5:3

by missing how one of the *texts* of "ancient Judaism" (i.e., Genesis) actually *does* "offer a real analogy for the modeling of believers on the paradigm of Adam, in this way becoming similar to him"[181] (i.e., Gen. 5:3), van Kooten constructs a "necessary background" that shares more affinities with Philo's treatment of Gen. 1:27 than with Paul's actual argument. He "supplements" the "insufficient" ancient Jewish background[182] with a Graeco-Roman philosophical context "from Plato to Plotinus."[183] Accordingly, Paul treats Christ as "the second God" who, like Philo's Word, "acts as a model for assimilation to God."[184] Van Kooten writes: "It is this language of becoming like a particular god that – to my knowledge – provides the best explanation for Paul's view about Christ-believers sharing the image and forms of Christ and becoming like him."[185] This imports a faulty view of how Christ was "the image of God" in 2 Cor. 4:4 backwards into 1 Cor. 15:49, treating Christ as metaphysical "image" the way Philo treats Word as "image" (see above). It also misses how Paul treats the "image" of Adam/Christ in vv. 48–49.

Yet merely recognizing a reference to Gen. 5:3 does not necessarily clarify what Paul means in vv. 48–49. As we saw above, it is easy to interpret Adam's "image" in 5:3 as a reference to the "image" which Adam bore, i.e., "God's image" (5:1–2). From this perspective, saying that one bears "Adam's image" might actually mean that he, e.g., Seth or the murder victims in Gen. 9:6, was born according to *God's* image. This basically treats a reference to 5:3 *as* a reference to 1:27, and many scholars would feel justified in their interpretation of 1 Cor. 15:49.[186] But this is not the only way

---

205–06, etc.), even calling v. 49 a reference to Gen. 1:27 (271). His two references to Gen. 5:3 (pp. 2, 10) do not refer to Paul's passages.

[181] Van Kooten, 2008, 206.
[182] Van Kooten, 2008, 219.
[183] Van Kooten, 2008, 125. Plato writes: "there is nothing so like him [*sc.* God: αὐτῷ ὁμοιότερον] as the one who becomes most nearly perfect in righteousness," *Theaetetus* 176c; "by virtue to be likened to God [ὁμοιοῦσθαι θεῷ]," *Republic* 613a-b; cf. *Phaedrus* 253a-b (van Kooten, 2008, 129–32). Tobin (1983) explains the "likeness of assimilation to God" (ὁμοίωσις θεῷ), e.g., in Plato's *Theaetetus* 176b as "the standard Middle Platonic formulation of the purpose of life, the goal of ethics" (18). Van Kooten adds between Plato and Plotinus Plutarch's *Antonius* 75.6 (133) and Alcinous (154–58), the latter of whom he applies most directly to Philo (158, 181–99; cf. Black, 1954, 172 n. 1) and then in a similar way to Paul (158, 199–218).
[184] Van Kooten, 2008, 133.
[185] Van Kooten, 2008, 133.
[186] See our note above for some scholars who see Gen. 1:27 behind Paul's use of "image" (p. 234 n. 178). Van Kooten (2008) writes that in 1 Cor. 15:49 Paul "speaks of human beings carrying the image of God: first the distorted image of the first Adam, which is only in a remote sense still an image of God, but subsequently the image of the second Adam" (73). One could specifically interpret Paul's genitival phrase "image of…" epex-

to interpret Gen. 5:3. When Philo explicitly treated 5:3, he did not interpret it in this way (see *QG* 1.81, above). He considered Seth as being *like Adam* without specific likeness to God in view. Within the text itself, when "image" is seen in light of the previous description of Adam's son in 5:3, "according to his *appearance*" (τὴν ἰδέαν), it is also possible to interpret 5:3 as conveying (simplistically) that Seth looked like Adam. To put it slightly less physically, Adam's son had the same qualities as his father: like father, like son.[187]

This latter construal of bearing Adam's "image" is Paul's in 1 Cor. 15:49. That Paul principally means "like father, like son" rather than "like God" is made clear from his introduction to v. 49 in v. 48. As "the dusty one" is such (οἷος), so too (τοιοῦτοι καί) are "the dusty ones" (v. 48a). Paul has in mind Adam's bodily construction. Philo had demonstrated the solidarity between Adam and his descendants by describing them in terms and labels drawn from the texts concerning Adam's own life and existence, including his creation in Gen. 2:7. Similarly, in v. 48 Paul draws a parallel between the initial man and his followers. Like Philo, he uses the textual terms and labels from Adam's creation in Gen. 2:7 ("soulish," "dusty") to describe Adam's descendants: like him they also are "soulish" and "dusty."

Based on this build-up in v. 48, when Paul then uses the language of bearing "the image" of this "dusty one" (i.e., Adam) in v. 49, he means by Adam's "image" something roughly like his "appearance" (e.g., like κατὰ τὴν ἰδέαν αὐτοῦ).[188] In response to the query, "In what type of *body* will the resurrected corpses come?" (v. 35), part of Paul's purpose in vv. 42–49 is to highlight what the God-given ontology of our pre-resurrected bodies has been like due to the creation of Adam. In parallel to this – but in a far surpassing way, and based upon this protological principle of family resemblance with Adam – Paul grants to the Corinthians glimpses of what

---

egetically (Hughes, 1989, 27 – concerning Rom. 8:29; cf. Dunn, 1988, 1.483; Scroggs, 1966, 69–70), and end up at the same theological conclusion (but see below). Ridderbos (1975) parenthetically notes Gen. 5:3 as a possible referent in v. 49, but mainly develops the link with Gen. 1:27 (72–73).

[187] See e.g., Wenham, 1987, 30; Kline, 1980, 23 n. 34; McCasland, 1950, 89.

[188] For something in the Graeco-Roman popular or technical philosophy to be a "real analogy" with 1 Cor. 15:48–49, it *must* be about humans sharing the same bodily constitution as the human from whom it is derived. Otherwise it fails to help illuminate Paul. Kim (1980) recognizes a "'material' connotation" as well as "the sense of 'likeness'" in Paul's use of "image" in 1 Cor. 15:49 (219), though he does not mention Gen. 5:3. He does, however, rightly apply this to 2 Cor. 4:4 (and Col. 1:15): "the conception of Christ as the εἰκὼν τοῦ θεοῦ... clearly conveys the sense that Christ is the (visible, therefore material) manifestation of (the invisible) God" (219). Cf. Dunn, 1980, 127.

the God-given ontology of our resurrected bodies will be like due to the resurrection of the last Adam and the propagation of his "image."[189]

(b) The Glory of the New Adamic "Image" (2 Cor. 3:18)

In 2 Cor. 3:18, Paul writes that by beholding the Lord's glory as in a mirror, Christians are "transformed into the same image" (τὴν αὐτὴν εἰκόνα).[190] Paul again sets "image" in terms of "glory." Here in 2 Corinthians 3, however, Paul writes nothing about the original Adam as he had in 1 Cor. 15:48a, 49a. In context, he is discussing Exodus 34 and Moses' shining face which reflected the Lord's glory when receiving and delivering the law. It is true that he then employs the texts of the beginning of humanity (4:4) and of the world (4:6), and one might wonder exactly when in his Mosaic discussion Genesis' protological texts entered his mind. When writing of being transformed into the same "image" as "the glory of the Lord," does Paul actually have the principle of Gen. 5:3 in mind?

Despite the absence of Genesis in 2 Corinthians 3, there exists a natural connection between Exodus 34 and Gen. 1:27.[191] Moses' face transformed into glory as he reflected God's glory (3:7; cf. Ex. 34:29–30).[192] Moses was a mirror-image (such as a statue, coin, picture, or mirror) of the Lord's glory insofar as he accurately conveyed something about the Lord from whose presence he was emerging.[193] For the onlookers, to behold Moses' face was to know something true about the Lord; it was to know specifically his "glory." This concept is similar to that found in 1 Cor. 11:7, which Paul clearly associates with and draws from Gen. 1:27 and Genesis 2. There it was the manner in which the "image" appeared (i.e., covering

---

[189] Lorenzen (2008), having recognized Paul's reference to Gen. 5:3 rather than 1:27 (e.g., pp. 161, 178), writes that all of the terms from 1 Cor. 15:42–48 (glory, incorruptibility, immortality, power, Spiritual) "describe the properties of both the resurrection-body of Christ and of his supporters. The wearing of the εἰκών of the heavenly one [sc. in 1 Cor. 15:49] therefore refers to "the bodily identity between Christ and his followers'" (196; translation mine: "All diese Bezeichnungen beschreiben sowohl die Eigenschaften des Auferstehungskörpers Christi als auch seiner Anhänger. Das Tragen der εἰκών des Himmlischen bezieht sich daher auf 'die somatische Identität von Christus und seinen Nachfolgern'").

[190] On the "conceptual background" that has been offered for Paul's notion of transformation to Christ-likeness in 2 Cor. 3:18 see Thrall, 1994, 1.294–95.

[191] Among all of the "conceptual backgrounds" mentioned by Thrall (1994) for Paul's transformation into Christ-likeness in 3:18, she highlights that the Moses narrative of Exodus 34 gave natural rise to the notions of "mirror," "glory," "transformation," and "image" (1.294; cf. Lorenzen, 2008, 166 n. 102). In 1 Corinthians, each of these concepts is related to creation (Gen. 1:27 and 5:3).

[192] Concerning the "glory" that arose from Moses' face-to-face (mirror-like) encounter with the Lord see Watson, 2004, 293; Thrall, 1994, 1.243; Richardson, 1994, 158.

[193] Segal, 1990, 60.

or not covering a man's head) that gave to onlookers a certain impression of the one imaged (God). This was either for "shame" and "dishonor" or, as intended, for "glory." The "image" motif in 2 Cor. 3:18, though not immediately arising from a reading of Genesis but rather from Exodus 34, is nevertheless of one conceptual piece with Paul's "image" motif as he draws it from the beginning of Genesis. It is not a shock that he does, in fact, draw attention to the beginning of Genesis a few verses later (4:4, 6).

Moses' bearing of "the glory of the Lord" in his face, the concept from which Paul draws his point in 2 Cor. 3:18, is therefore reminiscent of Paul's reading of Gen. 1:27, where a person is "the image and glory of God." Yet, if one will recall, above I likened 2 Cor. 3:18 to Paul's application of Gen. 5:3, not 1:27. When regarding Paul's application of Gen. 5:3 in 1 Cor. 15:48–49 I somewhat *distanced* it from Gen. 1:27 since Paul wrote that we reflect *Adam's* (and thus *Christ's*) nature and appearance more specifically than *God's*. Are we merely running in circles? No.

Paul's subsequent references in 2 Cor. 4:4 ("Christ, the image of God") and 4:6 ("the glory of God" in the "face of Christ") help clarify his use of "image" of "the glory of the Lord" in 3:18. When one beholds "the glory of the Lord" a certain "image" is seen, as if the form in a mirror. It is in accord with that beheld "image" that those looking are transformed. Even if "the Lord" in 3:18 refers more generally to Yahweh (the *Lord* in Exodus 34) rather than specifically to "Jesus Christ, *Lord*" (2 Cor. 4:5), what exactly is "the same image" as that Lord's "glory" but Jesus?[194] Paul shifts naturally from mentioning our transformation into "the same image" as "the Lord's glory" to mentioning Jesus as the (new Adamic) "image of God" who reveals in his resurrected "face" the "glory" of the God who spoke creation into being. In this sense, while Paul's theme in 4:4 is certainly culled from Gen. 1:27, his statement in 3:18 really is intimately related (conceptually and lexically) to Gen. 5:3. For "the same image" that Christians see when beholding the Lord's glory – i.e., Jesus' face, that "image" into which Christians are transformed – is the mid-way point between the Creator-Lord and those who are transformed into said "image" of his glory.[195]

---

[194] For the association between 3:18, 4:4, and 4:6 and the conclusion thereupon that the "image" to which Christians are conformed is Jesus cf. Meyer, 2009, 101 n. 138; Nguyen, 2008, 176–77; Fee, 2007, 180–85 (cf. *idem*, 1994, 317–18); Matera, 2003, 102; Watson, 1997, 301 n. 7; Thrall, 1994, 1.283; Hays, 1993, 153; Kim, 1980, 232. It is through "unveiled beholding" that believers see the mirror-"image" of "the glory of the Lord" (3:18) while unbelievers are "veiled" and "blinded" to "the glory of Christ, who is the image of God" and in whose "face" shines "the glory of God" (4:4–6).

[195] Fee (2007) argues that "the *impetus* for the language in this case [*sc*. in 4:4] lies *not* with Christ as the second Adam but with the mirror imagery that Paul uses in 3:18, which in turn holds the three sentences [*sc*. 3:18, 4:4, 6] together" (184). As I posited

3.3 The Image of Adam: Genesis 5:3

But one should not jump too quickly to Philo's concept of human assimilation to God through the incorporeal "second God," the Word, or to Wisdom's incorporeal "wisdom." In Paul's discussion, the "face" of God's "image" should keep our attention on the *human* "image of God." This keeps us rooted not only in Paul's own argument, but in Paul's employment of Gen. 5:3 by which he conveys our assimilation to Christ's "image." The resurrected Jesus himself is the Adamic "image of God."

Here Paul actually reflects *both* readings of Genesis 5 that I mentioned above, and to miss this is to remain confused. The family of Adam (beginning with Seth) was the "image" of Adam (5:3), who himself was the "image of God" (5:1; 1:27). Therefore Seth (and subsequent humans in Gen. 9:6 [and in 1 Cor. 11:7b]) could be likened to *God* via Adam. In 1 Cor. 15:48–49, Paul did not have God-likeness in mind but *only* Adamic-likeness. His view was narrowly focused on bodily ontology. Here in 2 Cor. 3:18, however, Paul has combined the two themes more explicitly: 1) the assimilation of subsequent humans to God 2) via their assimilation to their Adam. In the context of 2 Corinthians 3–4, just as Moses was likened to the Lord as an image of glory, so also Christians are likened to the glory of the Creator,[196] but this is so only through looking like the man who is, within the new ministry of the Spirit and within the new creation of light, the Creator's new Adam, the glorious "image" of God.

Once Paul has introduced the "transformation" into the "image" of the seminal person of the "new,"[197] which is granted by "the Lord, the Spirit,"[198] in 2 Cor. 3:18, there follows a cord of interwoven beginnings and new beginnings (4:4, 6). Each is cast in the language and conceptuality drawn from *the* Beginning. Though Paul's context had not been directly about the creation, his approach was similar to his hermeneutic of creation elsewhere. He argued about a former person (and event and ministry) to whom God had given "glory" but whom God had overshadowed by a subsequent person (and event and ministry) whose surpassing "glory" eclipsed the former into non-glory. In this context of comparison, it is the latter "image" who is "the appropriate goal for the Christians' transformation of

---

above, it is the Moses narrative (a natural correlate being the mirror-motif, hence Fee) that prompts 3:18, but something prompts the clear Adam/creation-language in 4:4–6, and it is precisely in 3:18 where the Moses/mirror imagery prompts Gen. 5:3 and conformity with the "image" of Jesus – and this is a "second Adam" theme. Thus Fee concludes that "lying behind the present passage is a *new-creation* theology" (184).

[196] Thrall (1994) argues that in 3:17 "our" unveiled faces are contrasted to Moses' now-veiled-now-unveiled face (1.283). Cf. Watson, 2004, 291–96; Childs, 1974, 618–19; Harris, 2005, 293.

[197] Cf. 1 Cor. 15:49.

[198] Cf. 1 Cor. 15:45, 51–52.

identity,"[199] who is the "goal of (human-) history."[200] According to Rom. 8:29, this image and conformity was "marked out" *before* history.

(c) The New Adamic "Image," the Cosmos, and the Before (Rom. 8:29)

It is well known that Paul discusses "predestination" in Rom. 8:29–30. But it is important for us to discuss more than this theological topic. There are hermeneutical issues involved as well.[201] To establish the surety of hope, that despite the present suffering "all things" really do work together "for good" for "those who love God," i.e., for "those being called according to [God's] purpose" (Rom. 8:28), Paul turns the Roman Christians to the Beginning and (especially) Before:

> Those whom [God] pre-knew [προέγνω], [for them] he also pre-marked out [προώρισεν] to be conformed to the image of his Son [συμμόρφους τῆς εἰκόνος τοῦ υἱοῦ αὐτοῦ] so that he would be firstborn [πρωτότοκον] among many brothers. And whom he pre-marked out [προώρισεν], these he also called... justified... and glorified [ἐδόξασεν]. (8:29–30)

Paul builds his central statement of the Before on the principle of the Beginning, which in 1 Cor. 15:48–49 he had drawn from Gen. 5:3. Many recognize certain elements of the Adamic protology behind Paul's reference to "image" in v. 29, especially since this statement follows closely on the heels of Paul's use of Genesis 1–3 in vv. 19–23.[202] "God's Son" has an "image," i.e., an appearance, and those who become his family members share the form (defining characteristics) of this "image."[203] As in 1 Cor. 15:49, here Paul is not attempting to compare people to God, although

---

[199] Nguyen, 2008, 182.

[200] Lindemann, 1997, 163.

[201] Thus though it is true that "foreknew" and "pre-marked out" do "speak of God's purpose prior to the creative acts of Genesis 1" (Reymond, 1998, 711; contra Eskola, 1998, 165–77, esp. 170–71, 173, 175 n. 34), this does not say enough. The fact that Paul uses the text's word "image" (and concept of similitude with Adam) within his presentation of the content of this "prior purpose" confirms that a hermeneutical investigation would be illuminating.

[202] Cf. Dunn, 1998A, 237–38 (cf. *idem,* 1988, 1.483–84); Moo, 1996, 534 n. 151; Fee, 1994, 318. For recognition of "the Adam story" behind Paul's discussion in Romans 8 cf. e.g., Witherington, 2004, 230; Eskola, 1998, 171–72; Byrne, 1996, 272–73; Ziesler, 1989, 227; Käsemann, 1980, 244–45; Cranfield, 1975, 1.432.

[203] Lorenzen (2008) considers "form" and "image" to be mutually interpretive, together referring to "the outward" (i.e., "bodily") "appearance of Christ" (207–08; cf. Michaelis, 1968, 877 n. 37). This is a criticism of the epexegetical rendering of 8:29 (as in Dunn, 1988, 1.483; Hughes, 1989, 27).

such a relationship could be deduced,[204] but is attempting to liken certain people to the qualities of the preeminent "brother."[205]

Paul's use of Gen. 5:3 is again based upon a positive appraisal of the protological principle. This should not be overlooked. Bearing the "image" of *an* Adam is not itself negative, even though Paul sees a negative outworking of it from the beginning until now. Paul does not criticize or deny the principle, even using it in 1 Cor. 15:49b and 2 Cor. 3:18 to describe the glorious and heavenly assimilation of believers to the head of their new creation and covenant. It is this same principle that Paul re-employs again here in Rom. 8:29 to show that, as Douglas Moo summarizes, "it is God's purpose to imprint on all those who belong to Christ the 'image' of the 'second Adam'."[206]

Yet again Paul's application of Gen. 5:3 takes a slightly different form than it had in its other two variations. In both 1 Corinthians 15 and 2 Corinthians 3, Paul's application of the creational theme of assimilation to Adam had differed slightly due to context. Rom. 8:29 is no different. Regarding 1 Cor. 15:49, within the context of exegesis of creation and Adam himself Paul labeled Jesus as "the last Adam." Regarding 2 Cor. 3:18, where Paul's argument involved the Moses-story of the glorious Lord's reflective presence, Paul labeled Jesus the "image" of "the glory of the Lord" and then "the image of God." By the time v. 29 appears in Romans 8, Paul has already been arguing that Christ's followers are "God's children" (τέκνα θεοῦ, 8:16). They are "sons of God" (υἱοὶ θεοῦ, v. 14) who are "co-heirs" with him (συγκληρονόμοι) and who will be "co-glorified" with him (συνδοξασθῶμεν) if they first "co-suffer" with him

---

[204] As do Byrne, 1996, 272–73 and Dunn, 1988, 1.483–84.

[205] Lorenzen (2008) does not think that the "Adam-Christ-typology" is in Paul's mind, though she acknowledges that it is a possibility. She is careful to add, however, that "*if* the thought of Adam-Christ-typology is present, it would be – as in 1 Corinthians 15 – not primarily Gen. 1:26f but 5:1–3 that is in the background" (210 n. 54; translation mine: "*Wenn* aber der Gedanke der Adam-Christus-Typologie vorliegt, dann stünde – wie in 1Kor 15 – nicht primär Gen 1, 26f, sondern Gen 5, 1.3 im Hintergrund"). This is a helpful recognition, and I will develop it below.

Concerning Paul's language of "brothers" in 8:29, Paul's switch from the father/son imagery of Gen. 5:3 (and 1 Cor. 15:49) to that of siblings in Rom. 8:29 may cause confusion (e.g., cf. Byrne, 1996, 153, 269, and 272–73). Käsemann (1980), however, helpfully refers to Heb. 2:11ff in which "the Son creates sons and recognizes them as brothers" (245). He says, "We obviously have here the established tradition of the eschatological Adam as the prototype of the sons of God" (245). When set within the context of the relationship between God the Father and Jesus as Son (and believers "in him" as Jesus' "siblings" under God the Father), the relationship that Paul understood between Jesus (as last Adam) and believers (as "Adamic" descendants) would certainly be rendered capable of great flexibility within the new creation.

[206] Moo, 1996, 534 n. 151.

(συμπάσχομεν) (8:17). In v. 29, it is not surprising that he casts the basic principle of Gen. 5:3 as "co-formity" (σύμμορφος) with the image of God's "Son" (τοῦ υἱοῦ). This contextual difference should not cause us to lose sight of its referent in the anthropogonic text of Genesis. This is especially since among some of Paul's contemporaries, there was a close connection between Adam, his descendants, and being considered "children," "sons," or "offspring" of the Creator, particularly when the texts of Genesis' beginning are in mind, and especially Genesis 5. For example, Luke referred to Adam as "son of God" (υἱός... τοῦ θεοῦ) while implementing the genealogy from Genesis 5 (Luke 3:38).[207] Philo himself considered Seth's placement in Adam's lineage as "image" testimony to his new status as successor and firstborn son. Paul's own use of "Son" (and "sonship") in Rom. 8:29 is a most appropriate title for an Adam.[208]

In something of a similar interpretation of Gen. 5:3 to Philo's, in Rom. 8:29 Paul portrays the rights of "inheritance" coming to the one who is conformed to the "image" of the "Son of God."[209] God's "Son" thereby becomes "firstborn" while those conformed to his Son's image are "co-heirs" with him as those who "will be co-glorified" with him (8:17; cf. 8:30). Paul has again added a nuance to his timing of the Adamic "image"-bearing. In 1 Cor. 15:49 it was in the future. In 2 Cor. 3:18 it had a predominantly present aspect. In Rom. 8:29 the actual act of conformity is perhaps present[210] and certainly (also) future.[211] But Paul now adds another dimension – the Before.

The process of Gen. 5:3 itself was "marked out" (-ὁρίζω) by God "before" (προ-) creation. Paul is not claiming here that God merely thought

---

[207] Seebaß, 1975, 84–87 finds Luke's reference in 3:38 similar to Paul's quotation of Aratus in Acts 17:28 (85). In Acts 17:24–28, Luke also presents Paul as arguing (in similar language to 1 Cor. 15:35–49) from the beginning of the world ("the God who made the cosmos [ὁ θεὸς ὁ ποιήσας τὸν κόσμον] and all that is in it") to the beginning of Adamic humanity ("gives [διδούς] to all life [ζωήν] and breath [πνοήν] and all things... having made out of one [human] [ἐξ ἑνός] all nations of humans") and God's sovereignty over all nations ("having marked out [ὁρίσας]" where and how long they should live), to general humanity as "offspring of God" (γένος...τοῦ θεοῦ). Cf. Kline, 1980, 23 n. 33.

[208] Cf. Mathews, 1996, 170; Kline, 1980, 23 (mentioning Rom. 8:29 in 23 n. 34); McCasland, 1950, 98 (comparing "son" [of God] and "image" with Philo [92–93] and Epictetus [96]). This does not deny that "sonship" (υἱοθεσίας, 8:15) appears connected to what had been given to Israel (ἡ υἱοθεσία, Rom. 9:4) (so Lorenzen, 2008, 211; Dunn, 1988, 1.467).

[209] On a slightly different comparison between Philo (*Conf.* 146) and Rom. 8:29 see Siegert, 2009, 187.

[210] E.g., Käsemann, 1980, 244.

[211] E.g., Lorenzen, 2008, 210–11. Jewett (2004) considers the aorist in Rom. 8:30 to convey "the initial evidence of this glory that will one day fill the creation (cf. 2 Cor. 3:18)" (34).

through the mechanics of progeny-production before enacting it in Seth. It is the conformity of God-lovers to the *last* Adam, God's Son, that Paul claims to have been marked before Gen. 5:3 – before creation in Gen. 1:1.

In chapter 1 we saw that Paul's use of "pre-marked out" (προώρισεν) referred to the "time" before creation. This was clear in 1 Cor. 2:7 where Paul used this word in an allusion to Prov. 8:23 and to the "wisdom" that God established before Gen. 1:1–2. The shape of Rom. 8:29 looks as if Paul took his own idea concerning Prov. 8:23 from 1 Cor. 2:7 and blended it with his own idea concerning Gen. 5:3 from 1 Cor. 15:49.[212] Thus:

	Origin		Goal		Means of Attainment
1 Cor. 2:7 discusses	προορίζω	for	(eschat.) δόξα		–
1 Cor. 15 discusses	–		(eschat.) δόξα	via	εἰκών (Gen. 5:3)
Rom. 8:29–30 unites	προορίζω	for	(eschat.) δοξάζω	via	εἰκών (Gen. 5:3)

In 1 Corinthians, God's pre-creational determinations (2:7; cf. Prov. 8:23) were written in a different context than was the method of its attainment (15:49; cf. Gen. 5:3). In Romans, these two concepts are compressed into the same statement. Paul has expanded his reference to God's pre-creational plan. It is no longer only the crucifixion of the last Adam that was marked out before the first Adam was created (1 Cor. 2:7), but it is the Gen. 5:3-process itself (Rom. 8:29) as well as the recipients of this "image" (8:30) which and whom Paul sees in God's wise determination before the beginning. "Glory" has also been expanded from the benefit of "us" to its benefit to the whole cosmos.

In Prov. 8:22–23, God's wisdom was marked out "for [the benefit of] his works" (εἰς ἔργα αὐτοῦ). In Romans 8, Paul portrays the pre-marked out recipients of the glory that God destined before the beginning as themselves something of mediators of a cosmic and glorious freedom. The benefit of God's created works, i.e., "freedom" from the slavery of corruptibility, comes when "the glory of God's children," the "sons of God," are "revealed." When Paul applies the principle of Gen. 5:3 in v. 29, he is already thinking about all of creation, particularly as it appears in the broader text of creation (Genesis 1–2) and fall (Genesis 3).[213]

---

[212] Cf. Bruce, 1971, 38; Dunn, 1988, 1.483.

[213] It is easy to merely mention Genesis 3 since Paul specifically refers to God's curse on the earth due to Adam's disobedience (Gen. 3:17–19). Only by sweat and hard work will the earth produce and Paul takes this as a struggle for the earth as much as for humans (Rom. 8:20). But Paul has more of the Beginning in mind, referring not merely to "the earth" (as in Gen. 3) but to "the creation" (ἡ κτίσις, i.e., the actual act of God in the beginning [cf. Rom. 1:20; see J. Moo, 2008, 75–77 and 75 n. 6]), and assuming behind his description of the burdened cosmos a time when it had been free from the slavery of corruptibility (i.e., in Gen. 1–2).

Here Paul shows an intertwining of the three strands in his interpretation of creation. Paul grants hope by way of conformity with the image of God's Son. This process is rooted in a scope of hope that is no less cosmic and cosmogonic than Genesis 1 and Proverbs 8.[214] Then Paul casts the Before in the language of the Beginning. Cosmic hope comes to God's creation through the glory of God's children. These children were marked out before creation to receive glory through the pre-creationally marked out method which God subsequently initiated in Gen. 5:3.

(d) Summary: Paul's Reading of Genesis 5:3,
in Comparison with Philo's Readings

Genesis 5:3 furthers the understanding of humanity's beginnings. This furtherance could be in terms of Adam's progeny bearing the otherwise inaccessible "image of God" that had been given to Adam. Paul gives a hint of this in 2 Cor. 3:18 where the goal is a reflection of *God's* glory, but this is only accessible through conformity with his "image" – not Moses, nor even Adam, but the resurrected Jesus. The anthropological furtherance provided by Gen. 5:3 can also be seen in terms of likeness with Adam himself – humanity "modeled on the paradigm of Adam." This seemed to be Philo's trend, to compare subsequent humanity with Adam in ontological body and soul. In a broadly similar way, Paul draws upon Gen. 5:3 in such a way in 1 Cor. 15:48a and 49a, reasoning that Adam's family is "such as" he was in terms of appearance or bodily structure (v. 48a), bearing his "image" of dust (v. 49a). Paul extends this in vv. 48b, 49b to "the last Adam" and to his subsequent family.

To explain something about the resurrection of the body to Corinthians who have questioned it, Paul firstly turns them to the cosmogonic "desire" and causative action of God in Genesis 1 regarding diverse bodies, fleshes, and glories (vv. 37–41). He then points out the created nature of soulish dustiness of the first human, Adam, in Gen. 2:7 (vv. 45–47). He thirdly guides their skeptical thinking to contemplate the original principle of the first Adam's relationship to subsequent humanity in Gen. 5:3 (vv. 48–49). Though the contexts of 2 Corinthians 3 and Romans 8 are different, and Paul's language of Gen. 5:3 is slightly recast accordingly, Paul mimics his own hermeneutic by setting this same anthropogonic principle of the new beginning within the grander scope of the God who created light and who cares for the freedom of his whole creation. He will free all of his creation through this very process whereby God-lovers bear the "image" of the

---

[214] "Cosmic" should not be confused with indiscriminate. As Jewett (2004) argues, "creation" in Romans 8 excludes "non-Christian believers" and "the angelic forces" that are opposed to God (35 n. 45)

glory of the Son of God, the last Adam. For Paul, the anthropological principle of Gen. 5:3 provides both despair, which sees the first man as connected to his subsequent family, but also hope, which recognizes the glory, power, incorruptibility, and immortality of the second first-man as fitted-clothing shared with his subsequent family. Unlike with Philo's treatment, their honor is not like Seth's, who found it in mirroring the ethics of the Adam of Genesis 5, but rather in mirroring the suffering and then glory of the Adam who was crucified for their sins and raised for their glory. And it was both this latter Adam and conformity to his "image" that were pre-creationally determined for the glory of those who love his Father and for the freedom of his Father's creation.

3.4 Comparisons and Conclusions
Philo and Paul on the Beginning of Humanity

The texts of the beginning of humanity – Gen. 1:27, 2:7, and 5:3 – are immeasurably important for the anthropology of both Philo and Paul. But they are not isolated texts, either in Genesis itself or in Philo's or Paul's interpretations and applications of them. These texts are mutually interpretive. Sometimes Philo interprets them together, sometimes he opposes them to each other. Paul always treats them as one. The texts are also set within the grander narrative of Genesis 1–5: creation of everything (Genesis 1), creation of Adam and Eve (Genesis 2), the story of Adam and his sons (Genesis 3–4), and the future of Adam's descendants (Genesis 5). Both Philo and Paul fit their readings of Genesis' human beginnings within the larger structure of Genesis' cosmic beginning. Recognition of this hermeneutic helped us interpret their complex readings of the texts.

For Philo, Adam himself is virtuous and perfect in mind and body. For Paul, all "bodies" on earth have "glory," and man in particular still reflects on God's reputation as his "image and glory." Philo and Paul consider the body of Adam to have been perfectly knit together by the divine Craftsman, molded in harmony of parts in perfect accord with God's previous "desire" and "purpose." For Philo and Paul this previous divine "purpose" and "desire" also created the entire world. But Philo and Paul also display negative interpretations of Adam's creation when comparing him with the Other, whether the bodiless and textual human of the Idealized Gen. 1:27 (so Philo) or the embodied Jesus of the resurrection and life-making Spirit (so Paul).

Some communities placed future hope in "the human situation following Genesis 3" being "restored to the situation of Genesis 1."[215] Some craved the return of "all the glory of Adam."[216] For Philo, Cain was deprived of the honor of the "image" and "appearance" of Adam because he was ethically nothing like that first father. One aspect of hope lies in mimicking that first cosmopolitan. For Paul, God-lovers who look to Christ, the last Adam, are not hoping for a return to such dust as the first Adam – even though he had been truly glorious and divinely arranged dust. Paul does look for all the glory of *an* Adam, but he craves movement into the Adam of the Beyond – beyond the grave to the image and glory of the new "Adam." That image, along with its Adam, his progeny, their conformation to him, and their shared glory with him were all intended and marked out by the Creator *before* the beginning for the freedom of the world.

---

[215] Minear, 1994, 78.

[216] On "all the glory of Adam" in Qumran literature see van Kooten, 2008, 15–27.

Conclusion

Paul's interpretation of creation in 1 and 2 Corinthians and Romans, like Philo's in his commentary on Genesis 1–2, contains three interwoven aspects: the beginning of the world, the beginning of humanity, and God's intentions before the beginning. Paul not only has an explicit Before, but its content is connected to his understanding of the Beginning according to Genesis. This has become especially clear as we have compared Paul's briefer comments with those more full treatments of the same creation-texts by Philo in his formal commentary. Philo perceives the Before to be God's noetic structural design for the ontic beauty of the world and humanity. Paul also considers the Before to include God's intentions ("desires") for the diverse ontological structures within his creation, e.g., the fleshes and glories of all things in heaven and earth. But Paul also perceives the Before to contain a salvific, historical design for the freedom of the world through the cross-shaped glory of a Christ-conformed people.

To be clear, the main task above has neither been to present a full synthesis of Paul's and Philo's theologies of the Beginning and Before, nor to present a full comparison of Paul and Philo. I have certainly not refrained from detailed analyses and comparisons and contrasts. These are very important implications of this study, and they can be reviewed in the appropriate sections in each chapter above. The primary task has been somewhat more modest in its scope: to lay bare the interwoven nature of the Before and the Beginning in the apostle Paul as in the commentator Philo. As we have seen, Philo's interpretation of the beginning of Genesis was certainly informed by a notion of God's intentions before the creation of the sense-perceptible realm. This Before was significantly shaped according to Plato's *Timaeus*, and yet his reading of the Beginning was not subject to *merely* an imposition of a fully formed presupposition. Rather, his reading of Genesis also helped shape and fill out his Before. Thus, for example, Philo could claim that the "pre-existent" noetic paradigm was "made" and "became," and this claim was because his scripture, not Plato, told him so. For Paul, also, his interpretation of the protological text was certainly informed by a notion of God's wise intentions before creation, and this Before was significantly shaped according to Prov. 8:22–31. But his reading of the Beginning of Genesis also added shape and content to his communication of God's Before. Thus, for example, Paul could claim that God had not merely "marked out" a general "wisdom" before creation, but that God had "pre-marked out" family-members for the "pre-marked out" last Adam and had even "pre-marked out" the manner of conformity with that Adam's "image." Paul expressed the Before in the wording and motifs of the Beginning (e.g., Gen. 5:3). For Paul, as for Philo, the Before and the text of the Beginning were reciprocally interpretive, interlocked themes within his thoughts on creation.

Also in a manner similar to Philo's fuller treatment of the text of Genesis, Paul treated the creation of the whole world according to Genesis as the appropriate setting for the creation of the more particular humanity according to Genesis. The cosmic perspective of each man even helped us interpret some of their more difficult discussions of the creation of humanity, e.g., regarding who the "image of God" is, how good or bad Adam was by virtue of his creation, and why there was flexibility for both interpreters regarding Adam's glory. These two aspects of the Beginning itself – cosmic and anthropic – are also tightly wound together.

I demonstrated that God's intentions *before* creation – e.g., his "purposes" and "desires" – become manifest for both interpreters not only in certain explicit statements (analyzed in chapter 1), but also implicitly throughout the whole of their respective interpretations of the beginning of the world (analyzed in chapter 2) and the beginning of humanity (analyzed in chapter 3). Thus it is the case that Paul, like Philo, displays three interconnected facets to his interpretation of creation. Like an interwoven cord not easily unraveled is Paul's reading of the Beginning and Before.

There are theological implications of Paul's interpretation of creation. Though these implications are not part of what I set out to establish in this project, two particular theological implications nonetheless will be interesting to present here at the end – or is it now the beyond – of this study of Paul's Beginning and Before. The first regards Paul's more specific relationship between the first and last Adams. The second concerns Paul's application of the Beginning in general.

At various points in the history of Christian thought a certain construal of Paul's relationship between Adam and Christ has been repeated. This understanding places Christ as the "model" for Adam,[1] "the anthropology of Christ" as "primary and prior to that of Adam,"[2] the first Adam as "the

---

[1] Nicholas Cabasilas (14th century), *The Life in Christ* 6.91–94; as quoted in Bouteneff, 2008, 176 and as followed by Bouteneff, 45 (who there also quotes Barth, 1962, 46–47 as support). See also Haffner, 1995, 139–40 on the relationship between Jesus' incarnation and the Fall according to John Duns Scotus (1266 – 1308 CE).

[2] Scroggs, 1966, 101. Cf. K. Barth, 1962, 5. The quotation above is actually Scroggs' favorable summary of Barth's thought. Cf. Barth, 1962, 16.

imitation of the second"³ and "made in the image of the incarnate Christ."⁴ Paul's concept of the Before – that Jesus' crucifixion, and therefore obviously his human nature, was marked out by God *before* he created the first human (Adam) – could seem to confirm these interpretations of Paul. It is worthwhile to notice that this construal of Paul's relationship between Jesus and Adam, while seeming to have affirmation in Paul's language of "pre-destination," actually reverses Paul's main method of argumentation.

Most of these perspectives are arguing from Rom. 5:14: "Adam is a 'type' [τύπος] of the coming one." That statement, as is well known, could be taken to mean that Adam was the "impression" of the prior (pre-existent) stamp who is Christ, or that Adam was the prior "example" of the particular aspect of the human Christ's mission that Paul is discussing. The samples of Paul's Christ-Adam thought just quoted opt for the first construal. I did not analyze Rom. 5:12–21 since it has to do with Paul's understanding of Adam as a sinner rather than with the pre-sin creation. Yet in each of Paul's uses of creation at which we looked throughout this study, Paul does not define Adam as anything like a "pre-Christ." In other words, the portrayals cited above would seem to suggest that such was Paul's thought regarding Adam, that he defined Adam in a Christic manner, as if one could not understand the anthropology of Adam without first and necessarily understanding that of the incarnate Christ. Paul's movement of language and conceptuality, however, actually goes the other direction. Adam was originally "Adam" for Paul, and he then explains *Christ* as the last "*Adam*." As Adam was first the "image of God," so the risen (post-Mosaic) Christ is called the "image of God." As Adam "became" something that had to do with life in the beginning (i.e., a soul that lives), so Christ is said to have "become" something that has to do with life in the end (i.e., a Spirit that life-makes). These are each *Adamic* words and concepts – "Adam," "image," "became" – that Paul employs to explain something about Jesus. As we have seen, Paul's direction of thought constantly takes Adam as the model, and describes Jesus accordingly.

Though there is still room to debate both what Paul meant in Rom. 5:14 and how to put across the panorama of Pauline thought in a systematic way, Paul's typical dynamic of portraying Christ in *Adamic* categories and language, and not the other way around, is hardly best conveyed by saying that for Paul "Christ was the model for Adam," etc. As Francis Watson argues, "In Paul, scripture is not overwhelmed by the light of an autonomous Christ-event needing no scriptural mediation. It is scripture that shapes the contours of the Christ-event."⁵ Though Watson was not referring to Paul's

---

³ Cabasilas, *The Life in Christ* 6.91–94 (quoted in Bouteneff, 2008, 176).
⁴ Irenaeus's interpretation of Rom. 5:14 as summarized by Bouteneff, 2008, 176.
⁵ Watson, 2004, 17.

particular use of the scriptural creation account, what has been demonstrated above confirms this pattern: Paul uses the scripture's Adamic (and more broadly creational) texts to "shape the contours" both of Christ as last "Adam" and "image of God" and also of our assimilation to his (Adamic) "image."[6] Though the raised Jesus is certainly different than the created Adam in many respects – even as a plant from a seed – and though it is important that Paul does not portray Christ in *only* Adamic terms, Paul's movement of understanding does not have him teaching the Corinthians that Christ is the model of Adam. Even though Paul saw Christ's (crucified) humanness in God's wisdom *before* creation (and therefore before Adam), and even though Paul understood the Son of God as the mediator of the original creation itself (and therefore of Adam himself), Paul's actual practice of describing *Jesus* by way of *Adamic* texts rather than the other way around should have a different impact on the shape of discussion about Pauline Christology than has sometimes been the case.

A second theological implication can be posited here in the "beyond" of this study regarding Paul's broader use of creation language. Little systematic study of Paul's protology has been attempted. What has been written is typically narrowed to Adam and is almost exclusively concerned with him as Sinner. Much of the scholarship has taken Paul's protological thoughts in the wrong direction. The skew normally comes from insufficient engagement with the appropriate data in Paul; sometimes it is also due to inappropriate comparisons between Paul and Philo. A prime reason given for Paul's alleged lack of "knowledge" of or "interest" in the creation of the world[7] and of the (pre-sin) creation of Adam[8] is Paul's vested interest in Christ and the *new* creation. Supposedly these interests render contemplation on and discussion of the "old" virtually pointless. It often follows that Adam was therefore not God's image and glory and that he did not display God's "intent." Christ alone bears those honors and Adam is "only" the bringer of sin and death. The world is simply "passing away" due to Adam's sin and the dawned End in Christ. The "old" was thus only of secondary importance. Paul therefore had very little to say about it.

The simple list of passages from 1–2 Corinthians and Romans in which Paul refers to creation, as laid out in the beginning of this study, should have automatically cast doubt on the suppositions that Paul's understanding of sin and the End somehow precludes a deep reflection on pre-sin cre-

---

[6] Regard Paul's basic hermeneutical practice of the beginning of humanity, the texts concerning Adam's beginning are (to use the words of Hays, 1989) some of "the 'determinate subtext[s] that play a constitutive role' in shaping [Paul's] literary production" about Christ (18).

[7] So Reumann's (and Aymer's) and Witherington's more passing comments.

[8] So the fuller statements of e.g., Scroggs, Kim, (earlier Dunn), Bouteneff.

ation. As this study has demonstrated from three different (interwoven) angles, it is precisely within the contexts of his discussion of sin, death, and the End in Christ that Paul most readily introduces the original creation of the world and humanity. It is in Paul's response to the blinding effects of "the god of this world" on those who are perishing as well as to the vain glory of clinging to an eclipsed ministry of condemnation and death that Paul presents his truly glorious Christology according to the beginning of humanity ("image of God") and the beginning of the world ("God said out of darkness, 'Light will shine'") (2 Cor. 4:4–6). It is precisely when Paul puts forward sin's fatality and corruption in the human (1 Corinthians 15) and in the world (Romans 8) that he intensely employs and applies Genesis' language and motifs concerning the world's and humanity's Beginning. The End does not render needless or unimportant Paul's contemplation on the Beginning. It is precisely because God has *begun* the End that Paul repeatedly turns followers of Christ to reflect on how God originally *began* the world and humanity, and even on God's intentions *before*.

Beginnings are generally important for Paul, but *the* Beginning has a special and abiding quality for Paul's theology. The original creation, as described in the beginning of Genesis, provides the divinely "desired" structure according to which the End – i.e., the New Beginning – had been marked out by the Creator. The Creator's activity of giving "bodies," "fleshes," and "glories" was not abandoned once the New Beginning began. Neither was God's "shining" of "light" left behind, nor the name and category "Adam," nor the God-intended title and function "image of God," nor even the propagation of an Adam's own "image" to his subsequent family. All of these concepts, titles, and motifs are from the Beginning, and by them Paul expresses the End, the New Beginning – the Beyond. Even though this Beyond had been marked out *Before* the Original began, since Paul employs the patterns of the Beginning to express the patterns of the Beyond in Christ, should we conclude that the Beginning was of little value for Paul or that he did not contemplate it in any depth? μὴ γένοιτο!

Paul's interpretation of creation, like Philo's in his commentary, intimately intertwines God's pre-creational desire and purpose with the beginning of the world and the beginning of humanity. Paul was so compelled by the beauty and design of the Beginning that he often casts even his Christocentric eschatology in its words and motifs. Yet though Paul expresses the Beyond according to the Beginning, the hope Paul offers is not a return to the Beginning *per se*. "What does new creation look like?" one might ask. One could hear Paul answer, "It looks like old creation, *only more so*."[9] Paul's Christian hope is an arrival beyond the Beginning to the "more so": to a scene of glory for humans, and therefore to a scene of free-

---

[9] Bartlett, 2000, 232 (emphasis added).

dom for the world – a free glory which, by God's original and wise design, had not yet been experienced even in the faultless, exceedingly good Beginning. Forever like God's design in the Beginning, however, this Beyond will be and has already begun to become just as God had always desired. The Beyond already is and forever will be just as the Creator had wisely marked out for his crucified-for-sin and resurrected New Adam, for this Son's redeemed, transformed, and therefore glorious family, and for his gloriously liberated world – marked out in the Before, initiated in the Beginning.

Bibliography

Primary Literature: Translations, Reference Works

Aristotle. 1938–60. Translated by H.P. Cooke et al. 23 vols. Loeb Classical Library. London: Heinemann; Cambridge: Harvard University Press.
Borgen, P., K. Fuglseth, and R. Skarsten, eds. 2000. *The Philo Index: A Complete Greek Word Index to the Writings of Philo of Alexandria.* Leiden: Brill.
Brown, F., S. Driver, C. Briggs, eds. 1996. *The Brown-Driver-Briggs Hebrew and English Lexicon of the Old Testament.* Peabody, MA: Hendrickson Publishers.
Charlesworth, J.H., ed. 1983–85. *The Old Testament Pseudepigrapha: Apocalyptic Literature and Testaments.* 2 vols. Garden City, NY: Doubleday.
Cohn, L. 1889. *Philonis Alexandrini libellus De opificio mundi.* Breslau: G. Koebner.
Cohn, L. and P. Wendland. 1896–1915. *Philonis Alexandrini opera quae supersunt.* 6 vols. Berlin: Walter de Gruyter (1962).
Danker, F.W., ed. 2000. *A Greek-English Lexicon of the New Testament and Other Early Christian Literature*, 3rd ed. Chicago: University of Chicago Press.
Epictetus. 1925–28. Translated by W.A. Oldfather. 2 vols. Loeb Classical Library. London: Heinemann.
Friberg, T., B. Friberg, N.F. Miller, eds. 2000. *Analytical Lexicon of the Greek New Testament.* Barker's Greek New Testament Library. Grand Rapids: Baker Books.
Holladay, C.R. 1995. *Fragments from Hellenistic Jewish Authors: Aristobulus*, vol. 3. Texts and Translations 39; Pseudepigrapha Series 13. Atlanta: Scholars Press.
Josephus. 1926-. Translated by H.St.J. Thackeray et al. 10 vols. Loeb Classical Library. London: Heinemann; Cambridge: Harvard University Press.
Elliger, K. and W. Rudolph. 1997. *Biblia Hebraica Stuttgartensia*, 5th ed. Stuttgart: Deutsche Bibelgesellschaft.
Liddell, H.G., R. Scott, H.S. Jones, eds. 1996. *A Greek-English Lexicon, with Revised Supplements.* Oxford: Clarendon Press.
Louw, J.P. and E.A. Nida, eds. 1988. *Greek-English Lexicon of the New Testament: Based on Semantic Domains*, 2nd ed. New York: United Bible Societies.
Metzger, B.M. 1994. *A Textual Commentary on the Greek New Testament.* 2nd ed. New York: United Bible Societies.
Philo. 1929–62. Translated by F.H. Colson et al. 12 vols. Loeb Classical Library. London: Heinemann; Cambridge: Harvard University Press.
Plato. 1967–86. Translated by H.N. Fowler et al. 12 vols. Loeb Classical Library. London: Heinemann; Cambridge: Harvard University Press.
Pliny the Elder. Natural History. 1938–62. Translated by H. Rackham et al. 10 vols. Loeb Classical Library. London: Heinemann; Cambridge: Harvard University Press.
Plotinus. 1966–88. Translated by A.H. Armstrong et al. 7 vols. Loeb Classical Library. London: Heinemann; Cambridge: Harvard University Press.

Plutarch. 1927–2004. Translated by F.C. Babbit et al. 16 vols. Loeb Classical Library. London: Heinemann; Cambridge: Harvard University Press.
Rahlfs, A. and R. Hanhart, eds. 2006. *Septuaginta*, 2nd ed. Stuttgart: Deutsche Bibelgesellschaft.
Roberts, A. and J. Donaldson. 1989. *The Ante-Nicene Fathers: The Writings of the Fathers down to AD. 325*, in 10 vols. Edinburgh: T&T Clark.
St. Thomas Aquinas, *Summa Theologiae: A Concise Translation*. 1989. Edited by T. McDermott. Christian Classics. London: Eyre & Spottiswoode.
Tertullian. 1931. Translated by T.R. Glover and G.H. Rendall. Loeb Classical Library: London: Heinemann.
Thayer, J.H. 1996. *Thayer's Greek-English Lexicon of the New Testament*. Peabody, MA: Hendrickson Publishers.
Wallace, D.B. 1996. *Greek Grammar Beyond the Basics: An Exegetical Syntax of the New Testament*. Grand Rapids: Zondervan Publishing House.
Wevers, J.W., ed. 1974. *Septuaginta: Vetus Testamentum Graecum, 1: Genesis*. Göttingen: Vandenhoeck & Ruprecht.
Yonge, C.D. 1993. *The Works of Philo. Complete and Unabridged*. Peabody, MA: Hendrickson Publishers.

Secondary Literature

Adams, E. 2000. *Constructing the World: A Study in Paul's Cosmological Language*. Edinburgh: T&T Clark.
–. 2002. "Paul's Story of God and Creation." Pages 19–43 in *Narrative Dynamics in Paul: A Critical Assessment*. Edited by B.W. Longenecker. Louisville: Westminster John Knox Press.
Agourides, S. 1980. Response to U. Wilckens, "Das Kreuz Christi als die Tiefe der Weisheit Gottes: Zu 1. Kor 2,1–16." Pages 101–02 in *Paolo a Una Chiesa Divisa [1 Co 1–4]*. Edited by L. De Lorenzi. Colloquium Oecumenicum Paulinum 5. Rome: Abbey St. Paul.
Alexander, P. 2002. "Enoch and the Beginning of Jewish Interest in Natural Science." Pages 223–44 in *The Wisdom Texts from Qumran and the Development of Sapiential Thought*. Edited by C. Hempel, A. Lange, and H. Lichtenberger. Leuven: Leuven University Press.
Allen, L. 1970. "The Old Testament Background of [ΠΡΟ] ‛ΟΡΙΖΕΙΝ in the New Testament," *New Testament Studies* 17: 104–08.
Alter, R. 1996. *Genesis: Translation and Commentary*. New York: W.W. Norton & Company.
Anderson, B.W. 1994. *From Creation to New Creation: Old Testament Perspectives*. Minneapolis: Augsburg Fortress.
Arichea, D.C. 1999. "1 Corinthians 15:1–58: An Asian Perspective." Pages 193–99 in *Return to Babel: Global Perspectives on the Bible*. Edited by J.R. Levison and P. Pope-Levison. Westminster John Knox Press.
Arnold, B.T. 2009. *Genesis*. The New Cambridge Bible Commentary. Cambridge: Cambridge University Press.
Asher, J. 2000. *Polarity and Change in 1 Corinthians 15: A Study in Metaphysics, Rhetoric, and Resurrection*. Hermeneutische Untersuchungen zur Theologie 42. Tübingen: Mohr Siebeck.

–. 2001. "Σπείρεται in 1 Cor 15:42–44," *Journal of Biblical Literature* 120.1 (Spring): 101–22.
Aymer, A.J.D. 1985. *Paul's Understanding of 'KAINE KTISIS': Continuity and Discontinuity in Pauline Eschatology*. Ann Arbor, MI: University Microfilms International.
Baer, R.A. 1970. *Philo's Use of the Categories Male and Female*. Leiden: Brill.
Balla, P. 2007. "2 Corinthians." Pages 753–83 in *Commentary on the New Testament Use of the Old Testament*. Edited by G.K. Beale and D.A. Carson. Grand Rapids: Baker Academic.
Barbour, R.S. 1979. "Wisdom and the Cross in 1 Corinthians 1 and 2." Pages 57–71 in *Theologia Crucis – Signum Crucis: Festschrift für Erich Dinkler zum 70. Geburtstag*. Edited by E. Dinkler, C. Andresen, and G. Klein. Tübingen: J.C.B. Mohr (Mohr Siebeck).
Barclay, J.M.G. 1992. "Thessalonica and Corinth: Social Contrasts in Pauline Christianity," *Journal for the Study of the New Testament* 47: 49–74.
–. 1996A. *Jews in the Mediterranean Diaspora: From Alexander to Trajan (323 BCE – 117 CE)*. Edinburgh: T&T Clark.
–. 1996B. "The Resurrection in Contemporary New Testament Scholarship." Pages 13–30 in *Resurrection Reconsidered*. Edited by G. D'Costa. Oxford: Oneworld.
–. 1997. *Colossians and Philemon*. Sheffield: Sheffield Academic Press.
–. 2004. "πνευματικός in the Social Dialect of Pauline Christianity." Pages 157–67 in *The Holy Spirit and Christian Origins: Essays in Honor of James D.G. Dunn*. Edited by G.N. Stanton, B.W. Longenecker, and S. Barton. Grand Rapids: Eerdmans.
–. 2006. "'By the Grace of God I am what I am': Grace and Agency in Philo and Paul." Pages 140–57 in *Divine and Human Agency in Paul and his Cultural Environment*. Edited by J.M.G. Barclay and S.J. Gathercole. London: T&T Clark.
Barclay, W. 1954. *The Letters to the Corinthians*. Edinburgh: The Saint Andrew Press.
Barrett, C.K. 1962. *From First Adam to Last: Study in Pauline Theology*. London: Adam and Charles Black.
–. 1968. *The First Epistle to the Corinthians*. London: Adam and Charles Black.
–. 1993. *The Second Epistle to the Corinthians*. Black's New Testament Commentary. Peabody, MA: Hendrickson Publishers.
Barth, K. 1957–75. *Church Dogmatics*. Translation edited by G.W. Bromiley and T.F. Torrence. Edinburgh: T&T Clark.
–. 1962. *Christ and Adam: Man and Humanity in Romans 5*, eds. T.F. Torrance and J.K.S. Reid. Translated by T.A. Smail. New York: Harper & Brothers Publishing.
Bartlett, D.L. 2000. "Creation Waits with Eager Longing." Pages 229–50 in *God Who Creates: Essays in Honor of W. Sibley Towner*. Edited by W.P. Brown and S.D. McBride. Grand Rapids: Eerdmans.
Batto, B.F. 1992. "Creation Theology in Genesis." Pages 16–38 in *Creation in the Biblical Traditions*. Edited by R.J. Clifford and J.J. Collins. Catholic Biblical Quarterly Monograph Series 24. Washington D.C.: The Catholic Biblical Association of America.
Beasley-Murray, P. 1980. "Colossians 1:15–20: An Early Christian Hymn Celebrating the Lordship of Christ." Pages 169–83 in *Pauline Studies: Essays presented to Professor F. F. Bruce on his 70th Birthday*. Edited by D.A. Hagner and M.J. Harris. Grand Rapids: Eerdmans.
Becker, J. 2007. *Die Auferstehung Jesu Christi nach dem Neuen Testament: Ostererfahrung und Osterverständnis im Urchristentum*. Tübingen: Mohr Siebeck.
Bedale, S. 1954. "The Meaning of κεφαλή in the Pauline Epistles," *Journal for Theological Studies* 5: 211–15.

Beker, J.C. 1980. *Paul the Apostle: The Triumph of God in Life and Thought*. Edinburgh: T&T Clark.
Belleville, L.L. 1991. *Reflections of Glory: Paul's Polemical Use of the Moses-Doxa Tradition in 2 Corinthians 3.1–18*. Journal for the Study of the New Testament Supplement Series 52. Sheffield: Sheffield Academic Press.
Berchman, R.M. 2000. "Philo and Philosophy." Pages 49–70 in *Judaism in Late Antiquity: Part 2, Volume 3, Where We Stand: Issues and Debates in Ancient Judaism*. Edited by J. Neusner and A.J. Avery-Peck. Leiden: Brill.
Best, E. 1998. *A Critical and Exegetical Commentary on Ephesians*. International Critical Commentary. Edinburgh: T&T Clark.
Bird, P.A. 1995. "Sexual Differentiation and Divine image in the Genesis Creation Texts." In *The Image of God: Gender Models in Judaeo-Christian Tradition*, ed. K.E. Børresen, 5–28. Minneapolis: Fortress Press.
Black, M. 1954. "The Pauline Doctrine of the Second Adam," *Scottish Journal of Theology* 7: 170–79.
Blomberg, C. 1995. *1 Corinthians*. The NIV Application Commentary. Grand Rapids: Zondervan.
Bonhoeffer, D. 1959. *Creation and Fall: A Theological Interpretation of Genesis 1–3*. Translated by D.S. Bax. London: SCM Press.
–. 1986. *Meditating on the Word*. Translated by D.M. Gracie. Cambridge, MS: Cowley Publications.
Borgen, P. 1987. *Philo, John and Paul: New perspectives on Judaism and early Christianity*. Brown Judaic Studies 131. Atlanta: Scholars Press.
–. 1995. "Man's Sovereignty over Animals and Nature According to Philo of Alexandria." In *Texts and Contexts: Biblical Texts in their Textual and Situational Contexts, Essays in Honor of Lars Hartman*, eds. T. Fornberg and D. Hellholm, 369–89. Oslo: Scandinavian University Press.
–. 1997. *Philo of Alexandria, An Exegete for His Time*. Novum Testamentum Supplement Series 86. Leiden: Brill.
Bornkamm, G. 1967. "μυστήριον." In *Theological Dictionary of the New Testament*, vol. 4, eds. G. Kittel, G. Friedrich, G.W. Bromiley, 802–28. Grand Rapids: Eerdmans.
–. 1985. "μυστήριον." In *Theological Dictionary of the New Testament: Abridged*, ed. G.W. Bromily, 617–19. Grand Rapids: Eerdmans.
Bouteneff, P.C. 2008. *Beginnings: Ancient Christian Readings of the Biblical Creation Accounts*. Grand Rapids: Baker Academic.
Bremmer, J.N. 2002. *The Rise and Fall of the Afterlife: The 1995 Read-Tuckwell Lectures at the University of Bristol*. London: Routledge.
–. 2005. "Canonical and Alternative Creation Myths in Ancient Greece." In *Creation of Heaven and Earth: Re-Interpretation of Genesis 1 in the Context of Judaism, Ancient Philosophy, Christianity, and Modern Physics*, ed. G. van Kooten, 73–96. Themes in Biblical Narrative 8. Leiden: Brill.
Brown, R.E. 1958. "The Semitic Background of the New Testament *Mysterion*," *Biblica* 39: 426–48.
Bruce, F.F. 1971. *1 and 2 Corinthians*. The New Century Bible Commentary. London: Oliphants.
–. 1977. *Paul: Apostle of the Heart Set Free*. Grand Rapids: Eerdmans.
Bultmann, R. 1969. *Faith and Understanding*. Translation by L.P. Smith. London: SCM Press.
–. 2007. *Theology of the New Testament, with a New Introduction by Robert Morgan*. Translated by K. Grobel. Waco, TX: Baylor University Press.

Burrell, D. 2004. *Faith and Freedom: An Interfaith Perspective*. Malden, MA: Blackwell Publishers.
Byrne, B. 1996. *Romans*. Sacra Pagina Series 6. Collegeville, MN: The Liturgical Press.
Carmichael, C.M. 1996. *The Story of Creation: Its Origin and Its Interpretation in Philo and the Fourth Gospel*. Ithaca: Cornell University Press.
Carnley, P.F. 1997. "Response by Peter F. Carnley." In *The Resurrection: An Interdisciplinary Symposium on the Resurrection of Jesus*, eds. S.T. Davis, D. Kendall, G. O'Collins, 29–40. Oxford: Oxford Uni. Press.
Carr, W. 1977. "The Rulers of this Age – 1 Corinthians 2.6–8," *New Testament Studies* 23: 20–35.
Carson, D.A., D.J. Moo, and L. Morris. 1992. *An Introduction to the New Testament*. Leicester: Inter-Varsity; Grand Rapids: Zondervan.
Cassuto, U. 1961. *A Commentary on the Book of Genesis 1–6: From Adam to Noah*. Translation by I. Abrahams. Jerusalem: Magnes Press.
Chester, A. 2001. "Resurrection and Transformation." In *Auferstehung – Resurrection: The Fourth Durham-Tübingen Research Symposium; Resurrection, Transfiguration, and Exaltation in Old Testament, Ancient Judaism and Early Christianity*, eds. F. Avemarie and H. Lichtenberger, 47–78. Wissenschaftliche Untersuchungen zum Neuen Testament 135. Tübingen: Mohr Siebeck.
Childs, B.S. 1974. *The Book of Exodus: A Critical, Theological Commentary*. Old Testament Library. Louisville: The Westminster Press.
–. 1992. *Biblical Theology of the Old and New Testaments: Theological Reflection on the Christian Bible*. Minneapolis: Fortress Press.
Ciampa, R. and B. Rosner. 2007. "1 Corinthians." In *Commentary on the New Testament Use of the Old Testament*, eds. G.K. Beale and D.A. Carson, 695–752. Grand Rapids: Baker Academic.
Clarke, W.K.L. 1952. *Concise Bible Commentary*. London: SPCK.
Clifford, R.J. 1992. "Creation in the Psalms." In *Creation in the Biblical Traditions*, ed. R.J. Clifford, J.J. Collins, 57–69. Catholic Biblical Quarterly Monograph Series 24. Washington D.C.: The Catholic Biblical Association of America.
–. 1994. *Creation Accounts in the Ancient Near East and the Bible*. Catholic Biblical Quarterly 26. Washington, D.C.: The Catholic Biblical Association of America.
Clifford, R.J. and J.J. Collins. 1992. "Introduction: The Theology of Creation Traditions." In *Creation in the Biblical Traditions*, eds. R.J. Clifford, J.J. Collins, 1–15. Catholic Biblical Quarterly Monograph Series 24. Washington D.C.: The Catholic Biblical Association of America.
Collins, J.J. 1997. *Jewish Wisdom in the Hellenistic Age*. Edinburgh: T&T Clark.
Collins, R.F. 1999. *First Corinthians*. Sacra Pagina Series 7. Collegeville, MN: The Liturgical Press.
Conzelmann, H. 1964. "Die Mutter der Weisheit." In *Zeit und Geschichte: Dankesgabe an R. Bultmann zum 80. Geburtstag*, ed. E. Dinkler, 225–34. Tübingen.
–. 1971. "The Mother of Wisdom." In *The Future of our Religions Past: Essays in Honour of Rudolf Bultmann*, ed. J.M. Robinson, 230–43. London: SCM Press.
–. 1975. *1 Corinthians: A Commentary on the First Epistle to the Corinthians*. Translated by J.W. Leitch. Hermeneia. Philadelphia: Fortress Press.
Cook, J. 1982. "Genesis 1 in the Septuagint as Example of the Problem: Text and Tradition," *Journal of Northwest Semitic Languages* 10: 25–36.
–. 1997. *The Septuagint of Proverbs: Jewish and/or Hellenistic Proverbs? Concerning the Hellenistic Colouring of the LXX Proverbs*. Leiden: Brill.

–. 2001. "The Septuagint of Genesis: Text and/or Interpretation." In *Studies in the Book of Genesis: Literature, Redaction and History*, ed. A. Wénin, 315–29. Leuven: Leuven University Press.

Cotter, D.W. 2003. *Genesis*. Berit Olam: Studies in Hebrew Narrative and Poetry. Collegeville, MN: The Liturgical Press.

Cox, R. 2005. "By the Same Word: The Intersection of Cosmology and Soteriology in Hellenistic Judaism, Early Christianity and 'Gnosticism' in the Light of Middle Platonic Intermediary Doctrine." PhD diss., Notre Dame.

–. 2007. *By the Same Word: Creation and Salvation in Hellenistic Judaism and Early Christianity*. Berlin: Walter de Gruyter.

Cranfield, C.E.B. 1975–79. *A Critical and Exegetical Commentary on the Epistle to the Romans*. 2 vols. International Critical Commentary. Edinburgh: T&T Clark.

Currid, J. 1997. *Ancient Egypt and the Old Testament*. Grand Rapids: Baker Books.

Dahlberg, B.T. 1998. "Genesis." In *Pentateuch/Torah*. Mercer Commentary on the Bible, vol. 1. Macon, GA: Mercer University Press.

Davis, J.A. 1984. *Wisdom and Spirit: An Investigation of 1 Corinthians 1.18–3.20 against the Background of Jewish Sapiential Traditions in the Greco-Roman Period*. Lanham, MD: University Press of America.

De Boer, M. 1988. *Defeat of Death: Apocalyptic Eschatology in 1 Corinthians 15 and Romans 5*. Journal for the Study of the New Testament Supplement Series 22. Sheffield: JSOT Press.

Delitzsch, F. 1894. *A New Commentary on Genesis*. Translated by S. Taylor. Edinburgh: T&T Clark.

Delobel, J. 1986. "1 Cor 11:2–16: Towards a Coherent Explanation." In *L'Apotre Paul: Personnalité, style et conception du ministère*, ed. A. Vanhoye, 369–89. Bibliotheca ephemeridum theologicarum lovaniensium 73. Leuven: Leuven University Press.

Dillon, J.M. 1977. *The Middle Platonists: a Study of Platonism 80 B.C. to A.D. 220*. London: Duckworth.

–. 1990. "The Theory of Three Classes of Men in Plotinus and in Philo." In *The Golden Chain: studies in the Development of Platonism and Christianity*, by J. Dillon, XX.69–76. London: Variorum.

–. 1993. *Alcinous, The Handbook of Platonism. Translation with an Introduction and Commentary*. Clarendon Later Ancient Philosophers. Oxford: Clarendon Press.

–. 1997. "Reclaiming the Heritage of Moses: Philo's Confrontation with Greek Philosophy." In *The Great Tradition: Further Studies in the Development of Platonism and Early Christianity*, by J. Dillon, IV.109–23. Variorum Collected Studies Series. Aldershot: Ashgate.

–. 2005. "Cosmic Gods and Primordial Chaos in Hellenistic and Roman Philosophy: The Context of Philo's Interpretation of Plato's *Timaeus* and the Book of Genesis." In *Creation of Heaven and Earth: Re-Interpretation of Genesis 1 in the Context of Judaism, Ancient Philosophy, Christianity, and Modern Physics*, ed. G. van Kooten, 97–107. Themes in Biblical Narrative 8. Leiden: Brill.

Dorsey, D.A. 1999. *The Literary Structure of the Old Testament: A Commentary on Genesis-Malachi*. Grand Rapids: Baker Academic.

Driver, S.R. 1926. *The Book of Genesis, with Introduction and Notes*, 12th ed. London: Methuen.

Dunn, J.D.G. 1973. "1 Corinthians 15:45 – last Adam, life-giving spirit." In *Christ and Spirit in the New Testament*, eds. B. Lindars and S. Smalley, 127–41. Cambridge: Cambridge University Press.

–. 1980. *Christology in the Making: A New Testament Inquiry into the Origins of the Doctrine of the Incarnation*. London: SCM Press.
–. 1988. *Romans*. Word Bible Commentary 38, 2 vols. Dallas: Word Books.
–. 1993. "Pauline Christology: Shaping the Fundamental Structures." In *Christology in Dialogue*, ed. R.F. Berkey and S.A. Edwards, 96–107. Cleveland: Pilgrim.
–. 1995. *1 Corinthians*. Sheffield: Sheffield Academic Press.
–. 1996. "Deutero-Pauline letters." In *Early Christian Thought in its Jewish Context*, eds. J.M.G. Barclay and J.P.McM. Sweet, 130–44. Cambridge: Cambridge University Press.
–. 1998A. *The Christ and the Spirit: Collected Essays of James D.G. Dunn*, vol. 1 "Christology." Edinburgh: T&T Clark.
–. 1998B. *The Theology of Paul the Apostle*. Grand Rapids: Eerdmans.
Dupont, J. 1960. *Gnosis. La connaissance religieuse dans les épitres de saint Paul*, 2nd ed. Paris: Gabalda.
Ellingworth, P. and H. Hatton. 1994. *A Handbook on Paul's First Letter to the Corinthians*. New York: United Bible Society.
Ellis, E. E. 1978. *Prophecy and Hermeneutic in Early Christianity: New Testament Essays*. Wissenschaftliche Untersuchungen zum Neuen Testament 18. Tübingen: J.C.B. Mohr (Paul Siebeck).
Endo, M. 2002. *Creation and Christology: A Study in the Johannine Prologue in Light of Early Jewish Creation Accounts*. Wissenschaftliche Untersuchungen zum Neuen Testament 149. Tübingen: Mohr-Siebeck.
Endsjø, D. 2008. "Immortal Bodies, before Christ: Bodily Continuity in Ancient Greece and 1 Corinthians," *Journal for the Study of the New Testament* 30.4: 417–36.
Eskola, T. 1998. *Theodicy and Predestination in Pauline Soteriology*, Wissenschaftliche Untersuchungen zum Neuen Testament 100. Tübingen: Mohr Siebeck.
Fee, G.D. 1987. *The First Epistle to the Corinthians*. New International Commentary on the New Testament. Grand Rapids: Eerdmans.
–. 1994. *God's Empowering Presence: The Holy Spirit in the Letters of Paul*. Peabody, MA: Hendrickson Publishers.
–. 2007. *Pauline Christology: An Exegetical-Theological Study*. Peabody, MA: Hendrickson Publishers.
Fergusson, D. 1998. *The Cosmos and the Creator: An Introduction to the Theology of Creation*. London: SPCK.
Feuillet, A. 1966. *Le Christ: Sagesse de Dieu*. Paris: J. Gabalda.
–. 1973. "La dignité et le rôle de la femme d'après quelques textes pauliniens," *New Testament Studies* 21: 157–91.
Fitzmyer, J.A. 1993. *Romans: A New Translation with Introduction and Commentary*. Anchor Bible 33. New York: Doubleday.
Frick, P. 1999. *Divine Providence in Philo of Alexandria*. Texts and Studies in Ancient Judaism 77. Tübingen: Mohr Siebeck.
Frid, B. 1985. "The Enigmatic ΑΛΛΑ in 1 Corinthians 2 9," *New Testament Studies* 31: 603–11.
Früchtel, L. 1937. "Griechische Fragmente zu Philons Quaestiones in Genesin et in Exodum," *Zeitschrift für die alttestementliche Wissenschaft* N.F. 14: 108–15.
Furnish, V.P. 1984. *II Corinthians*. Anchor Bible 32A. New York: Doubleday.
–. 1999. *The Theology of the First Letter to the Corinthians*. Cambridge: Cambridge University Press.
Gaffin, R. 1978. *Resurrection and Redemption*. New Jersey: P&R Publishing Company.

Garland, D.E. 1999. *2 Corinthians: An Exegetical and Theological Exposition of Holy Scripture*. The New American Commentary 29. Nashville: Broadman & Holman.
–. 2003. *1 Corinthians*. Baker Exegetical Commentaries on the New Testament. Grand Rapids: Baker Academic.
Garr, W.R. 2003. *In His Own Image and Likeness: Humanity, Divinity and Monotheism*. Culture and History of the Ancient Near East 15. Leiden: Brill.
Garrett, D. 2000. *Rethinking Genesis: The Sources and Authorship of the First Book of the Pentateuch*. Fearn, Great Britain: Christian Focus Publications.
Gelander, S. 1997. *The Good Creator: Literature and Theology in Genesis 1–11*. Atlanta: Scholars Press.
Gibbs, J.G. 1971. *Creation and Redemption: A Study in Pauline Theology*. Supplements to Novum Testamentum 26. Leiden: Brill.
Goldstein, J.A. 1983. *II Maccabees*. Anchor Bible 41. Garden City: Doubleday & Company.
Goodenough, E.R. 1935. *By Light, Light: The Mystic Gospel of Hellenistic Judaism*. New Haven: Yale University Press.
–. 1962. *An Introduction to Philo Judaeus*. Brown Classics in Judaica. Oxford: Blackwell.
Goulder, M.D. 2001. *Paul and the Competing Mission in Corinth*. Peabody, MA: Hendrickson Publishers.
Grudem, W. 1990. "The Meaning of Κεφαλή: A Response to Recent Studies," *Trinity Journal* 11: 3–72.
Gundry-Volf, J.M. 1994. "Male and Female in Creation and New Creation: Interpretations of Galatians 3.28c in 1 Corinthians 7." In *To Tell the Mystery: Essays on New Testament Eschatology in Honor of Robert H. Gundry*, eds. T.E. Schmidt and M. Silva, 95–121. Journal for the Study of the New Testament Supplement Series 100. Sheffield: JSOT Press.
–. 1997. "Gender and Creation in 1 Corinthians 11:2–16: A Study in Paul's Theological Method." In *Evangelium, Schriftauslegung Kirche: Festschrift für Peter Stuhlmacher zum 65. Geburtstag*, eds. J. Adna, S.J. Haffemann, O. Hofius, 151–71. Göttingen: Vandenhoeck & Ruprecht.
Gunkel, H. 1984. "The Influence of Babylonian Mythology Upon the Biblical Creation Story" (1895). In *Creation in the Old Testament*, ed. B.W. Anderson, 25–52. Philadelphia: Fortress Press; London: SPCK.
–. 1997. *Genesis*. Translated by M.E. Biddle (German ed. 1910). Macon, GA: Mercer University Press.
Gunton, C.E. 1998. *The Triune Creator: A Historical and Systematic Study*. New Studies in Constructive Theology III. Edinburgh: Edinburgh University Press.
Hafemann, S.J. 1995. *Paul, Moses, and the History of Israel: The Letter/Spirit Contrast and the Argument from Scripture in 2 Corinthians 3*. Wissenschaftliche Untersuchungen zum Neuen Testament 81. Tübingen: Mohr Siebeck.
Haffner, P. 1995. *Mystery of Creation*. Leominster: Gracewing.
Hamerton-Kelly, R.G. 1973. *Pre-Existence, Wisdom, and the Son of Man*. Cambridge: Cambridge University,.
Hanson, A.T. 1980A. "The Midrash in II Corinthians 3: A Reconsideration," *Journal for the Study of the New Testament* 9: 2–28.
–. 1980B. *The New Testament Interpretation of Scripture*. London: SPCK.
Hardy, D.W. 1997. "Creation and Eschatology." In *The Doctrine of Creation: Essays in Dogmatics, History and Philosophy*, ed. C. Gunton, 105–33. Edinburgh: T&T Clark.
Hargreaves, J. 1978. *A Guide to 1 Corinthians*. London: SPCK.

Harrington, D.J. 1996. *Wisdom Texts from Qumran*. London: Routledge.
–. 2002. "Two Early Jewish Approaches to Wisdom: Sirach and Qumran Sapiental Work A." In *The Wisdom Texts from Qumran and the Development of Sapiential Thought*, eds. C. Hempel, A. Lange, H. Lichtenberger, 263–76. Leuven: Leuven University Press.
Harris, M.J. 2005. *The Second Epistle to the Corinthians: A Commentary on the Greek Text*. New International Greek Testament Commentary. Grand Rapids: Eerdmans.
Harris, R.L., G.I. Archer, Jr., B.K. Waltke, eds. 1980. *Theological Wordbook of the Old Testament*. Chicago: Moody Publishers.
Harrisville, R.A. 1987. *1 Corinthians*. Augsburg Commentary on the New Testament. Minneapolis: Augsburg Fortress Publishing.
Hartley, J.E. 2000. *Genesis*. New International Biblical Commentary: Old Testament Series 1. Peabody, MA: Hendrickson Publishers.
Hawking, S. 1988. *A Brief History of Time: From the Big Bang to Black Holes*. London: Bantam Press.
Hay, D.M. 2004. "Philo's Anthropology, the Spiritual Regimen of the Therapeutae, and a Possible Connection with Corinth." In *Philo und das Neue Testament: Wechselseitige Wahrnehmungen – Internationales Symposium zum Corpus Judaeo-Hellenisticum, 1.-4. Mai 2003, Eisenach/Jena*, eds. R. Deines, K.-W. Niebuhr, 126–42. Wissenschaftliche Untersuchungen zum Neuen Testament 172. Tübingen: Mohr Siebeck.
Hays, R.B. 1989. *Echoes of Scripture in the Letters of Paul*. New Haven: Yale University Press.
–. 1995. "Adam, Israel, Christ: The Question of Covenant in the Theology of Romans: A Response to Leander E. Keck and N.T. Wright." In *Pauline Theology, Vol. III: Romans*, eds. D.M. Hay and E.E. Johnson, 68–86. Minneapolis: Fortress Press.
–. 1997. *First Corinthians*. Interpretation Bible Commentary. Louisville: John Knox Press.
Heckel, Th.K. 2002. "Body and Soul in Saint Paul." In *Psyche and Soma: Physicians and Metaphysicians on the Mind-Body Problem from Antiquity to Enlightenment*, eds. J.P. Wright and P. Potter, 117–31. Oxford: Oxford University Press.
Heil, J.P. 2005. *The Rhetorical Role of Scripture in 1 Corinthians*. Society of Biblical Literature Monograph Series 15. Atlanta: Society of Biblical Literature.
Hengel, M. 1974. *Judaism and Hellenism: Studies in Their Encounter in Palestine during the Early Hellenistic Period*. Translated by J. Bowden. London: SCM Press.
–. 2001. *The Pre-Christian Paul*. Philadelphia: Trinity Press International.
Héring, J. 1962. *The First Epistle of Saint Paul to the Corinthians*. Translated by A.W. Heathcote and P. J. Allcock. London: Epworth Press.
Hillar, M. 1998. "The Logos and its Function in the Writings of Philo of Alexandria: Greek Interpretation of the Hebrew Myth and Foundations of Christianity," *A Journal from the Radical Reformation: A Testimony to Biblical Unitarianism* 7.3, Part I (Spring 1998): 22–37; 7.4, Part II (Summer): 36–53.
Hoekema, A. 1986. *Created in God's Image*. Grand Rapids: Eerdmans.
Hooker, M.D. 1964. "Authority on Her Head: An Examination of 1 Cor. 11:10," *New Testament Studies* 10: 410–16.
–. 1990. *From Adam to Christ: Essays on Paul*. Cambridge: Cambridge University Press.
Horsley, R.A. 1976. "Pneumatikos vs. Psychikos: Distinctions of Spiritual Status among the Corinthians," *HTR* 69: 269–88.
–. 1977. "Wisdom of Word and Words of Wisdom in Corinth," *Catholic Biblical Quarterly* 39: 224–39.

–. 1978. "'How can some of you say that there is no Resurrection of the Dead?' Spiritual Elitism in Corinth," *Novum Testamentum* 20: 203–231.
–. 1998. *1 Corinthians*. Abingdon New Testament Commentary. Nashville: Abingdon.
–. 2004. "Gnosis in Corinth: 1 Corinthians 8.1–6." In *Christianity at Corinth: The Quest for the Pauline Church*, eds. E. Adams and D.G. Horrell, 119–28. Louisville: Westminster John Knox Press.
House, P.R. 1998. *Old Testament Theology*. Downers Grove: InterVarsity Press.
Houston, J.M. 1980. *I Believe in the Creator*. Grand Rapids: Eerdmans.
Hubbard, M.V. 2002. *New Creation in Paul's Letters and Thought*. Cambridge: Cambridge University Press.
Hughes, P.E. 1989. *The True Image: The Origin and Destiny of Man in Christ*. Grand Rapids: Eerdmans.
Hultgren, S. 2003. "The Origin of Paul's Doctrine of the Two Adams in 1 Corinthians 15.45–49," *Journal for the Study of the New Testament* 25: 344–45.
Hurley, J.B. 1981. *Man and Woman in Biblical Perspective*. Grand Rapids: Zondervan Publishing House.
Hurtado, L.W. 2003. *Lord Jesus Christ: Devotion to Jesus in Earliest Christianity*. Grand Rapids: Eerdmans.
–. 2004. "Does Philo Help Explain Early Christianity?" In *Philo und das Neue Testament: Wechselseitige Wahrnehmungen – Internationales Symposium zum Corpus Judaeo-Hellenisticum, 1.-4. Mai 2003, Eisenach/Jena*, eds. R. Deines, K.-W. Niebuhr, 73–92. Wissenschaftliche Untersuchungen zum Neuen Testament 172. Tübingen: Mohr Siebeck.
Jacobson, H. 1996. *A Commentary on Pseudo-Philo's* Liber Antiquitatum Biblicarum, *with Latin Text and English Translation*, vol. 1–2. Arbeiten zur Geschichte des antiken Judentums und des Urchristentums 31. Leiden: Brill.
Jaubert, A. 1971–72. "Le Voile des Femmes (1 Cor 11.2–16)," *New Testament Studies* 18: 419–30.
Jenson, R. 1999. *Systematic Theology, Vol. 2: The Works of God*. Oxford: Oxford University Press.
Jeremias, J. 1964. "Αδάμ." In *Theological Dictionary of the New Testament*, eds. G. Kittel, G. Friedrich, G.W. Bromily, I.141–43. Grand Rapids: Eerdmans.
Jervell, J.S. 1960. *Imago Dei: Gen 1,26f. im Spätjudentum, in der Gnosis und in den paulinischen Briefen*. Forschungen zur Religion und Literatur des Alten und Neuen Testaments H. 76. Göttingen: Vandenhoeck & Ruprecht.
Jewett, P. 1985. *Election and Predestination*. Grand Rapids: Eerdmans.
Jewett, R. 2004. "The Corruption and Redemption of Creation: Reading Rom 8:18–23 within the Imperial Context." In *Paul and the Roman Imperial Order*, ed. R.A. Horsley, 25–46. Harrisburg: Trinity Press International.
–. 2007. *Romans: A Commentary*. Hermeneia. Minneapolis: Fortress Press.
Jobes, K. 2000. "Sophia-Christology: The Way of Wisdom?" In *The Way of Wisdom: Essays in Honour of Bruce K. Waltke*, eds. J.I. Packer and S.K. Soderlund, 226–50. Grand Rapids: Zondervan.
Johnston, P.S. 2002. *Shades of Sheol: Death and Afterlife in the Old Testament*. Leicester: Apollos.
Jónsson, G.A. 1988. *The Image of God: Genesis 1:26–28 in a Century of Old Testament Research*, Coniectanea Biblica Old Testament Series 26. Stockholm: Almqvist & Wiksell International.

Kammler, H.-C. 2003. *Kreuz und Weisheit: Eine exegetische Untersuchung zu 1 Kor 1,10–3,4*. Wissenschaftliche Untersuchungen zum Neuen Testament 159. Tübingen: Mohr Siebeck.
Käsemann, E. 1980. *Commentary on Romans*. Translated and edited by G.W. Bromiley. Grand Rapids: Eerdmans.
Kidner, D. 1967. *Genesis*. Tyndale Old Testament Commentary. Downers Grove: InterVarsity Press.
Kim, S. 1980. *The Origin of Paul's Gospel*. Wissenschaftliche Untersuchungen zum Neuen Testament 2.4. Tübingen: Mohr Siebeck.
–. 2002. *Paul and the New Perspective: Second Thoughts on the Origin of Paul's Gospel*. Grand Rapids: Eerdmans.
Kim, Y.S. 2008. *Christ's Body in Corinth: the Politics of a Metaphor*. Minneapolis: Fortress Press.
Kistemaker, S. 1993. *Exposition of the First Epistle to the Corinthians*. New Testament Commentary. Grand Rapids: Baker Academic.
Kline, M.G. 1980. *Images of the Spirit*. Eugene, OR: Wipf and Stoic.
Knibb, M.A. 1989. "The Adam Literature," *The Expository Times* 101.1: 29–30.
Kraus, H.-J. 1993. *Psalm 1–59*. Translated by H.C. Oswald. Continental Commentaries. Minneapolis: Fortress Press.
Kremer, J. 1997. *Der Erste Brief an die Korinther*. Regensburger Neues Testament. Regensburg.
Kugel, J.L. 1998. *Traditions of the Bible: A Guide to the Bible as it Was at the Start of the Christian Era*. Cambridge: Harvard University Press.
Kuschel, K.-J. 1992. *Born Before All Time? The Dispute over Christ's Origin*. Translated by J. Bowden. London: SCM Press.
Lambrecht, J. 1981. "Paul's Christological Use of Scripture in 2 Cor. 15.20–28," *New Testament Studies* 28: 502–527.
Lampe, G.W.H. 1964. "The New Testament Doctrine of *KTISIS*," *Scottish Journal of Theology* 17: 449–62.
Lampe, P. 1990. "Theological Wisdom and the 'Word About the Cross': The Rhetorical Scheme in 1 Corinthians 1–4," *Interpretation* 44 (January): 117–31.
Lange, A. 1995. *Weisheit und Prädestination: Weisheitliche Urordnung und Prädestination in den Textfunden von Qumran*. Studies on the Texts of the Desert of Judah 18. Leiden: Brill.
Laporte, J. 1976. "Philo in the Tradition of Biblical Wisdom Literature." In *Aspects of Wisdom in Judaism and Early Christianity*, ed. R.L. Wilken, 103–41. Notre Dame: University of Notre Dame Press.
Lee, A.C.C. 1993. "Genesis 1 from the Perspective of a Chinese Creation Myth." In *Understanding Poets and Prophets: Essays in Honour of George Wishart Anderson*, ed. A.G. Auld, 186–98. Journal for the Study of the Old Testament Supplement Series 152. Sheffield: Sheffield Academic Press.
Leonhardt-Balzer, J. 2004A. "Creation, the Logos and the Foundation of a City: A Few Comments on *Opif.* 15–25." In *Philo und das Neue Testament: Wechselseitige Wahrnehmungen – Internationales Symposium zum Corpus Judaeo-Hellenisticum, 1.-4. Mai 2003, Eisenach/Jena*, eds. R. Deines, K.-W. Niebuhr, 324–44. Wissenschaftliche Untersuchungen zum Neuen Testament 172. Tübingen: Mohr Siebeck.
–. 2004B. "Der Logos und die Schöpfung: Streiflichter bei Philo (Op 20–25) und im Johannesprolog (Joh 1,1–18)." In *Kontexte des Johannesevangeliums: Das vierte Evangelium in religions- und traditionsgeschichtlicher Perspektive*, eds. J. Frey, U.

Schnelle, 295–319. Wissenschaftliche Untersuchungen zum Neuen Testament 175. Tübingen: Mohr Siebeck.

–. 2009. "Heilsgeschichte bei Philo? Die Aufnahme der Zweigeisterlehre in QE I 23." In *Heil und Geschichte: Die Geschichtsbezogenheit des Heils und das Problem der Heilsgeschichte in der biblishen Tradition und in der theologischen Deutung*, eds. J. Frey, S. Krauter, H. Lichtenberger, 129–47. Wissenschaftliche Untersuchungen zum Neuen Testament 248. Tübingen: Mohr Siebeck.

Levison, J.R. 1988. *Portraits of Adam in Early Judaism: From Sirach to 2 Baruch*. Journal for the Study of the Pseudepigrapha Supplement Series 1. Sheffield: Sheffield Academic Press.

Lewis, S. 1999. "So that God may be All in All: 1 Corinthians 15:12–34," *Liber Annuus* 49: 195–210.

Lincoln, A. 1990. *Ephesians*. Word Biblical Commentary. Dallas: Word Books.

Lindemann, A. 1997. "Die Auferstehung der Toten: Adam und Christus nach 1.Kor 15." In *Eschatologie und Schöpfung, Festschrift für Erich Gräßer*, eds. M. Evang, H. Merklein, M. Wolter, 155–67. Berlin: Walter de Gruyter.

Link-Salinger, R., ed. 1989. *Of Scholars, Savants, and their Texts: Studies in Philosophy and Religious Thought, Essays in Honor of Arthur Hyman*. New York: Peter Lang.

Loader, W. 2004. *The Septuagint, Sexuality, and the New Testament: Case Studies on the Impact of the LXX in Philo and the New Testament*. Grand Rapids: Eerdmans.

Lockwood, G. 2000. *1 Corinthians: A Theological Exposition of Sacred Scripture*. Concordia Commentary. Saint Louis, MO: Concordia Publishing House.

Longman, T., III. 2006. *Proverbs*. Baker Commentary on the Old Testament Wisdom and Psalms. Grand Rapids: Baker Academic.

Lorenzen, S. 2008. *Das paulinische Eikon-Konzept: Semantische Analysen zur Sapientia Salomonis, zu Philo und den Paulusbriefen*. Wissenschaftliche Untersuchungen zum Neuen Testament 2.250. Mohr Siebeck.

Lumbala, F.K. 1999. "1 Corinthians 15:1–58: An African Perspective." In *Return to Babel: Global Perspectives on the Bible*, eds. J.R. Levison and P. Pope-Levison, 189–92. Westminster John Knox Press.

Luther, M. 1883–1993. *Dr. Martin Luthers Werke*. 65 vols. Weimar: H. Böhlau.

Luz, U. 1969. "The Image of God in Christ and Mankind: New Testament Perspectives," *Concilium* 10.5 (December): 41–46.

Marcus, R. 1948. "Notes on the Armenian Text of Philo's *Quaestiones in Genesin*, Books I-III," *Journal of Near Eastern Studies* 7.2 (April): 111–15.

Martin-Achard, R. 1960. *From Death to Life: A Study of the Development of the Doctrine of the Resurrection in the Old Testament*. Edinburgh: Oliver & Boyd.

Martin, D. 1992. *The Corinthian Body*. New Haven: Yale University Press.

Martin, R.P. 1983. *Carmen Christi: Philippians ii.5–11 in recent interpretation and in the setting of Early Christian Worship*. Grand Rapids: Eerdmans.

Martin, T.W. 2005. "Veiled Exhortations Regarding the Veil: Ethos as the Controlling Proof in Moral Persuasion (1 Cor. 11:2–16)." In *Rhetoric, Ethic, and Moral Persuasion in Biblical Discourse*, eds. T.H. Olbricht and A. Eriksson, 255–73. New York: T&T Clark International.

Martin, W.J. 1970. "I Corinthians 11:2–16: An Interpretation." In *Apostolic History and the Gospel: Biblical and Historical Essays presented to F. F. Bruce on his 60th Birthday*, eds. W. Ward Gasque and R.P. Martin, 231–41. Exeter: Paternoster.

Matera, F.J. 2003. *II Corinthians: A Commentary*. New Testament Library. Louisville: Westminster John Knox.

Mathews, K.A. 1996. *Genesis 1–11:26: An Exegetical and Theological Exposition of Holy Scripture NIV Text*. The New American Commentary 1A. Nashville: Broadman & Holman Publishers.
May, G. 1994. *Creatio Ex Nihilo: The Doctrine of "Creation out of Nothing" in Early Christian Thought*. Translated by A.S. Worrall. Edinburgh: T&T Clark.
McCasland, S.V. 1950. "The Image of God According to Paul," *Journal of Biblical Literature* 69.2: 85–100.
McGinn, S.E. 1996. "'*Exousia echein epi tês kephalês*:' 1 Cor 11:10 and the Ecclesial Authority of Women," *Listening: Journal of Religion and Culture* 31.2 (Spring): 91–104.
Meier, J.P. 1978. "On the Veiling of Hermeneutics (1 Cor. 2:2–16)," *Catholic Biblical Quarterly* 40: 212–26.
Meyer, J.C. 2009. *The End of the Law: Mosaic Covenant in Pauline Theology*. Nashville: B&H Academic.
Michaelis, W. 1968. "πρωτότοκος." In *Theological Dictionary of the New Testament*, eds. G. Kittel, G. Friedrich, G.W. Bromily, VI.871–82. Grand Rapids: Eerdmans.
Mickelsen, B. and A. Mickelsen. 1986. "What Does *Kephale* Mean in the New Testament?" In *Women, Authority and the Bible*, ed. A. Mickelsen, 97–110. Downers Grove: InterVarsity.
Minear, P.S. 1994. *Christians and New Creation: Genesis Motifs in the New Testament*. Louisville: Westminster John Knox Press.
Mitchell, M.M. 1991. *Paul and the Rhetoric of Reconciliation: An Exegetical Investigation of the Language and Composition of 1 Corinthians*. Hermeneutische Untersuchungen zur Theologie 28. Tübingen: Mohr Siebeck.
Moffatt, J. 1938. *The First Epistle of Paul to the Corinthians*. London: Hodder and Stoughton.
Moiser, J. 1992. "1 Corinthians 15," *Irish Biblical Studies* 14 (January): 10–30.
Moltmann, J. 1985. *God in Creation: An Ecological Doctrine of Creation*. London: SCM Press.
Moo, D.J. 1996. *The Epistle to the Romans*. New International Commentary on the New Testament. Grand Rapids: Eerdmans.
–. 2006. "Nature in the New Creation: New Testament Eschatology and the Environment," *Journal of the Evangelical Theological Society* 49: 449–88.
Moo, J. 2008. "Romans 8.19–22 and Isaiah's Cosmic Covenant," *New Testament Studies* 54: 74–89.
Morissette, R. 1972A. "La citation du Psaume VIII,7b dans 1 Corinthiens XV,27a," *Science et Esprit* 24: 313–42.
–. 1972B. "La condition de ressuscité. 1 Corinthiens 15,35–49: structure littéraire de la péricope," *Biblica* 53: 208–28.
Morris, L. 1985. *The First Epistle of Paul to the Corinthians: An Introduction and Commentary*. Tyndale New Testament Commentaries. Grand Rapids: Eerdmans.
Muddiman, J. 1994. "'I Believe in the Resurrection of the Body'," in *Resurrection: Essays in Honour of Leslie Houlden*, eds. S. Barton and G. Stanton, 128–38. London: SPCK.
Murphy-O'Connor, J. 1978A. "1 Cor. 8:6: Cosmology or Soteriology," *Revue Biblique* 85: 253–67.
–. 1978B. "Freedom or the Ghetto (1 Co8,1–13;10,23–11,1)," *Revue Biblique* 85:543–74.
–. 1980. "Sex and Logic in 1 Corinthians," *Catholic Biblical Quarterly* 42: 482–500.
Murphy, R.E. 1985. "Wisdom and Creation," *Journal of Biblical Literature* 104.1: 3–11.

Murray, J. 1959. *The Epistle to the Romans: The English Text with Introduction, Exposition and Notes.* New Testament Commentary. Grand Rapids: Eerdmans.
Neusner, J. 1978. "Review of E.P. Sanders, *Paul and Palestinian Judaism,*" *History of Religions* 18: 177–91.
Newman, C.C. 1992. *Paul's Glory-Christology: Tradition and Rhetoric.* Leiden: Brill.
Nguyen, V.H.T. 2008. *Christian Identity in Corinth: A Comparative Study of 2 Corinthians, Epictetus and Valerius Maximus.* Wissenschaftliche Untersuchungen zum Neuen Testament 2.243. Tübingen: Mohr Siebeck.
Nickelsburg, G.W.E. 1981. *Jewish Literature Between the Bible and the Mishnah: A Historical and Literary Introduction.* London: SCM Press.
–. 2004. "Philo among Greeks, Jews and Christians." In *Philo und das Neue Testament: Wechselseitige Wahrnehmungen – Internationales Symposium zum Corpus Judaeo-Hellenisticum, 1.-4. Mai 2003, Eisenach/Jena*, eds. R. Deines, K.-W. Niebuhr, 53–72. Wissenschaftliche Untersuchungen zum Neuen Testament 172. Tübingen: Mohr Siebeck.
Nikiprowetzky, V. 1977. *Le commentaire de L'Écriture chez Philon d'Alexandrie.* Leiden: Brill.
Noort, E. 2000. "The Creation of Man and Woman in Biblical and Ancient Near Eastern Traditions." In *The Creation of Man and Woman: Interpretations of the Biblical Narratives in Jewish and Christian Traditions*, ed. G.P. Luttikhuizen, 1–18. Themes in Biblical Narrative: Jewish and Christian Traditions I. Leiden: Brill.
–. 2005. "The Creation of Light in Genesis 1:1–5: Remarks on the Function of Light and Darkness in the Opening Verses of the Hebrew Bible." In *Creation of Heaven and Earth: Re-Interpretation of Genesis 1 in the Context of Judaism, Ancient Philosophy, Christianity, and Modern Physics*, ed. G. van Kooten, 3–20. Themes in Biblical Narrative 8. Leiden: Brill.
Norden, E. 1923. *Agnostos Theos: Untersuchungen zur Formgeschichte religiöser Rede.* Teubner: Leipzig.
O'Collins, G. 1997. "The Resurrection: The State of the Questions." In *The Resurrection: An Interdisciplinary Symposium on the Resurrection of Jesus*, eds. S.T. Davis, D. Kendall, G. O'Collins, 5–28. Oxford: Oxford Uni. Press.
Orr, W.F and J.A. Walther. 1976. *1 Corinthians: A New Translation; Introduction with a Study of the Life of Paul, Notes, and Commentary.* Anchor Bible 32. Garden City, NY: Doubleday & Company.
Paas, S. 2003. *Creation & Judgment: Creation Texts in Some Eighth Century Prophets.* Leiden: Brill.
Padgett, A.G. 1984. "Paul on Women in the Church: The Contradiction of Coiffure in 1 Cor 11.2–16," *Journal for the Study of the New Testament* 20: 69–86.
–. 2002. "The Body in Resurrection: Science and Scripture on the 'Spiritual Body' (1 Cor 15:35–58)," *Word and World* 22.2: 155–63.
Parker, K.I. 2005. "Adam: The Postmodernist Bourgeois Liberal?," *Journal for the Study of the Old Testament* 29.4: 439–53
Pearce, V. 1969. *Who Was Adam?* Exeter: Paternoster Press.
Pearson, B.A. 1973. *The Pneumatikos-Psychikos Terminology in 1 Corinthians: A Study in the Theology of the Corinthian Opponents of Paul and its Relation to Gnosticism.* Dissertation Series (Society of Biblical Literature) 12. Missoula, MT: Scholars Press.
–. 1975. "Hellenistic-Jewish Wisdom Speculation and Paul." In *Aspects of Wisdom in Judaism and Early Christianity*, ed. R. Wilken, 43–66. Notre Dame: University of Notre Dame.

–. 1984. "Philo and Gnosticism." In *Aufstieg und Niedergang der römischen Welt* II.21.1: *Religion*, ed. W. Haase, 295–342. Hellenistisches Judentum in römischen Zeit: Philon und Josephus. Berlin: Walter de Gruyter.
Peerbolte, L.J. 2000. "Man, Woman, and the Angels in 1 Cor 11:2–16," In *The Creation of Man and Woman: Interpretations of the Biblical Narratives in Jewish and Christian Traditions*, ed. G.P. Luttikhuizen, 76–92. Themes in Biblical Narrative: Jewish and Christian Traditions I. Leiden: Brill.
Penner, T. and C. Vander Stichele. 2005. "Unveiling Paul: Gender *Ethos* in 1 Corinthians 11:2–16." In *Rhetoric, Ethic, and Moral Persuasion in Biblical Discourse*, eds. T.H. Olbricht and A. Eriksson, 214–37. New York: T&T Clark International.
Perdue, L.G. 1994. *Wisdom and Creation: The Theology of Wisdom Literature*. Nashville: Abingdon Press.
Petit, F. 1973. *L'ancienne version latine des Questions sur la Genèse de Philon d'Alexandre*. Berlin : Akademie-Verlag.
Piper, O. 1954. "Review of G. Lindeskog, *Studien zum neutestamentlichen Schöpfungsgedanken* (Uppsala: Uppsala University, 1952)," *Journal of Religion* 34.3: 218–19.
Polkinghorne, J. 1994. *Science and Christian Belief: Theological Reflections of a Bottom-Up Thinker*. London: SPCK Publishing.
Porter, S. 1999. "Resurrection, the Greeks and the New Testament." In *Resurrection*, eds. S. Porter, M. Hayes, D. Tombs, 52–81. Journal for the Study of the New Testament Supplement Series 186. Sheffield: Sheffield Academic Press.
Poythress, V.S. 2006. *Redeeming Science: A God-Centered Approach*. Wheaton: Crossway Books.
Prior, D. 1985. *The Message of 1 Corinthians*. Downers Grove: InterVarsity Press.
Probst, H. 1991. *Paulus und der Brief: Die Rhetorik des antiken Briefes als Form der paulinischen Korintherkorrespondenz (1 Kor 8–10)*. Wissenschaftliche Untersuchungen zum Neuen Testament 2.45. Tübingen: Mohr (Siebeck).
Quek, S.-H. 1980. "Adam and Christ According to Paul." In *Pauline Studies: Essays presented to Professor F. F. Bruce on his 70th Birthday*, eds. D.A. Hagner and M.J. Harris, 67–79. Grand Rapids: Eerdmans.
Radice, R. 1989. *Platonismo e creazionismo in Filone di Alessandria*. Milan: Vita e Pensiero.
–. 1991. "Observations on the Theory of the Ideas as the Thoughts of God in Philo of Alexandria." In *Heirs of the Septuagint. Philo, Hellenistic Judaism and Early Christianity: Festschrift for Earle Hilgert*, eds. D.T. Runia, D.M. Hay, D. Winston, 126–34. Brown Judaic Studies 230. Atlanta: Scholars Press.
–. 2009. "Philo's Theology and Theory of Creation." In *The Cambridge Companion to Philo*, ed. A. Kamesar, 124–45. Cambridge: Cambridge University Press.
Rainbow, P.A. 1991. "Jewish Monotheism as the Matrix for New Testament Christology: A Review Article," *Novum Testamentum* 32.1: 78–91.
Reiling, J. 1988. "Wisdom and the Spirit: An Exegesis of 1 Corinthians 2,6–16." In *Text and Testimony: Essays in New Testament and Apocalyptic Literature in Honour of A. F. J. Klijn*, eds. Baarda, Hilhorst, Luttikhuizen, and van der Woude, 200–11. Kampen: Uitgeversmaatschappij J. H. Kok.
Reumann, J. 1973. *Creation and New Creation: The Past, Present, and Future of God's Creative Activity*. Minneapolis: Augsburg Publishing House.
Reymond, R.L. 1998. *A New Systematic Theology of the Christian Faith*. Nashville: Thomas Nelson Publishers.
Richardson, N. 1994. *Paul's Language about God*. Journal for the Study of the New Testament Supplement Series 99. Sheffield: Sheffield Academic Press.

Ridderbos, H. 1975. *Paul: An Outline of His Theology*. Translated by J.R. de Witt. Grand Rapids: Eerdmans.
Ringe, S. 1999. *Wisdom's Friends: Community and Christology in the Fourth Gospel*. Louisville: Westminster John Knox Press.
Robertson, A., and A. Plummer. 1911. *A Critical and Exegetical Commentary on the First Epistle of St Paul to the Corinthians*. International Critical Commentary. Edinburgh: T&T Clark.
Rösel, M. 1994. *Übersetzung als Vollendung der Auslegung: Studien zur Genesis-Septuaginta*. Beihefte zur Zeitschrift für die altestamentliche Wissenschaft 223. Berlin: de Gruyter.
Rowe, C.K. 2005. "New Testament Iconography? Situating Paul in the Absence of Material Evidence." In *Picturing the New Testament: Studies in Ancient Visual Images*, eds. A. Weissenrieder, F. Wendt, P. von Gemünden, 289–312. Wissenschaftliche Untersuchungen zum Neuen Testament 2.193. Tübingen: Mohr Siebeck.
Ruef, J. 1977. *Paul's First Letter to Corinth*. London: SCM Press.
Runes, D.D., ed. 2001. *The Dictionary of Judaism*. Philosophical Library: Concise Dictionaries. New York: Kensington Publishing Corporation.
Runia, D.T. 1986. *Philo of Alexandria and the* Timaeus *of Plato*. Philosophia Antiqua 44. Leiden: Brill.
–. 1990. "Philo, Alexandrian and Jew." In *Exegesis and Philosophy: Studies on Philo of Alexandria*, by D.T. Runia, I.1–18. Collected Studies 332. London: Variorum.
–. 1990. "How to Read Philo." In *Exegesis and Philosophy: Studies on Philo of Alexandria*, by D.T. Runia, II.185–98. Collected Studies 332. London: Variorum.
–. 1990. "Naming and Knowing: Themes in Philonic Theology with Special Reference to the *De Mutatione Nominum*." In *Exegesis and Philosophy: Studies on Philo of Alexandria*, by D.T. Runia, XI. Collected Studies 332. London: Variorum.
–. 1993. "Was Philo a Middle Platonist?" *Studia Philonica Annual* 5: 112–140.
–. 2000. *Philo of Alexandria: an Annotated Bibliography 1987–1996*. Supplements to Vigiliae Christianae 57. Leiden: Brill.
–. 2001. *Philo of Alexandria: On the Creation of the Cosmos according to Moses; Introduction, Translation and Commentary*. Philo of Alexandria Commentary Series 1. Leiden: Brill.
Runia, D.T. and R. Radice. 1988. *Philo of Alexandria: an Annotated Bibliography 1937–1986*. Supplements to Vigiliae Christianae 8. Leiden: Brill.
Sacks, R.D. 1990. *A Commentary on the Book of Genesis*. Ancient Near Eastern Texts and Studies 6. Lewiston, NY: Edwin Mellen Press.
Sailhamer, J.H. 1990. "Genesis." The Expositor's Bible Commentary, vol. 2. Grand Rapids: Zondervan.
–. 1992. *Pentateuch as Narrative: A Biblical Theological Commentary*. Grand Rapids: Zondervan.
Sanday, W. and A.C. Headlam. 1896. *A Critical and Exegetical Commentary on the Epistle to the Romans*. International Critical Commentary. Edinburgh: T&T Clark.
Sanders, E.P. 1992. *Judaism: Practice and Belief 63BCE – 66 CE*. London: SCM Press.
Sanders, J.T. 1971. *The New Testament Christological Hymns: Their Historical Religious Background*. Cambridge: Cambridge University Press.
Sandmel, S. 1983. "Philo Judaeus: An Introduction to the Man, his Writings, and his Significance." In *Aufstieg und Niedergang der römischen Welt: Geschichte und Kultur Roms im Spiegel der neueren Forschung*, eds. H. Temporini and W. Haase, 3–46. Berlin: Walter de Gruyter.

Schaller, B. 1990. "Ἀδάμ." In *Exegetical Dictionary of the New Testament*, vol. 1, eds. H. Betz and G. Schneider, 27–28. Grand Rapids: Eerdmans.
–. 2004. "Adam und Christus bei Paulus. Oder: Über Brauch und Fehlbrauch von Philo in der neutestamentlichen Forschung." In *Philo und das Neue Testament: Wechselseitige Wahrnehmungen – Internationales Symposium zum Corpus Judaeo-Hellenisticum, 1.-4. Mai 2003, Eisenach/Jena*, eds. R. Deines, K.-W. Niebuhr, 53–72. Wissenschaftliche Untersuchungen zum Neuen Testament 172. Tübingen: Mohr Siebeck.
Schmid, J. 1959. "Die alttestamentlichen Zitate bei Paulus und die Theoria vom sensus plenior," *Biblische Zeitschrift* 3: 161–73.
Schnabel, E. 1985. *J. Law and Wisdom from Ben Sira to Paul: A Tradition Historical Enquiry into the Relation of Law, Wisdom, and Ethics*. Wissenschaftliche Untersuchungen zum Neuen Testament 2.16. Tübingen: J. C. B. Mohr (Paul Siebeck).
Schrage, W. 1991–2001. *Der erste Brief an die Korinther*. 4 vols. Evangelisch-Katholischer Kommentar zum Neuen Testament. Zürich: Benziger; Neukirchener-Vluyn: Neukirchener Verlag.
–. 1997. "Das messianische Zwischenreich bei Paulus." In *Eschatologie und Schöpfung, Festschrift für Erich Gräßer*, eds. M. Evang, H. Merklein, M. Wolter, 343–54. Berlin: Walter de Gruyter.
Schreiner, T.R. 1991. "Head Coverings, Prophecies and the Trinity: 1 Corinthians 11:2–16." In *Recovering Biblical Manhood and Womanhood: A Response to Evangelical Feminism*, eds. J. Piper and W. Grudem, 124–39. Wheaton: Crossway.
–. 1998. *Romans*. Baker Exegetical Commentaries on the New Testament 6. Grand Rapids: Baker Academic.
–. 2006. *Paul, Apostle of God's Glory in Christ: A Pauline Theology*. Downers Grove, InterVarsity Press.
Schüle, A. 2005. "Made in the 'Image of God': The Concepts of Divine Images in Gen 1–3," *Zeitschrift für die alttestamentliche Wissenschaft* 117: 1–20.
Schüssler-Fiorenza, E. 1983. *In Memory of Her: A Feminist Theological Reconstruction of Christian Origins*. New York: Crossroads.
Schwarz, H. 2002. *Creation*. Grand Rapids: Eerdmans.
Scott, J.M. 1997. "Paul's *Imago Mundi*' and Scripture." In *Evangelium, Schriftauslegung, Kirche. Festschrift für Peter Stuhlmacher*, eds. J. Adna, S.J. Hafemann, O. Hofius, 366–81. Göttingen: Vandenhoeck & Ruprecht.
Scott, R.B.Y. 1965. *Proverbs and Ecclesiastes*. Anchor Bible 18. Garden City: Doubleday.
Scroggs, R. 1966. *The Last Adam: A Study in Pauline Anthropology*. Oxford: Basil Blackwell.
–. 1967–68. "Paul: ΣΟΦΟΣ and ΠΝΕΥΜΑΤΙΚΟΣ," *New Testament Studies* 14: 33–55.
–. 1972. "Paul and the Eschatological Woman," *Journal of the American Academy of Religion* 40.3: 283–303.
–. 1974. "Paul and the Eschatological Woman: Revisited," *Journal of the American Academy of Religion* 42.3: 532–37.
Seebaß, H. 1975. "Ἀδάμ." In *The New International Dictionary of New Testament Theology*, ed. C. Brown, I.84–87. Exeter: The Paternoster Press.
–. 1996. *Genesis I: Urgeschichte (1,1–11,26)*. Neukirchener: Neukirchen-Vluyn.
Segal, A. 1990. *Paul the Convert: The Apostolate and Apostasy of Saul the Pharisee*. New Haven: Yale University Press.
Seifrid, M. 2007. "Romans." In *Commentary on the New Testament Use of the Old Testament*, eds. G.K. Beale and D.A. Carson, 607–94. Grand Rapids: Baker Academic.

Sellin, G. 1986. *Der Streit um die Auferstehung der Toten: Eine religionsgeschichtliche und exegetische Untersuchung von 1 Korinther 15*. Forschungen zur Religion und Literatur des Alten und Neuen Testaments 138. Göttingen: Vandenhoeck & Ruprecht.

Senft, C. 1979. *La Première Épitre de Saint-Paul aux Corinthiens*. Paris: Delachaux & Niestle Editeurs.

Sheppard, G.T. 1980. *Wisdom as a Hermeneutical Construct: A Study in the Sapientalizing of the Old Testament*. Berlin: Walter de Gruyter.

Sider, R.J. 1975. "The Pauline Conception of the Resurrection Body in 1 Corinthians 15.35–54," *New Testament Studies* 21: 428–39.

–. 1977. "St. Paul's Understanding of the Nature and Significance of the Resurrection in 1 Corinthians XV 1–19," *Novum Testamentum* 19: 124–41.

Siegert, F. 2009. "Philo and the New Testament." In *The Cambridge Companion to Philo*, ed. A. Kamesar, 175–209. Cambridge Companions to Philosophy. Cambridge: Cambridge University Press.

Simon, W.G.H. 1959. *The First Epistle to the Corinthians*. London: SCM Press.

Skehan, P.W. 1979. "Structures in Poems on Wisdom: Proverbs 8 and Sirach 24," *Catholic Biblical Quarterly* 41: 365–79.

Skehan, P.W. and A.A. Di Lella. 1987. *The Wisdom of Ben Sira: A New Translation with Notes*. Anchor Bible 39. New York: Doubleday.

Skinner, J. 1910. *A Critical and Exegetical Commentary on Genesis*. The International Critical Commentary. Edinburgh: T&T Clark.

Stanley, C.D. 1992. *Paul and the Language of Scripture: Citation Technique in the Pauline Epistles and Contemporary Literature*. Society for New Testament Studies Monograph Series 69. Cambridge: Cambridge University Press.

Steenburg, D. 1988. "The Case Against the Synonymity of *Morphe* and *Eikon*," *Journal for the Study of the New Testament* 34: 77–86.

–. 1990. "The Worship of Adam and Christ as the Image of God." *Journal for the Study of the New Testament* 39: 95–109.

Sterling, G.E. 1995. "Wisdom Among the Perfect: Creation Traditions in Alexandrian Judaism and Corinthian Christianity," *Novum Testamentum* 37.4: 355–84.

–. 1997. "Prepositional Metaphysics in Jewish Wisdom Speculation and Early Christian Liturgical Texts," *Studia Philonica Annual* 9: 220–21.

–. 1999. "Review of G.J. Warne, *Hebrew Perspectives on the Human Person in the Hellenistic Era: Philo and Paul*, Mellen Biblical Press Series 35. Lewiston, NY: Mellen, 1995," *Review of Biblical Literature* (15 February).

–. 2004. "The Place of Philo of Alexandria in the Study of Christian Origins." In *Philo und das Neue Testament: Wechselseitige Wahrnehmungen–Internationales Symposium zum Corpus Judaeo-Hellenisticum, 1.–4. Mai 2003, Eisenach/Jena*, eds. R. Deines, K.-W. Niebuhr, 21–52. Wissenschaftliche Untersuchungen zum Neuen Testament 172. Tübingen: Mohr Siebeck, 2004.

Stockhausen, C.K. 1989. *Moses' Veil and the Glory of the New Covenant: The Exegetical Substructure of II Cor. 3,1–4,6*. Rome: Editrice Pontificio Istituto Biblico.

Stordalen, T. 1992. "Genesis 2,4: Restudying a *locus classicus*," *Zeitschrift für die alttestamentliche Wissenschaft* 104: 163–77.

Stuckenbruck, L. 2001. "Why Should Women Cover Their Heads Because of the Angels? (1 Corinthians 11:10)," *Stone-Campbell Journal* 4.2: 205–34.

–. 2002. "4QInstruction and the Possible Influence of Early Enoch Traditions: An Evaluation." In *The Wisdom Texts from Qumran and the Development of Sapiential Thought*, eds. C. Hempel, A. Lange, H. Lichtenberger, 245–61. Leuven: Leuven University Press.

Stuhlmacher, P. 1987. "The Hermeneutical Significance of 1 Cor. 2:6–16." In *Tradition and Interpretation in the New Testament: Essays in Honor of E. Earle Ellis for His 60th Birthday*, eds. G.F. Hawthorne and O. Betz, 328–47. Grand Rapids: Eerdmans/Tübingen: J.C.B. Mohr (Paul Siebeck).
–. 1994. *Paul's Letter to the Romans: A Commentary*. Translated by S.J. Hafemann. Louisville: Westminster/John Knox Press.
Talbert, C.H. 2002. *Reading Corinthians: A Literary and Theological Commentary on 1 and 2 Corinthians*. Macon, GA: Smyth & Helwys Publishing.
Tamez, E. 1999. "1 Corinthians 15:1–58: A Latin American Perspective." In *Return to Babel: Global Perspectives on the Bible*, eds. J.R. Levison and P. Pope-Levison, 185–88. Westminster John Knox Press.
Thackeray, H.St.J. 1921. *The Septuagint and Jewish Worship: A Study in Origins*. London: Oxford University Press.
Theissen, G. 1987. *Psychological Aspects of Pauline Theology*. Translation by J.P. Galvin. Edinburgh: T&T Clark.
Thielman, F. 2005. *Theology of the New Testament: A Canonical and Synthetic Approach*. Grand Rapids: Zondervan.
Thiselton, A.C. 1978. "Realized Eschatology in Corinth," *New Testament Studies* 24: 510–26.
–. 2000. *The First Epistle to the Corinthians*. New International Greek Testament Commentary. Grand Rapids: Eerdmans.
–. 2006A. *First Corinthians: a shorter exegetical and pastoral commentary*. Grand Rapids: Eerdmans.
–. 2006B. "The Significance of Recent Research on 1 Corinthians for Hermeneutical Appropriation of this Epistle Today," *Neotestamenica* 40.2: 320–52.
Thrall, M.E. 1973. "Christ Crucified or Second Adam? A Christological Debate between Paul and the Corinthians." In *Christ and Spirit in the New Testament*, eds. B. Lindars and S. Smalley, 143–56. Cambridge: Cambridge University Press.
–. 1994–2000. *A Critical and Exegetical Commentary on the Second Epistle to the Corinthians*. 2 vols. International Critical Commentary. Edinburgh: T&T Clark.
Tigchelaar, E.J.C. 2005. "'Lights Serving as Signs for Festivals' (Genesis 1:14b) in Enuma Elis and Early Judaism." In *Creation of Heaven and Earth: Re-Interpretation of Genesis 1 in the Context of Judaism, Ancient Philosophy, Christianity, and Modern Physics*, ed. G. van Kooten, 31–48. Themes in Biblical Narrative 8. Leiden: Brill.
Trible, P. 1993. "Treasures Old and New: Biblical Theology and the Challenge of Feminism." In *The Open Text: New Directions For Biblical Studies?* ed. F. Watson, 32–56. London: SCM Press.
Tobin, T. 1983. *The Creation of Man: Philo and the History of Interpretation*. Catholic Biblical Quarterly Monograph Series 14. Washington, D.C.: The Catholic Biblical Association.
–. 1992. "Interpretations of the Creation of the World in Philo of Alexandria." In *Creation in the Biblical Traditions*, eds. R.J. Clifford and J.J. Collins, 108–28. Catholic Biblical Quarterly Monograph Series 24.
Toews, B.G. 2002. "Genesis 1–4: The Genesis of Old Testament Instruction." In *Biblical Theology: Retrospect and Prospect*, ed. S. Hafemann, 38–52. Downers Grove: InterVarsity Press.
Tsumura, D.T. 2005. *Creation and Destruction: A Reappraisal of the* Chaoskampf *Theory in the Old Testament*. Indiana: Eisenbrauns.
Usami, K. 1976. "'How are the Dead Raised?' (1 Cor. 15,25–58)," *Biblica* 57: 468–93.

Van den Hoek, A. 2000. "Endowed with Reason or Glued to the Senses: Philo's Thought on Adam and Eve." In *The Creation of Man and Woman: Interpretations of the Biblical Narratives in Jewish and Christian Traditions*, ed. G.P. Luttikhuizen, 63–75. Themes in Biblical Narrative: Jewish and Christian Traditions I. Leiden: Brill.

Van der Horst, P.W. 2006. "Philo and the Rabbis on Genesis: Similar Questions, Different Answers." In *Jews and Christians in Their Graeco-Roman Context: Selected Essays on Early Judaism, Samaritanism, Hellenism, and Christianity*, by P.W. van der Horst, 114–27. Wissenschaftliche Untersuchungen zum Neuen Testament 196. Tübingen: Mohr Siebeck.

Van Kooten, G.H. 2003. *Cosmic Christology in Paul and the Pauline School: Colossians and Ephesians in the Context of Graeco-Roman Cosmology, with a New Synopsis of the Greek Text*. Wissenschaftliche Untersuchungen zum Neuen Testament 2.171. Tübingen: Mohr Siebeck.

–. 2005. "The 'True Light Which Enlightens Everyone' (*John* 1:9): John, *Genesis*, the Platonic Notion of the 'True, Noetic Light,' and the Allegory of the Cave in Plato's *Republic*." In *Creation of Heaven and Earth: Re-Interpretation of Genesis 1 in the Context of Judaism, Ancient Philosophy, Christianity, and Modern Physics*, ed. G. van Kooten, 149–94. Themes in Biblical Narrative 8. Leiden: Brill.

–. 2008. *Paul's Anthropology in Context: The Image of God, Assimilation to God, and Tripartite Man in Ancient Judaism, Ancient Philosophy and Early Christianity*. Wissenschaftliche Untersuchungen zum Neuen Testament 232. Tübingen:Mohr Siebeck.

Van Till, H.J. 1986. *The Fourth Day: What the Bible and the Heavens are Telling us about the Creation*. Grand Rapids: Eerdmans.

Van Ruiten, J.T.A.G.M. 2000. "The Creation of Man and Woman in Early Jewish Literature." In *The Creation of Man and Woman: Interpretations of the Biblical Narratives in Jewish and Christian Traditions*, ed. G.P. Luttikhuizen, 34–62. Themes in Biblical Narrative: Jewish and Christian Traditions I. Leiden: Brill.

Van Wolde, E. 1996A. *Stories of the Beginning: Genesis 1–11 and Other Creation Stories*. London: SCM Press.

–. 1996B. "The Text as an Eloquent Guide: Rhetorical, Linguistic and Literary Features in Genesis 1." In *Literary Structure and Rhetorical Strategies in the Hebrew Bible*, eds. L.J. de Regt, J. de Waard, J.P. Fokkelman, 134–51. Assen: Van Gorcum.

Vervenne, M. 2001. "Genesis 1,1–2,4: The Compositional Texture of the Priestly Overture to the Pentateuch." In *Studies in the Book of Genesis: Literature, Redaction and History*, ed. A. Wénin, 35–79. Leuven: Leuven University Press.

Von Rad, G. 1956. *Genesis*. Translated by J.H. Marks. London: SCM Press.

–. 1965. "Das theologische Problem des alttestamentlichen Schöpfungsglaubens" (1936). In *Gesammelte Studien zum Alten Testament*, von Rad, 3rd ed., 136–47. Theologische Bücherei 8. München: Kaiser.

–. 1966. "The Theological Problem of the Old Testament Doctrine of Creation." In *The Problem of the Hexateuch and Other Essays*, 131–43. Translated by E.W. Trueman Dicken. London: Oliver & Boyd.

Vorholt, R. 2008. *Der Dienst der Versöhnung: Studien zur Apostolatstheologie bei Paulus*. Wissenschaftliche Monographien zum Alten und Neuen Testament 118. Neukirchen-Vluyn: Neukirchener Verlag.

Vos, G. 1930. *The Pauline Eschatology*. Phillipsburg: P&R Publishing.

Wallace, H.N. 1990. "The Toledot of Adam," in *Studies in the Pentateuch*, ed. J.A. Emerton, 17–33. Leiden: Brill.

Waltke, B. 1975. "The Creation Account of Gen. 1:1–3. Part 4: The Theology of Genesis 1," *Bibliotheca Sacra* 132: 327–42.
Watson, F. 1992. "Strategies of Recovery and Resistance: Hermeneutical Reflections On Genesis 1–3 and Its Pauline Reception," *Journal for the Study of the New Testament* 14.45: 79–103.
–. 1994. *Text, Church and World: Biblical Interpretation in Theological Perspective.* Grand Rapids: Eerdmans.
–. 1997. *Text and Truth: Redefining Biblical Theology.* Edinburgh: T&T Clark.
–. 2000A. *Agape, Eros, Gender: Towards a Pauline Sexual Ethic.* Cambridge: Cambridge University Press.
–. 2000B. "The Authority of the Voice: A Theological Reading of 1 Cor. 11.2–16," *New Testament Studies* 46: 520–36.
–. 2002. "Is there a Story in these Texts?" In *Narrative Dynamics in Paul: A Critical Assessment*, ed. B.W. Longenecker, 231–39. Louisville: Westminster John Knox Press.
–. 2004. *Paul and the Hermeneutics of Faith.* London: T&T Clark.
Watson, N. 1992. *The First Epistle to the Corinthians.* London: Epworth Press.
Wedderburn, A.J.M. 1971. "The Body of Christ and Related Concepts in 1 Corinthians," *Scottish Journal of Theology* 24: 74–96.
–. 1973A. "ἐν τῇ σοφίᾳ τοῦ θεοῦ – 1 Kor. 1.21," *Zeitschrift für die neutestamentliche Wissenschaft* 64: 132–4.
–. 1973B. "Philo's 'Heavenly Man'," *Novum Testamentum* 15.4 (October): 301–26.
–. 1987. *Baptism and Resurrection: Studies in Pauline Theology against Its Graeco-Roman Background*, Wissenschaftliche Untersuchungen zum Neuen Testament 44. Tübingen: Mohr Siebeck.
–. 2004. "Pauline Pneumatology and Pauline Theology." In *The Holy Spirit and Christian Origins: Essays in Honor of James D.G. Dunn*, eds. G.N. Stanton, B.W. Longenecker, S. Barton, 144–56. Grand Rapids: Eerdmans.
Weiss, J. 1910. *Der erste Korintherbrief.* Göttingen: Vandenhoeck & Ruprecht.
Welborn, L.L. 2005. *Paul, the Fool of Christ: A Study of 1 Corinthians 1–4 in the Comic-Philosophic Tradition.* Edinburgh: T&T Clark.
Wenham, G. 1987. *Genesis 1–15.* Word Biblical Commentary. Waco: Word Book.
Westermann, C. 1984. *Genesis 1–11: A Continental Commentary.* Minneapolis: Augsburg Publishing House.
–. 1987. *Genesis: A Practical Commentary.* Grand Rapids: Eerdmans.
Wevers, J.W. 1993. *Notes on the Greek Text of Genesis.* Septuagint and Cognate Studies Series 35. Society of Biblical Literature. Atlanta: Scholars Press.
Whiteley, D.E.H. 1964. *The Theology of St. Paul.* Oxford: Basil Blackwell.
Wilckens, U. 1959. *Weisheit und Torheit: Eine exegetisch-religionsgeschichtliche Untersuchung zu 1 Kor. 1,18 – 2,16.* Beiträge zur historischen Theolgie 26. Tübingen: Mohr.
–. 1971. "σοφία." In *Theological Dictionary of the New Testament*, eds. G. Kittel, G. Friedrich, G.W. Bromiley, VII.496–526. Grand Rapids: Eerdmans.
–. 1975. "Christus der 'letzte Adam' und der Menschensohn. Theologische Überlegungen zum überlieferungsgeschichtlichen Problem der paulinischen Adam-Christus-Anthithese." In *Jesus der Menschensohn: Festschrift für Anton Vögtle*, eds. R. Pesch and R. Schnackenburg, 387–402. Freiburg: Herder.
–. 1979. "Zu 1.Kor 2,1–16." In *Theologia Crucis – Signum Crucis: Festschrift für Erich Dinkler zum 70. Geburtstag*, eds. E. Dinkler, C. Andresen, G. Klein, 501–37. Tübingen: J.C.B. Mohr (Mohr Siebeck).

Williams, H.H.D., III. 2001. *"The Wisdom of the Wise": The Presence and Function of Scripture within 1 Cor. 1:18–3:23*. Arbeiten zur Geschichte des antiken Judentums und des Urchristentums 49. Leiden: Brill.

Williamson, R. 1989. *Jews in the Hellenistic World: Philo*. Cambridge: Cambridge University Press.

Willis, W.L. 1985. *Idol Meat in Corinth: The Pauline Argument in 1 Corinthians 8 and 10*, Society of Biblical Literature Dissertation Series 68. Chico: Scholars Press.

Willms, H. 1935. *EIKΩN: eine begriffsgeschichtliche Untersuchung zum Platonismus, I. Teil: Philon von Alexandreia, mit einer Einleitung über Platon und die Zwischenzeit*. Münster: Aschendorff.

Winston, D. 1979. *The Wisdom of Solomon*. Anchor Bible 43. Garden City: Doubleday.

–. 1983. "Philo's Doctrine of Free Will." In *Two Treatises of Philo of Alexandria*, eds. D. Winston and J. Dillon, 181–95. Brown Judaic Studies 25. Chico: Scholars Press.

–. 2001. "Philo's Theory of Eternal Creation: *De Prov.* 1.6–9." In *The Ancestral Philosophy: Hellenistic Philosophy in Second Temple Judaism: Essays of David Winston*, ed. G.E. Sterling, 117–27. Providence, RI: Brown Judaic Studies.

Winter, B.W. 1997. *Philo and Paul Among the Sophists: Alexandrian and Corinthian Responses to a Julio-Claudian Movement*. Cambridge: Cambridge University Press.

Witherington, B., III. 1994. *Paul's Narrative Thought World: The Tapestry of Tragedy and Triumph*. Louisville: Westminster/John Knox Press.

–. 1995. *Conflict and Community in Corinth: A Socio-Rhetorical Commentary on 1 and 2 Corinthians*. Grand Rapids: Eerdmans.

–. 1998. *The Many Faces of the Christ: The Christologies of the New Testament and Beyond*. New York: The Crossroad Publishing Company.

–. 2000. *Jesus the Sage: The Pilgrimage of Wisdom*. Edinburgh: T&T Clark.

–. 2004. *Paul's Letter to the Romans: A Socio-Rhetorical Commentary*. Grand Rapids: Eerdmans.

Wolfson, H.A. 1947. *Philo*. 2 vols. Cambridge: Harvard University Press.

Wright, N.T. 1991. *The Climax of the Covenant: Christ and the Law in Pauline Theology*. London: T&T Clark Ltd..

–. 2002. "The Letter to the Romans." In *The New Interpreter's Bible*, vol. 10, 395–770. Nashville: Abingdon.

–. 2003. *The Resurrection of the Son of God*. Christian Origins and the Question of God 3. Minneapolis: Fortress Press.

–. 2005. *Paul: In Fresh Perspective*. London: SPCK.

Wuellner, W. 1970. "Haggadic Homily Genre in 1 Corinthians 1–3," *Society of Biblical Literature*: 199–204.

Yates, J.W. 2008. *The Spirit and Creation in Paul*, Wissenschaftliche Untersuchungen zum Neuen Testament 2.251. Tübingen: Mohr Siebeck.

Yee, G. 1992. "The Theology of Creation in Proverbs 8:22–31." In *Creation in the Biblical Traditions*, eds. R.J. Clifford, J.J. Collins, 85–96. Catholic Biblical Quarterly Monograph Series 24. Washington D.C.: The Catholic Biblical Association of America.

Zeller, E. 1962. *Outlines of the History of Greek Philosophy*. 13th edition revised by W. Nestle. Translated by L.R. Palmer. New York: Meridian Books, the World Publishing Company (first edition 1883).

Ziesler, J. 1989. *Paul's Letter to the Romans*. New Testament Commentaries. London: SCM Press.

Index of Ancient Sources

1. Old Testament

Genesis

1	6, 7, 11, 19, 21–7, 28–31, 34–8, 41–5, 46–4, 69, 71, 78, 79, 81, 82, 83, 84, 85, 86, 91–4, 97, 98, 99, 101–07, 110–12, 115–8, 120, 121–34, 135–7, 140, 146, 147–151, 164, 165, 173, 175, 202, 203–04
1–2	2, 3, 5–8, 16, 23–4, 38, 43, 44, 46–9, 81, 93, 142–4, 153–5, 162, 168, 170, 175, 179, 185–7, 202, 205
1–3	8, 10, 14, 28, 199
1–5	126, 186, 203
1:1	22, 24, 25, 29, 31, 33, 37, 39, 48, 61, 62, 94, 95, 100, 104, 107, 164, 201
1:1–2	24, 31, 40, 61, 102–3, 201
1:1–3	29, 31, 84
1:1–5	19, 31, 33, 35, 36, 37, 38, 39, 40, 41, 43, 45, 84, 88, 99, 108, 150, 151
1:1–25	17, 164
1:1–27	19
1:1–31	179
1:1–2:3	42, 43
1:1–2:5	172
1:1–2:7	14
1:2	25, 28, 29, 30, 31, 39, 40, 44, 61, 84, 87, 94, 95, 101, 165, 168, 169, 182
1:2–3	2, 16, 19, 83, 89, 90, 91, 92, 94, 96, 133
1:2–5	39, 79, 81–98, 136
1:3	30, 80, 81–98, 135
1:3ff	62
1:3–4	81, 98
1:3–5	83, 84, 85, 86, 87, 88
1:3–13	90
1:3–31	30
1:4	35–6, 80–7, 98, 110, 136
1:4–5	87
1:5	29, 84, 87
1:6	38–41, 98, 99, 100, 148
1:6–7	80
1:6–8	99, 100, 128
1:6–10	94
1:6–13	125
1:6–25	19, 41
1:6–31	38, 41, 79, 81, 84, 88, 95, 98, 99, 115, 135, 136, 143
1:8	100
1:9	80, 102, 103
1:9–10	95, 148, 149, 170
1:9–13	100, 164
1:10	104, 105, 149
1:10–12	104
1:11	80, 104, 122
1:11–12	105, 106, 120, 122, 123, 124, 126, 135
1:11–13	101, 105, 107, 121, 134, 145, 146
1:12	104, 105, 106, 112, 122
1:14	110, 111
1:14–15	110
1:14–19	62, 83–96, 107, 109, 126, 128, 131–4, 135, 146
1:16	111
1:20	80, 112, 168
1:20–21	2, 112, 164

1:20–23	112, 124	2:8–9	15
1:20–24	94, 188	2:15–16	155
1:20–25	127, 145, 164	2:18	151, 154, 156
1:20–27	95, 127, 128, 135	2:19	15, 114, 144, 170
1:21	112, 113, 168	2:21–22	179, 180
1:22	25	2:21–23	2, 14, 152, 156, 180
1:24	79, 80, 113, 144, 168	2:24	2, 163
1:24–25	2, 113, 144, 188	3	1, 2, 3, 8, 126, 143, 165, 191, 202, 204
1:24–26	113		
1:25	79, 113	3–4	204
1:26	12, 114, 127, 139, 140, 144, 164, 174, 186, 187	3:1–24	15
		3:17	42
1:26–27	74, 154, 185, 199	3:17–19	202
1:26–28	2, 17, 38, 41, 44, 62, 115, 126, 137, 141, 142, 146, 151, 170, 174, 185, 186	3:19	165
		3:22	155, 165, 166
		4:1	152, 157, 162, 180
		4:25	190
1:27	14, 16, 18, 42, 72, 85, 91, 139–64, 166–72, 174, 175, 179, 185–6, 188–203	5	165, 189–90, 197, 200, 203
		5:1	42, 139, 185, 192
		5:1–2	185, 191
1:27–28	143	5:1–3	17, 74, 185, 186, 199
1:28	114, 140, 143–7, 174, 185	5:3	2, 17, 18, 69–75, 126, 137, 139, 154, 185–203, 206
1:28–30	25		
1:29–30	80	5:3–5	187
1:30	168	6	63
1:31	25, 28, 35, 80, 81, 83, 139	6:3	165
		7:11	103
2	8, 15, 38, 43, 71, 81, 148–9, 152–6, 172–4, 184, 185, 196, 203	8:21	147
		8:22	107
		9:6	139, 161, 186, 193, 197
2–3	164, 191	9:27	93
2–4	42, 185, 186	9:29	187
2:1	33, 105, 110	10	126
2:1–2	33	17:5	5, 6
2:1–3	25, 34	18:15	73
2:4	41, 42, 43, 164, 185	18:19	73
2:4–5	38, 41–5, 99, 147–9, 151	49:17	93
2:4–6	17		
2:4–7	43	*Exodus*	
2:5	41, 43	3:14–15	46
2:5–6	164	9:9	93
2:6	44, 61, 148–51, 164, 172	10:21–22	93
2:7	2, 9, 11–14, 16–18, 44, 48, 49, 73, 102, 118, 126, 137, 139, 142–51, 161, 164–85, 186, 191–194, 202, 203	10:21–23	82
		10:23	81
		19:16	87
		20:21	87
		27:20	81
2:7–23	162	33:11	89

34	195		
34:29	87, 130, 157	*Job*	
34:29–30	195–96	10:8–9	48, 96
34:29–35	89	27:3	167
35:14	81	28	58, 59
39:16	81	29:3	83
		32:8	167
Leviticus		33:4	167
19:18	93	34	167, 168
24:2	81	34:13	167
		34:14–15b	167
Numbers		34:15c	167
4:16	81	36:6	121
6:25	82, 89	37:3	83
33:52	139	37:11	83
		37:15	83, 91
Deuteronomy		37:21–22	83
4:11	87	38:14	48
30:11–14	63		
		Psalms (LXX)	
Judges		2	48, 58
6:38, 40	81	2:2	48
21:14	120	2:7	48
		2:9	48
1 Samuel		4:7	83
6:5, 11	139	8	140, 177, 182
		8:3–6	140
2 Samuel		8:4–6	176
22:16	165	8:6	149, 182
22:29	82	8:6–7	115, 149
23:4	82	8:6–9	176
		8:7	127, 176
2 Kings		17:29	83
5:7	120	23	58
7:20	81	24 MT	24
11:18	139	26	86
15:12	81	26:1	86
		30:17	83
1 Chronicles		32:6	167
6	190	32:6–9	25
		32:8–9	79
2 Chronicles		35:10	83, 85
4:20	81	36:6	83
23:17	139	42:3	83
		54:20	46, 48, 58, 61
Nehemiah		66:1	83
9:6	120	70:20	121, 141
		73:12	46
Esther		73:13–18	46
8:16	82	79:4	83

79:8	83		8:30	25
79:20	83		9:1–6	59
88:16	83		11:16	156
89:2	22, 46		13:9	82
94:3–6	25		20:27	82
95:5	25			
96:11	83		*Ecclesiastes*	
103	167, 168		1:10	61
103:1-5	25		2:13	83, 88
103:1–22	167		3:11	32
103:2	83		7:8	32
103:24–30	167		7:12	121
103:29	167		8:1	83
103:30	167		10:13	32
104 MT	24		12:7	167
111:4	83			
118:105	83		*Isaiah*	
118:130	83		2:5	82
118:135	83		9	91
134:6	125		9:1	82, 90, 91, 92, 93, 95
135:7	83		9:1–6	91, 92
138:11–12	83		9:2	91
145	95		9:3–4	91
145:5	95		9:5–6	91
145:6	95		19:5	32
145:7–9	95		26:9	82
148:3	83		29:14	48, 54, 57
148:5–6	83		29:16	48
			30:26	82
Proverbs			36–37	54
3:18–20	24		41:25	48
3:19	24		42:5	165
4:6–9	59		42:6	82
4:18	82		42:16	82, 90
6:23	82		43:1	93, 95
8	23–28, 51–64, 69, 75, 202		44:2	93, 95
			45	94
8:22	24, 60, 68, 69, 72		45–46	49
8:22ff	59, 63		45:4–	
8:22–31	20–2, 23–28, 51, 58–64, 75, 82, 205		46:13	48
			45:7	48, 82, 90
8:22–25	24, 25, 59, 63		45:7–8	93
8:22–23	23, 26, 28, 60–4, 202		45:9	48, 49
8:23	23–6, 47–50, 57–71, 201		45:12	48
8:23–24	25		45:18	48
8:23–25	24, 25		46:9–10	48
8:24	25, 61		49:6	82
8:26–31	25		50:10	82
8:27	62		51:4–5	82
8:27–29	61		51:5	82

53:11	82
57:16	165
58:8	82
58:10	82
59–60	90
59:21–60:21	90
60:1	89
60:1–3	82
60:19–20	82
62:1	82
64:3 LXX	68
64:4	49
64:8	48, 49

Jeremiah
1:5	74
4:23	40, 88, 91
9:24	55
10:12–13	83
13:16	88, 91
18:4	49
28:15–28:16 LXX	83
31:35	83
38:36 LXX	83
51:15–16	83

Ezekiel
1:26–28	90
7:20	141
16:17	141
23:14	141
32:7–8	88, 91
37:9–10	167
37:14	185
42:17	83

Daniel
2–3	139
2:19–23	57
2:22	82
12:3	133

Hosea
6:5	82
10:12	82
13:2	139

Amos
| 5:18–20 | 87 |
| 5:26 | 139 |

Micah
| 7:8–9 | 82 |

Zechariah
| 12:1 | 165 |

2. Philo

De Abrahamo (Abr.)
2	42
41	141, 145
42–44	103
68–71	28
71	169
87	142
153	85
156	84
156–63	83, 110
162–63	131
258	42

De aeternitate mundi (Aet.)
1	87, 95
4	33
13–19	106, 123
17–18	102, 103
18	101
18–19	103
19	109
52	32
63	106
83	27

De agricultura (Agr.)
| 129 | 111 |

De cherubim (Cher.)
14	169
28	101
113	168
124–27	100

De confusione linguarum (Conf.)
| 12.5–9 | 29 |

62	101, 168	1.8	110
146	203	1.10	191
168–82	146	1.19–20	43
170	146	1.20	38
172	40	1.22	44
173	134	1.31ff	170
174	110	1.31–32	152
175–79	171	1.31–35	169
176–78	170	1.32	142
177	170	1.36–42	170
177–78	171	1.42	169, 170
179	170	1.43	161
		1.88	169

De congressu eruditionis gratia (Cong.)

20	169	1.92	169
79	28	1.95	169
		1.105–06	193

De decalogo (Dec.)

58	108, 124	2.2	28
101	38, 144	2.3	32
105	86	2.12–13	44, 146
		2.22–24	170

De ebrietate (Ebr.)

30–31	23, 26, 28, 64	3.95–96	142, 168
31	61	3.95–99	141
37–45	84	3.96	100, 143, 147
44	84	3.100–01	141
69	168	3.101	86
		3.161	143, 170

De fuga et inventione (Fug.)

De migratione Abrahami (Migr.)

12	100	6	100
63	147	34–35	85
68–72	146	36–42	28
69–70	170, 171	38–42	84
71–72	171	40–42	84
94–102	28	178–94	110
95	101	181	110
109	28	183	5, 28
134	170	192	30
178	42	220	171

De gigantibus (Gig.)

De mutatione nominum (Mut.)

8	109, 132	12	46, 60
33	168	27	28, 46
		27–28	121

Legum allegoriarum libri (Leg.)

1.2	32, 38	27–32	144
1.3	85	30	109
1.5	122	30–31	168, 169
1.5–7	107	46	28, 46
		219	167

Index of Ancient Sources 239

223	141, 143, 166	38	101, 102, 103
		38–39	100–05, 148–9, 164, 170
De opificio mundi (*Op.*)		38–44	100–07
1–12	14	40	104, 105
3	33, 170	40–44	105–07
8	30, 104	41	105
8–9	30, 101, 102, 103, 104	42	104, 105, 106
9	30, 35, 101	43	104, 106
9–11	76	43–44	188
11	30	44	106, 107, 122–4, 146
12	169	45	108, 145
13	33, 34, 36, 112	45–46	108–09
13–14	108	45–61	107–12
13–28	38	46	109
13–35	148	47	108, 109
13–128	99, 142–3, 147–8, 167	47–52	108, 110
13–147	14	51	84
15	39, 84	53	110
15–16	88	53–54	82
15–25	85	53–61	108, 110–12
16	19, 29, 31, 34–8, 39, 84–88, 107, 109, 140, 145–9	54	110
		55	108, 110, 111
16–35	150	56	110, 111
17	85	56–57	109
17–20	40, 85	58	111
18	40, 85	58–59	109, 110
18–19	172	59	111
21	146, 171	59–60	109
21–22	30, 101, 102, 103, 167	60	110, 111
22	101	61	99, 110, 111
23	28, 86	62	112, 122, 124
24–25	85, 141	62–63	112–13
25	29, 85, 140, 145	63	113, 167, 188
26	32	63–64	127
26–28	29, 31–4, 38, 39	64	113, 122, 144, 188
26–29	19	64–68	113–15, 128
27	36, 109	65	28, 114, 146
29	29, 38–41, 44, 84, 103, 150, 169	66	28, 114, 146
		67	108, 114
29–32	87	68	115
30	35, 36, 84, 86, 92, 168	69	141–5, 150, 171
30–35	19, 82, 83–9	69–71	143–5, 149
31	83, 84, 85, 86	69–75	114
33	86, 87	69–88	18, 41, 115, 142–9
33–34	87	69–128	144
34	86, 88	70–71	145
36	40, 84, 88, 100	71	141, 145, 188, 189
36–37	99–100	72–75	144
36–68	19, 41, 98, 148	77	145, 146
36–88	41	77–78	115, 145–6

77–82	143	153–69	14
77–88	145	165	191
78	146	167	191
79	142	170–72	14
79–81	191	172	28
82	142, 147, 169		
83–88	146	*De plantation (Plant.)*	
84–85	114, 146–7, 174	2–4	112
88	142	7	5, 108, 131
89	33	8	112
129	41, 42, 43, 44, 147, 169	8–10	123
129–30	19, 38, 41–5, 99, 147, 148	10	105, 112, 149
		11–15	113
129ff	144, 167	12	108, 131
129–50	44, 142, 143	14–27	166, 169
130	43, 44	16–17	142, 168
131	105, 148, 168	18–20	140
131–33	44, 148–9, 164	18–22	143
131–50	43	20–22	142
133	149	27	83
134	142, 143, 147, 148, 149–150, 166, 167, 171, 189	31	121
		40	82
134–35	50, 142, 147–50, 166–70	42–43	167
134–36	142	43	168
134–50	18, 44, 143	44–46	166
135	149, 150, 167, 168, 169, 188	45	169
136	169, 170, 188	*De posteritate Caini (Post.)*	
136–38	170	14–15	87
136–41	170	58	170
136–47	170	64–65	42, 148
136–50	166, 170–2	170–71	119
137	171, 188	170–85	190
138	169, 171, 177, 178, 181	175	119
139	141, 170, 171, 188, 189		
140	169	*De praemiis et poenis (Praem.)*	
140–41	188	1	147
140–44	170	144	168
142	169		
142–50	170	*De providentia (Prov.)*	
144	142, 189	1.23	100
145	18, 169, 188–90	1.40	172
145–46	170	1.77–88	110
146	141, 145, 169, 189		
147	170	*De sacrificiis Abelis et Caini (Sacr.)*	
148	169	8	101
148–50	14, 170	126	168
151	142, 169		
151–52	14	*De somniis (Somn.)*	
151–69	14	1.21–24	109, 111, 132, 133

1.34	143		4.187	5, 88, 102, 114, 168
1.53–54	109, 111, 132, 133		4.187–88	143
1.63–64	5		4.188	192
1.65	28			
1.65–71	84			

Quaestiones in Genesim (QG)

1.1	42, 43
1.2	44
1.4	151, 170
1.5	169
1.7	83
1.11	28
1.81	18, 191–92, 195
2.18	104
2.19	104
2.47	38
2.56	151
2.62	142, 143, 146, 167

1.66	28
1.68–69	169
1.72	84
1.73–75	143
1.75	86, 87
1.82	88
1.83–84	84
1.85	86
1.85–86	86, 88
1.91	88
1.116	132
1.135	109, 132
2.45	100
2.242	28

Quis rerum divinarum heres sit (Her.)

55–57	144
88	171
96–99	28
97	110
113–22	107
115	107
117	107
119	107
134–35	102
155	171
164	190
181	141
199	26
230–31	167
231	146

De specialibus legibus (Spec.)

1.13–14	112
1.13–20	110
1.16–19	110
1.19	110
1.36–37	84
1.39	109, 111
1.54	84, 88
1.59–63	110
1.66	109, 132
1.80–81	167
1.81	100
1.92	110
1.171	144, 167
1.209	110
1.279	87
1.327–29	104
1.329	88, 168
2.64	167
2.165	110
3.83	142, 146, 167
3.180	85, 110
3.207	142, 146
3.208	167
4.123	169, 170
4.186–96	84

Quod deterius potiori insidiari soleat (Det.)

54	28
80–90	167
83	142, 144
84–85	143, 169
86–87	146, 173
87–90	146
90	142, 170

Quod deus sit immutabilis (Deus)

3	88
47–48	115
48	143

57	100	*John*	
111	192	1:1–5	87
131–35	88	1:14	87
160	28	2:18	55
		3:19	87
De virtutibus (Virt.)		4:48	55
55–65	28	5:21	120
62	26	6:30	55
164	88	6:63–65	120
168	143	8:12	87
203	173	9:5	87
203–05	144	12:46	87
204–05	146, 173	17:5	48
205	192	17:24	48
De vita Mosis (Mos.)		*Acts*	
1.158	88	2:23	48
		4:27–28	48
2.63	104	4:28	67
2.70	88	9:3	89
2.100	5	10:42	48
2.127	171	17:24–28	200
2.135	171	17:28	200
2.267	5	17:31	48
		18	55
		18:5	55
		18:27–28	55
3. New Testament		21:21	89
		22:11	89
Matthew		26:13	89
12:38	56	26:18	87
16:1	56		
22:20	140	*Romans*	
22:20–21	140	1:18–25	10
		1:20	1, 77, 201
Mark		1:21–22	117
8:11	55	2:17–20	82
12:16–17	140	3:23	7, 10
13:24–25	90	4:17	4, 5, 6, 19, 73, 116, 120
		5:12–21	1, 10, 11, 94, 207
Luke		5:14	207
1:79	82	8	17, 65, 68, 70, 71, 74,
3:38	200		198, 199, 201, 202, 209
8:17	82	8–11	56
11:15–16	55	8:9	183
20:24–25	140	8:11	120
22:22	48	8:16	199
23:8	55	8:17	200
		8:18	70
		8:18–22	71

8:19–23	94, 198	2	74
8:20	201	2:2–8	67
8:21	70, 74	2:6	46
8:28	71, 198	2:6–7	52, 65
8:28–29	56	2:6–8	57, 60
8:28–30	49	2:6–9	22, 46
8:29	2, 3, 10, 12, 18, 49, 61, 70, 72, 73, 74, 154, 191, 194, 198, 199, 200, 201	2:6–10	64
		2:6–16	59, 65, 66, 67, 68
		2:6–3:23	65
8:29–30	19, 50, 51, 55, 56, 64, 69, 70, 71, 72, 73, 198, 201	2:7	23, 26, 46, 47, 48, 49, 50, 51–64, 65–9, 70, 72, 73, 201
8:30	70, 72, 73, 200, 201	2:7–8	70
8:38–39	94	2:7–9	20, 49, 53, 64, 72
9:4	200	2:8	65, 68, 74
9:11	49, 56	2:9	48, 49, 56, 62, 65, 68, 71
9:12	49	2:9–10	66
9:16	49	2:9–16	68
9:17	49	2:10	65
9:18	49	2:11	116
9:18–23	49	2:12	56, 65
9:19	49	2:12–14	183
9:19–23	48, 49, 198	3:6–7	106, 119, 120
9:23	49, 50, 56, 62	3:16	183
9:29	47	4:7	56
10:6–8	58, 63	5:8	86
11:2	56, 73	6:11	183
11:36	1, 134	6:16	2, 162
12:3–8	176	6:17	116
16:25–27	57	6:19–20	183
		7:3–4	177
1 Corinthians		7:31	4
1	55	8:6	1, 4, 5, 6, 18, 58, 66, 94, 134, 158, 160
1–2	56, 59, 64, 65, 66, 68		
1–4	51, 52, 58, 60	9:1	89
1:10	177	10:4	58, 59
1:10–11ff	153	10:11	60
1:18	53, 56	11	177
1:18–25	55	11–14	47
1:18–2:5	51, 53–7, 65, 66, 67	11:2–16	152, 153
1:18–2:16	59, 66	11:3	153, 154, 158
1:19	48, 53	11:4–5	153
1:21	54, 58	11:4–6	153
1:22–23	54	11:4–7	152
1:22–24	53, 54, 56	11:4–12	153
1:23–24	54, 66	11:7	1, 8, 11, 12, 18, 151, 152, 154, 155, 156, 158, 159, 160, 161, 176, 180, 196, 197
1:24	65, 66, 67		
1:26–31	55, 56		
1:29	55		
1:30	55, 65, 66, 67	11:7–9	2, 18, 153, 160, 173,

	174–175, 179, 180, 193		160, 200
11:7–10	153, 161, 162	15:36	120
11:7–12	2, 5, 10, 17, 151, 152–7, 162, 177, 179–80, 185	15:36–37	119
		15:36–38	118–21
11:8	152, 153	15:36–41	118, 119, 175
11:8–9	153, 156	15:36–49	116
11:9	152, 153, 156	15:37	116, 118, 119, 120, 122
11:10	153	15:37–38	1, 106, 124, 135, 157
11:11	153	15:37–41	17, 95, 134, 135, 160, 164, 179, 180, 181, 192
11:11–12	153, 162, 177, 178, 179–180	15:37–42	176, 177, 179
11:12	1, 5, 97, 135, 151, 152, 153, 156–7, 176, 180	15:37–47	71
		15:38	117, 118–25, 146, 178
12–14	177	15:38–41	76, 121–34, 178, 180, 185
12:1–30	177		
12:3	183	15:39	1, 2, 127–8, 175
12:4	116	15:39–40	18, 173, 175–7, 180, 185
12:11	177, 178, 179	15:39–41	125–34
12:12	177, 178	15:40	1, 2, 128–31, 133, 176
12:12–20	179	15:40–41	132, 133
12:12–26	2	15:41	1, 131–4
12:12–30	18, 172, 173, 176, 177–180, 185	15:42	70, 179, 180
		15:42–43	70, 180, 181
12:13	183	15:42–44	180
12:14–20	177	15:42–47	192
12:18	177, 178	15:42–48	195
12:21	177	15:42–49	70, 130, 135
12:21–26	177, 179	15:43	70
12:22–26	177	15:44	116, 181
12:24	177, 178	15:44–46	132
12:27–30	177, 178, 179	15:44–47	2, 16, 18, 180, 181, 185
12:28	177, 178	15:44–49	70
14:14	116	15:45	3, 11, 13, 15, 120, 160, 173, 175, 181, 182, 183, 198
15	65, 66, 70, 71, 74, 116, 118, 127, 136, 159, 177, 200, 201, 211		
		15:45–47	10, 126, 160, 164, 173, 180
15:3	176	15:45–49	14, 100, 184, 187, 192, 193
15:5–7	89		
15:8	89	15:46	182
15:8–10	1	15:47	12, 182
15:12	115	15:47–49	132
15:17	176	15:48	2, 182, 194, 195, 203
15:21–22	1, 10, 11, 126, 174	15:48–49	2, 16, 18, 126, 187, 192–195, 196, 197, 199
15:21–23	193		
15:22	120	15:49	2, 10, 11, 12, 50, 51, 65, 69, 70, 71, 72, 74, 75, 155, 160, 182, 192, 193, 194, 195, 198, 199, 200, 201, 203
15:24–28	126		
15:27	174		
15:35	115, 116, 117, 118, 194		
15:35–41	19, 115–36		
15:35–49	17, 69, 70, 71, 97, 135,		

15:51–52	198	*Ephesians*	
15:52–54	70, 123	1:3–14	94
15:54–57	70	1:4	48, 53
15:56	176	1:4–6	48
		1:5	56
2 Corinthians		1:11	56
1:12	87	1:18	82
3	195, 199, 202	2:7	60
3–4	158, 197	2:10	56
3:3	183	3:11	56, 67
3:6	120	4:24	11, 155
3:7	130	5:8	82
3:7–10	157	5:8–9	87
3:7–4:6	89, 133		
3:10	130	*Philippians*	
3:10–4:6	130	1:10	86
3:18	2, 10, 11, 18, 70, 139,	1:19	183
	154, 157, 160, 191, 195–	2:6	158, 159
	198, 199, 200, 202	2:6–11	58, 94
3:18–4:6	159	2:15	132
4	158, 161		
4:2	96	*Colossians*	
4:4	1, 3, 10, 18, 83, 91, 92,	1:12–13	82, 87
	151, 152, 154, 157, 158–	1:15	12, 158, 159, 194
	161, 162, 163, 184, 193,	1:15–16	4, 59
	194, 196, 197	1:15–20	4, 58, 194
4:4–6	10, 17, 157–62, 209	3:10	11, 155
4:5	157, 196		
4:6	1, 3, 10, 19, 83, 89–98,	*1 Thessalonians*	
	133, 151, 161–2, 184,	3:4	47
	196, 197	4:6	47
5:17–18	97	5:5	87
5:18	1, 134	5:23	181, 183
6:14	89		
7:3	47	*1 Timothy*	
9:5	47	6:16	82
13:2	47		
		2 Timothy	
Galatians		1:9	48
1:4	57, 60		
1:9	47	*Titus*	
2:8	56	1:2	48
3:2	183		
3:2–3	1	*Hebrews*	
3:8	47	1:3	12
3:14	183	2:11ff	199
3:17–19	1	7:3	32
3:21	120		
5:21	47	*1 Peter*	
		1:20	48

2:9	82	3:32–35	113
3:18	120	3:33	82

2 Peter
3:1	86

2 Baruch
14:17	22
21:8	46
51:10	132
54:1	22, 46
54:1–5	46

1 John
1:5	82
1:7	81
2:9–10	81

Revelation
20:22–25	90
21:6	32
22:13	32

Clement of Alexandria
  Excerpta ex Theodoto
54	186–87

1 Enoch
9:11	22
39:11	22, 46
46:1–2	22
47:3	22
48:3–7	22
48:6–7	22
106	186

4. Other Ancient Literature

Alcinous
  Handbook on Platonism (Did.)
7.4	40, 169

2 Enoch
25:3	22
31.3	174
33:3	22

Aristobulus (apud Eusebius)
  Praeparatio Evangelica 13
12.9–11	23, 63
12.11f	32
12.13	33

4 Ezra
6:1–6	22
6:38	29
7:70	22
8:52	22

Aristotle
  Metaphysics
7.7	99
983b7	99

Eusebius
  Praeparatio Evangelica 13
12.9–11	23, 63
12.11f	32
12.13	33

  Physics
2.3–9	99

Hesiod
  Theogony
116–17	102

Baruch
3	63
3–4	26, 58
3:9–13	63
3:14–15	63
3:16	57
3:16–23	63
3:24–28	63
3:29–31	63
3:32–34	63
4:1–2	81
5:9	82

Life of Adam and Eve
  The Apocalypse of Moses (Greek)
10.3	187
12.1–2	187
13	160

Index of Ancient Sources

Vita Adam et Evae (Latin)
37.3   187

Irenaeus
  Adversus haereses (*Haer.*)
  1.23.1, 5   81
  1.24.1–2   81

Josephus
  Antiquities
  1.27   29, 40
  1.34   165

Jubilees
  2:2   29

1 Maccabees
  1:21   81

2 Maccabees
  1:24–25   95
  1:32   81
  7:23   5, 102
  7:28   5, 102

Origen
  Commentarius in Johannem
  I.17.103   102

  De principiis
  II.1.5   102

Plato
  Phaedrus
  245–246   27
  246–249   147
  253a–b   195

  Republic
  500c   142
  509a   86
  529b   40, 172
  613a–b   195
  613b   142

  Sophist
  246b   40, 172

  Theaetetus
  176b   195

  176c   195

  Timaeus
  27a   147
  28a–b   34, 37, 150
  28a–29a   99
  29e   106, 146
  30a   30, 31, 35, 83, 101, 169
  30c   106
  30d   106
  31b   99, 100, 169
  32b   169
  34b–35a   27
  36   100
  36e   169
  37d   105
  37e   111
  39c   111
  39e   37, 140
  40d–47e   151
  41a–b   107
  41a–44d   144
  45b–46b   85
  50c–d   37, 140
  52a   169
  53a–b   83, 101
  90–91   142
  90c   142

Plotinus
  Ennead III.2 (On Providence)
  7.24   27

  Ennead IV.3 (On Difficulties)
  13.23   27

  Ennead V.9 (On Intellect)
  5.22   27, 46

Plutarch
  Antonius
  75.6   195

  Moralia XIII
  1014B.8   27
  1016C.6   27
  1016D.10   27

  Table-talk
  670B   88

To an Uneducated Ruler
780e–f   86

Pseudo-Aristotle
 De Mundo (Mund.)
 2   106
 392b12   106

Pseudo-Philo
 Biblical Antiquities
 50.7   189

Proclus
 Hymn to Helios
 1.33–35   86

Qumran
 1QH^a (1QHodayoth^a)
 1[9].7ff   22

 1QS (*Rule of the Community*)
 3.15–18   22
 3.16   46
 11.22   48

 4Q418 (4Q Instruction^d)
 81.1–3   176

 4Q504 (*Words of the Luminaries*)
              143

Sibylline Oracles
 8.442–45   176

Sirach
 1   26, 58
 1:10   57
 17:1–8   143
 17:7   141
 24   26, 58, 61–62
 24:3   61
 24:5   61
 24:8   61
 24:9   62, 46
 24:23ff   82
 24:27   82
 24:32   82
 33:11–13   49
 33:10   49
 33:13   48
 36:17   60
 42–43   62
 42:15–
 43:33   46, 62
 42:21   46, 62
 42:17   62
 42:25   62
 42:28   62
 43   92, 133–34
 43:1–10   62, 92, 133, 134
 43:2–5   134
 43:5   62, 134
 43:6–8   134
 43:8–9   92, 133
 43:9   134
 43:9–10   134
 43:10   134
 50:29   82

Testament of Moses
 1:12–13   22

Testament of Naphthali
 2:2   48
 2:4   48

Theodoret of Cyrrhus
 Quaestiones in Genesis
 9   40

Tobit
 6:18   46
 8:6   155

Wisdom of Solomon
 2:23   145, 156
 2:24   145
 3:7   133
 6:22   60
 7:1   145
 7:10   83
 7:17   32
 7:25   88
 7:25–31   83
 7:26   87, 141, 160
 7:27   83
 8–10   60
 8:1   83
 9   27, 60, 62–63

9:1–2	145	13	48
9:2	63	14:5	141
9:8	63	14:17	142
9:9–18	60	15:5	49
9:10–18	63	15:7	48, 49
9:15	145	15:8	49
9:17	58	15:11	49, 167
10:1	63, 145	18:4	83, 84
10:17	161		
11:17	103		

Index of Modern Authors

Adams, E. 1, 5, 17, 33, 98, 176
Agourides, S. 67
Alexander, P. 58
Allen, L. 48, 58
Alter, R. 103
Anderson, B.W. 42
Asher, J. 118, 119, 120, 127, 177, 182
Baer, R.A. 143, 144, 145, 149, 151, 152, 167
Balla, P. 91
Barbour, R.S. 26, 52, 53, 55, 59, 65, 66, 67, 68
Barclay, J.M.G. 14, 40, 52, 64, 84, 89, 90, 97, 98
Barclay, W. 129
Barrett, C.K. 7, 8, 9, 11, 12, 14, 17, 52, 70, 118, 153, 160, 175, 176, 183
Barth, K. 159, 208
Bartlett, D.L. 209
Batto, B.F. 31, 101, 106
Becker, J. 5, 93, 116, 117, 126, 132, 134, 135
Beker, J.C. 17, 69, 70, 180
Berchman, R.M. 15, 82, 85, 105, 110
Best, E. 53
Bird, P.A. 174
Black, M. 9, 159, 160, 181, 191, 193
Blomberg, C. 52
Bonhoeffer, D. 45, 135
Borgen, P. 114, 147, 174
Bornkamm, G. 52, 67, 70
Bouteneff, P.C. 6, 7, 11, 12, 143, 172, 173, 174, 206, 207, 208
Bremmer, J.N. 101
Brown, R.E. 51, 56
Bruce, F.F. 69, 70, 71, 201
Bultmann, R. 51, 65
Byrne, B. 5, 48, 49, 72, 198, 199

Carmichael, C.M. 132
Cassuto, U. 42, 107
Chester, A. 165
Childs, B.S. 42, 78, 94, 95, 97, 174, 197
Ciampa, R. 57
Clarke, W.K.L. 102
Clifford, R.J. 6, 101, 102
Collins, J.J. 6, 61, 102
Collins, R.F. 46, 52, 57, 69, 72, 97, 116, 120, 122, 123, 125, 126, 128, 133, 135, 152, 154, 158, 173, 175, 181, 192
Conzelmann, H. 52, 62, 71, 108, 116, 117, 119, 122, 126, 131, 139, 152, 158, 173, 180, 181, 192
Cook, J. 26, 40, 59, 79, 122
Cotter, D.W. 42
Cox, R. 4, 5, 35, 84, 99, 100, 160
Cranfield, C.E.B. 5, 72, 74, 154, 158, 198
Currid, J. 78, 99, 101, 107, 140
Dahlberg, B.T. 42
Davis, J.A. 14, 27, 51, 52, 54, 56, 65, 68, 82
De Boer, M. 116
Delitzsch, F. 30, 30, 99, 123
Di Lella, A.A. 61, 62
Dillon, J.M. 30, 32, 36, 40, 83, 101, 109, 187
Dorsey, D.A. 42
Driver, S.R. 78
Dunn, J.D.G. 5, 7, 8, 9–12, 14, 47, 52, 56, 70, 71, 713, 141, 159, 160, 172, 173, 174, 180, 181, 183, 185, 191, 194, 198, 199, 200, 201, 208
Dupont, J. 168, 182
Ellingworth, P. 52, 121
Ellis, E. E. 52

Endo, M. 22, 29, 40
Eskola, T. 55, 56, 57, 58, 65, 70, 72, 73, 74, 198
Fee, G.D. 5, 9–11, 15, 24, 26, 27, 48, 52, 61, 65, 67, 68, 70, 71, 115, 117, 120, 121, 126, 128, 129, 152, 153, 154, 162, 173, 174, 178, 180, 181, 182, 183, 191, 192, 196, 197, 198
Fergusson, D. 6, 102
Feuillet, A. 56, 154, 155, 156, 157
Frick, P. 88, 95, 107, 111, 123
Furnish, V.P. 126, 132, 181, 192
Garland, D.E. 52, 68, 69, 70, 117, 119, 135, 180
Garr, W.R. 78
Gelander, S. 30, 33, 81, 108, 133
Gibbs, J.G. 4, 94
Goldstein, J.A. 6, 102
Goodenough, E.R. 82
Gundry-Volf, J.M. 151, 152, 153, 156, 175
Gunkel, H. 101, 165
Haffner, P. 5, 79, 102, 206
Hamerton-Kelly, R.G. 65
Hanson, A.T. 157, 158, 159, 186
Hardy, D.W. 97
Harrington, D.J. 23, 58, 146
Harris, M.J. 89, 91, 93, 94, 130, 158, 159, 197
Harris, R.L 99, 174
Harrisville, R.A. 117, 124, 125, 180
Hartley, J.E. 29, 42
Hatton, H. 52, 121
Hawking, S. 21, 32
Hay, D.M. 142, 143, 192
Hays, R.B. 13, 15, 46, 52, 67, 91, 92, 134, 141, 196, 208
Headlam, A.C. 5
Heil, J.P. 72, 126
Hengel, M. 22, 23, 25, 28, 32, 33, 58, 63
Héring, J. 69, 70, 117, 122, 129
Hillar, M. 38
Hoekema, A. 186
Hooker, M.D. 153, 173
Horsley, R.A. 14, 52, 53, 58, 117, 126, 192
House, P.R. 27
Hubbard, M.V. 81, 91, 93
Hughes, P.E. 73, 193, 198

Hultgren, S. 14, 143, 154, 169, 181, 182
Hurley, J.B. 152, 154
Hurtado, L.W. 13
Jaubert, A. 153, 156, 157, 173, 174
Jenson, R. 22
Jervell, J.S. 14, 141, 157, 166, 192
Jewett, P. 74
Jewett, R. 70, 140, 200, 202
Jobes, K. 26, 59
Johnston, P.S. 132. 134
Jónsson, G.A. 144
Kammler, H.-C. 48, 56, 57, 58, 65, 67, 70, 71
Käsemann, E. 5, 65, 70, 72, 158, 191, 198, 199, 200
Kidner, D. 29, 78, 101, 102
Kim, S. 8–9, 11–12, 17, 89, 155, 157, 158, 159, 162, 169, 173, 174, 194, 196, 208
Kim, Y.S. 120
Kistemaker, S. 117, 119, 121, 122, 123, 128, 129, 180
Kline, M.G. 165, 188, 194, 200
Kraus, H.-J. 174
Kremer, J. 58, 67, 70, 126
Kugel, J.L. 23, 27, 92, 141
Kuschel, K.-J. 5, 160
Lambrecht, J. 116, 126, 132, 174, 181, 182, 192
Lampe, G.W.H. 146
Lange, A. 26, 59
Laporte, J. 28
Lee, A.C.C. 101
Leonhardt-Balzer, J. 35, 37, 83, 84, 85, 96, 103, 140
Levison, J.R. 14, 142, 143, 166, 168, 170, 186, 189
Lincoln, A. 53
Lindemann, A. 180, 181, 182, 192, 198
Loader, W. 15, 148, 154, 166, 167
Lockwood, G. 119, 120, 121, 122, 123, 128, 134, 135, 180
Longman, T., III. 25, 61
Lorenzen, S. 26, 70, 73, 83, 112, 175, 176, 181, 185, 192, 195, 198, 199, 200
Luther, M. 22
Luz, U. 154, 158, 160, 192

Martin, D. 17, 51, 52, 100, 116, 117, 125, 128, 131, 132, 134, 169, 176, 177, 179, 181
Martin, R.P. 158, 173
Matera, F.J. 98, 158, 159, 162, 191, 196
Mathews, K.A. 31, 79, 97, 102, 139, 158, 174, 186, 200
May, G. 5, 102
McCasland, S.V. 140, 144, 154, 166, 173, 186, 191, 194, 200
McGinn, S.E. 153
Meier, J.P. 173
Meyer, J.C. 91, 92, 94, 162, 196
Michaelis, W. 73, 191, 198
Minear, P.S. 90, 91, 97, 119, 165, 174, 180, 185, 204
Mitchell, M.M. 52
Moffatt, J. 116, 117, 121, 126, 178, 180, 181, 182, 183
Moiser, J. 117
Moltmann, J. 140
Moo, D.J. 5, 48, 49, 102, 161, 192, 199
Moo, J. 202
Morissette, R. 115, 117, 119, 175, 181, 182, 183
Morris, L. 5, 52, 119, 121, 125, 129
Muddiman, J. 116
Murphy-O'Connor, J. 5, 161
Murphy, R.E. 26, 58, 59
Murray, J. 5
Neusner, J. 14
Newman, C.C. 91
Nguyen, V.H.T. 89, 91, 140, 155, 157, 159, 160, 162, 196, 198
Nickelsburg, G.W.E. 14, 132
Nikiprowetzky, V. 43
Noort, E. 31, 40, 79, 80, 89, 95, 101, 104, 132, 185, 186
Norden, E. 99
Orr, W.F 56
Padgett, A.G. 126, 174
Parker, K.I. 81, 123
Pearce, V. 105
Pearson, B.A. 63, 65, 68, 70, 169, 181, 182, 192
Peerbolte, L.J. 154, 177
Penner, T. 178
Perdue, L.G. 27
Plummer, A. 55, 56, 67, 70, 116, 121, 128, 181

Polkinghorne, J. 146
Poythress, V.S. 107
Prior, D. 52
Probst, H. 117, 184
Radice, R. 85, 87, 99, 101, 102, 104, 109, 120, 125, 128, 143, 145, 167, 168, 169, 172
Reiling, J. 26, 51, 52, 58, 70
Reymond, R.L. 198
Richardson, N. 89, 195
Ridderbos, H. 4, 9, 158, 159, 194
Ringe, S. 27
Robertson, A., 55, 56, 67, 70, 116, 121, 128, 181
Rösel, M. 27, 34, 39, 40, 42, 79, 99, 122, 169
Rosner, B. 58
Rowe, C.K. 155, 160
Runia, D.T. 5, 14, 15, 17, 27, 29, 30, 31, 36, 37, 39, 40, 42, 43, 44, 83, 84, 85, 86, 87, 99, 100, 101, 102, 103, 104, 105, 107, 108, 109, 113, 123, 131, 142, 143, 144, 145, 147, 148, 150, 166, 167, 168, 169, 171, 174, 183, 189
Sacks, R.D. 6, 31, 33, 79, 102
Sailhamer, J.H. 29, 31, 78, 86, 97, 102, 107
Sanday, W. 5
Sanders, E.P. 14
Sandmel, S. 17, 40, 169
Schaller, B. 14, 16, 142, 169, 192
Schmid, J. 184, 185
Schnabel, E. 22, 52
Schrage, W. 48, 57, 70, 72, 117, 153, 154, 173
Schreiner, T.R. 5, 116, 117
Schüle, A. 139, 140
Schwarz, H. 5, 102
Scott, J.M. 126
Scott, R.B.Y. 24
Scroggs, R. 7–12, 13, 22, 51, 59, 71, 78, 91, 140, 151, 153, 157, 165, 173, 181, 182, 183, 184, 191, 194, 206, 208
Seebaß, H. 104, 200
Segal, A. 89, 195
Seifrid, M. 48, 50
Sellin, G. 14, 126, 129, 132, 165, 168, 181, 182, 183, 191, 191

Senft, C. 69, 70, 118, 126, 181, 192
Sheppard, G.T. 61
Sider, R.J. 117, 121, 122
Siegert, F. 89, 99, 139, 200
Simon, W.G.H. 119, 120, 126
Skehan, P.W. 58, 61, 62
Skinner, J. 42, 78, 100, 102, 186
Stanley, C.D. 126, 181
Steenburg, D. 17, 23, 155, 157, 160, 169, 173, 174
Sterling, G.E. 14, 51, 52, 58, 72, 99, 182, 183
Stockhausen, C.K. 91, 92, 94
Stordalen, T. 1992. 43
Stuckenbruck, L. 153, 174
Stuhlmacher, P. 5, 51, 55, 65, 66
Talbert, C.H. 180
Theissen, G. 14, 46, 52, 57, 58, 59, 60, 65, 66, 192
Thielman, F. 81
Thiselton, A.C. 5, 46, 54, 55, 62, 70, 72, 92, 116, 117, 119, 121, 122, 125, 129, 132, 133, 135, 139, 152, 153, 154, 155, 160, 173, 177, 178, 180, 181
Thrall, M.E. 87, 89, 91, 158, 159, 162, 195, 196, 198
Tigchelaar, E.J.C. 62, 92, 132, 133
Tobin, T. 17, 28, 34, 35, 36, 42, 43, 44, 63, 64, 84, 86, 99, 100, 138, 142, 143, 144, 145, 147, 148, 150, 166, 168, 169, 193
Tsumura, D.T. 31, 101
Usami, K. 95, 116, 122, 126, 128, 182, 183, 192
Van den Hoek, A. 17, 142, 145, 166, 167, 169
Van der Horst, P.W. 92
Vander Stichele, C. 178
Van Kooten, G.H. 9, 10, 14, 15, 35, 40, 82, 83, 84, 85, 87, 100, 109, 140, 141, 142, 144, 145, 154, 158, 165, 173, 174, 181, 183, 186, 187, 191, 192, 193, 194, 204
Van Till, H.J. 86, 107
Van Ruiten, J.T.A.G.M. 154

Van Wolde, E. 78, 102, 112
Von Rad, G. 42, 43, 58, 100, 101, 102, 107, 109, 132, 140, 164, 165, 168, 174, 186
Vorholt, R. 89, 91
Vos, G. 116, 120, 121, 125, 129, 175, 181
Wallace, H.N. 185, 186
Walther, J.A. 56
Waltke, B. 31, 87
Watson, F. 13, 14, 15, 16, 21, 22, 41, 42, 47, 78, 79, 80, 81, 89, 91, 97, 107, 117, 130, 139, 141, 142, 151, 152, 153, 158, 162, 174, 177, 195, 196, 198, 207
Watson, N. 120, 126, 135
Wedderburn, A.J.M. 38, 54, 112, 169, 173, 181, 187
Welborn, L.L. 51, 52, 67, 71
Wenham, G. 22, 29, 30, 31, 42, 78, 80, 89, 101, 102, 107, 139, 140, 174, 194
Westermann, C. 29, 30, 33, 40, 42, 78, 80, 81, 86, 97, 100, 101, 102, 107, 123, 132, 139, 174
Wevers, J.W. 40, 105, 122, 181, 182
Whiteley, D.E.H. 7
Wilckens, U. 51, 52, 65, 66, 67, 181, 182
Williams, H.H.D., III. 52, 57, 58, 68
Williamson, R. 40, 41
Willms, H. 189
Winston, D. 6, 38, 86, 102, 114
Winter, B.W. 51
Witherington, B., III. 4, 5, 7, 9, 48, 50, 52, 61, 67, 68, 72, 73, 89, 91, 160, 192, 198, 208
Wolfson, H.A. 6, 102, 143, 150
Wright, N.T. 5, 10, 14, 116, 117, 126, 129, 132, 133, 134, 174, 180, 192
Wuellner, W. 52
Yates, J.W. 165
Yee, G. 26, 59
Ziesler, J. 5, 72, 198

Index of Subjects

Adam
- as glorious in Paul 152–7, 173–80
- as glorious in Philo 170–2, 188–91
- as image of God in Genesis 139–41
- as image of God in Paul 151–62, 162–164, 173, 180–5, 195–8
- as image of Word in Philo 141–51, 162–4, 166–70, 188–90
- as son of God 200
- dominion/rule of 62, 108, 139–40, 143, 146, 174
- dust, out of 2, 11, 12, 19, 71, 101, 103, 135, 139, 164–86, 188, 192–5, 203, 204, 206
- fall of 4, 6, 7, 8, 9, 10, 11, 62, 169, 173, 175, 176, 201, 206
- first 10, 12, 131, 157, 160, 163, 165, 175, 180–5, 185–8, 190, 192–5, 202–203, 205, 208–10
- formation of 164–85
- last/second 9, 10, 13, 71, 72, 75, 78, 157–64, 166, 180–185, 188, 189, 191–203, 205–10
- negative interpretation, Paul 180–4
- negative interpretation, Philo 166–70
- positive interpretation, Paul 173–80
- positive interpretation, Philo 170–2

Age/Ages (Aeons)
- before the age 23–7, 28, 46, 61–4, 68
- before the ages 45–75, 198–202
- until the age(s) 22, 46, 61

Angels 108, 109, 202
Anthropocentrism 99, 110–11, 115, 146
Anthropology 2, 16, 18, 44, 87, 117, 135, 138–204, 206–7
Anthropogony (see Beginning – of humanity)
Aristobulus
- on creation and before 32, 63
- on Proverbs 23, 58, 63

Aristotle 27, 99, 108, 131
Augustine 29, 32
Autonomy (non-) 153–4, 177

Baruch
- on creation and before 63
- on Proverbs 8 26, 58, 63
Before, The
- by Paul 45–75, 77, 137
- by Philo 27–45, 136
- explicit 19–20, 21–77, 98, 107, 136, 146, 205, 206
- implicit 19–20, 23, 36, 45, 50, 78, 107, 115, 123, 127, 135, 136, 157, 206
- in Proverbs 8 23–27, 60–4
Beginning, The (see also Creation)
- of humanity in Genesis 138–41, 164–166, 185–88, 203–04
- of humanity in Paul 151–64, 172–85, 191–203, 203–04
- of humanity in Philo 141–51, 166–72, 188–91, 203–04
- of world in Genesis 21–7, 78–81, 136–7
- of world in Paul 89–98, 115–37, 156–157, 161–2, 176–80
- of world in Philo 38–45, 81–9, 98–115, 136–7, 148–9
Ben Sira (see also Sirach)
- on Adam 14, 49, 142, 146
- on creation and before 46, 61–2
- on Proverbs 8 23, 26, 58, 61–2, 63
- on stars 61, 92, 132, 133
Beyond, The 204, 209–10
Body
- dusty 164–85, 191–5, 203
- earthly 100, 128–31, 132–4, 134–6, 166–70, 175–6, 180–4, 190

– formation of 142–7, 149–51, 152–7, 164–85, 203–04
– heavenly 69–75, 83–9, 89–98, 100, 107–12, 126, 130, 131–4, 135, 146, 147, 166–70, 176–80, 180–4, 195, 199
– natural (see Body – soulish)
– of animals 113–15, 127–8
– of Christ 115–18, 135–6, 176–80, 180–5
– of fish and birds 112–13, 127–8
– of plants 1, 22, 33, 80, 100, 105–07, 108, 118–24, 135, 145, 157, 183, 184, 185, 187, 208
– of seeds 1, 80, 100, 105–07, 113, 114, 118–24, 125, 127, 135, 156, 178, 183–4, 185, 208
– resurrection of 115–18, 135–6, 180–185
– soulish 114, 180–4, 192–5, 202
– Spiritual 70, 116, 180–5, 195

Calling 49, 55–6, 94, 113, 162–3
Causation 1, 5, 6, 34, 84, 90, 109, 112, 119, 120, 124, 126, 148, 152, 156, 157, 162
Christ, Jesus
– as image of God 157–64, 195–8
– as last/second Adam 13, 72, 75, 78, 157–64, 166, 180–5, 188, 189, 191–203, 205–211
– as wisdom of God 64–9
– conformity to 69–77, 185–8, 192–204
– crucifixion/death of 45, 53–7, 65–75, 75–7, 201, 205, 207
– greater than Adam 180–5, 192–5, 205–10
– greater than Moses 89, 130, 157–9, 161, 162, 164, 195–6, 197
– mediation of creation 5, 18, 59, 66, 159, 208
– pre-existence 5, 18, 48, 59, 66, 159, 208
– Son of God 48, 198–202, 203, 208
Christocentrism 74, 209
Christology (see Christ, Jesus)
Coin 142–3, 198
Commentary 2, 3, 14–16, 18, 20, 23, 26, 28, 38, 43–5, 50, 64, 81, 83, 87, 92, 95, 101, 107, 120–4, 127–8, 137–138, 142, 150, 167, 178, 205, 209–10
Comparison (of Paul and Philo)
– of the Before 75–7
– of the Beginning of humanity 203–4
– of the Beginning of the world 136–7
– method of 13–18
Condemnation 167, 211
Conformation
– conformation to Adam's image 185–203
– conformation to Christ's image 191–203
– conformation to God's image 195–8
Conversion 90, 91
Corporeality (see also Sensory) 27, 35, 37, 40–1, 44, 84–85, 88–9, 97, 98–100, 103, 136, 142, 167–70, 185
Corpses
– decay of 117–18, 168
– resurrection of 116, 120, 125, 132, 133, 135, 136, 177, 181, 183, 185, 196
Cosmology 98–136, 167, 176, 180
Cosmogony (see Beginning – of world)
Cosmos 7, 16, 17, 19, 28, 30–1, 32–3, 34–8, 39, 41, 46, 62, 75, 85, 87–8, 99–100, 106–07, 111, 113, 115, 118, 124, 125–6, 129, 131, 134, 135–7, 145, 149, 150, 169, 170, 176, 178, 187, 188, 198, 201
Covenants
– new 73, 132, 200
– old 73, 95, 96, 132
Creation (see also Beginning)
– by fiat/word 4, 34, 36, 79–81, 81–3, 89–98, 101, 136
– ex nihilo (from nothing) 4, 5–6, 73, 79, 102, 116–17, 134–5
– from matter 27, 29, 30–1, 36–7, 39, 84, 100–05, 140
– groaning of 4, 130, 176
– mediation of Christ 5, 18, 59, 66, 159, 208
– mediation of Wisdom 26, 59, 66, 159
– of Adam 164–85
– of animals 113–15, 127–8
– of birds 112–13, 127–8
– of Eve 2, 77, 152–7, 173–5, 203
– of fish 112–13, 127–8

– of humanity 138–41, 141–51, 151–164, 164–166, 166–72, 172–85, 185–188, 188–91, 191–203, 203–04
– of light 79–81, 81–98, 115, 134–6, 136–7
– of luminaries 107–12, 131–4, 175–6
– of plants 1, 22, 33, 80, 100, 105, 106, 107, 108, 120, 121, 123, 124–7, 135, 145, 157, 183, 184, 185, 187, 208
– of seeds 1, 80, 100, 105–07, 113, 114, 118–21, 121–4, 125, 127, 135, 156, 178, 183–4, 185, 208
– of sun, moon, stars 107–12, 131–4, 175–6
– of water 24–5, 39–40, 61, 79, 100–105, 112–13, 114, 125, 148–49, 164, 170, 188

Damascus Christophany 90, 91, 159
Darkness 24, 29, 30, 39, 40, 79, 82, 83, 87–8, 89–98, 157, 160–61, 209
Days
– as a-temporal 31–4, 34, 38–41,43
– in general 6, 19, 25, 77–8
– 1 in Paul 79–83, 89–98
– 1 in Philo 35–6, 38–41, 43, 63, 79–83, 83–9
– 2 in Paul 128–31, 124–6
– 2 in Philo 99–100
– 3 in Paul 115–24
– 3 in Philo 100–07
– 4 in Paul 124–6, 131–4
– 4 in Philo 107–12
– 5 in Paul 124–6, 127–8
– 5 in Philo 112–13
– 6 in Paul 124–6, 127–8, 151–7, 162–164, 173–5
– 6 in Philo 113–15, 141–7, 151
– seventh 63
Death
– in Adam 1, 8, 11, 164–5, 167, 172, 175, 176, 185, 187, 208–09
– salvation from 76, 107, 118–19
Desire (see Divine)
Dishonor (see also Shame) 129–31, 140, 152, 155–6, 180, 196
Diversity
– of body parts 176–80
– of gifts 177

Divine
– desire 19, 21, 23, 49, 50–1, 54, 57, . 69, 71, 78, 79–81, 93, 98, 113, 118, 121–4, 125–7, 132, 134–5, 136–7, 138, 166, 173–4, 175–6, 177–80, 184, 202–04, 205–10
– plan 19, 21, 22, 23, 25, 27, 29, 31, 33, 35, 36, 38, 41, 45, 47, 49, 50, 51, 54, 56, 67, 68, 69, 76–7, 81, 85, 123, 180, 201
– power 1, 5, 6, 7, 46, 53–5, 77, 78, 79, 91, 108, 109, 116, 117, 118, 135, 140, 155, 180, 181, 195, 203
– purpose 1, 19, 21, 23, 25, 27–9, 34–8, 45, 49, 50–1, 55–7, 60–1, 67–68, 76-7, 78, 83, 88, 98, 104–05, 106–07, 108, 110–12, 113, 115, 119, 121, 123–4, 136–7, 138, 143–4, 146–147, 151, 154–5, 156, 166, 169, 171–172, 178–80, 184, 198–9, 204, 206–209
– will 53–4, 57, 67, 139, 154–5, 165–6
Dust 2, 11, 12, 19, 71, 101, 103, 135, 139, 164–86, 188, 192–5, 203, 204, 206

Election (see also Pre-destination) 49, 55–6, 74, 94, 170–1
Eschatology (see also New Creation) 2, 31–2, 46, 69–70, 71, 72, 74–5, 97–8, 117, 130, 154, 160, 162, 184, 186, 188, 201, 209–10

Face
– of Adam 164, 171–2, 183
– of Christ 82, 89, 96, 97, 136, 157–9, 159–62, 164, 196
– of Christians 197
– of God 89
– of kings 140–1
– of Moses 89, 130, 157–9, 160–1, 195–6, 197
– of waters 61
Faith 1, 50, 137, 181
Fall (see also Sin) 4, 6, 7, 8, 9, 10, 11, 62, 169, 173, 175, 176, 201, 206
Female 152–7, 173–5
First Adam 10, 12, 131, 157, 160, 163, 165, 175, 180–5, 185–8, 190, 192–5, 202–03, 205, 208–10

Index of Subjects

Fore-knowledge 46, 72–3, 88, 96, 99, 104, 105, 108, 109, 110, 114, 115, 135, 136, 147, 178
Fore-ordination (see Pre-destination)
Forms (see also Ideas and Paradigm) 27, 37, 39, 44, 186, 187, 190

Gentiles (see Greeks)
Glory (see also Honor) 2, 7, 8, 9, 10, 12, 18, 45, 46, 49, 50, 56, 60, 65–75, 76, 77, 82, 89, 90, 92, 96, 97, 124, 125, 127, 128, 129, 130–1, 131–4, 135, 137, 138, 140, 151–2, 152–6, 156–64, 172, 173–80, 180–5, 188, 195–203, 203–04, 205, 206, 208, 209, 210
Glorification (see Glory)
Gnosticism 51–2, 81, 186–7
God
– Cause 1, 5, 6, 34, 84, 90, 109, 112, 119, 120, 124, 126, 148, 152, 156, 157, 162
– Creator 1, 5, 19–20, 27, 28, 34–5, 36, 37, 62, 75, 81, 92, 94, 95, 97, 98, 109, 111, 118, 131, 132, 135, 136, 137, 156, 157, 161, 163, 164, 166, 171, 184, 197, 200, 204, 209–10
– Savior in Paul 54–5, 67, 76, 83, 89, 93–4, 95, 96, 136, 205
– Savior in Philo 83, 87, 89, 96, 97, 107, 136
– Shiner in Paul 89–98, 134–6
– Shiner iin Philo 83–89, 134–6
Gospel 4, 9, 51, 53, 54, 55, 87, 140, 156, 157, 161, 184
Greeks 32, 53–5, 67, 101, 108, 111, 144, 158

Hardening 49–50
Head coverings 152–7
Hellenism 110, 132, 158
– Jewish creation-tradition 52
– Jewish wisdom-tradition 52, 58–60
Hermeneutics 3–20, 23, 26, 38, 40, 41, 44–5, 47, 51, 53, 56, 64, 69, 75–7, 79, 83, 87–8, 92, 94, 97, 99, 100, 115, 130, 136, 138, 140–5, 147–8, 149–152, 158, 161–3, 166–7, 170, 173, 179, 184–5, 197–8, 202–03, 208
History 21, 54, 55, 58, 76–7, 197–8

History-of-religion 16
Honor (see also Glory) 18, 114, 129–31, 133, 138, 152, 155–6, 157, 163–4, 174, 175, 177, 180, 190–1, 203–04, 208
Humanity (see also Beginning and Creation) 138–41, 141–51, 151–64, 164–166, 166–72, 172–85, 185–88, 188–91, 191–203, 203–04

Ideas (see also Forms and Paradigm) 28–9, 33–4, 37, 39, 43–4, 48, 84, 98, 143–4, 149–51, 167, 169, 172, 185, 188, 189, 191, 203
– as created 37–8, 44, 83, 205
Image
– Adam as God's 142–7, 147–51, 152–157, 173–5
– Christ as God's 157–62
– conformation to Adam's 185–203
– conformation to Christ's 191–203
– conformation to God's 195–8
– of Adam 185–203
– of Christ 191–203
– of God 139–163
Immortality 11, 70, 106–07, 123–4, 165, 167, 169, 183, 185, 195, 203
Incorporeality (see also Noetic) 37, 39–41, 43, 44–5, 83–5, 86, 88, 98, 99–100, 103, 136, 149–50, 167–70, 172, 181, 185, 197
Incorruptibility 70, 74, 82, 116, 147, 149, 166–7, 180, 185, 195, 203
Interdependence 2, 176–9
Invisibile 24, 30, 38–45, 83, 84, 87, 101, 105, 139, 145, 148, 155, 159, 160, 169, 170, 188–9, 195
Irenaeus 81, 141, 207

Jesus (see Christ, Jesus)
Josephus 14, 29, 31, 40, 167

Last/Second Adam 9, 10, 13, 71, 72, 75, 78, 157–64, 166, 180–185, 188, 189, 191–203, 205–10
Law 1, 81, 82, 108, 109, 111–12, 130, 170, 181, 195
Light
– in Genesis 1 79–83
– in Paul 89–98

– in Philo 83–9
Logos (see also Word) 28, 30, 83, 84, 85–6, 87, 88, 96–7, 99, 158, 159, 172, 185, 189
Luminaries
– in Genesis 1 108–09
– in Paul 131–4
– in Philo 107–12
– in Sirach 61, 92, 132, 133

Male 152–7, 173–5
Matter 27, 29, 30–1, 36–7, 39, 52, 84, 87, 100–05, 108, 131, 140, 167
Mercy 49–50, 82
Messiah (see Christ, Jesus)
Middle Platonism (see also Plato/Platonism) 31, 35, 99, 150, 193
Mirror (see also Reflection) 86, 90, 140, 159, 165, 197, 198, 204
Moses 23–4, 89, 130, 157–9, 161, 162, 195–6, 197, 199, 202
Mystery religions/cults 51–2
Mystery, The 46, 51–2, 57–8, 70

New Creation (see also Eschatology) 7, 9, 10, 46, 82, 97, 129–30, 161–2, 163, 183–4, 187, 197, 199, 208–09
Noetic (see also Incorporeal) 29, 35, 36, 37, 39, 40, 42, 44–5, 75, 83–9, 99–100, 106, 107, 140, 143, 148–51, 163, 165, 167, 169–70, 172, 189, 205

Old Creation (see Beginning and Creation)
Origen 6, 102

Paradigm (see also Ideas and Forms) 29, 34–8, 40, 45, 75, 76, 81, 83, 84–6, 88–9, 93–4, 95–6, 99, 106, 108, 109, 143, 149–50, 205
Paul
– on the Before 45–75, 77, 137
– on the Beginning of humanity 151–164, 172–85, 191–203, 203–04
– on the Beginning of the world 89–98, 115–37, 156–157, 161–2, 176–80
– on the Resurrection 115–36, 175–85
– on the Spirit 1, 62, 65, 68, 116, 157, 160, 164, 178, 181–6, 198, 204, 207

Philo
– on the Before 27–45, 136
– on the Beginning of humanity 141–151, 166–72, 188–91, 203–04
– on the Beginning of the world 38–45, 81–9, 98–115, 136–7, 148–9
– on the spirit 39, 84, 96, 114, 166, 168–9, 185
Philosophy 14, 15, 17, 21, 27, 32, 36, 38, 44, 50, 52, 58, 63, 72, 73, 82–3, 85, 86, 99, 104, 105, 108, 110, 111, 113, 125–6, 132, 134, 145, 146, 158, 165, 177, 189–90, 193, 195
Plan (see Divine)
Plato/Platonism 14, 19, 26, 27, 29, 30, 31, 34, 35, 36, 37, 38, 39–40, 45, 52, 63, 76, 84, 86, 99–100, 101, 104, 106, 107, 108, 110, 111, 131, 140, 141–2, 149, 150, 158, 169, 189, 193, 205
Polarity 130
Potter/Pottery 49, 164
Power (see Divine)
Pre-deliberation (see Pre-destination, Pre-determination, Pre-marked out) 21, 36, 41, 55, 75–7
Pre-destination (see Pre-marked out, Pre-deliberation, Pre-determination)
– of Christ's crucifixion 65–9, 75–7
– of conformation to Christ's image 69–75, 75–7, 198–202
– of people 75–7, 198–202
– pre-marked out 45–77, 96, 132, 198–204, 206
Pre-determination (see Pre-deliberation, Pre-destination, Pre-marked out) 35, 36, 38, 45–46, 54, 62, 65, 69, 73–4, 76, 77, 103
Pre-existence 5, 18, 23, 27, 46, 48, 59, 60, 66, 159, 208
Pre-marked out (see Pre-destination, Pre-deliberation, Pre-determination) 45–77, 96, 132, 198–204, 206
Prepositional Metaphysics 99
Pre-protology (see Before, The)
Prophecy 48–50, 54, 57, 90–3, 152–3, 156
Protology (see Beginning, The)
Proverbs 8
– and Genesis 1 23–7

- in Aristobulus 23, 58, 63
- in Baruch 8 26, 58, 63
- in Philo 23, 26, 27–8, 61, 64
- in Paul 45–75
- in Sirach 23, 26, 58, 61–2, 63
- in Wisdom of Solomon 23, 26, 60

Providence 108, 120, 121–2, 124, 127, 136

Psalm 8 (see also Adam – dominion) 115, 127, 140, 149, 176, 177, 182

Purpose (see Divine)

Qumran
- Adam's glory 174, 205
- Adam's mortality 170
- predestination (the Before) 22
- Proverbs 8 22

Reflection (see also Mirror) 86, 90, 140, 159, 165, 197, 198, 204

Resurrection 116, 120, 125, 132, 133, 135, 136, 177, 181, 183, 185, 196

Rhetoric 31, 51–2, 117, 133, 190

Rulers 46, 48, 57, 64, 65, 68, 70, 83

Seal 37, 44, 149–50, 166, 189

Sensory/Sense-Perceptible/Sensible (see also Corporeality) 29, 35–8, 41, 43, 44, 86–8, 98, 99–100, 110, 111, 112, 114–15, 142, 143, 146–7, 148–51, 163, 166, 167, 168, 169, 172, 205

Shame (see also Dishonor) 55, 152, 155–7, 163, 196

Sin (see also Fall) 1–2, 4, 8, 14, 172, 174–5, 176, 208–09

Sirach (see also Ben Sira)
- on Adam 14, 49, 142, 146
- on creation and before 46, 61–2
- on Proverbs 8 23, 26, 58, 61–2, 63
- on stars 61, 92, 132, 133

Space-Time 31–4

Spirit
- as breath of life 165, 181–4
- as eschatological 184, 186
- as life-giving 160, 182–4, 204, 207
- in Genesis 24, 61, 165
- in Paul 1, 62, 65, 68, 116, 157, 160, 164, 178, 181–6, 198, 204, 207
- in Philo 39, 84, 96, 114, 166, 168–9, 185

- Spiritual body 70, 116, 181–2

Statue 141, 142–3, 147, 149, 157–8, 166, 173, 198

Theocentrism 28, 62, 75, 88–9, 90, 93–99, 104–08, 110–12, 115, 118, 120, 127, 135–7, 151, 156–7, 176, 190

Time
- and space-time 31–4
- temporality/a-temporarlity 28, 32–4, 36, 37–8, 47, 49, 50, 55, 56, 57, 60, 61, 66–7, 72, 73, 112, 169

Timaeus 19, 26, 27, 29–38, 39, 75, 104, 105, 106, 111, 147, 150, 205

Toledoth 41–2

Two-Men Scheme
- in Paul 44, 157–63, 180–4
- in Philo 44, 147–51, 166–70

Unity 66, 168–9, 176–9

Universalism 55–6

Visible 19, 28, 30–1, 33–4, 35–8, 38–45, 75, 84, 100, 101, 107, 109, 133, 139, 146, 157–9, 160, 169–70, 195

Will (see Divine)

Wisdom
- in 1 Corinthians 1–4 45–77
- in Jewish literature 61–4
- in Proverbs 8 24–6
- of God 45–77
- of the cross 45–77
- mediation in creation 26, 59, 66, 159
- traditions 52, 58–60

Wisdom of Solomon
- and 1 Cor. 1–4 52, 58–60, 62
- on Adam 62, 142–3, 169
- on creation and before 60, 62
- on "image" 142–3, 158
- on Proverbs 8 23, 26, 60
- on life-giving Spirit 62, 165
- on wisdom 58, 60, 82, 97, 159

Woman (see Female)

Word (of God)
- in Genesis 1 22, 29, 78–81, 86, 88, 90, 98, 135
- in Paul 90–1, 92, 94, 95, 96–7, 151, 157, 161, 196

– in Philo (see also Logos) 28, 30, 83, 84, 85–6, 87, 88, 96–7, 99, 158, 159, 172, 185, 189

Worship 1, 109, 132, 139, 152–3, 157, 162

Wissenschaftliche Untersuchungen zum Neuen Testament
Alphabetical Index of the First and Second Series

Ådna, Jostein: Jesu Stellung zum Tempel. 2000. *Vol. II/119.*
Ådna, Jostein (Ed.): The Formation of the Early Church. 2005. *Vol. 183.*
- and *Kvalbein, Hans* (Ed.): The Mission of the Early Church to Jews and Gentiles. 2000. *Vol. 127.*
Ahearne-Kroll, Stephen P., Paul A. Holloway, and *James A. Kelhoffer* (Ed.): Women and Gender in Ancient Religions. 2010. *Vol. 263.*
Aland, Barbara: Was ist Gnosis? 2009. *Vol. 239.*
Alexeev, Anatoly A., Christos Karakolis and *Ulrich Luz* (Ed.): Einheit der Kirche im Neuen Testament. Dritte europäische orthodox-westliche Exegetenkonferenz in Sankt Petersburg, 24.–31. August 2005. 2008. *Vol. 218.*
Alkier, Stefan: Wunder und Wirklichkeit in den Briefen des Apostels Paulus. 2001. *Vol. 134.*
Allen, David M.: Deuteronomy and Exhortation in Hebrews. 2008. *Vol. II/238.*
Anderson, Charles A.: Philo of Alexandria's Views of the Physical World. 2011. *Vol. II/309.*
Anderson, Paul N.: The Christology of the Fourth Gospel. 1996. *Vol. II/78.*
Appold, Mark L.: The Oneness Motif in the Fourth Gospel. 1976. *Vol. II/1.*
Arnold, Clinton E.: The Colossian Syncretism. 1995. *Vol. II/77.*
Ascough, Richard S.: Paul's Macedonian Associations. 2003. *Vol. II/161.*
Asiedu-Peprah, Martin: Johannine Sabbath Conflicts As Juridical Controversy. 2001. *Vol. II/132.*
Attridge, Harold W.: Essays on John and Hebrews. 2010. *Bd. 264.*
- see *Zangenberg, Jürgen.*
Aune, David E.: Apocalypticism, Prophecy and Magic in Early Christianity. 2006. *Vol. 199.*
Avemarie, Friedrich: Die Tauferzählungen der Apostelgeschichte. 2002. *Vol. 139.*
Avemarie, Friedrich and *Hermann Lichtenberger* (Ed.): Auferstehung – Ressurection. 2001. *Vol. 135.*
- Bund und Tora. 1996. *Vol. 92.*
Baarlink, Heinrich: Verkündigtes Heil. 2004. *Vol. 168.*
Bachmann, Michael: Sünder oder Übertreter. 1992. *Vol. 59.*

Bachmann, Michael (Ed.): Lutherische und Neue Paulusperspektive. 2005. *Vol. 182.*
Back, Frances: Verwandlung durch Offenbarung bei Paulus. 2002. *Vol. II/153.*
Backhaus, Knut: Der sprechende Gott. 2009. *Vol. 240.*
Baker, William R.: Personal Speech-Ethics in the Epistle of James. 1995. *Vol. II/68.*
Bakke, Odd Magne: 'Concord and Peace'. 2001. *Vol. II/143.*
Balch, David L.: Roman Domestic Art and Early House Churches. 2008. *Vol. 228.*
Baldwin, Matthew C.: Whose *Acts of Peter*? 2005. *Vol. II/196.*
Balla, Peter: Challenges to New Testament Theology. 1997. *Vol. II/95.*
- The Child-Parent Relationship in the New Testament and its Environment. 2003. *Vol. 155.*
Baltes, Guido: Hebräisches Evangelium und synoptische Überlieferung. 2011. *Bd. II/312.*
Bammel, Ernst: Judaica. Vol. I 1986. *Vol. 37.*
- Vol. II 1997. *Vol. 91.*
Barclay, John M.G.: Pauline Churches and Diaspora Jews. 2011. *Vol. 275.*
Barreto, Eric D.: Ethnic Negotiations. 2010. *Vol. II/294.*
Barrier, Jeremy W.: The Acts of Paul and Thecla. 2009. *Vol. II/270.*
Barton, Stephen C.: see *Stuckenbruck, Loren T.*
Bash, Anthony: Ambassadors for Christ. 1997. *Vol. II/92.*
Bauckham, Richard: The Jewish World around the New Testament. Collected Essays Volume I. 2008. *Vol. 233.*
Bauer, Thomas Johann: Paulus und die kaiserzeitliche Epistolographie. 2011. *Vol. 276.*
Bauernfeind, Otto: Kommentar und Studien zur Apostelgeschichte. 1980. *Vol. 22.*
Baum, Armin Daniel: Pseudepigraphie und literarische Fälschung im frühen Christentum. 2001. *Vol. II/138.*
Bayer, Hans Friedrich: Jesus' Predictions of Vindication and Resurrection. 1986. *Vol. II/20.*
Becker, Eve-Marie: Das Markus-Evangelium im Rahmen antiker Historiographie. 2006. *Vol. 194.*
Becker, Eve-Marie and *Peter Pilhofer* (Ed.): Biographie und Persönlichkeit des Paulus. 2005. *Vol. 187.*

- and *Anders Runesson* (Ed.): Mark and Matthew I. 2011. *Vol. 271.*
Becker, Michael: Wunder und Wundertäter im frührabbinischen Judentum. 2002. *Vol. II/144.*
Becker, Michael and *Markus Öhler* (Ed.): Apokalyptik als Herausforderung neutestamentlicher Theologie. 2006. *Vol. II/214.*
Bell, Richard H.: Deliver Us from Evil. 2007. *Vol. 216.*
- The Irrevocable Call of God. 2005. *Vol. 184.*
- No One Seeks for God. 1998. *Vol. 106.*
- Provoked to Jealousy. 1994. *Vol. II/63.*
Bennema, Cornelis: The Power of Saving Wisdom. 2002. *Vol. II/148.*
Bergman, Jan: see *Kieffer, René*
Bergmeier, Roland: Das Gesetz im Römerbrief und andere Studien zum Neuen Testament. 2000. *Vol. 121.*
Bernett, Monika: Der Kaiserkult in Judäa unter den Herodiern und Römern. 2007. *Vol. 203.*
Betho, Benjamin: see *Clivaz, Claire.*
Betz, Otto: Jesus, der Messias Israels. 1987. *Vol. 42.*
- Jesus, der Herr der Kirche. 1990. *Vol. 52.*
Beyschlag, Karlmann: Simon Magus und die christliche Gnosis. 1974. *Vol. 16.*
Bieringer, Reimund: see *Koester, Craig.*
Bittner, Wolfgang J.: Jesu Zeichen im Johannesevangelium. 1987. *Vol. II/26.*
Bjerkelund, Carl J.: Tauta Egeneto. 1987. *Vol. 40.*
Blackburn, Barry Lee: Theios Aner and the Markan Miracle Traditions. 1991. *Vol. II/40.*
Blackwell, Ben C.: Christosis. 2011. *Vol. II/314.*
Blanton IV, Thomas R.: Constructing a New Covenant. 2007. *Vol. II/233.*
Bock, Darrell L.: Blasphemy and Exaltation in Judaism and the Final Examination of Jesus. 1998. *Vol. II/106.*
- and *Robert L. Webb* (Ed.): Key Events in the Life of the Historical Jesus. 2009. *Vol. 247.*
Bockmuehl, Markus: The Remembered Peter. 2010. *Vol. 262.*
- Revelation and Mystery in Ancient Judaism and Pauline Christianity. 1990. *Vol. II/36.*
Bøe, Sverre: Cross-Bearing in Luke. 2010. *Vol. II/278.*
- Gog and Magog. 2001. *Vol. II/135.*
Böhlig, Alexander: Gnosis und Synkretismus. Vol. 1 1989. *Vol. 47* – Vol. 2 1989. *Vol. 48.*
Böhm, Martina: Samarien und die Samaritai bei Lukas. 1999. *Vol. II/111.*
Börstinghaus, Jens: Sturmfahrt und Schiffbruch. 2010. *Vol. II/274.*
Böttrich, Christfried: Weltweisheit – Menschheitsethik – Urkult. 1992. *Vol. II/50.*

- and *Herzer, Jens* (Ed.): Josephus und das Neue Testament. 2007. *Vol. 209.*
Bolyki, János: Jesu Tischgemeinschaften. 1997. *Vol. II/96.*
Bosman, Philip: Conscience in Philo and Paul. 2003. *Vol. II/166.*
Bovon, François: New Testament and Christian Apocrypha. 2009. *Vol. 237.*
- Studies in Early Christianity. 2003. *Vol. 161.*
Brändl, Martin: Der Agon bei Paulus. 2006. *Vol. II/222.*
Braun, Heike: Geschichte des Gottesvolkes und christliche Identität. 2010. *Vol. II/279.*
Breytenbach, Cilliers: see *Frey, Jörg.*
Broadhead, Edwin K.: Jewish Ways of Following Jesus Redrawing the Religious Map of Antiquity. 2010. *Vol. 266.*
Brocke, Christoph vom: Thessaloniki – Stadt des Kassander und Gemeinde des Paulus. 2001. *Vol. II/125.*
Brunson, Andrew: Psalm 118 in the Gospel of John. 2003. *Vol. II/158.*
Büchli, Jörg: Der Poimandres – ein paganisiertes Evangelium. 1987. *Vol. II/27.*
Bühner, Jan A.: Der Gesandte und sein Weg im 4. Evangelium. 1977. *Vol. II/2.*
Burchard, Christoph: Untersuchungen zu Joseph und Aseneth. 1965. *Vol. 8.*
- Studien zur Theologie, Sprache und Umwelt des Neuen Testaments. Ed. by D. Sänger. 1998. *Vol. 107.*
Burnett, Richard: Karl Barth's Theological Exegesis. 2001. *Vol. II/145.*
Byron, John: Slavery Metaphors in Early Judaism and Pauline Christianity. 2003. *Vol. II/162.*
Byrskog, Samuel: Story as History – History as Story. 2000. *Vol. 123.*
Calhoun, Robert M.: Paul's Definitions of the Gospel in Romans 1. 2011. *Vol. II/316.*
Cancik, Hubert (Ed.): Markus-Philologie. 1984. *Vol. 33.*
Capes, David B.: Old Testament Yaweh Texts in Paul's Christology. 1992. *Vol. II/47.*
Caragounis, Chrys C.: The Development of Greek and the New Testament. 2004. *Vol. 167.*
- The Son of Man. 1986. *Vol. 38.*
- see *Fridrichsen, Anton.*
Carleton Paget, James: The Epistle of Barnabas. 1994. *Vol. II/64.*
- Jews, Christians and Jewish Christians in Antiquity. 2010. *Vol. 251.*
Carson, D.A., O'Brien, Peter T. and *Mark Seifrid* (Ed.): Justification and Variegated Nomism.
Vol. 1: The Complexities of Second Temple Judaism. 2001. *Vol. II/140.*

Vol. 2: The Paradoxes of Paul. 2004.
Vol. II/181.
Caulley, Thomas Scott and *Hermann Lichtenberger* (Ed.): Die Septuaginta und das frühe Christentum – The Septuagint and Christian Origins. 2011. *Vol. 277.*
– see *Lichtenberger, Hermann.*
Chae, Young Sam: Jesus as the Eschatological Davidic Shepherd. 2006. *Vol. II/216.*
Chapman, David W.: Ancient Jewish and Christian Perceptions of Crucifixion. 2008. *Vol. II/244.*
Chester, Andrew: Messiah and Exaltation. 2007. *Vol. 207.*
Chibici-Revneanu, Nicole: Die Herrlichkeit des Verherrlichten. 2007. *Vol. II/231.*
Ciampa, Roy E.: The Presence and Function of Scripture in Galatians 1 and 2. 1998. *Vol. II/102.*
Classen, Carl Joachim: Rhetorical Criticsm of the New Testament. 2000. *Vol. 128.*
Claußen, Carsten (Ed.): see *Frey, Jörg.*
Clivaz, Claire, Andreas Dettwiler, Luc Devillers, Enrico Norelli with *Benjamin Bertho* (Ed.): Infancy Gospels. 2011. *Vol. 281.*
Colpe, Carsten: Griechen – Byzantiner – Semiten – Muslime. 2008. *Vol. 221.*
– Iranier – Aramäer – Hebräer – Hellenen. 2003. *Vol. 154.*
Cook, John G.: Roman Attitudes Towards the Christians. 2010. *Vol. 261.*
Coote, Robert B. (Ed.): see *Weissenrieder, Annette.*
Coppins, Wayne: The Interpretation of Freedom in the Letters of Paul. 2009. *Vol. II/261.*
Crump, David: Jesus the Intercessor. 1992. *Vol. II/49.*
Dahl, Nils Alstrup: Studies in Ephesians. 2000. *Vol. 131.*
Daise, Michael A.: Feasts in John. 2007. *Vol. II/229.*
Deines, Roland: Die Gerechtigkeit der Tora im Reich des Messias. 2004. *Vol. 177.*
– Jüdische Steingefäße und pharisäische Frömmigkeit. 1993. *Vol. II/52.*
– Die Pharisäer. 1997. *Vol. 101.*
Deines, Roland, Jens Herzer and *Karl-Wilhelm Niebuhr* (Ed.): Neues Testament und hellenistisch-jüdische Alltagskultur. III. Internationales Symposium zum Corpus Judaeo-Hellenisticum Novi Testamenti. 21.–24. Mai 2009 in Leipzig. 2011. *Vol. 274.*
– and *Karl-Wilhelm Niebuhr* (Ed.): Philo und das Neue Testament. 2004. *Vol. 172.*
Dennis, John A.: Jesus' Death and the Gathering of True Israel. 2006. *Vol. 217.*

Dettwiler, Andreas and *Jean Zumstein* (Ed.): Kreuzestheologie im Neuen Testament. 2002. *Vol. 151.*
– see *Clivaz, Claire.*
Devillers, Luc: see *Clivaz, Claire.*
Dickson, John P.: Mission-Commitment in Ancient Judaism and in the Pauline Communities. 2003. *Vol. II/159.*
Dietzfelbinger, Christian: Der Abschied des Kommenden. 1997. *Vol. 95.*
Dimitrov, Ivan Z., James D.G. Dunn, Ulrich Luz and *Karl-Wilhelm Niebuhr* (Ed.): Das Alte Testament als christliche Bibel in orthodoxer und westlicher Sicht. 2004. *Vol. 174.*
Dobbeler, Axel von: Glaube als Teilhabe. 1987. *Vol. II/22.*
Docherty, Susan E.: The Use of the Old Testament in Hebrews. 2009. *Vol. II/260.*
Dochhorn, Jan: Schriftgelehrte Prophetie. 2010. *Vol. 268.*
Downs, David J.: The Offering of the Gentiles. 2008. *Vol. II/248.*
Dryden, J. de Waal: Theology and Ethics in 1 Peter. 2006. *Vol. II/209.*
Dübbers, Michael: Christologie und Existenz im Kolosserbrief. 2005. *Vol. II/191.*
Dunn, James D.G.: The New Perspective on Paul. 2005. *Vol. 185.*
Dunn, James D.G. (Ed.): Jews and Christians. 1992. *Vol. 66.*
– Paul and the Mosaic Law. 1996. *Vol. 89.*
– see *Dimitrov, Ivan Z.*
–, *Hans Klein, Ulrich Luz,* and *Vasile Mihoc* (Ed.): Auslegung der Bibel in orthodoxer und westlicher Perspektive. 2000. *Vol. 130.*
Ebel, Eva: Die Attraktivität früher christlicher Gemeinden. 2004. *Vol. II/178.*
Ebertz, Michael N.: Das Charisma des Gekreuzigten. 1987. *Vol. 45.*
Eckstein, Hans-Joachim: Der Begriff Syneidesis bei Paulus. 1983. *Vol. II/10.*
– Verheißung und Gesetz. 1996. *Vol. 86.*
–, *Christoph Landmesser* and *Hermann Lichtenberger* (Ed.): Eschatologie – Eschatology. The Sixth Durham-Tübingen Research Symposium. 2011. *Vol. 272.*
Ego, Beate: Im Himmel wie auf Erden. 1989. *Vol. II/34.*
Ego, Beate, Armin Lange and *Peter Pilhofer* (Ed.): Gemeinde ohne Tempel – Community without Temple. 1999. *Vol. 118.*
– and *Helmut Merkel* (Ed.): Religiöses Lernen in der biblischen, frühjüdischen und frühchristlichen Überlieferung. 2005. *Vol. 180.*
Eisele, Wilfried: Welcher Thomas? 2010. *Vol. 259.*
Eisen, Ute E.: see *Paulsen, Henning.*

Elledge, C.D.: Life after Death in Early Judaism. 2006. *Vol. II/208.*
Ellis, E. Earle: Prophecy and Hermeneutic in Early Christianity. 1978. *Vol. 18.*
– The Old Testament in Early Christianity. 1991. *Vol. 54.*
Elmer, Ian J.: Paul, Jerusalem and the Judaisers. 2009. *Vol. II/258.*
Endo, Masanobu: Creation and Christology. 2002. *Vol. 149.*
Ennulat, Andreas: Die 'Minor Agreements'. 1994. *Vol. II/62.*
Ensor, Peter W.: Jesus and His 'Works'. 1996. *Vol. II/85.*
Eskola, Timo: Messiah and the Throne. 2001. *Vol. II/142.*
– Theodicy and Predestination in Pauline Soteriology. 1998. *Vol. II/100.*
Farelly, Nicolas: The Disciples in the Fourth Gospel. 2010. *Vol. II/290.*
Fatehi, Mehrdad: The Spirit's Relation to the Risen Lord in Paul. 2000. *Vol. II/128.*
Feldmeier, Reinhard: Die Krisis des Gottessohnes. 1987. *Vol. II/21.*
– Die Christen als Fremde. 1992. *Vol. 64.*
Feldmeier, Reinhard and *Ulrich Heckel* (Ed.): Die Heiden. 1994. *Vol. 70.*
Felsch, Dorit: Die Feste im Johannesevangelium. 2011. *Vol. II/308.*
Finnern, Sönke: Narratologie und biblische Exegese. 2010. *Vol. II/285.*
Fletcher-Louis, Crispin H.T.: Luke-Acts: Angels, Christology and Soteriology. 1997. *Vol. II/94.*
Förster, Niclas: Marcus Magus. 1999. *Vol. 114.*
Forbes, Christopher Brian: Prophecy and Inspired Speech in Early Christianity and its Hellenistic Environment. 1995. *Vol. II/75.*
Fornberg, Tord: see *Fridrichsen, Anton.*
Fossum, Jarl E.: The Name of God and the Angel of the Lord. 1985. *Vol. 36.*
Foster, Paul: Community, Law and Mission in Matthew's Gospel. *Vol. II/177.*
Fotopoulos, John: Food Offered to Idols in Roman Corinth. 2003. *Vol. II/151.*
Frank, Nicole: Der Kolosserbrief im Kontext des paulinischen Erbes. 2009. *Vol. II/271.*
Frenschkowski, Marco: Offenbarung und Epiphanie. Vol. 1 1995. *Vol. II/79* – Vol. 2 1997. *Vol. II/80.*
Frey, Jörg: Eugen Drewermann und die biblische Exegese. 1995. *Vol. II/71.*
– Die johanneische Eschatologie. Vol. I. 1997. *Vol. 96.* – Vol. II. 1998. *Vol. 110.* – Vol. III. 2000. *Vol. 117.*
Frey, Jörg, Carsten Claußen and *Nadine Kessler* (Ed.): Qumran und die Archäologie. 2011. *Vol. 278.*

– and *Cilliers Breytenbach* (Ed.): Aufgabe und Durchführung einer Theologie des Neuen Testaments. 2007. *Vol. 205.*
– *Jens Herzer, Martina Janßen* and *Clare K. Rothschild* (Ed.): Pseudepigraphie und Verfasserfiktion in frühchristlichen Briefen. 2009. *Vol. 246.*
– *Stefan Krauter* and *Hermann Lichtenberger* (Ed.): Heil und Geschichte. 2009. *Vol. 248.*
– and *Udo Schnelle (Ed.):* Kontexte des Johannesevangeliums. 2004. *Vol. 175.*
– and *Jens Schröter* (Ed.): Deutungen des Todes Jesu im Neuen Testament. 2005. *Vol. 181.*
– Jesus in apokryphen Evangelienüberlieferungen. 2010. *Vol. 254.*
–, *Jan G. van der Watt,* and *Ruben Zimmermann* (Ed.): Imagery in the Gospel of John. 2006. *Vol. 200.*
Freyne, Sean: Galilee and Gospel. 2000. *Vol. 125.*
Fridrichsen, Anton: Exegetical Writings. Edited by C.C. Caragounis and T. Fornberg. 1994. *Vol. 76.*
Gadenz, Pablo T.: Called from the Jews and from the Gentiles. 2009. *Vol. II/267.*
Gäbel, Georg: Die Kulttheologie des Hebräerbriefes. 2006. *Vol. II/212.*
Gäckle, Volker: Die Starken und die Schwachen in Korinth und in Rom. 2005. *Vol. 200.*
Garlington, Don B.: 'The Obedience of Faith'. 1991. *Vol. II/38.*
– Faith, Obedience, and Perseverance. 1994. *Vol. 79.*
Garnet, Paul: Salvation and Atonement in the Qumran Scrolls. 1977. *Vol. II/3.*
Gemünden, Petra von (Ed.): see *Weissenrieder, Annette.*
Gese, Michael: Das Vermächtnis des Apostels. 1997. *Vol. II/99.*
Gheorghita, Radu: The Role of the Septuagint in Hebrews. 2003. *Vol. II/160.*
Gordley, Matthew E.: The Colossian Hymn in Context. 2007. *Vol. II/228.*
– Teaching through Song in Antiquity. 2011. *Vol. II/302.*
Gräbe, Petrus J.: The Power of God in Paul's Letters. 2000, ²2008. *Vol. II/123.*
Gräßer, Erich: Der Alte Bund im Neuen. 1985. *Vol. 35.*
– Forschungen zur Apostelgeschichte. 2001. *Vol. 137.*
Grappe, Christian (Ed.): Le Repas de Dieu / Das Mahl Gottes. 2004. *Vol. 169.*
Gray, Timothy C.: The Temple in the Gospel of Mark. 2008. *Vol. II/242.*
Green, Joel B.: The Death of Jesus. 1988. *Vol. II/33.*

Gregg, Brian Han: The Historical Jesus and the Final Judgment Sayings in Q. 2005. *Vol. II/207.*

Gregory, Andrew: The Reception of Luke and Acts in the Period before Irenaeus. 2003. *Vol. II/169.*

Grindheim, Sigurd: The Crux of Election. 2005. *Vol. II/202.*

Gundry, Robert H.: The Old is Better. 2005. *Vol. 178.*

Gundry Volf, Judith M.: Paul and Perseverance. 1990. *Vol. II/37.*

Häußer, Detlef: Christusbekenntnis und Jesusüberlieferung bei Paulus. 2006. *Vol. 210.*

Hafemann, Scott J.: Suffering and the Spirit. 1986. *Vol. II/19.*
– Paul, Moses, and the History of Israel. 1995. *Vol. 81.*

Hahn, Ferdinand: Studien zum Neuen Testament.
Vol. I: Grundsatzfragen, Jesusforschung, Evangelien. 2006. *Vol. 191.*
Vol. II: Bekenntnisbildung und Theologie in urchristlicher Zeit. 2006. *Vol. 192.*

Hahn, Johannes (Ed.): Zerstörungen des Jerusalemer Tempels. 2002. *Vol. 147.*

Hamid-Khani, Saeed: Relevation and Concealment of Christ. 2000. *Vol. II/120.*

Hannah, Darrel D.: Michael and Christ. 1999. *Vol. II/109.*

Hardin, Justin K.: Galatians and the Imperial Cult? 2007. *Vol. II/237.*

Harrison, James R.: Paul and the Imperial Authorities at Thessolanica and Rome. 2011. *Vol. 273.*
– Paul's Language of Grace in Its Graeco-Roman Context. 2003. *Vol. II/172.*

Hartman, Lars: Text-Centered New Testament Studies. Ed. von D. Hellholm. 1997. *Vol. 102.*

Hartog, Paul: Polycarp and the New Testament. 2001. *Vol. II/134.*

Hasselbrook, David S.: Studies in New Testament Lexicography. 2011. *Vol. II/303.*

Hays, Christopher M.: Luke's Wealth Ethics. 2010. *Vol. 275.*

Heckel, Theo K.: Der Innere Mensch. 1993. *Vol. II/53.*
– Vom Evangelium des Markus zum viergestaltigen Evangelium. 1999. *Vol. 120.*

Heckel, Ulrich: Kraft in Schwachheit. 1993. *Vol. II/56.*
– Der Segen im Neuen Testament. 2002. *Vol. 150.*
– see *Feldmeier, Reinhard.*
– see *Hengel, Martin.*

Heemstra, Marius: The Fiscus Judaicus and the Parting of the Ways. 2010. *Vol. II/277.*

Heiligenthal, Roman: Werke als Zeichen. 1983. *Vol. II/9.*

Heininger, Bernhard: Die Inkulturation des Christentums. 2010. *Vol. 255.*

Heliso, Desta: Pistis and the Righteous One. 2007. *Vol. II/235.*

Hellholm, D.: see *Hartman, Lars.*

Hemer, Colin J.: The Book of Acts in the Setting of Hellenistic History. 1989. *Vol. 49.*

Henderson, Timothy P.: The Gospel of Peter and Early Christian Apologetics. 2011. *Vol. II/301.*

Hengel, Martin: Jesus und die Evangelien. Kleine Schriften V. 2007. *Vol. 211.*
– Die johanneische Frage. 1993. *Vol. 67.*
– Judaica et Hellenistica. Kleine Schriften I. 1996. *Vol. 90.*
– Judaica, Hellenistica et Christiana. Kleine Schriften II. 1999. *Vol. 109.*
– Judentum und Hellenismus. 1969, ³1988. *Vol. 10.*
– Paulus und Jakobus. Kleine Schriften III. 2002. *Vol. 141.*
– Studien zur Christologie. Kleine Schriften IV. 2006. *Vol. 201.*
– Studien zum Urchristentum. Kleine Schriften VI. 2008. *Vol. 234.*
– Theologische, historische und biographische Skizzen. Kleine Schriften VII. 2010. *Vol. 253.*
– and *Anna Maria Schwemer:* Paulus zwischen Damaskus und Antiochien. 1998. *Vol. 108.*
– Der messianische Anspruch Jesu und die Anfänge der Christologie. 2001. *Vol. 138.*
– Die vier Evangelien und das eine Evangelium von Jesus Christus. 2008. *Vol. 224.*

Hengel, Martin and *Ulrich Heckel* (Ed.): Paulus und das antike Judentum. 1991. *Vol. 58.*
– and *Hermut Löhr* (Ed.): Schriftauslegung im antiken Judentum und im Urchristentum. 1994. *Vol. 73.*
– and *Anna Maria Schwemer* (Ed.): Königsherrschaft Gottes und himmlischer Kult. 1991. *Vol. 55.*
– Die Septuaginta. 1994. *Vol. 72.*
–, *Siegfried Mittmann* and *Anna Maria Schwemer* (Ed.): La Cité de Dieu / Die Stadt Gottes. 2000. *Vol. 129.*

Hentschel, Anni: Diakonia im Neuen Testament. 2007. *Vol. 226.*

Hernández Jr., Juan: Scribal Habits and Theological Influence in the Apocalypse. 2006. *Vol. II/218.*

Herrenbrück, Fritz: Jesus und die Zöllner. 1990. *Vol. II/41.*

Herzer, Jens: Paulus oder Petrus? 1998. *Vol. 103.*

- see *Böttrich, Christfried.*
- see *Deines, Roland.*
- see *Frey, Jörg.*
Hill, Charles E.: From the Lost Teaching of Polycarp. 2005. *Vol. 186.*
Hoegen-Rohls, Christina: Der nachösterliche Johannes. 1996. *Vol. II/84.*
Hoffmann, Matthias Reinhard: The Destroyer and the Lamb. 2005. *Vol. II/203.*
Hofius, Otfried: Katapausis. 1970. *Vol. 11.*
- Der Vorhang vor dem Thron Gottes. 1972. *Vol. 14.*
- Der Christushymnus Philipper 2,6–11. 1976, ²1991. *Vol. 17.*
- Paulusstudien. 1989, ²1994. *Vol. 51.*
- Neutestamentliche Studien. 2000. *Vol. 132.*
- Paulusstudien II. 2002. *Vol. 143.*
- Exegetische Studien. 2008. *Vol. 223.*
- and *Hans-Christian Kammler:* Johannesstudien. 1996. *Vol. 88.*
Holloway, Paul A.: Coping with Prejudice. 2009. *Vol. 244.*
- see *Ahearne-Kroll, Stephen P.*
Holmberg, Bengt (Ed.): Exploring Early Christian Identity. 2008. *Vol. 226.*
- and *Mikael Winninge* (Ed.): Identity Formation in the New Testament. 2008. *Vol. 227.*
Holtz, Traugott: Geschichte und Theologie des Urchristentums. 1991. *Vol. 57.*
Hommel, Hildebrecht: Sebasmata. Vol. 1 1983. *Vol. 31.*
Vol. 2 1984. *Vol. 32.*
Horbury, William: Herodian Judaism and New Testament Study. 2006. *Vol. 193.*
Horn, Friedrich Wilhelm and *Ruben Zimmermann* (Ed.): Jenseits von Indikativ und Imperativ. Vol. 1. 2009. *Vol. 238.*
Horst, Pieter W. van der: Jews and Christians in Their Graeco-Roman Context. 2006. *Vol. 196.*
Hultgård, Anders and *Stig Norin* (Ed): Le Jour de Dieu / Der Tag Gottes. 2009. *Vol. 245.*
Hume, Douglas A.: The Early Christian Community. 2011. *Vol. II/298.*
Hvalvik, Reidar: The Struggle for Scripture and Covenant. 1996. *Vol. II/82.*
Jackson, Ryan: New Creation in Paul's Letters. 2010. *Vol. II/272.*
Janßen, Martina: see *Frey, Jörg.*
Jauhiainen, Marko: The Use of Zechariah in Revelation. 2005. *Vol. II/199.*
Jensen, Morten H.: Herod Antipas in Galilee. 2006; ²2010. *Vol. II/215.*
Johns, Loren L.: The Lamb Christology of the Apocalypse of John. 2003. *Vol. II/167.*
Jossa, Giorgio: Jews or Christians? 2006. *Vol. 202.*

Joubert, Stephan: Paul as Benefactor. 2000. *Vol. II/124.*
Judge, E. A.: The First Christians in the Roman World. 2008. *Vol. 229.*
- Jerusalem and Athens. 2010. *Vol. 265.*
Jungbauer, Harry: „Ehre Vater und Mutter". 2002. *Vol. II/146.*
Kähler, Christoph: Jesu Gleichnisse als Poesie und Therapie. 1995. *Vol. 78.*
Kamlah, Ehrhard: Die Form der katalogischen Paränese im Neuen Testament. 1964. *Vol. 7.*
Kammler, Hans-Christian: Christologie und Eschatologie. 2000. *Vol. 126.*
- Kreuz und Weisheit. 2003. *Vol. 159.*
- see *Hofius, Otfried.*
Karakolis, Christos: see *Alexeev, Anatoly A.*
Karrer, Martin und *Wolfgang Kraus* (Ed.): Die Septuaginta – Texte, Kontexte, Lebenswelten. 2008. *Vol. 219.*
- see *Kraus, Wolfgang.*
Kelhoffer, James A.: The Diet of John the Baptist. 2005. *Vol. 176.*
- Miracle and Mission. 2000. *Vol. II/112.*
- Persecution, Persuasion and Power. 2010. *Vol. 270.*
- see *Ahearne-Kroll, Stephen P.*
Kelley, Nicole: Knowledge and Religious Authority in the Pseudo-Clementines. 2006. *Vol. II/213.*
Kennedy, Joel: The Recapitulation of Israel. 2008. *Vol. II/257.*
Kensky, Meira Z.: Trying Man, Trying God. 2010. *Vol. II/289.*
Kessler, Nadine (Ed.): see *Frey, Jörg.*
Kieffer, René and *Jan Bergman* (Ed.): La Main de Dieu / Die Hand Gottes. 1997. *Vol. 94.*
Kierspel, Lars: The Jews and the World in the Fourth Gospel. 2006. *Vol. 220.*
Kim, Seyoon: The Origin of Paul's Gospel. 1981, ²1984. *Vol. II/4.*
- Paul and the New Perspective. 2002. *Vol. 140.*
- "The 'Son of Man'" as the Son of God. 1983. *Vol. 30.*
Klauck, Hans-Josef: Religion und Gesellschaft im frühen Christentum. 2003. *Vol. 152.*
Klein, Hans, Vasile Mihoc und *Karl-Wilhelm Niebuhr* (Ed.): Das Gebet im Neuen Testament. Vierte, europäische orthodox-westliche Exegetenkonferenz in Sambata de Sus, 4. – 8. August 2007. 2009. Vol. 249.
- see Dunn, James D.G.
Kleinknecht, Karl Th.: Der leidende Gerechtfertigte. 1984, ²1988. *Vol. II/13.*
Klinghardt, Matthias: Gesetz und Volk Gottes. 1988. *Vol. II/32.*
Kloppenborg, John S.: The Tenants in the Vineyard. 2006, student edition 2010. *Vol. 195.*

Koch, Michael: Drachenkampf und Sonnenfrau. 2004. *Vol. II/184.*
Koch, Stefan: Rechtliche Regelung von Konflikten im frühen Christentum. 2004. *Vol. II/174.*
Köhler, Wolf-Dietrich: Rezeption des Matthäusevangeliums in der Zeit vor Irenäus. 1987. *Vol. II/24.*
Köhn, Andreas: Der Neutestamentler Ernst Lohmeyer. 2004. *Vol. II/180.*
Koester, Craig and *Reimund Bieringer* (Ed.): The Resurrection of Jesus in the Gospel of John. 2008. *Vol. 222.*
Konradt, Matthias: Israel, Kirche und die Völker im Matthäusevangelium. 2007. *Vol. 215.*
Kooten, George H. van: Cosmic Christology in Paul and the Pauline School. 2003. *Vol. II/171.*
- Paul's Anthropology in Context. 2008. *Vol. 232.*
Korn, Manfred: Die Geschichte Jesu in veränderter Zeit. 1993. *Vol. II/51.*
Koskenniemi, Erkki: Apollonios von Tyana in der neutestamentlichen Exegese. 1994. *Vol. II/61.*
- The Old Testament Miracle-Workers in Early Judaism. 2005. *Vol. II/206.*
Kraus, Thomas J.: Sprache, Stil und historischer Ort des zweiten Petrusbriefes. 2001. *Vol. II/136.*
Kraus, Wolfgang: Das Volk Gottes. 1996. *Vol. 85.*
- see *Karrer, Martin.*
- see *Walter, Nikolaus.*
- and *Martin Karrer* (Hrsg.): Die Septuaginta – Texte, Theologien, Einflüsse. 2010. *Bd. 252.*
- and *Karl-Wilhelm Niebuhr* (Ed.): Frühjudentum und Neues Testament im Horizont Biblischer Theologie. 2003. *Vol. 162.*
Krauter, Stefan: Studien zu Röm 13,1-7. 2009. *Vol. 243.*
- see *Frey, Jörg.*
Kreplin, Matthias: Das Selbstverständnis Jesu. 2001. *Vol. II/141.*
Kuhn, Karl G.: Achtzehngebet und Vaterunser und der Reim. 1950. *Vol. 1.*
Kvalbein, Hans: see *Ådna, Jostein.*
Kwon, Yon-Gyong: Eschatology in Galatians. 2004. *Vol. II/183.*
Laansma, Jon: I Will Give You Rest. 1997. *Vol. II/98.*
Labahn, Michael: Offenbarung in Zeichen und Wort. 2000. *Vol. II/117.*
Lambers-Petry, Doris: see *Tomson, Peter J.*
Lampe, Peter: Die stadtrömischen Christen in den ersten beiden Jahrhunderten. 1987, ²1989. *Vol. II/18.*
Landmesser, Christof: Wahrheit als Grundbegriff neutestamentlicher Wissenschaft. 1999. *Vol. 113.*
- Jüngerberufung und Zuwendung zu Gott. 2000. *Vol. 133.*
- see *Eckstein, Hans-Joachim.*
Lange, Armin: see *Ego, Beate.*
Lau, Andrew: Manifest in Flesh. 1996. *Vol. II/86.*
Lawrence, Louise: An Ethnography of the Gospel of Matthew. 2003. *Vol. II/165.*
Lee, Aquila H.I.: From Messiah to Preexistent Son. 2005. *Vol. II/192.*
Lee, Pilchan: The New Jerusalem in the Book of Relevation. 2000. *Vol. II/129.*
Lee, Sang M.: The Cosmic Drama of Salvation. 2010. *Vol. II/276.*
Lee, Simon S.: Jesus' Transfiguration and the Believers' Transformation. 2009. *Vol. II/265.*
Lichtenberger, Hermann: Das Ich Adams und das Ich der Menschheit. 2004. *Vol. 164.*
- see *Avemarie, Friedrich.*
- see *Eckstein, Hans-Joachim.*
- see *Frey, Jörg.*
- and *Thomas Scott Caulley* (Ed.): Die Septuaginta und das frühe Christentum – The Septuagint and Christian Origins. 2011. *Vol. 277.*
Lierman, John: The New Testament Moses. 2004. *Vol. II/173.*
- (Ed.): Challenging Perspectives on the Gospel of John. 2006. *Vol. II/219.*
Lieu, Samuel N.C.: Manichaeism in the Later Roman Empire and Medieval China. ²1992. *Vol. 63.*
Lindemann, Andreas: Die Evangelien und die Apostelgeschichte. 2009. *Vol. 241.*
- Glauben, Handeln, Verstehen. Studien zur Auslegung des Neuen Testaments. 2012. *Vol. 2/282.*
Lincicum, David: Paul and the Early Jewish Encounter with Deuteronomy. 2010. *Vol. II/284.*
Lindgård, Fredrik: Paul's Line of Thought in 2 Corinthians 4:16–5:10. 2004. *Vol. II/189.*
Livesey, Nina E.: Circumcision as a Malleable Symbol. 2010. *Vol. II/295.*
Loader, William R.G.: Jesus' Attitude Towards the Law. 1997. *Vol. II/97.*
Löhr, Gebhard: Verherrlichung Gottes durch Philosophie. 1997. *Vol. 97.*
Löhr, Hermut: Studien zum frühchristlichen und frühjüdischen Gebet. 2003. *Vol. 160.*
- see *Hengel, Martin.*
Löhr, Winrich Alfried: Basilides und seine Schule. 1995. *Vol. 83.*
Lorenzen, Stefanie: Das paulinische Eikon-Konzept. 2008. *Vol. II/250.*

Luomanen, Petri: Entering the Kingdom of Heaven. 1998. *Vol. II/101.*
Luz, Ulrich: see *Alexeev, Anatoly A.*
– see *Dunn, James D.G.*
Mackay, Ian D.: John's Raltionship with Mark. 2004. *Vol. II/182.*
Mackie, Scott D.: Eschatology and Exhortation in the Epistle to the Hebrews. 2006. *Vol. II/223.*
Magda, Ksenija: Paul's Territoriality and Mission Strategy. 2009. *Vol. II/266.*
Maier, Gerhard: Mensch und freier Wille. 1971. *Vol. 12.*
– Die Johannesoffenbarung und die Kirche. 1981. *Vol. 25.*
Markschies, Christoph: Valentinus Gnosticus? 1992. *Vol. 65.*
Marshall, Jonathan: Jesus, Patrons, and Benefactors. 2009. *Vol. II/259.*
Marshall, Peter: Enmity in Corinth: Social Conventions in Paul's Relations with the Corinthians. 1987. *Vol. II/23.*
Martin, Dale B.: see *Zangenberg, Jürgen.*
Maston, Jason: Divine and Human Agency in Second Temple Judaism and Paul. 2010. *Vol. II/297.*
Mayer, Annemarie: Sprache der Einheit im Epheserbrief und in der Ökumene. 2002. *Vol. II/150.*
Mayordomo, Moisés: Argumentiert Paulus logisch? 2005. *Vol. 188.*
McDonough, Sean M.: YHWH at Patmos: Rev. 1:4 in its Hellenistic and Early Jewish Setting. 1999. *Vol. II/107.*
McDowell, Markus: Prayers of Jewish Women. 2006. *Vol. II/211.*
McGlynn, Moyna: Divine Judgement and Divine Benevolence in the Book of Wisdom. 2001. *Vol. II/139.*
McNamara, Martin: Targum and New Testament. 2011. *Vol. 279.*
Meade, David G.: Pseudonymity and Canon. 1986. *Vol. 39.*
Meadors, Edward P.: Jesus the Messianic Herald of Salvation. 1995. *Vol. II/72.*
Meißner, Stefan: Die Heimholung des Ketzers. 1996. *Vol. II/87.*
Mell, Ulrich: Die „anderen" Winzer. 1994. *Vol. 77.*
– see *Sänger, Dieter.*
Mengel, Berthold: Studien zum Philipperbrief. 1982. *Vol. II/8.*
Merkel, Helmut: Die Widersprüche zwischen den Evangelien. 1971. *Vol. 13.*
– see *Ego, Beate.*
Merklein, Helmut: Studien zu Jesus und Paulus. Vol. 1 1987. *Vol. 43.* – Vol. 2 1998. *Vol. 105.*
Merkt, Andreas: see *Nicklas, Tobias*

Metzdorf, Christina: Die Tempelaktion Jesu. 2003. *Vol. II/168.*
Metzler, Karin: Der griechische Begriff des Verzeihens. 1991. *Vol. II/44.*
Metzner, Rainer: Die Rezeption des Matthäusevangeliums im 1. Petrusbrief. 1995. *Vol. II/74.*
– Das Verständnis der Sünde im Johannesevangelium. 2000. *Vol. 122.*
Mihoc, Vasile: see *Dunn, James D.G.*
– see *Klein, Hans.*
Mineshige, Kiyoshi: Besitzverzicht und Almosen bei Lukas. 2003. *Vol. II/163.*
Mittmann, Siegfried: see *Hengel, Martin.*
Mittmann-Richert, Ulrike: Magnifikat und Benediktus. 1996. *Vol. II/90.*
– Der Sühnetod des Gottesknechts. 2008. *Vol. 220.*
Miura, Yuzuru: David in Luke-Acts. 2007. *Vol. II/232.*
Moll, Sebastian: The Arch-Heretic Marcion. 2010. *Vol. 250.*
Morales, Rodrigo J.: The Spirit and the Restorat. 2010. *Vol. 282.*
Mournet, Terence C.: Oral Tradition and Literary Dependency. 2005. *Vol. II/195.*
Mußner, Franz: Jesus von Nazareth im Umfeld Israels und der Urkirche. Ed. von M. Theobald. 1998. *Vol. 111.*
Mutschler, Bernhard: Das Corpus Johanneum bei Irenäus von Lyon. 2005. *Vol. 189.*
– Glaube in den Pastoralbriefen. 2010. *Vol. 256.*
Myers, Susan E.: Spirit Epicleses in the Acts of Thomas. 2010. *Vol. 281.*
Nguyen, V. Henry T.: Christian Identity in Corinth. 2008. *Vol. II/243.*
Nicklas, Tobias, Andreas Merkt und *Joseph Verheyden* (Ed.): Gelitten – Gestorben – Auferstanden. 2010. *Vol. II/273.*
– see *Verheyden, Joseph*
Niebuhr, Karl-Wilhelm: Gesetz und Paränese. 1987. *Vol. II/28.*
– Heidenapostel aus Israel. 1992. *Vol. 62.*
– see *Deines, Roland.*
– see *Dimitrov, Ivan Z.*
– see *Klein, Hans.*
– see *Kraus, Wolfgang.*
Nielsen, Anders E.: "Until it is Fullfilled". 2000. *Vol. II/126.*
Nielsen, Jesper Tang: Die kognitive Dimension des Kreuzes. 2009. *Vol. II/263.*
Nissen, Andreas: Gott und der Nächste im antiken Judentum. 1974. *Vol. 15.*
Noack, Christian: Gottesbewußtsein. 2000. *Vol. II/116.*
Noormann, Rolf: Irenäus als Paulusinterpret. 1994. *Vol. II/66.*

Norelli, Enrico: see *Clivaz, Claire.*
Norin, Stig: see *Hultgård, Anders.*
Novakovic, Lidija: Messiah, the Healer of the Sick. 2003. *Vol. II/170.*
Obermann, Andreas: Die christologische Erfüllung der Schrift im Johannesevangelium. 1996. *Vol. II/83.*
Öhler, Markus: Barnabas. 2003. *Vol. 156.*
− see *Becker, Michael.*
− (Ed.): Aposteldekret und antikes Vereinswesen. 2011. *Vol. 280.*
Okure, Teresa: The Johannine Approach to Mission. 1988. *Vol. II/31.*
Onuki, Takashi: Heil und Erlösung. 2004. *Vol. 165.*
Oropeza, B. J.: Paul and Apostasy. 2000. *Vol. II/115.*
Ostmeyer, Karl-Heinrich: Kommunikation mit Gott und Christus. 2006. *Vol. 197.*
− Taufe und Typos. 2000. *Vol. II/118.*
Pao, David W.: Acts and the Isaianic New Exodus. 2000. *Vol. II/130.*
Park, Eung Chun: The Mission Discourse in Matthew's Interpretation. 1995. *Vol. II/81.*
Park, Joseph S.: Conceptions of Afterlife in Jewish Insriptions. 2000. *Vol. II/121.*
Parsenios, George L.: Rhetoric and Drama in the Johannine Lawsuit Motif. 2010. *Vol. 258.*
Pate, C. Marvin: The Reverse of the Curse. 2000. *Vol. II/114.*
Paulsen, Henning: Studien zur Literatur und Geschichte des frühen Christentums. Ed. von Ute E. Eisen. 1997. *Vol. 99.*
Pearce, Sarah J.K.: The Land of the Body. 2007. *Vol. 208.*
Peres, Imre: Griechische Grabinschriften und neutestamentliche Eschatologie. 2003. *Vol. 157.*
Perry, Peter S.: The Rhetoric of Digressions. 2009. *Vol. II/268.*
Pierce, Chad T.: Spirits and the Proclamation of Christ. 2011. *Vol. II/305.*
Philip, Finny: The Origins of Pauline Pneumatology. 2005. *Vol. II/194.*
Philonenko, Marc (Ed.): Le Trône de Dieu. 1993. *Vol. 69.*
Pilhofer, Peter: Presbyteron Kreitton. 1990. *Vol. II/39.*
− Philippi. Vol. 1 1995. *Vol. 87.* − Vol. 2 ²2009. *Vol. 119.*
− Die frühen Christen und ihre Welt. 2002. *Vol. 145.*
− see *Becker, Eve-Marie.*
− see *Ego, Beate.*
Pitre, Brant: Jesus, the Tribulation, and the End of the Exile. 2005. *Vol. II/204.*

Plümacher, Eckhard: Geschichte und Geschichten. 2004. *Vol. 170.*
Pöhlmann, Wolfgang: Der Verlorene Sohn und das Haus. 1993. *Vol. 68.*
Poirier, John C.: The Tongues of Angels. 2010. *Vol. II/287.*
Pokorný, Petr and *Josef B. Souček:* Bibelauslegung als Theologie. 1997. *Vol. 100.*
− and *Jan Roskovec* (Ed.): Philosophical Hermeneutics and Biblical Exegesis. 2002. *Vol. 153.*
Popkes, Enno Edzard: Das Menschenbild des Thomasevangeliums. 2007. *Vol. 206.*
− Die Theologie der Liebe Gottes in den johanneischen Schriften. 2005. *Vol. II/197.*
Porter, Stanley E.: The Paul of Acts. 1999. *Vol. 115.*
Prieur, Alexander: Die Verkündigung der Gottesherrschaft. 1996. *Vol. II/89.*
Probst, Hermann: Paulus und der Brief. 1991. *Vol. II/45.*
Puig i Tàrrech, Armand: Jesus: An Uncommon Journey. 2010. *Vol. II/288.*
Rabens, Volker: The Holy Spirit and Ethics in Paul. 2010. *Vol. II/283.*
Räisänen, Heikki: Paul and the Law. 1983, ²1987. *Vol. 29.*
Rehkopf, Friedrich: Die lukanische Sonderquelle. 1959. *Vol. 5.*
Rein, Matthias: Die Heilung des Blindgeborenen (Joh 9). 1995. *Vol. II/73.*
Reinmuth, Eckart: Pseudo-Philo und Lukas. 1994. *Vol. 74.*
Reiser, Marius: Bibelkritik und Auslegung der Heiligen Schrift. 2007. *Vol. 217.*
− Syntax und Stil des Markusevangeliums. 1984. *Vol. II/11.*
Reynolds, Benjamin E.: The Apocalyptic Son of Man in the Gospel of John. 2008. *Vol. II/249.*
Rhodes, James N.: The Epistle of Barnabas and the Deuteronomic Tradition. 2004. *Vol. II/188.*
Richards, E. Randolph: The Secretary in the Letters of Paul. 1991. *Vol. II/42.*
Riesner, Rainer: Jesus als Lehrer. 1981, ³1988. *Vol. II/7.*
− Die Frühzeit des Apostels Paulus. 1994. *Vol. 71.*
Rissi, Mathias: Die Theologie des Hebräerbriefs. 1987. *Vol. 41.*
Röcker, Fritz W.: Belial und Katechon. 2009. *Vol. II/262.*
Röhser, Günter: Metaphorik und Personifikation der Sünde. 1987. *Vol. II/25.*
Rose, Christian: Theologie als Erzählung im Markusevangelium. 2007. *Vol. II/236.*
− Die Wolke der Zeugen. 1994. *Vol. II/60.*
Roskovec, Jan: see *Pokorný, Petr.*

Rothschild, Clare K.: Baptist Traditions and Q. 2005. *Vol. 190.*
– Hebrews as Pseudepigraphon. 2009. *Vol. 235.*
– Luke Acts and the Rhetoric of History. 2004. *Vol. II/175.*
– see *Frey, Jörg.*
Rudolph, David J.: A Jew to the Jews. 2011. *Vol. II/304.*
Rüegger, Hans-Ulrich: Verstehen, was Markus erzählt. 2002. *Vol. II/155.*
Rüger, Hans Peter: Die Weisheitsschrift aus der Kairoer Geniza. 1991. *Vol. 53.*
Ruf, Martin G.: Die heiligen Propheten, eure Apostel und ich. 2011. *Vol. II/300.*
Runesson, Anders: see *Becker, Eve-Marie.*
Sänger, Dieter: Antikes Judentum und die Mysterien. 1980. *Vol. II/5.*
– Die Verkündigung des Gekreuzigten und Israel. 1994. *Vol. 75.*
– see *Burchard, Christoph*
– and *Ulrich Mell* (Ed.): Paulus und Johannes. 2006. *Vol. 198.*
Salier, Willis Hedley: The Rhetorical Impact of the Semeia in the Gospel of John. 2004. *Vol. II/186.*
Salzmann, Jörg Christian: Lehren und Ermahnen. 1994. *Vol. II/59.*
Samuelsson, Gunnar: Crucifixion in Antiquity. 2011. *Vol. II/310.*
Sandnes, Karl Olav: Paul – One of the Prophets? 1991. *Vol. II/43.*
Sato, Migaku: Q und Prophetie. 1988. *Vol. II/29.*
Schäfer, Ruth: Paulus bis zum Apostelkonzil. 2004. *Vol. II/179.*
Schaper, Joachim: Eschatology in the Greek Psalter. 1995. *Vol. II/76.*
Schimanowski, Gottfried: Die himmlische Liturgie in der Apokalypse des Johannes. 2002. *Vol. II/154.*
– Weisheit und Messias. 1985. *Vol. II/17.*
Schlichting, Günter: Ein jüdisches Leben Jesu. 1982. *Vol. 24.*
Schließer, Benjamin: Abraham's Faith in Romans 4. 2007. *Vol. II/224.*
Schnabel, Eckhard J.: Law and Wisdom from Ben Sira to Paul. 1985. *Vol. II/16.*
Schnelle, Udo: see *Frey, Jörg.*
Schröter, Jens: Von Jesus zum Neuen Testament. 2007. *Vol. 204.*
– see *Frey, Jörg.*
Schutter, William L.: Hermeneutic and Composition in I Peter. 1989. *Vol. II/30.*
Schwartz, Daniel R.: Studies in the Jewish Background of Christianity. 1992. *Vol. 60.*
Schwemer, Anna Maria: see *Hengel, Martin*
Scott, Ian W.: Implicit Epistemology in the Letters of Paul. 2005. *Vol. II/205.*

Scott, James M.: Adoption as Sons of God. 1992. *Vol. II/48.*
– Paul and the Nations. 1995. *Vol. 84.*
Shi, Wenhua: Paul's Message of the Cross as Body Language. 2008. *Vol. II/254.*
Shum, Shiu-Lun: Paul's Use of Isaiah in Romans. 2002. *Vol. II/156.*
Siegert, Folker: Drei hellenistisch-jüdische Predigten. Teil I 1980. *Vol. 20* – Teil II 1992. *Vol. 61.*
– Nag-Hammadi-Register. 1982. *Vol. 26.*
– Argumentation bei Paulus. 1985. *Vol. 34.*
– Philon von Alexandrien. 1988. *Vol. 46.*
Siggelkow-Berner, Birke: Die jüdischen Feste im Bellum Judaicum des Flavius Josephus. 2011. *Vol. II/306.*
Simon, Marcel: Le christianisme antique et son contexte religieux I/II. 1981. *Vol. 23.*
Smit, Peter-Ben: Fellowship and Food in the Kingdom. 2008. *Vol. II/234.*
Smith, Julien: Christ the Ideal King. 2011. *Vol. II/313.*
Snodgrass, Klyne: The Parable of the Wicked Tenants. 1983. *Vol. 27.*
Söding, Thomas: Das Wort vom Kreuz. 1997. *Vol. 93.*
– see *Thüsing, Wilhelm.*
Sommer, Urs: Die Passionsgeschichte des Markusevangeliums. 1993. *Vol. II/58.*
Sorensen, Eric: Possession and Exorcism in the New Testament and Early Christianity. 2002. *Vol. II/157.*
Souček, Josef B.: see *Pokorný, Petr.*
Southall, David J.: Rediscovering Righteousness in Romans. 2008. *Vol. 240.*
Spangenberg, Volker: Herrlichkeit des Neuen Bundes. 1993. *Vol. II/55.*
Spanje, T.E. van: Inconsistency in Paul? 1999. *Vol. II/110.*
Speyer, Wolfgang: Frühes Christentum im antiken Strahlungsfeld. Vol. I: 1989. *Vol. 50.*
– Vol. II: 1999. *Vol. 116.*
– Vol. III: 2007. *Vol. 213.*
Spittler, Janet E.: Animals in the Apocryphal Acts of the Apostles. 2008. *Vol. II/247.*
Sprinkle, Preston: Law and Life. 2008. *Vol. II/241.*
Stadelmann, Helge: Ben Sira als Schriftgelehrter. 1980. *Vol. II/6.*
Stein, Hans Joachim: Frühchristliche Mahlfeiern. 2008. *Vol. II/255.*
Stenschke, Christoph W.: Luke's Portrait of Gentiles Prior to Their Coming to Faith. *Vol. II/108.*
Stephens, Mark B.: Annihilation or Renewal? 2011. *Vol. II/307.*
Sterck-Degueldre, Jean-Pierre: Eine Frau namens Lydia. 2004. *Vol. II/176.*

Stettler, Christian: Der Kolosserhymnus. 2000. Vol. II/131.
- Das letzte Gericht. 2011. Vol. II/299.
Stettler, Hanna: Die Christologie der Pastoralbriefe. 1998. Vol. II/105.
Stökl Ben Ezra, Daniel: The Impact of Yom Kippur on Early Christianity. 2003. Vol. 163.
Strobel, August: Die Stunde der Wahrheit. 1980. Vol. 21.
Stroumsa, Guy G.: Barbarian Philosophy. 1999. Vol. 112.
Stuckenbruck, Loren T.: Angel Veneration and Christology. 1995. Vol. II/70.
−, Stephen C. Barton and Benjamin G. Wold (Ed.): Memory in the Bible and Antiquity. 2007. Vol. 212.
Stuhlmacher, Peter (Ed.): Das Evangelium und die Evangelien. 1983. Vol. 28.
- Biblische Theologie und Evangelium. 2002. Vol. 146.
Sung, Chong-Hyon: Vergebung der Sünden. 1993. Vol. II/57.
Svendsen, Stefan N.: Allegory Transformed. 2009. Vol. II/269.
Tajra, Harry W.: The Trial of St. Paul. 1989. Vol. II/35.
- The Martyrdom of St.Paul. 1994. Vol. II/67.
Tellbe, Mikael: Christ-Believers in Ephesus. 2009. Vol. 242.
Theißen, Gerd: Studien zur Soziologie des Urchristentums. 1979, ³1989. Vol. 19.
Theobald, Michael: Studien zum Corpus Iohanneum. 2010. Vol. 267.
- Studien zum Römerbrief. 2001. Vol. 136.
- see Mußner, Franz.
Thornton, Claus-Jürgen: Der Zeuge des Zeugen. 1991. Vol. 56.
Thüsing, Wilhelm: Studien zur neutestamentlichen Theologie. Ed. von Thomas Söding. 1995. Vol. 82.
Thurén, Lauri: Derhethorizing Paul. 2000. Vol. 124.
Thyen, Hartwig: Studien zum Corpus Iohanneum. 2007. Vol. 214.
Tibbs, Clint: Religious Experience of the Pneuma. 2007. Vol. II/230.
Toit, David S. du: Theios Anthropos. 1997. Vol. II/91.
Tolmie, D. Francois: Persuading the Galatians. 2005. Vol. II/190.
Tomson, Peter J. and Doris Lambers-Petry (Ed.): The Image of the Judaeo-Christians in Ancient Jewish and Christian Literature. 2003. Vol. 158.
Toney, Carl N.: Paul's Inclusive Ethic. 2008. Vol. II/252.
Trebilco, Paul: The Early Christians in Ephesus from Paul to Ignatius. 2004. Vol. 166.

Treloar, Geoffrey R.: Lightfoot the Historian. 1998. Vol. II/103.
Troftgruben, Troy M.: A Conclusion Unhindered. 2010. Vol. II/280.
Tso, Marcus K.M.: Ethics in the Qumran Community. 2010. Vol. II/292.
Tsuji, Manabu: Glaube zwischen Vollkommenheit und Verweltlichung. 1997. Vol. II/93.
Twelftree, Graham H.: Jesus the Exorcist. 1993. Vol. II/54.
Ulrichs, Karl Friedrich: Christusglaube. 2007. Vol. II/227.
Urban, Christina: Das Menschenbild nach dem Johannesevangelium. 2001. Vol. II/137.
Vahrenhorst, Martin: Kultische Sprache in den Paulusbriefen. 2008. Vol. 230.
Vegge, Ivar: 2 Corinthians – a Letter about Reconciliation. 2008. Vol. II/239.
Verheyden, Joseph, Korinna Zamfir and Tobias Nicklas (Ed.): Prophets and Prophecy in Jewish and Early Christian Literature. 2010. Vol. II/286.
- see Nicklas, Tobias
Visotzky, Burton L.: Fathers of the World. 1995. Vol. 80.
Vollenweider, Samuel: Horizonte neutestamentlicher Christologie. 2002. Vol. 144.
Vos Johan S.: Die Kunst der Argumentation bei Paulus. 2002. Vol. 149.
Waaler, Erik: The Shema and The First Commandment in First Corinthians. 2008. Vol. II/253.
Wagener, Ulrike: Die Ordnung des „Hauses Gottes". 1994. Vol. II/65.
Wagner, J. Ross: see Wilk, Florian.
Wahlen, Clinton: Jesus and the Impurity of Spirits in the Synoptic Gospels. 2004. Vol. II/185.
Walker, Donald D.: Paul's Offer of Leniency (2 Cor 10:1). 2002. Vol. II/152.
Walter, Nikolaus: Praeparatio Evangelica. Ed. von Wolfgang Kraus und Florian Wilk. 1997. Vol. 98.
Wander, Bernd: Gottesfürchtige und Sympathisanten. 1998. Vol. 104.
Wardle, Timothy: The Jerusalem Temple and Early Christian Identity. 2010. Vol. II/291.
Wasserman, Emma: The Death of the Soul in Romans 7. 2008. Vol. 256.
Waters, Guy: The End of Deuteronomy in the Epistles of Paul. 2006. Vol. 221.
Watt, Jan G. van der (Ed.): Eschatology of the New Testament and Some Related Documents. 2011. Vol. II/315.
- see Frey, Jörg
- see Zimmermann, Ruben
Watts, Rikki: Isaiah's New Exodus and Mark. 1997. Vol. II/88.

Webb, Robert L.: see *Bock, Darrell L.*
Wedderburn, Alexander J.M.: Baptism and Resurrection. 1987. *Vol. 44.*
– Jesus and the Historians. 2010. *Vol. 269.*
Wegner, Uwe: Der Hauptmann von Kafarnaum. 1985. *Vol. II/14.*
Weiß, Hans-Friedrich: Frühes Christentum und Gnosis. 2008. *Vol. 225.*
Weissenrieder, Annette: Images of Illness in the Gospel of Luke. 2003. Vol. II/164.
–, and *Robert B. Coote* (Ed.): The Interface of Orality and Writing. 2010. *Vol. 260.*
–, *Friederike Wendt* and *Petra von Gemünden* (Ed.): Picturing the New Testament. 2005. *Vol. II/193.*
Welck, Christian: Erzählte ‚Zeichen'. 1994. *Vol. II/69.*
Wendt, Friederike (Ed.): see *Weissenrieder, Annette.*
Wiarda, Timothy: Peter in the Gospels. 2000. *Vol. II/127.*
Wifstrand, Albert: Epochs and Styles. 2005. *Vol. 179.*
Wilk, Florian and *J. Ross Wagner* (Ed.): Between Gospel and Election. 2010. *Vol. 257.*
– see *Walter, Nikolaus.*
Williams, Catrin H.: I am He. 2000. *Vol. II/113.*
Wilson, Todd A.: The Curse of the Law and the Crisis in Galatia. 2007. *Vol. II/225.*
Wilson, Walter T.: Love without Pretense. 1991. *Vol. II/46.*
Winn, Adam: The Purpose of Mark's Gospel. 2008. *Vol. II/245.*
Winninge, Mikael: see *Holmberg, Bengt.*
Wischmeyer, Oda: Von Ben Sira zu Paulus. 2004. *Vol. 173.*
Wisdom, Jeffrey: Blessing for the Nations and the Curse of the Law. 2001. *Vol. II/133.*
Witmer, Stephen E.: Divine Instruction in Early Christianity. 2008. *Vol. II/246.*
Wold, Benjamin G.: Women, Men, and Angels. 2005. *Vol. II/2001.*
Wolter, Michael: Theologie und Ethos im frühen Christentum. 2009. *Vol. 236.*
– see *Stuckenbruck, Loren T.*
Worthington, Jonathan: Creation in Paul and Philo. 2011. *Vol. II/317.*
Wright, Archie T.: The Origin of Evil Spirits. 2005. *Vol. II/198.*
Wucherpfennig, Ansgar: Heracleon Philologus. 2002. *Vol. 142.*
Yates, John W.: The Spirit and Creation in Paul. 2008. *Vol. II/251.*
Yeung, Maureen: Faith in Jesus and Paul. 2002. *Vol. II/147.*
Young, Stephen E.: Jesus Tradition in the Apostolic Fathers. 2011. *Vol. II/311.*
Zamfir, Corinna: see *Verheyden, Joseph*
Zangenberg, Jürgen, Harold W. Attridge and *Dale B. Martin* (Ed.): Religion, Ethnicity and Identity in Ancient Galilee. 2007. *Vol. 210.*
Zimmermann, Alfred E.: Die urchristlichen Lehrer. 1984, ²1988. *Vol. II/12.*
Zimmermann, Johannes: Messianische Texte aus Qumran. 1998. *Vol. II/104.*
Zimmermann, Ruben: Christologie der Bilder im Johannesevangelium. 2004. *Vol. 171.*
– Geschlechtermetaphorik und Gottesverhältnis. 2001. *Vol. II/122.*
– (Ed.): Hermeneutik der Gleichnisse Jesu. 2008. *Vol. 231.*
– and *Jan G. van der Watt* (Ed.): Moral Language in the New Testament. Vol. II. 2010. *Vol. II/296.*
– see *Frey, Jörg.*
– see *Horn, Friedrich Wilhelm.*
Zugmann, Michael: „Hellenisten" in der Apostelgeschichte. 2009. *Vol. II/264.*
Zumstein, Jean: see *Dettwiler, Andreas*
Zwiep, Arie W.: Christ, the Spirit and the Community of God. 2010. *Vol. II/293.*
– Judas and the Choice of Matthias. 2004. *Vol. II/187.*

For a complete catalogue please write to the publisher
Mohr Siebeck • P.O. Box 2030 • D–72010 Tübingen/Germany
Up-to-date information on the internet at www.mohr.de